THE PACIFIC NORTHWEST'S

BEST TRIPS

32 AMAZING ROAD TRIPS

This edition written and researched by

**Becky Ohlsen, Celeste Brash, John Lee, Brendan
Sainsbury, Ryan Ver Berkmoes**

SYMBOLS IN THIS BOOK

✓	Top Tips	📖	History & Culture	📷	Essential Photo
🔗	Link Your Trips	👫	Family	🚶	Walking Tour
💬	Tips from Locals	🍷	Food & Drink	🍴	Eating
↱	Trip Detour	🌳	Outdoors	🛏	Sleeping

☏	Telephone Number	@	Internet Access	📖	English-Language Menu
☺	Opening Hours	🛜	Wi-Fi Access	👶	Family-Friendly
P	Parking	🥗	Vegetarian Selection	🐾	Pet-Friendly
⊘	Nonsmoking	🏊	Swimming Pool		
❄	Air-Conditioning				

MAP LEGEND

Routes
- Trip Route
- Trip Detour
- Linked Trip
- Walk Route
- Tollway
- Freeway
- Primary
- Secondary
- Tertiary
- Lane
- Unsealed Road
- Plaza/Mall
- Steps
-)= = Tunnel
- Pedestrian Overpass
- Walk Track/Path

Boundaries
- --- International
- ---- State/Province
- ⌐⌐⌐ Cliff

Hydrography
- River/Creek
- Intermittent River
- Swamp/Mangrove
- Canal
- Water
- Dry/Salt/ Intermittent Lake
- Glacier

Route Markers
- 🔳97 US National Hwy
- 🔳5 US Interstate Hwy
- 🔳44 State Hwy

Trips
- 1 Trip Numbers
- 9 Trip Stop
- 🔳 Walking tour
- ↱ Trip Detour

Population
- ✪ Capital (National)
- ◉ Capital (State/Province)
- ● City/Large Town
- ○ Town/Village

Areas
- Beach
- Cemetery (Christian)
- Cemetery (Other)
- Park
- Forest
- Reservation
- Urban Area
- Sportsground

Transport
- ✈ Airport
- Ⓑ BART station
- Ⓣ Boston T station
- Ⓒ Cable Car/ Funicular
- Ⓜ Metro/Muni station
- Ⓟ Parking
- Ⓢ Subway station
- Ⓡ Train/Railway
- Ⓣ Tram
- Ⓤ Underground station

Note: Not all symbols displayed above appear on the maps in this book

---

PLAN YOUR TRIP

ON THE ROAD

CONTENTS

British Columbia
p267

Washington
p53

Oregon
p157

3

Contents cont.

Vancouver Capilano Suspension Bridge

WELCOME TO
THE PACIFIC NORTHWEST

What's the Pacific Northwest got that other regions don't? Plenty. Start with hundreds of miles of coastline and throw in a stunning natural landscape: thousands of years of geological events have dramatically shaped this region, leaving behind snow-capped mountain ranges, rocky islands, hundreds of waterfalls, natural hot springs and one particularly lovely gorge.

Because almost every drive in the Pacific Northwest is a scenic one, there's no better way to see it than by road trip. The great stops along the way range from historical sites to natural wonders to roadside attractions.

You can cruise along the coast, explore volcanic remnants, sample regional wines, or even travel in the footsteps of Lewis and Clark.

And if you've only got time for one trip, make it one of our Classic Trips, which take you to the very best of the Pacific Northwest.

THE PACIFIC NORTHWEST HIGHLIGHTS

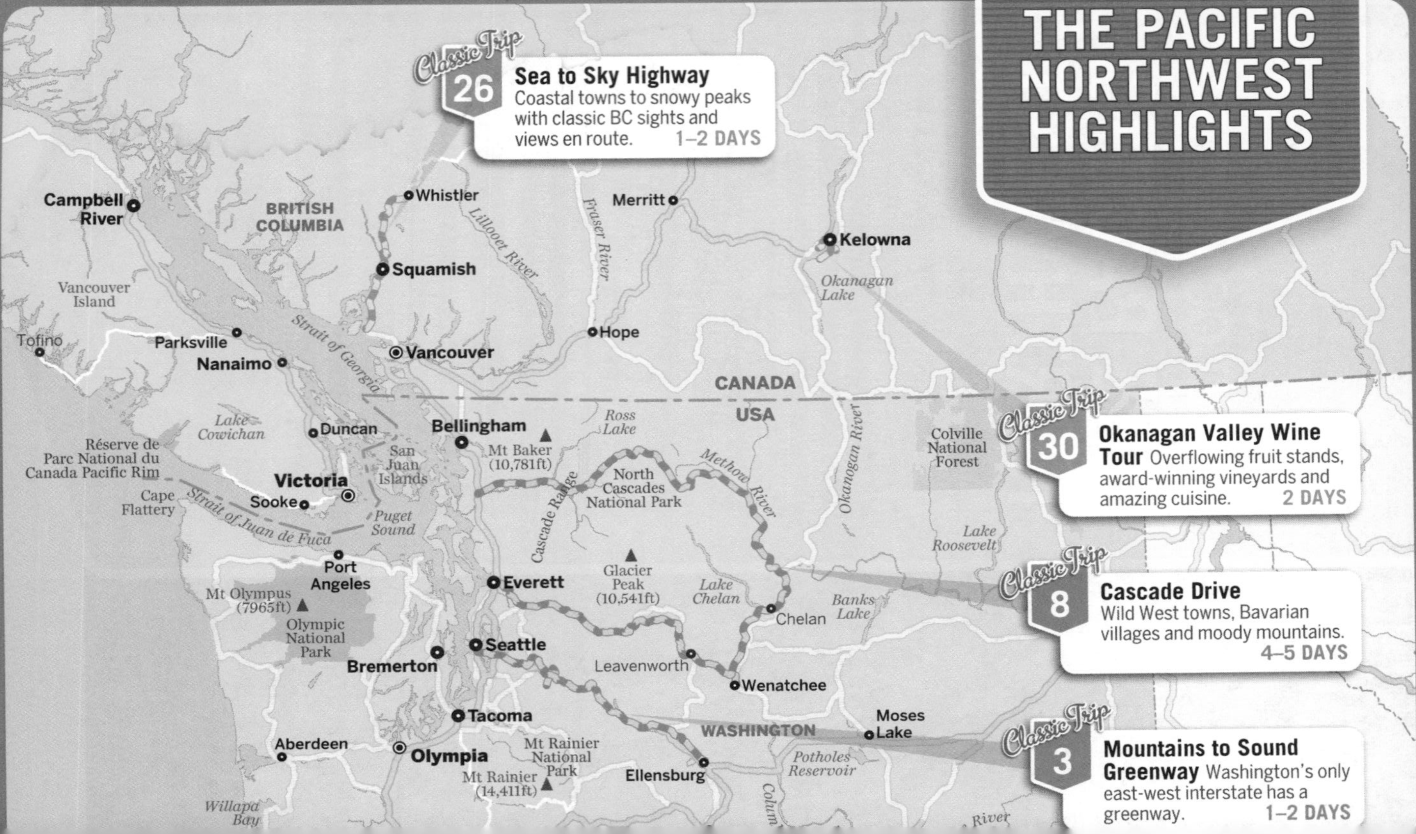

Classic Trip 26
Sea to Sky Highway Coastal towns to snowy peaks with classic BC sights and views en route. 1–2 DAYS

Classic Trip 30
Okanagan Valley Wine Tour Overflowing fruit stands, award-winning vineyards and amazing cuisine. 2 DAYS

Classic Trip 8
Cascade Drive Wild West towns, Bavarian villages and moody mountains. 4–5 DAYS

Classic Trip 3
Mountains to Sound Greenway Washington's only east-west interstate has a greenway. 1–2 DAYS

BRITISH COLUMBIA

CANADA
USA

WASHINGTON

Campbell River
Tofino
Parksville
Nanaimo
Duncan
Victoria
Sooke
Vancouver Island
Lake Cowichan
Cape Flattery
Réserve de Parc National du Canada Pacific Rim
Strait of Juan de Fuca
Port Angeles
Mt Olympus (7965ft)
Olympic National Park
Aberdeen
Willapa Bay
Bremerton
Olympia
Tacoma
Seattle
Puget Sound
San Juan Islands
Strait of Georgia
Vancouver
Squamish
Whistler
Lillooet River
Merritt
Hope
Fraser River
Bellingham
Mt Baker (10,781ft)
Cascade Range
Ross Lake
North Cascades National Park
Glacier Peak (10,541ft)
Everett
Methow River
Chelan
Lake Chelan
Leavenworth
Wenatchee
Banks Lake
Moses Lake
Potholes Reservoir
Ellensburg
Mt Rainier National Park
Mt Rainier Park (14,411ft)
Kelowna
Okanagan Lake
Okanagan River
Colville National Forest
Lake Roosevelt
Colum...
River

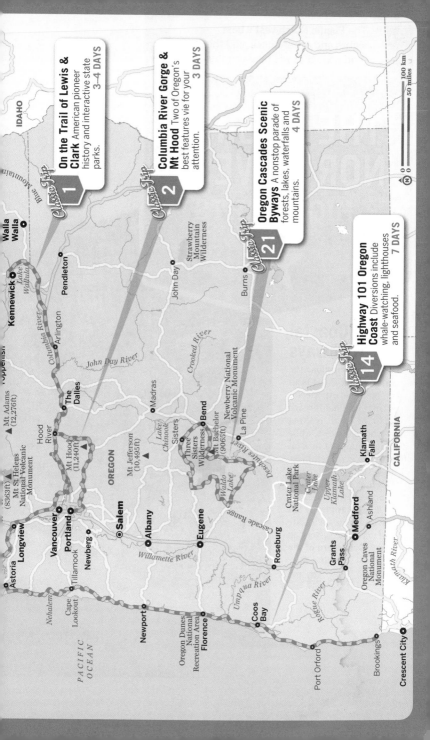

Classic Trip 1
On the Trail of Lewis & Clark American pioneer history and interactive state parks. **3–4 DAYS**

Classic Trip 2
Columbia River Gorge & Mt Hood Two of Oregon's best features vie for your attention. **3 DAYS**

Classic Trip 21
Oregon Cascades Scenic Byways A nonstop parade of forests, lakes, waterfalls and mountains. **4 DAYS**

Classic Trip 14
Highway 101 Oregon Coast Diversions include whale-watching, lighthouses and seafood. **7 DAYS**

IDAHO

Walla Walla

Lake Wallula

Kennewick

Pendleton

Blue Mountains

Columbia River

Arlington

John Day River

John Day

Strawberry Mountain Wilderness

Crooked River

Burns

The Dalles

Madras

Hood River

Mt Adams (12,276ft) ▲

Mt St Helens National Volcanic Monument ▲

(8363ft) ▲

Mt Hood (11,240ft) ▲

Lake Chinook

Sisters

Bend

Newberry National Volcanic Monument

La Pine

Deschutes River

OREGON

Mt Jefferson (10,495ft) ▲

Three Sisters Wilderness

Mt Bachelor (9065ft) ▲

Waldo Lake

Longview

Vancouver

Portland

Newberg

Salem ◉

Albany

Eugene

Willamette River

Cascade Range

Crater Lake National Park

Crater Lake

Roseburg

Upper Klamath Lake

Klamath Falls

CALIFORNIA

Astoria

Cape Lookout

Tillamook

Nehalem

Newport

Oregon Dunes National Recreation Area

Florence

Umpqua River

Coos Bay

Rogue River

Grants Pass

Oregon Caves National Monument

Medford

Ashland

PACIFIC OCEAN

Port Orford

Brookings

Crescent City

Klamath River

100 km
50 miles

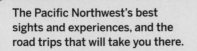

The Pacific Northwest's best sights and experiences, and the road trips that will take you there.

THE PACIFIC NORTHWEST

HIGHLIGHTS

Coastal Highways

Cruising along the stunning Pacific Coast is an unforgettable experience. Lofty headlands reach out to the ocean, offering spectacular views, while steep mountains of rock jut offshore like giant sentinels. Stroll beaches, explore tide pools, watch for whales and eat your fill of fresh seafood on **Trip 14: Highway 101 Oregon Coast**, or get a taste of maritime history on **Trip 5: Graveyard of the Pacific Tour**.

TRIPS 5 14

Oregon Highway 101

North Cascades Picture Lake

The Cascade Mountains

You don't have to leave the cities to enjoy the Cascades: snow-capped peaks make natural backdrops to the urban bustle in Seattle, Portland and Vancouver. Explore the northern Cascades on **Trip 8: Cascade Drive** and on **Trip 12: Mt Baker & Lummi Island**. Get to know the Oregon Cascades on **Trip 21: Oregon Cascades Scenic Byways**.

TRIPS 8 12 21

John Day Fossil Beds

Within the soft rocks and crumbly soils of eastern Oregon's John Day region lies one of the world's greatest fossil collections. Over 2200 plant and animal species dating back millions of years have been identified at the John Day Fossil Beds, and the amazing rock formations make **Trip 17: Journey Through Time Scenic Byway** particularly memorable.

TRIP 17

Back Roads & Byways

Ditching the interstate is richly rewarded around these parts. Experience one of the West Coast's most spectacular coastal back roads on **Trip 7: Chuckanut Drive & Whidbey Island**. Get lost in a maze of forests, lakes and hot springs on **Trip 21: Oregon Cascades Scenic Byways**. Or go back in time with the amazing **Trip 17: Journey Through Time Scenic Byway**.

TRIPS 7 17 21

Willamette Valley Wine grapes

BEST ROADSIDE FUN

Oregon Vortex Defy physics at a classic roadside attraction. **Trips** 22 23

Prehistoric Gardens Where the dinosaurs are more fun than ferocious. **Trip** 14

Stonehenge Washington's answer to the UK monument. **Trips** 1 17

The Glass House A quirky house made of embalming fluid bottles. **Trip** 13

Marsh's Free Museum Right across from the World's Largest Frying Pan. **Trip** 5

Willamette Wineries

Pinot Noir lovers unite! It's Oregon's most famous grape, finicky as a superstar and the foundation for some exceptional wine. Cruise around the towns of Newberg, Dundee and McMinnville and sample the local favorite, along with Chardonnay, Riesling and Pinot Gris. Bring a designated driver and hit all the high points on **Trip 16: Willamette Valley Wine Tour**.

TRIP 16

Crater Lake National Park Volcanic landscape

Volcanoes & Craters

Volcanoes have a way of wreaking havoc upon the landscape, but give them an eon or two to settle down and you get some gorgeous results. The eruption of Mt Mazama left behind the unique geological gift of Crater Lake, which you'll see on **Trip 23: Crater Lake Circuit**, or you can witness more recent volcanic aftermath on **Trip 10: Mt St Helens Volcano Trail**.

TRIPS 10 23

BEST HOT SPRINGS

Terwilliger Hot Springs A popular place at Cougar Reservoir. **Trips** 20 21

Breitenbush Lovely, developed springs with on-site accommodations. **Trip** 20

Bonneville A luxurious spa complex on the Lewis and Clark Trail. **Trips** 1 2

Umpqua An unbeatable location, perched above the Umpqua River. **Trip** 23

Belknap A resort built around two giant pools. **Trip** 21

HIGHLIGHTS
★

Columbia River Gorge Multnomah Falls

Olympic National Park Black-tailed deer

Columbia River Gorge

Carved out by the mighty Columbia as the Cascades uplifted, the Columbia River Gorge is a geological marvel. With Washington state on its north and Oregon to its south, the gorge provides both states with dramatic views, countless waterfalls and great hikes. Take your time following the gorge on **Trip 2: Columbia River Gorge & Mt Hood**.

TRIP

Olympic National Park

Within this park you can hike through old-growth forests, waltz through flower-filled meadows, swim in pure mountain lakes or try to summit Mt Olympus. You can even go trout fishing, beachcombing, hot-spring soaking and skiing. Learn about some of the park's best features, including the intensely green Hoh Rainforest, on **Trip 4: Olympic Peninsula Loop**.

TRIP 4

Waterfalls

Tiered falls, plunging falls, curtain falls, ribbon falls – hundreds of waterfalls in the Pacific Northwest give you ample opportunity to witness firsthand all the variations in the waterfall vernacular. You'll find abundant waterfall-peeping opportunities on **Trip 2: Columbia River Gorge & Mt Hood**, and you can even hit 10 falls within one state park on **Trip 20: To Bend & Back**.

TRIPS

17

HIGHLIGHTS ★

Microbreweries

Love beer? Welcome to paradise. The Pacific Northwest has some of the best microbrews in the world and plenty of them. In fact, Portland (aka 'Beervana') holds the distinguished record of 'most microbreweries of any city in the world.' Almost any city worth its malt has multiple brews to sample; head out to Bend and check out their nine local microbreweries in **Trip 20: To Bend & Back**.

TRIPS

Foodie Fun

The Pacific Northwest has some of the most inventive restaurants in the country, with chefs known for making the most of the region's bounteous produce and fresh seafood. Sample the latter on **Trip 14: Highway 101 Oregon Coast**, or go inland for decadent pairings of wine and fine dining on **Trip 16: Willamette Valley Wine Tour**. For a taste of urban foodie hot spots, check out **Trip 22: Essential I-5**.

TRIPS

(left) **Haida Gwaii** Shoreline at low tide

(below) **Portland** Craft brewery

Island Exploration

Hundreds of islands litter the Pacific Northwest coastline, ranging from uninhabited to barely inhabited, and you'll feel like you've left the world behind the moment you drive onto the ferry. Go off the grid on **Trip 6: San Juan Islands Scenic Byway**, or make your escape with **Trip 31: Haida Gwaii Adventure**.

TRIPS

BEST SKIING

Whistler Follow in the ski tracks of the 2010 Winter Olympians. **Trip** 26

Methow Valley A cross-country skier's paradise with over 125 miles of groomed trails. **Trip** 8

Crystal Mountain Washington's largest ski resort, with more than 50 named runs. **Trip** 9

Mt Hood You can ski here every month of the year. **Trip** 2

19

IF YOU LIKE...

Alert Bay Namgis Burial Grounds

History

History buffs can follow in the footsteps of Native Americans, explorers, pioneers and gold rush prospectors, and the area's maritime history is reflected all along the Pacific Coast. Too recent? Explore fossil beds that date back millions of years.

1 On the Trail of Lewis & Clark Follow the trail of America's greatest explorers.

5 Graveyard of the Pacific Tour Lighthouses, nautical museums and shipwrecks illuminate maritime history.

17 Journey Through Time Scenic Byway Dig deep into Oregon history with fossil beds, ghost towns and more.

25 Vancouver & the Fraser Valley East of Vancouver, learn more about British Columbia's pioneer past.

The Great Outdoors

It's no wonder the Pacific Northwest attracts outdoorsy types. The great outdoors is what the area is all about, whether you're trekking through forests, finding remote hot springs or biking down the coast.

2 Columbia River Gorge & Mt Hood This area reveals some of Oregon's most dramatic work.

4 Olympic Peninsula Loop From beaches to mountains, explore the treasures of the Olympic Peninsula.

6 San Juan Islands Scenic Byway Whale-watching, kayaking and biking are the main attractions in these islands off Washington's coast.

21 Oregon Cascades Scenic Byways Waterfalls, hot springs and lakes break up the almost nonstop greenery.

Food & Drink

The Pacific Northwest leads the continent in locally grown, sustainable and organic products. And since great wine demands great food, you can get your fill of both in the wine regions of Oregon, Washington and British Columbia, where tasting is an art form.

7 Chuckanut Drive & Whidbey Island Nosh your way from cheese shops to oyster farms and farm-to-plate restaurants.

11 Washington Wine Tour Columbia Valley's laid-back wine country is emerging as a major winemaking destination.

16 Willamette Valley Wine Tour Oregon's wine country showcases some of the area's best food and wine.

30 Okanagan Valley Wine Tour Explore Canada's hill-lined, lakeside wine region.

North Cascades National Park Ross Lake

Family Travel

From aquariums full of sea life to cowboys riding bucking broncos, the Pacific Northwest will spark a child's imagination. Whether you head to the coast, the mountains or farmland, you'll be greeted with kindness by locals who know how to treat families right.

3 **Mountains to Sound Greenway** Waterfalls, aquariums and interesting museums make this trip fun for everyone.

14 **Highway 101 Oregon Coast** Enjoy tide pools, ocean surf and lots of small-town stops along the way.

22 **Essential I-5** This trip packs in the fun, with stops that range from roadside attractions to light history.

26 **Sea to Sky Highway** The Britannia Mining Museum is a hit with road-weary kids.

Off the Beaten Track

No one does remote like the Pacific Northwest. It's easy to lose yourself out here, with undeveloped land masses that stretch on and on, from the unpopulated eastern regions of Washington and Oregon to the vast expanses of British Columbia.

13 **International Selkirk Loop** Find the forgotten corners of Washington, Idaho and British Columbia.

17 **Journey Through Time Scenic Byway** If ghost towns and a wide horizon are what you're after, this is the place.

19 **Hells Canyon Scenic Byway** Few roads access the canyons in this remote corner of Oregon.

29 **Vancouver Island's Remote North** Head north from Vancouver to see the less-well-known side of the island.

Mountains

One of the benefits of being in a geological area known for earthquakes and volcanoes is the landscape they leave behind. Snow-capped ranges dominate the landscape, providing scenic backdrops and abundant recreational opportunities – from skiing to hiking to searching for Bigfoot.

8 **Cascade Drive** This altitudinous route through the northern Cascades is alive with rugged beauty.

9 **Mt Rainier Scenic Byways** At 14,411ft, volcanic Mt Rainier is the highest peak in the Cascades.

10 **Mt St Helens Volcano Trail** See the destruction left behind after its 1980 eruption.

32 **Circling the Rockies** Get a taste of national parks, hot springs, and the Canadian Rockies.

NEED ᵀᴼ KNOW

CELL PHONES
The US and Canada use GSM-850 and GSM-1900 bands. SIM cards are relatively easy to obtain in both countries.

INTERNET ACCESS
Wi-fi is available in most lodgings and cafes; some larger hotels add $10 to $20 for access. Internet cafes charge $4 to $10 per hour.

FUEL
Gas stations are easy to find, except in national parks and some mountain areas. Expect to pay $2.50 to $4.50 per gallon.

RENTAL CARS
Budget (📞800-218-7992; www.budget.com)

Enterprise (📞800-261-7331; www.enterprise.com)

Hertz (📞800-654-3131; www.hertz.com)

IMPORTANT NUMBERS
Emergencies (📞911)

Local Directory Assistance (📞411)

American Automobile Association (AAA; 📞877-428-2277)

Canadian Automobile Association (📞800-222-4357)

Climate

Vancouver
GO Jun–Sep

Victoria
GO Jun–Sep

Seattle
GO Jun–Sep

Eastern Washington
GO May–Oct

Desert, dry climate

Warm to hot summers, mild winters

Mild to hot summers, cold winters

Portland
GO Jun–Sep

Eastern Oregon
GO May–Oct

Oregon Coast
GO Jun–Sep

When to Go

High Season (Jun–Sep)
» Sunny, warm days throughout the region.

» More crowds and higher prices for accommodations and sights.

» For ski resorts, busiest times are December to March.

Shoulder Season (Apr–May & Oct)
» Crowds and prices drop off.

» Temperatures remain mild.

» Services are more limited, but there's less competition for them.

Low Season (Nov–Mar)
» Colder days, less sunlight, more rain.

» Some services may close along the coast, and high passes can be blocked by snow.

» Indoor activities, such as theater and music, are at their best!

Your Daily Budget

Budget: Less than $100
» Inexpensive motel room/dorm bed: $85/30

» Food cart meal: $5-10

Midrange: $100-200
» Good hotel room: $125 a night

» Meal in a good restaurant: $20-35

Top End: More than $200
» Upscale hotel room: $200 & up

» Fine-dining meal: $35-75

Eating

Food trucks Cheap, creative and often delicious.

Cafes Pick up a pastry with your morning coffee.

Roadside diners Cheap and simple.

Restaurants All price ranges and cuisine types are represented.

Vegetarians Most restaurants offer vegetarian options.

Eating price indicators represent the cost of a main dish:

$	less than $10
$$	$10–$20
$$$	more than $20

Sleeping

Hostels Budget options let you share a room on the cheap.

Motels Cheaper than hotels and ubiquitous along highways.

B&Bs Personal service, often in former homes, breakfast included.

Hotels The higher the rate, the more amenities.

Sleeping price indicators represent the cost of a double room with private bathroom in high season. Lodging tax (6% to 16%) will be extra:

$	less than $100
$$	$100–$200
$$$	more than $200

Arriving in the Pacific Northwest

Portland International Airport
Rental Cars Reserve online and pick up at the airport.

Max Light Rail Connects to downtown Portland in 40 minutes; adult/child $2.50/1.25.

Shuttle Frequent services from $14 one way.

Taxis $35; around 20 minutes to downtown.

Sea-Tac Airport (Seattle)
Rental Cars Reserve online and pick up at the airport.

Link Light Rail Connects to downtown Seattle in 30 minutes; adult/child $3.25/1.50.

Shuttle Frequent services from $18 one way.

Taxi $45; about 25 minutes to downtown.

Vancouver International Airport
Rental Cars Reserve online and pick up at the airport.

SkyTrain Connects to downtown Vancouver in 25 minutes; from CAN$7.50/6.75.

Taxi CAN$35; around 30 minutes to downtown.

Money

ATMs are widely available. Credit cards accepted at most hotels, restaurants and shops.

Tipping

20% to 25% of restaurant bill; 10% to 15% for taxis; $1 per drink or 20% for bartenders; $1 to $2 per bag for valets; $2 daily for housekeeping.

Opening Hours

High-season hours.

Post offices & banks ◷8am or 9am-5pm Mon-Fri, some 8am or 9am-2pm Sat.

Restaurants ◷7-11:30am breakfast, 11:30am-2:30pm lunch, 5-9pm dinner.

Supermarkets ◷8am-10pm, 24hr in large cities.

Useful Websites

Lonely Planet (www.lonelyplanet.com/the-pacific-northwest)

Washington State Tourism (www.experiencewa.com)

Oregon Tourism Commission (www.traveloregon.com)

Tourism British Columbia (www.hellobc.com)

For more, see Road Trip Essentials (p346).

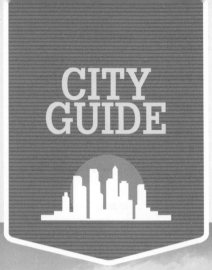

CITY GUIDE

SEATTLE

Lively, progressive and endlessly green, Seattle is Washington state's largest city. Rainy days are a great time to wander historic Pike Place Market or visit Seattle's most rocking museum, the Experience Music Project. When the sun comes out, head for the Olympic Sculpture Park or take our walking tour (p152).

Seattle Sunset over the Seattle skyline

Getting Around

Seattle traffic is chaotic, and downtown is hilly, with lots of one-way streets. All the city's taxicabs operate at the same rate, currently $2.60 at meter drop, then $2.70 per mile. Metro Transit buses (fares $2.50 to $2.75 for three hours) run 5am to 1:30am.

Parking

Downtown parking is scarce and expensive, and some hotels charge a premium overnight, so check before booking. Metered parking goes from 8am to 6pm and extends until 8pm in popular areas; Sundays are free if you can find a spot, although some high-traffic areas limit you to two or four hours per spot.

Where to Eat

Some of Seattle's favorite restaurants are in Pike Place Market, where you can also forage for picnic fixings. Historic Pioneer Square has a surprising number of budget-friendly options, and the International District has amazing Asian cuisine.

Where to Stay

Belltown and the Pike Place Market area offer lots of choices, ranging from hostels to boutiques to large chains. The University District offers more budget-conscious options, and Capitol Hill is a good choice for inns and B&Bs.

Useful Websites

Lonely Planet (www.lonelyplanet.com/usa/seattle)
Visit Seattle (www.visitseattle.org)

Trips through Seattle:

For more, check out our city and country guides. www.lonelyplanet.com

TOP EXPERIENCES

➡ **Browse in Pike Place Market**
Seattle's landmark is more than just a market – it's a living community, complete with flying fish, mysterious shops, buskers and a wall of chewing gum.

➡ **Speed Up the Space Needle**
On a clear day, views from this iconic 1962 World's Fair tower are well worth the price of admission.

➡ **Rock Out at the EMP**
Paul Allen's music museum introduces the musical legends who've shaped the Seattle sound for generations, from Bing Crosby to Jimi Hendrix to Kurt Cobain.

➡ **Sample the Coffee Culture**
This is, after all, the birthplace of Starbucks. Hundreds of micro-roasters, cafes, baristas and connoisseurs make sure the city's coffee culture keeps buzzing.

➡ **Explore Capitol Hill**
In Seattle's most colorful neighborhood, there's beer-flavored ice cream and coffee-flavored beer, dogs with dyed pink streaks in their fur, and enough vinyl and books to make you think Amazon.com never happened.

➡ **Chow Down in Belltown**
This funky little neighborhood, where grunge was born, is now known for its huge number and variety of restaurants. Most have a strong emphasis on 'locavore' cuisine, with ingredients sourced from Seattle's nearby waters and farms. It's a compact enough area to do a mini-tour through several menus.

Portland Downtown

PORTLAND

Laid-back Portland has a compact downtown and several charming residential neighborhoods. People-watching is a favorite pastime, best enjoyed while noshing at food carts, sipping microbrews at a sidewalk table, or wandering the aisles of Powell's Books. Check out all the city has to offer on our walking tour (p260).

Getting Around

Transit buses, the streetcar and the Max light-rail system all link up and can get you nearly everywhere (www.trimet. org). Bicycling is a great way to see Portland: there's a good network of bike lanes, and a new bike-share program (look for the bright-orange fleets).

Parking

You can get lucky with metered street parking, but there are six convenient SmartPark buildings downtown that charge $1.60 per hour. Check www. portlandonline.com/ smartpark for locations and hours.

Where to Eat

Downtown offers everything from fine dining to food carts where you can find the perfect combination of good, cheap and fast. For good midrange options, including great brunches and a mélange of ethnic cuisines, head across the river to northeast and southeast Portland.

Where to Stay

You'll find Portland's swankiest digs downtown, along with some nice midrange options. On the east side of town are some of the city's coolest independent hotels, as well as lots of midrange and budget chain offerings near the convention center.

Useful Websites

Travel Portland (www. travelportland.com) What to do, where to go, how to save.

Portland Mercury (www. portlandmercury.com) Alt-weekly paper with news and culture.

Willamette Week (www. wweek.com) Long-established news weekly with event listings.

Trips through Portland:

Vancouver Skyline at night

VANCOUVER

Vancouver is a sparkling, cosmopolitan city set against a backdrop of rugged natural beauty. Its welcoming downtown (see our walking tour, p340) is flanked by the forested seawall of Stanley Park, and its neighborhoods contain easily walkable shopping streets. Wander historic Gastown, artsy Granville Island and the colorful West End 'gayborhood.'

Getting Around

You don't really need a car in Vancouver: it's easy enough to get around on foot, by bus or by cab. TransLink network, which includes buses, SkyTrain and SeaBus, starts at CAN$2.75 for travel within one zone. An all-day, all-zone pass costs CAN$9.75.

Parking

Parking is at a premium downtown. Some streets have metered parking (up to CAN$6 per hour), but your best bet is to head for pay-parking lots (from CAN$5 per hour). For an interactive map of parking-lot locations, check EasyPark (www.easypark.ca).

Where to Eat

Top streets include downtown's Robson St for Japanese *izakaya,* Yaletown's Hamilton and Mainland Sts for splurge-worthy dinners, Gastown for resto-bars, Commercial Dr for ethnic-flavored joints, and the West End's Denman and Davie Sts for midrange options.

Where to Stay

Swanky sleepovers abound downtown, as do midrange options. To split the geographical difference between downtown and the great outdoors, head to the North Shore. Hostels are scattered across the city; there are good digs near the University of British Columbia.

Useful Websites

Tourism Vancouver (www.tourismvancouver.com) Official tourism site.

City of Vancouver (www.vancouver.ca) Resource-packed official city site.

Inside Vancouver (www.insidevancouver.ca) What to do in and around the city.

Trips through Vancouver: 25

THE PACIFIC NORTHWEST
BY REGION

Variety defines the Pacific Northwest: roads here will take you to coastal villages, lush rainforests, mountain peaks, wide-open wheat fields and arid deserts, plus some of the most appealing cities in the US. Here's your guide to each region.

British Columbia (p267)

Canada's westernmost province wows visitors with its mighty mountains, deep forests and dramatic coastlines. But there's much more to British Columbia than nature-hugging dioramas – take, for example, cosmopolitan Vancouver, a city that fuses cuisines and cultures from Asia and beyond. Wherever you head, the great outdoors will always call.

Explore Vancouver on Trip 25
Go island-hopping on Trip 28

Washington (p53)

Washington state is the heart of the Pacific Northwest, from the lush, green Olympic Peninsula to the white peaks of the Cascade Mountains and the whale-surrounded San Juan Islands. Further east, the state leans more cowboy than boutique. The biggest urban jolt is Seattle, but Spokane, Bellingham and Olympia are equally worthy.

Explore a rainforest on Trip 4
Peek at peaks on Trip 8

Oregon (p159)

Oregon's landscape ranges from rugged coastline and thick evergreen forests to barren, fossil-strewn deserts, volcanoes and glaciers. And then there are the towns: funky Portland, dramatic Ashland, beer-loving Bend and beyond.

Eat like royalty on Trip 16
Gaze upon Crater Lake on Trip 23

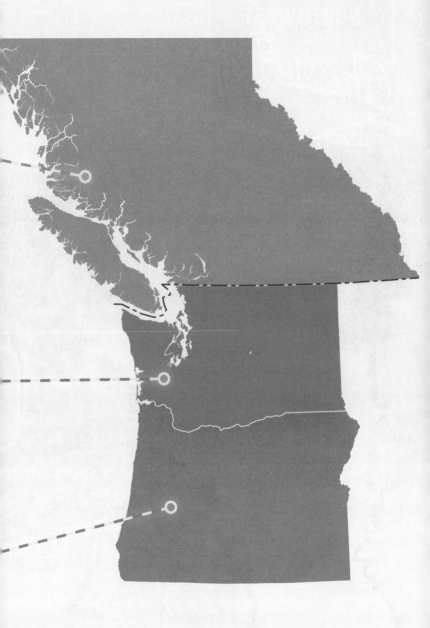

THE PACIFIC
NORTHWEST

Classic Trips

3

What is a Classic Trip?

All of our Pacific Northwest trips show you the best of the region, but we've chosen some as our all-time favorites. These are our Classic Trips – the ones that lead you to the most iconic sights, the top activities and the uniquely Pacific Northwest experiences.

eft: Sparks Lake
above: Snoqualmie Falls

31

Classic Trip

On the Trail of Lewis & Clark

1

Follow the Columbia River on this historic drive that marks the climax of Lewis and Clark's cross-continental 1805 journey as they stumbled toward the Pacific and instant immortality.

TRIP HIGHLIGHTS

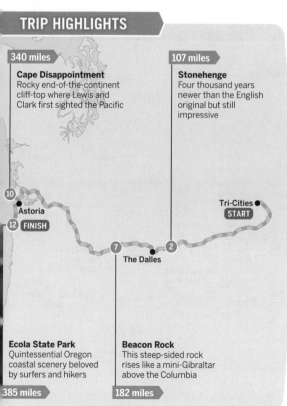

340 miles

Cape Disappointment
Rocky end-of-the-continent cliff-top where Lewis and Clark first sighted the Pacific

107 miles

Stonehenge
Four thousand years newer than the English original but still impressive

10
Astoria

12 FINISH

Tri-Cities ●
START

7
The Dalles

2

Ecola State Park
Quintessential Oregon coastal scenery beloved by surfers and hikers

385 miles

Beacon Rock
This steep-sided rock rises like a mini-Gibraltar above the Columbia

182 miles

3–4 DAYS
385 MILES/620KM

GREAT FOR...

BEST TIME TO GO
Year-round – if you don't mind frequent rain, the Columbia River valley is always open.

ESSENTIAL PHOTO
Indian Beach, Ecola State Park – the Oregon coast personified.

BEST FOR HISTORY
The Lewis & Clark Interpretive Center in Cape Disappointment State Park.

Classic Trip

1 On the Trail of Lewis & Clark

It would take most people their combined annual leave to follow the Lewis and Clark trek in its entirety from St Louis, MO, to Cape Disappointment. Focusing on the final segment, this trip documents the contradictory mix of crippling exhaustion and building excitement that the two explorers felt as they struggled, car-less and weather-beaten, along the Columbia River on their way to completing the greatest overland trek in American history.

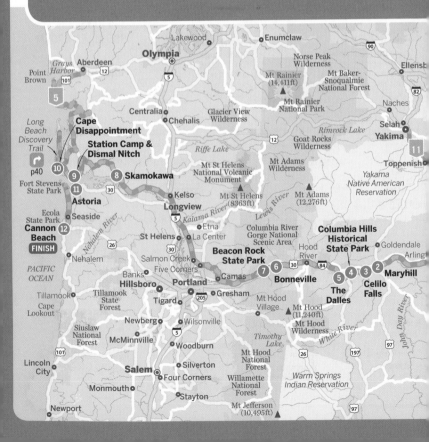

1 Tri-Cities

This trip's start point has a weighty historical significance. The arrival of Lewis and Clark and the Corps of Discovery at the confluence of the Snake and Columbia Rivers on October 16, 1805, marked a milestone achievement on their quest to map a river route to the Pacific. After a greeting by 200 Indians singing and drumming in a half circle, the band camped at this spot for two days, trading clothing for dried salmon. The **Sacajawea Interpretive Center** (📞509-545-2361; http://parks.state.wa.us/250/sacajawea; Sacajawea State Park, Pasco, WA; suggested donation $1; 🕙10am-5pm late Mar–Nov 1; 👶) situated at the river confluence 5 miles southeast of present-day Pasco, relates the story of the expedition through the eyes of Sacajawea, the Shoshone Native American guide and interpreter the Corps had recruited in North Dakota.

🍴 p41

The Drive » Head south on I-82 before switching west at the Columbia River on SR-14, aka the Lewis & Clark Hwy. Here, in dusty sagebrush country, you'll pass a couple of minor sites – Wallula Gap, where the Corps first spotted Mt Hood, and the volcanic bluff of Hat Rock, first named by William Clark. The next stop is 107 miles from Tri-Cities.

TRIP HIGHLIGHT

2 Maryhill

Conceived by great Northwest entrepreneur and road builder Sam Hill, the **Maryhill Museum of Art** (📞509-773-3733; www.maryhillmuseum.org; 35 Maryhill Museum Dr, WA; adult/child $9/3; 🕙10am-5pm mid-Mar–mid-Nov) occupies a mansion atop a bluff overlooking the Columbia River. Its eclectic art collection is enhanced by a small Lewis and Clark display, while its peaceful gardens are perfect for a classy picnic punctuated by exotic peacock cries. Interpretive signs point you to fine views down the Columbia Gorge to the riverside spot (now a state park) where Meriwether Lewis and William Clark camped on October 21, 1805. The park is just one of several along this trip where you can pitch a tent within a few hundred yards of the Corps' original camp.

Another of Hill's creations, a life-sized unruined replica of **Stonehenge** (US Hwy 97), lies 2 miles to the east.

LINK YOUR TRIP

5 Graveyard of the Pacific Tour

Lewis and Clark survived, but others didn't. Find out about the tumultuous maritime history of southwest Washington's coast.

11 Washington Wine Tour

After all that Lewis and Clark history you'll need a glass of wine. Break off in the Tri-Cities for some relaxed quaffing opportunities.

The Drive 》 Continue west from Maryhill on SR-14 for 5 miles to the site of the now submerged Celilo Falls.

❸ Celilo Falls

A vivid imagination can be as important as sunscreen when following the 'Trail.' One example of this is the turnout that's 5 miles west of Maryhill overlooks what was once the Indian salmon fishing center of Celilo Falls. The explorers spent two days here in late October 1805, lowering their canoes down the crashing falls on elk-skin ropes. A century and a half later the rising waters of the dammed Columbia drowned the falls – which were the sixth-most voluminous in the world – destroying a centuries-old Native American fishing site and rendering much of Clark's description of the region unrecognizable.

The Drive 》 Head west on SR-14, paralleling the mighty Columbia, for another 15 miles to Columbia Hills Historical State Park.

❹ Columbia Hills Historical State Park

Indian tribes like the Nez Perce, Clatsop and Walla Walla were essential to the success of the Lewis and Clark expedition, supplying them not only with food but also horses and guides. One of the best places to view tangible traces of the region's Native American heritage is the Temani Pesh-wa (Written on Rocks) Trail at **Columbia Hills Historical State Park** (📞509-439-9032; Hwy 14, mile 85; day-use fee $10; ⏰Apr-Oct), which highlights the region's best petroglyphs. Reserve a spot in advance on the free guided tours on Friday and Saturday at 10am to view the famous but fragile pictograph of the god Tsagaglal (She Who Watches). The park is also a popular site for rock climbers and windsurfers.

The Drive 》 Two miles west of Horsethief Lake, turn south onto US-197, which takes you across the Columbia River into the Dalles in Oregon. Two miles upriver sits the Dalles Dam, which completely submerged the once-magnificent Celilo Falls and rapids on its completion in 1957.

❺ The Dalles

Once the urban neighbor of the formidable Celilo Falls, the Dalles' image is more mundane these days. The local economy focuses on cherry-growing, computer technology and outdoor recreation. Notwithstanding, the town hosts one of the best Lewis and Clark–related museums along this stretch of the Columbia, sited in the **Columbia Gorge Discovery Center** (📞541-296-8600; www.gorgediscovery.org; 5000 Discovery Dr; adult/child $9/5; ⏰9am-5pm) on the western edge of the city. Displays detail the 30 tons of equipment the Corps dragged across the continent and the animals they had to kill to survive (including 190 dogs and a ferret). Kids will get a kick from dressing up in Lewis and Clark period costume.

🍴 🛏 p41

The Drive 》 You can continue west from the Dalles on either side of the Columbia (the expedition traveled straight down the middle by canoe) via SR-14 (Washington), or the slower, more scenic SR-30 (Oregon). En route to Bonneville, 46 miles away, look for the views down to macabre Memaloose Island, once a burial site for Native Americans who left their dead here in canoes of cedar.

❻ Bonneville

There are two Bonnevilles: Bonneville, Oregon, and North Bonneville, Washington. At this stage in their trip, Lewis and Clark were flea-infested and half-starved from a diet of dog meat and starchy wapato roots. Fortunately, 21st-century Bonneville, which is famous for its Depression-era dam completed in 1938, has some tastier culinary offerings to contemplate.

The Drive >> Just west of North Bonneville on SR-14 lies Beacon Rock State Park.

- - - - - - - - - - - - - - -

TRIP HIGHLIGHT

⑦ Beacon Rock State Park

On November 2, 1805, a day after passing modern Bonneville, Clark wrote about a remarkable 848ft-tall monolith he called Beaten Rock, changing the name on his return to Beacon Rock. Just over a century later, Henry Biddle bought the rock for the bargain price of $1 (!) and you can still hike his snaking 1-mile trail to the top of the former lava plug in **Beacon Rock State Park** (📞509-427-8265; http://parks.state.wa.us/474/Beacon-Rock; Hwy 14, Mile 35; day-use fee $10). As you enjoy the wonderful views, ponder the fact that you have effectively climbed up the inside of an ancient volcano. For the Corps, the rock brought a momentous discovery, for it was here that the excited duo first noticed the tide, proving at last that they were finally nearing their goal of crossing the American continent.

The Drive >> Your next stop along SR-14 should be the fantastic views of the flood-carved gorge and its impressive cascades from the Cape Horn overview. From here, it's a straight shot on I-5 to Kelso and

LEWIS & CLARK HISTORICAL PARK

The so-called **Lewis & Clark National Historical Park** (📞503-861-2471; www.nps.gov/lewi; 92343 Fort Clatsop Rd; adult/child $5/free; ⏱9am-6pm mid-Jun–Aug, to 5pm Sep–mid-Jun) combines 10 different historical sites clustered around the mouth of the Columbia River, each of which relates to important facts about the Corps of Discovery and its historic mission to map the American West. It was formed through the amalgamation of various state parks and historic sites in 2004, and is run jointly by the National Park Service and the states of Washington and Oregon. Highlights include Cape Disappointment, Fort Clatsop and the 6.5-mile **Fort to Sea trail** linking Clatsop and the ocean at Sunset Beach.

then over the Lewis and Clark Bridge to parallel the Columbia River westward on SR-4. Skamokawa is 103 miles in total from the state park.

- - - - - - - - - - - - - - -

⑧ Skamokawa

For most of their trip down the Columbia River, Lewis and Clark traveled not on foot but by canoe. There's nowhere better to paddle in the Corps' canoe wake than at **Pillar Rock**, where Clark wrote of his joy at finally being able to camp in view of the ocean. **Columbia River Kayaking** (📞360-747-1044; www.columbiariverkayaking.com; 957 Steamboat Slough Rd, Skamokawa; half-day tours from $65; ⏱noon-4pm Fri-Sun) in the town of Skamokawa offers one- or two-day kayak tours to this site, as well as Grays Bay.

The Drive >> Continue on SR-4 northwest out of Skamokawa. In Naselle, go southwest on

SR-401. From Skamokawa to Dismal Nitch is 35 miles, along the north bank of the Columbia River.

- - - - - - - - - - - - - - -

⑨ Station Camp & Dismal Nitch

Just east of the Astoria-Megler Bridge on the north bank of the Columbia River, a turnout marks Dismal Nitch, where the drenched duo were stuck in a pounding week-long storm that Clark described as the most disagreeable time he had ever experienced. The Corps finally managed to make camp at Station Camp, 3 miles further west, now an innocuous highway pullout, where they stayed for 10 days while the two leaders, no doubt sick of each other by now, separately explored the headlands around Cape Disappointment.

Classic Trip

STEVE ESTVANIK / SHUTTERSTOCK ©

WHY THIS IS A CLASSIC TRIP
BRENDAN SAINSBURY, WRITER

This retracing of the Corps of Discovery's transcontinental wilderness odyssey is as close as it gets to an American pilgrimage. Lewis and Clark were, without doubt, America's greatest explorers and the nation wouldn't be the same today without them. Meticulous, curious, brave and groundbreaking, they also came in peace; only one small incident on their return journey with the Blackfeet Indians marred the charitable spirit of the Corps' grail-like quest.

Top: Cape Disappointment
Left: Fort Clatsop, Lewis and Clark National Historical Park
Right: North Head Lighthouse, Cape Disappointment

OLENA YAKOBCHUK / SHUTTERSTOCK ©

The Drive ≫ You're nearly there! Contain your excitement as you breeze the last few miles west along Highway 101 to Ilwaco and the inappropriately named Cape Disappointment.

TRIP HIGHLIGHT

⑩ Cape Disappointment

Disappointment is probably the last thing you're likely to be feeling as you pull into blustery cliff-top **Cape Disappointment State Park** (☑360-642-3078; Hwy 100; ☉dawn-dusk). Find time to make the short ascent of Mackenzie Hill in Clark's footprints and catch your first true sight of the Pacific. You can almost hear his protracted sigh of relief over two centuries later.

Located on a high bluff inside the park not far from the Washington town of Ilwaco, the sequentially laid-out **Lewis & Clark Interpretive Center** (Hwy 100; adult/child $5/2.50; ☉10am-5pm Wed-Sun) faithfully recounts the Corps of Discovery's cross-continental journey using a level of detail the journal-writing explorers would have been proud of. Information includes everything from how to use an octant to what kind of underpants Lewis wore! A succinct 20-minute film backs up the permanent exhibits. Phone ahead and you can also tour the impressive end-of-continent **North**

THE PACIFIC NORTHWEST'S BEST TRIPS **1** ON THE TRAIL OF LEWIS & CLARK

GARY WEATHERS / GETTY IMAGES ©

Head Lighthouse (http://
northheadlighthouse.com;
tours $2.50; ☉10am-5pm)
nearby.

The Drive » From Ilwaco, take
Hwy 101 back east to the 4.1-
mile long Astoria-Megler Bridge,
the longest continuous truss
bridge in the US. On the other
side lies Astoria in Oregon, the
oldest US-founded settlement
west of the Mississippi.

- - - - - - - - - - - -

⑪ Astoria

After the first truly
democratic ballot in
US history (in which a
woman and a black slave
both voted), the party
elected to make their
winter bivouac across
the Columbia River in
present-day Oregon. A
replica of the original
Fort Clatsop (adult/
child $5/free; ☉9am-6pm
Jun-Aug, to 5pm Sep-May),
where the Corps spent
a miserable winter in
1805–6, lies 5 miles
south of Astoria. Also on
site are trails, a visitor
center and buckskin-clad
rangers who wander the
camp between mid-June
and Labor Day sewing
moccasins (the Corps
stockpiled an impressive
340 pairs for their return
trip), tanning leather and
firing their muskets.

 DETOUR:
LONG BEACH
DISCOVERY TRAIL

Start: ⑩ Cape Disappointment (p39)

Soon after arriving in 'Station Camp,' the
indefatigable Clark, determined to find a better
winter bivouac, set out with several companions
to continue the hike west along a broad sandy
peninsula, coming to a halt near present-day 26th
St in Long Beach, where Clark dipped his toe in
the Pacific and carved his name on a cedar tree for
posterity. The route of this historic three-day trudge
has been re-created in the Long Beach Discovery
Trail, a footpath that runs from the small town
of Ilwaco, adjacent to Cape Disappointment, to
Clark's 26th St turnaround. Officially inaugurated in
September 2009, the trail has incorporated some
dramatic life-size sculptures along its 8.2-mile
length. One depicts a giant gray whale skeleton,
another recalls Clark's recorded sighting of a
washed-up sea sturgeon, while a third re-creates in
bronze the original cedar tree (long since uprooted
by a Pacific storm).

 p41, p81, p174

The Drive » From Fort
Clatsop, take Hwy 101, aka
the Oregon Coast Hwy, south
through the town of Seaside to
Cannon Beach, 25 miles from
Astoria.

- - - - - - - - - - - -

TRIP HIGHLIGHT

⑫ Cannon Beach

Mission accomplished –
or was it? Curiosity (and
hunger) got the better of
the Corps in early 1806
when news of a huge
beached whale lured Clark
and Sacagawea from a salt
factory they had set up
near the present-day town
of Seaside down through
what is now Ecola State
Park to Cannon Beach.

Ecola State Park
(☎503-436-2844; www.
oregonstateparks.org; day use
$5) is the Oregon you may
have already visited in
your dreams: sea stacks,
crashing surf, hidden
beaches and gorgeous
pristine forest. Criss-
crossed by paths, it lies
1.5 miles north of Can-
non Beach, the high-end
'antiresort' so beloved by
Portlanders.

Clark found the whale
near **Haystack Rock**,
a 295ft sea stack that's
the most spectacular
landmark on the Oregon
coast and accessible from
the beach. After bartering
with the Tillamook tribe,
he staggered away with
300lb of whale blubber –
a feast for the half-starved
Corps of Discovery.

 p41

Eating & Sleeping

Tri-Cities ❶

✕ Atomic Ale Brewpub & Eatery Pub $$
(www.atomicalebrewpub.com; 1015 Lee Blvd, Richland; pizzas $9-14, sandwiches $8; ⏱11am-10pm Mon-Thu, to 11pm Fri & Sat, to 8pm Sun) Hanford-inspired 'gallows humor' pervades this cheery microbrewery, known for its wood-fired specialty pizzas and top-notch soup. Start with a locally crafted Half-Life Hefeweizen, Plutonium Porter or Atomic Amber. Real intellectuals grab an Oppenheimer Oatmeal Stout.

The Dalles ❺

✕ Baldwin Saloon American $$
(www.baldwinsaloon.com; 205 Court St; mains $11-20; ⏱11am-10pm Mon-Sat) This 1876 building, with the remnants of a rare cast-iron facade, has been a bar, a brothel and a coffin-storage warehouse. Today it's a casual establishment with a brick interior full of large oil paintings, and a historic dark-wood bar. Food choices include salads, sandwiches, burgers and pasta dishes.

🛏 Celilo Inn Motel $$
(☎541-769-0001; www.celiloinn.com; 3550 E 2nd St; d $119-164;) The beautifully remodeled Celilo Inn was once an old motel, but is now a slick and trendy stay with gorgeous contemporary rooms, many offering views of The Dalles' bridge and dam (worth it at only $10 to $20 more). Luxurious touches include flat-screen TVs and a cool pool for those guaranteed hot summer days. Discount on weekdays.

Bonneville ❻

🛏 Bonneville Hot Springs Resort & Spa Hotel $$$
(☎866-459-1678; www.bonnevilleresort.com; 1252 E Cascade Dr, North Bonneville, WA; r $129-229, pool per hour $10-15; 🐕❄@🛜🏊) With a grand, five-star lobby and 78 stylish rooms (nearly half with private-balcony hot tubs), this resort offers fine dining and full spa services. There's a 25m indoor pool filled with mineral water, plus indoor and outdoor Jacuzzis.

The resort is about 4 miles west of the Bridge of the Gods; look for the entrance road ('Hot Springs Way') across from the Bonneville Dam visitor center road. Weekday rates are lower.

Astoria ⓫

✕ T Paul's Urban Café International $$
(☎503-338-5133; www.tpaulsurbancafe.org; 1119 Commercial St; mains $15-24; ⏱11am-9pm Mon-Thu, to 10pm Fri & Sat) With a slick yet funky atmosphere, this popular cafe serves up a large variety of gourmet quesadillas, sandwiches, salads and pastas.

🛏 Commodore Hotel Boutique Hotel $$
(☎503-325-4747; www.commodoreastoria. com; 258 14th St; d with shared/private bath from $99/179; 🐕🛜) Hip travelers should make a beeline for this stylish hotel, which offers attractive but small, minimalist rooms. Choose either private bathrooms or go Euro-style (sinks in rooms, but baths down the hall; 'deluxe' rooms have better views). There's a great living-room-style lobby with cafe. Room 309 has the best river view.

Cannon Beach ⓬

✕ Newman's at 988 French, Italian $$$
(☎503-436-1151; www.newmansat988.com; 988 Hemlock St; mains $21-37; ⏱5:30-9pm daily Jul–mid-Oct, Tue-Sun mid-Oct–Jun) Expect a fine dining experience at this small, quality restaurant on the main drag. Award-winning chef John Newman comes up with a fusion of French and Italian dishes, such as marinated rack of lamb and char-grilled portobello mushrooms with spinach and gorgonzola. Desserts are sublime; reserve ahead.

🛏 Cannon Beach Hotel Historic Hotel $$
(☎503-436-1392; www.cannonbeachhotel.com; 1116 S Hemlock St; d from $160; 🐕🛜) If you don't need much space, check out this classy, centrally located hotel with just 10 rooms. Standard rooms are lovely, but very small; even the regular suites are tight. A good breakfast at the cafe on the premises is included.

Columbia River Gorge & Mt Hood

2

Towering waterfalls, excellent hiking, hot springs, fruit farms — what else could you want from a long weekend? Add shimmering lakes and snow-capped Mt Hood, and the diversity becomes surreal.

TRIP HIGHLIGHTS

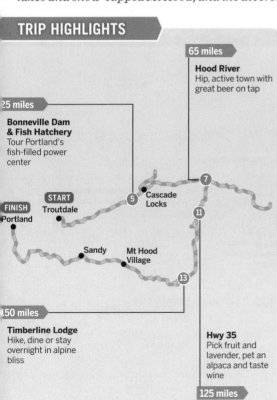

65 miles

Hood River
Hip, active town with great beer on tap

25 miles

Bonneville Dam & Fish Hatchery
Tour Portland's fish-filled power center

START Troutdale

FINISH Portland

5 Cascade Locks

7

11

Sandy   Mt Hood Village

13

150 miles

Timberline Lodge
Hike, dine or stay overnight in alpine bliss

Hwy 35
Pick fruit and lavender, pet an alpaca and taste wine

125 miles

3 DAYS
215 MILES/346KM

GREAT FOR...

BEST TIME TO GO

May to October: fruit is in season, everything is lush and all roads are open.

ESSENTIAL PHOTO

Multnomah Falls: get a top-to-bottom shot of one of the country's highest cascades.

BEST FOR VIEWS

Enjoy a panorama of the lushest part of the Columbia Gorge from Vista House.

2

Columbia River Gorge & Mt Hood

Few places symbolize the grandeur of the Pacific Northwest like the Columbia River Gorge and Mt Hood. Start along this massive cleft in the Cascade Range that measures up to 4000ft deep and is graced by 77 waterfalls. Meanwhile, great white Mt Hood peeks out from behind in all its 11,240ft glory. As you drive up the mountain from the gorge you'll be treated to a fertile foodie heaven of fruit farms and vineyards.

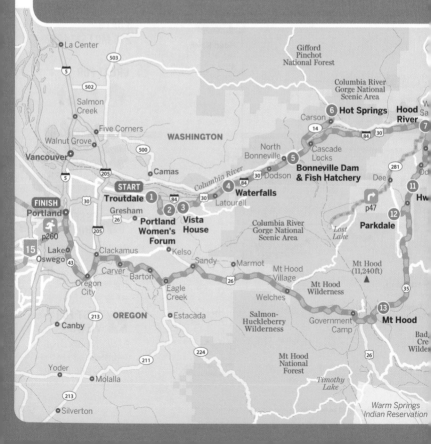

1 Troutdale

Although the metal arch over Troutdale (erected in 2010) isn't the official entrée to the Historic Route 30 (which starts a few miles west from here), this is the logical place to turn off the I-84 from Portland and begin a journey into Columbia Gorge's moss-covered wonderland. Troutdale's center is adorably early-20th-century and a pleasant place to stretch your legs before the drive.

🛏 p51

The Drive » Continue through town then turn right (inland) after the bridge, following the signs for Historic Route 30 toward Corbett. The road follows the forested Sandy River before veering left.

2 Portland Women's Forum

Pull into this parking lot for your first view of the Columbia Gorge. This spot was once the site of the Chanticleer Hotel, built in 1912. It was here, in 1913, that the plans were made for building Hwy 30, which would become Oregon's first modern paved road. Unfortunately, the hotel burned down in 1931 but the panoramas are as splendid as ever.

The Drive » Turn left from the parking lot, drive along the ridge and watch as Hwy 30 turns into classic Columbia Gorge country, with increasing mossy lushness.

3 Vista House

Built between 1916 and 1918, this stone roadside rotunda sits atop Crown Point, 733ft above the Columbia River, and offers magnificent 180-degree views. From the outside, the building looks like it only houses a small information center, but there's a worthwhile historica **museum** (📞503-695-2240; vistahouse.com; ⏰9am-4pm, to 6pm May-Sep) and gift shop hidden down a staircase underground. Weather permitting, you can also go upstairs to the fabulous outdoor viewing deck.

The Drive » Take a right directly out of the parking lot and head downhill as the road winds along the old highway and its stone barriers into increasing greenery.

4 Waterfalls

Welcome to a land so lush and vibrantly green that it looks more like something described in a fantasy novel than reality. This 9-mile section of Hwy 30 could easily be nicknamed 'Waterfall Alley' for the excessive number of spectacular cascades tumbling over

 LINK YOUR TRIP

15 Three Capes Loop
Head back through Portland and go west on Hwy 26 toward the coast.

17 Journey Through Time Scenic Byway
From The Dalles, it's about 30 miles east along Hwy 84 and the Columbia River Gorge to Maryhill.

Classic Trip

mossy basalt cliffs. The falls are at their gushiest in spring. If you're into hiking, you could easily spend a day or two exploring this area, or you can take short walks to the easier access places. **Multnomah Falls** is the highest in Oregon and the busiest stop – you'll find more peace and

quiet around the lesser-known spots.

The Drive » Keep heading east on Hwy 30 till it merges with I-84 shortly after Ainsworth State Park. After a few miles, take exit 40 toward Bonneville Dam.

TRIP HIGHLIGHT

❺ Bonneville Dam & Fish Hatchery

Upon its completion in 1938, Bonneville became the first dam on the Columbia River, permanently altering one of the

continent's mightiest rivers, as well as one of the world's most important salmon runs. It's worth stopping here to check out the **visitors center** (☎541-374-8820; I-84 exit 40; ⊙9am-5pm) that has good exhibits, free tours to the powerhouse throughout the day and a theater showing videos of the dam's history; the underwater viewing room into the fish ladder is a highlight. Afterwards, stroll the nearby fish hatchery, making sure you visit the gargantuan 10ft-long sturgeon named Herman.

The Drive » Get back on I-84 and drive about 3.5 miles upstream to exit 44, which leads you to the Bridge of the Gods (toll each way $1) into Washington State. Turn east on Hwy 14.

❻ Hot Springs

Feel like a nice warm soak to ease your car-stiff bum? **Carson Hot Springs Resort** (p51) is hardly fancy, but its modesty is its finest feature; the first-come, first-served mineral baths are a true escape from any kind of hype. To get there, turn left on Wind River Rd from Hwy 14, then take a right on Hot Springs Ave.

For a more luxurious experience, head to **Bonneville Hot Springs Resort & Spa** (p41), which has an elegant 25m indoor pool filled

TOP WATERFALLS

The following are all off Hwy 30, listed from west to east.

Latourell Falls (249ft) The first major waterfall as you come east on Hwy 30. Hike 10 minutes to reach it, or go a mile to the top.

Bridal Veil Falls (140ft) Two-tiered falls reached via an easy half-mile walk. A separate wheelchair-accessible trail passes through a meadow.

Wahkeena Falls (242ft) Hike up the Wahkeena Trail, join Trail No 441 and head down to Multnomah Falls. Return via the road for the 5-mile loop.

Multnomah Falls (642ft) The gorge's top attraction. Trail No 411 leads to the top (1 mile). Continue up foresty Multnomah Creek and the top of Larch Mountain (another 7 miles).

Oneonta Falls (75ft) Located within the lovely half-mile Oneonta Gorge. Carefully scamper over log jams and wade in water up to waist-high. Fun and worth it!

Horsetail Falls (176ft) Just east of Oneonta Gorge. A 4.5-mile loop begins here, passing through Ponytail Falls and Triple Falls. Walk a half-mile east on Hwy 30 (passing the Oneonta Gorge) to return.

Elowah Falls (289ft) More isolated but pretty falls located about a mile off the highway. Hike to the top, then take a 0.7-mile side trail to McCord Creek Falls (2.5 miles round-trip).

DETOUR:
LOST LAKE

Start: 7 Hood River

For a classic Mt Hood photo op, detour 25 miles south of Hood River to the spectacular Lost Lake. Flanked by forest, this stunning blue body of mountain water frames the white cone of Mt Hood like a perfect postcard. Along with fabulous views, the detour offers respite from the heat when the gorge gets too hot. To get there from Hood River, take Hwy 281 to Dee and follow the signs. Allow at least half a day for the excursion.

with mineral water, plus indoor and outdoor Jacuzzis. Look for the entrance road ('Hot Springs Way') across from the Washington Bonneville Dam visitor center road.

🛏 p41, p51

The Drive › Backtrack over the Bridge of the Gods, then head east on I-84.

TRIP HIGHLIGHT
7 Hood River

Your next stop is the windy riverside town of Hood River, one of the world's top windsurfing and kiteboarding destinations. It's also one very attractive town, thanks to its old homes and stunning setting on the banks of the Columbia River. Plus Mt Hood, with its hiking trails and ski runs, is only a stone's throw away. It should come as no surprise that Hood River has a youthful, adrenaline-hungry population and a main drag packed with good

restaurants, boutique shops and adventure sports stores.

✕ 🛏 p51

The Drive › Get back on I-84 E for around 10 miles, then take exit 69 to Mosier. This links you back up with Historic Route 30 for another incredibly scenic 9 miles.

---

8 Rowena Crest

The summit of this portion of Historic Route 30 has a parking lot with views over the Columbia Gorge, which at this point is losing its lushness to windy, barren hillsides and steep, stratified cliff faces. Here there are two hiking trails: the walk to **Tom McCall Point Trail** (3 miles round-trip) will get you glimpses over the rolling hills of the plateau and Mt Adams, while the easier **Rowena Plateau Trail** (2.5 miles round-trip) is a particular good spot for May wildflowers and leads to the waterfowl-filled **Rowena Pond**.

The Drive › Historic Route 30 winds down the hill back to river level. Follow the signs to the Columbia Gorge Discovery Center.

---

9 Columbia Gorge Discovery Center

The informative **Columbia Gorge Discovery Center** (📞541-296-8600; www.gorgediscovery.org; 5000 Discovery Dr; adult/child $9/5; ⏰9am-5pm) covers the history of the gorge from its creation by cataclysmic floods, through its Native American inhabitants, to the early pioneers, settlers and eventual damming of the river. Whether you're a gorge fanatic or a first-time visitor, the center will undoubtedly increase your appreciation for one of the Pacific Northwest's most amazing natural landscapes.

The Drive › Go back out to Historic Route 30 or I-84 (they run parallel to each other from here, but Historic Route 30 is more scenic), east a couple of miles to The Dalles.

Classic Trip

WHY THIS IS A CLASSIC TRIP
CELESTE BRASH, WRITER

Few routes take in this much
beauty in such a small space –
not only that but all this starts only a half-hour
from downtown Portland! The waterfall strip of the
Columbia Gorge is one of the most beautiful places
I know, and Mt Hood's sharp snowy peak is symbolic
of the region. The hiking is phenomenal, the people
you meet are down to earth, and you can pick fruit
and drink fabulous beer and wine.

Left: Hood River with view to Mt Hood
Right: Multnomah Falls

---

⑩ The Dalles

Though steadfastly
unglamorous, The
Dalles offers decent
camping and hiking,
and the fierce winds are
excellent for windsurf-
ing and kiteboarding.
Sights here include the
fascinating **Fort Dalles
Museum** (☎541-296-4547;
www.fortdallesmuseum.org;

TUSHARKOLEY / SHUTTERSTOCK ©

STAS MOROZ / SHUTTERSTOCK ©

500 W 15th St; adult/child $5/1; ⊙10am-5pm Mar-Oct, closed Mon-Thu Nov-Feb) it's Oregon's oldest museum and is full of historical items. Built in 1957, **The Dalles Dam & Lock** produces enough electricity to power a city of a million inhabitants. **The Dalles Dam Visitors Center** (☎541-296-9778; Clodfelter Way; ⊙9am-5pm May-Sep) contains the

expected homage to hydroelectricity, along with a fish cam to view migratory salmon – it's east on the frontage road from exit 87 off I-84.

✕ ⊨ p41

The Drive ≫ From here you'll backtrack on Historic Route 30 or I-84 (the faster option) to Hood River. Take exit 64 and follow the signs for Hwy 35, which leads inland toward Mt Hood.

TRIP HIGHLIGHT

⑪ Highway 35

The first 16.5 miles of Hwy 35 to Parkdale is the first leg of the 'Fruit Loop,' named for all its agriculture. Wind along scenic fertile lands, easy-to-spot family fruit stands, U-pick orchards, lavender fields, alpaca farms and winery tasting

rooms. There are blossoms in spring, berries in summer, and apples and pears in fall – with plenty of festivals and celebrations throughout the seasons (except for winter). It's a good way to sample the area's agricultural bounties while appreciating the local scenery too – try not to get in an accident from ogling the larger-than-life Mt Hood when it's in view.

The Drive >> Enjoy the scenery of endless orchards and vineyards, and stop whenever you feel the whim – there are over 30 businesses to choose from!

⑫ Parkdale

Your ascent ends at the little town of Parkdale, a great stop for lunch. You can also visit the tiny **Hutson Museum** (☏541-352-7434; 4967

Baseline Dr, Parkdale; $1; ☺ noon-2pm Thu-Sun Apr-Oct, hours vary) in a country-perfect red farmhouse. It has displays of rocks and minerals, Native American artifacts and local memorabilia – plus a garden of native plants.

✕ p51

The Drive >> Return to Hwy 35 and follow it south for 27 miles around grand, white-capped Mt Hood to Hwy 26.

TRIP HIGHLIGHT

⑬ Mt Hood

At 11,240ft, Mt Hood is the highest peak in Oregon. Its pyramid shape makes it peek out from behind many hills, ever enhancing the view. The best place to enjoy this alpine world is Timberline Lodge (p51), a handsome wooden gem from the 1930s, offering glorious shelter and refreshments to both guests and nonguests (and yes, some exterior shots of *The Shining* were

filmed here). In summer, wildflowers bloom on the mountainsides and hidden ponds shimmer in blue, making for some unforgettable hikes; in winter, downhill and cross-country skiing dominates people's minds and bodies.

From here there's also convenient access to the **Pacific Crest Trail** (PCT). Whether you hike 2 miles or 12 miles along the PCT, the views of Mt Hood are incredible. The trail is easy to find – follow the signs to the right of the lodge.

🛏 p51

MOUNT HOOD RAILROAD

If you're tired of the road, the **Mount Hood Railroad** (☏800-872-4661; www.mthoodrr.com; 110 Railroad Ave; Odell trip adult/child $30/25, brunch train $25/20, Polar Express $41/31) also starts here and runs scenically up a similar route to Hwy 35, past the towns of Odell and Dee before its terminus in Parkdale. The views are spectacular, the cars are beautifully restored and the food is memorable. You can also choose to go on special train excursions that include wine tasting and visits to museums.

Eating & Sleeping

Troutdale ❶

🛏 McMenamins Edgefield   Hotel $$

(📞503-669-8610; www.mcmenamins.com/54-edgefield-home; 2126 SW Halsey St, Troutdale; dm $30, s/d with shared bath from $50/140; 🐾🖥📶) This former county poor farm, restored by the McMenamin brothers, is now a one-of-a-kind, 38-acre hotel complex with a dizzying variety of services. There's a wine-tasting room, cinema, glassblowing studio, pitch-and-putt golf course (beer-in-hand), live music, gardens and restaurants.

Hot Springs ❻

🛏 Carson Hot Springs Resort   Hotel $$

(📞509-427-8292; www.carsonhotspringresort.com; 372 St Martin Rd, Carson; r $85-179, mineral bath & wrap $20-30) This rustic, locally loved resort has standard hotel rooms and a charming historic bathhouse where you can soak in a mineral bath and then be wrapped up like a burrito to sweat out your worries.

Hood River ❼

🍴 Celilo Restaurant & Bar   Northwestern $$

(📞541-386-5710; www.celilorestaurant.com; 16 Oak St; lunch mains $9-12, dinner mains $18-28; ⏱11:30am-3pm & 5-9pm) For upscale dining with an emphasis on locally sourced ingredients, there's Celilo, a modern and beautiful restaurant with walls that open to the sidewalk on warm afternoons. Main dishes include various house-made pastas, luscious salads, and lots of fish and seafood dishes (check the website for the current menu). Lunch is more affordable and casual.

🍴 Double Mountain Brewery   Pub Food $$

(📞541-387-0042; www.doublemountainbrewery.com; 8 4th St; sandwiches $6.50-10, pizzas $16-22; ⏱11am-11pm Sun-Thu, to midnight Fri & Sat) For a casual bite, step into this popular brewpub-restaurant for a tasty sandwich or excellent brick-oven pizza (try the Truffle Shuffle). The menu is limited, but the food is great and the beer even better. Live music on weekends.

🛏 Columbia Gorge Hotel   Hotel $$$

(📞800-345-1921; www.columbiagorgehotel.com; 4000 Westcliff Dr; r $134-289; 🐾❄ @📶🖥) Hood River's most famous place to stay is this historic Spanish-style hotel, set high on a cliff above the Columbia. The atmosphere is classy and the grounds lovely, and there's a fine restaurant on the premises. Rooms have antique beds and furnishings. River-view rooms cost more, but are worth it.

🛏 Inn of the White Salmon   Inn $$

(📞509-493-2335; www.innofthewhitesalmon.com; 172 West Jewett Blvd, White Salmon; r from $120; 🐾❄📶) Over in White Salmon, WA, is this very pleasant and contemporary 22-room, ecofriendly inn with sleek, modern rooms, bookish decor and a lovely patio-garden out back. There are also suites with kitchenettes.

Parkdale ⓬

🍴 Apple Valley BBQ   Barbecue $$

(4956 Baseline Dr, Parkdale; mains $10-18; ⏱11am-8pm Wed-Sun) Fill up on barbecue ribs, pulled pork, burgers, salads and homemade pie in a lively 1950s flashback setting. Tables out front make for excellent street viewing on a warm day.

Mt Hood ⓭

🛏 Timberline Lodge   Lodge $$

(📞800-547-1406; www.timberlinelodge.com; 27500 Timberline Rd; d from $135-245; 🐾📶 🎿) As much a community treasure as a hotel, this gorgeous historic lodge offers a variety of rooms, from dorms that sleep up to 10 to deluxe fireplace rooms. There's a year-round heated outdoor pool, and the **ski lifts** (📞503-272-3158; Government Camp; lift tickets from $44) are close by. Enjoy awesome views of Mt Hood, nearby hiking trails, two bars and a good dining room. Rates vary widely.

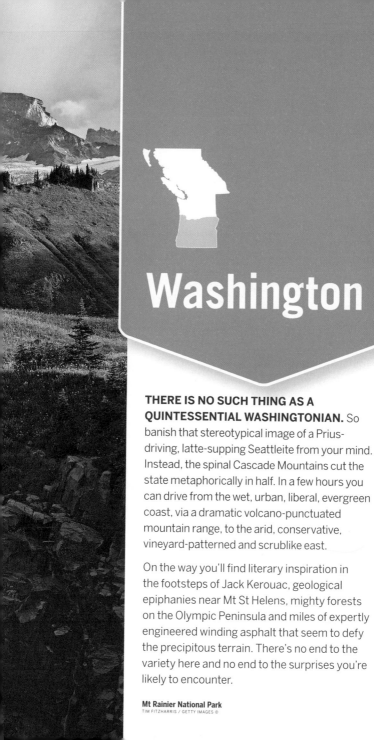

Washington

THERE IS NO SUCH THING AS A QUINTESSENTIAL WASHINGTONIAN. So banish that stereotypical image of a Prius-driving, latte-supping Seattleite from your mind. Instead, the spinal Cascade Mountains cut the state metaphorically in half. In a few hours you can drive from the wet, urban, liberal, evergreen coast, via a dramatic volcano-punctuated mountain range, to the arid, conservative, vineyard-patterned and scrublike east.

On the way you'll find literary inspiration in the footsteps of Jack Kerouac, geological epiphanies near Mt St Helens, mighty forests on the Olympic Peninsula and miles of expertly engineered winding asphalt that seem to defy the precipitous terrain. There's no end to the variety here and no end to the surprises you're likely to encounter.

Mt Rainier National Park
TIM FITZHARRIS / GETTY IMAGES ©

Washington Trips

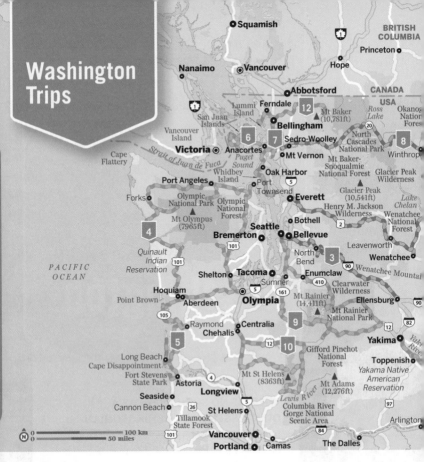

 3 Mountains to Sound Greenway 1–2 Days
Washington's only east–west interstate has a protected greenway. (p57)

4 Olympic Peninsula Loop 4 Days
Tolkien meets *Twilight* in surreal, wet forest. (p67)

5 Graveyard of the Pacific 2 Days
Fear not, this is more maritime history lesson than creepy cemetery. (p75)

6 San Juan Islands Scenic Byway 3 Days
More float than drive around the speckled greenery of a 'lost' America. (p83)

7 Chuckanut Drive & Whidbey Island 1–2 Days
An old-fashioned alternative to the interstate, shadowing Puget Sound. (p91)

8 Cascade Drive 4–5 Days
Wild West towns, Bavarian villages and moody mountains. (p99)

DON'T MISS

Ross Lake Resort

A floating hotel on a wilderness lake; no wonder Kerouac loved the cold, almost terrifying, beauty on Trip 8

Cape Disappointment

Few leave Cape Disappointment disappointed, thanks to its spectacular end-of-the-continent setting. Drop by on Trips 1 5

Leavenworth

German theme towns rarely work in the US except when the alpine backdrop *looks* positively German. See it on Trip 8

Northwest Railway Museum

Snoqualmie community saves a slice of American heritage: a moving museum on a train. Visit on Trip 3

North Woven Broom

Long before Harry Potter, North Woven Broom was making artisan broomsticks. Sweep by on Trip 13

Classic Trip

Mountains to Sound Greenway

3

Busy I-90 zaps you from the Yakima Valley to the metro sophistication of Seattle in less than two hours. But meander off the main road and more serendipitous adventures lurk.

TRIP HIGHLIGHTS

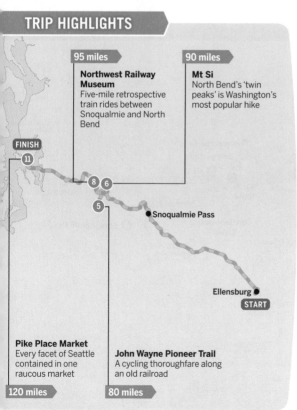

95 miles

Northwest Railway Museum
Five-mile retrospective train rides between Snoqualmie and North Bend

90 miles

Mt Si
North Bend's 'twin peaks' is Washington's most popular hike

FINISH
11

8 6
5
● Snoqualmie Pass

Ellensburg ●
START

Pike Place Market
Every facet of Seattle contained in one raucous market

120 miles

John Wayne Pioneer Trail
A cycling thoroughfare along an old railroad

80 miles

1–2 DAYS
120 MILES/193KM

GREAT FOR...

BEST TIME TO GO
May to September: open museums and predictable weather.

ESSENTIAL PHOTO
Snoqualmie Falls' raw power and *Twin Peaks* flashbacks.

BEST FOR FAMILIES
Northwest Railway Museum and its train rides.

3 Mountains to Sound Greenway

Dramatic changes in scenery and radically contrasting ecosystems are par for the course in Washington, a land bisected by the climate-altering Cascade Mountains. With I-90 as its main artery, this drive ferries you from the dry east to the wet west via 3046ft Snoqualmie Pass on an ostensibly busy road. But a mile or two off the interstate a parallel 'greenway' of bucolic trails and small-town preservation societies prevails.

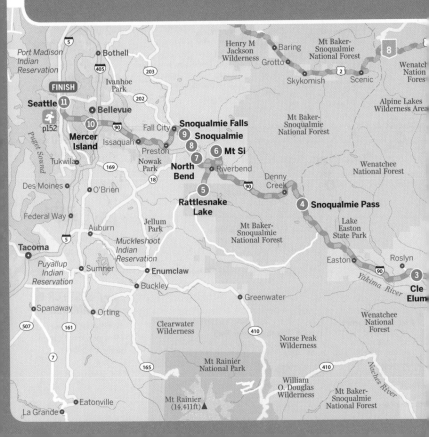

1 Ellensburg

Take an archetypal American rodeo town with a smattering of historic buildings and add a stately college. Welcome to Ellensburg, town of juxtapositions. Here, erudite college undergraduates rub shoulders with weekend cowboys in a small yet salubrious collegiate town where two-thirds of the 16,000 population are registered students. The town is at its busiest during the annual **Ellensburg Rodeo** (www.ellensburgrodeo.com;

⊙Labor Day weekend, Sep), the biggest of its kind in the Pacific Northwest. Like most Washington towns, Ellensburg has its fair share of peripheral motel/mall infestations, but body-swerve the familiar big boxes and you'll uncover a compact but select cluster of venerable red-bricked buildings in a downtown **historic district**. Also worth checking out is the **Kittitas County Historical Museum** (www.kchm.org; 114 E 3rd Ave; donations accepted; ⊙10am-4pm Mon-Sat), housed in the 1889 Cadwell Building, known mostly for its petrified-wood and gemstone collections, but also hosting a cleverly laid out history section documenting the backgrounds of Croatian, Arabic and Welsh immigrants.

✕ 🛏 p65

The Drive >> To avoid the clamor of the busy interstate, take US-97 northwest out of Ellensburg before branching onto SR-10 to the small rural settlement of Thorp, 9 miles from Ellensburg.

2 Thorp Grist Mill

In the small town of Thorp (population 264), the **Thorp Grist Mill** (www.thorp.org; 11640 N Thorp Hwy; ⊙tours Wed-Sun May-Aug) was once a de facto meeting place for local farmers. Today, its well-preserved shell gives an interesting insight into the pioneer farmers who plowed the fields of the Kittitas Valley in the late 19th century. Converted to a rural museum, the mill originally dates from 1883 when its primary purpose was to grind flour using water power from the nearby Yakima River. It ceased operation in 1946, but, thanks to the foresight of local community activists, was placed on the National Register of Historic Places in 1977.

The Drive >> Continue northwest on SR-10 through quiet bucolic farmland to Cle Elum, 18 miles from Thorp.

LINK YOUR TRIP

8 Cascade Drive
Both ends of this trip will deposit you close to entry points for the Cascade Drive, another mountain-punctuated driving extravaganza.

11 Washington Wine Tour
Do this drive backward starting in Seattle and the essence of local wine in Ellensburg might inspire you to travel on to Yakima and beyond.

Map

0 —— 20 km
0 —— 10 miles

Winton

Wenatchee National Forest

2

...s Club Park — Leavenworth

8

Cashmere

Sunnyslope

Wenatchee Confluence State Park

...natchee ...tional ...orest

97

Squilchuck State Park

Liberty

...stol

10

90

2 Thorp Grist Mill

Ellensburg 1 START

82

16 miles to 11

Classic Trip

❸ Cle Elum

Cle Elum's location on the cusp of the Eastern Cascades and the bald treeless grasslands of the Kittitas Valley pulls in two radically different types of visitor. Seattleites regularly cross Snoqualmie Pass to sup the local wine and enjoy seemingly endless summer sunshine. Easterners stop by to gaze west at the snowier, more topographically interesting mountains. A posh resort, the **Suncadia** (☎509-649-6400; www.suncadiaresort.com; 3600 Suncadia Trail; r from $169; 🛜🐾), just west of Cle Elum and complete with golf, spa and winery, caters for both groups.

Though small, the town has a couple of esoteric museums conceived and maintained by vivacious community groups.

Up the road 3.5 miles, **Roslyn** stood in for Alaska in the 1990s TV show *Northern Exposure* (plot spoiler: there's more TV nostalgia four stops further on).

The Drive » Time to brave I-90! Access the road at exit 84 and motor 30 miles progressively uphill to Snoqualmie Pass. Just before the summit you'll pass Keechelus Lake, the source of the Yakima River, on your left.

- - - - - - - -

❹ Snoqualmie Pass

One of the easier routes across the Cascades and the only one to carry an interstate (the I-90), Snoqualmie was first prospected by white settlers in the 1850s. By the 1930s a fledgling road was being plowed year-round and the pass had spawned a nascent ski area, which has since morphed into four separate areas known (and managed) communally as the **Summit at Snoqualmie** (www.summitatsnoqualmie.com; 1001 SR 906; day pass adult/youth $66/45; ⏱9am-10pm late Nov–Apr). This is the nearest day-use ski area to Seattle (read: long lines). Should you summit the pass in summer, consider a hike. The **Pacific Crest Trail** briefly descends to the hustle of the interstate here but blissful tranquillity stretches for many miles in either direction.

The Drive » Descend on I-90 until exit 32, 22 miles from the pass. Go south on 436th Ave SE, which becomes Cedar Falls Rd. Within 3 miles you'll be deposited at Rattlesnake Lake.

- - - - - - - -

TRIP HIGHLIGHT

❺ Rattlesnake Lake

An important nexus on the Mountains to Sound Greenway, tranquil Rattlesnake Lake was once a more tumultuous place. A town called Moncton existed here until 1915 before it was flooded, evacuated and condemned after an abortive damming project. From 1906 to 1980 an erstwhile railway, the 'Milwaukee Road,' passed through. The railroad bed has been reworked into a non-motorized thoroughfare known as the **John Wayne Pioneer Trail**, which is popular with cyclists. From here, with a bike or walking, you can descend to the lake, a journey that includes careering through the 2.3-mile Snoqualmie tunnel (bring headlamps). The lake is also the starting point for the **Snoqualmie Valley Trail** and a 4-mile round-trip hike up to Rattlesnake Ridge. There are toilets and a kayak launch lakeside and a small interpretive center.

The Drive » Return to I-90 but this time, rather than join it, head underneath on 436th Ave SE to the junction with E North Bend Way. Turn left and then go right on SE Mt Si Rd. This leg of the trip is 10 miles.

- - - - - - - -

TRIP HIGHLIGHT

❻ Mt Si

Brooding moodily behind the town of North Bend, 4167ft Mt Si is allegedly the most climbed mountain in the state (approximately 40,000 hike it every year) and an annual fitness test for many Seattleites. The trail starts 2.5 miles down SE Mt Si Rd from a parking lot and is an 8-mile round trip including 3150ft of ascent. Though popular and predictably crowded in summer, the switchbacking path is no cakewalk. Dress appropriately for the mountains and bring water. The lofty meadow that acts as the summit for most walkers (the actual summit is a precipitous haystack-shaped rock) is revered for its hard-earned Puget Sound views.

The Drive >> Retrace your route along SE Mt Si Rd to the intersection with E North Bend Way, where you turn right into North Bend.

---

7 North Bend

If your memory stretches back to pre-Clinton era America and/or you nurture a secret penchant for cult US TV miniseries, your first sight of North Bend could require an eerie double take. This is where David Lynch's weird and wonderful *Twin Peaks* was filmed in the early 1990s and the town – a sleepy, if salubrious, place these days – is still playing on the fact. **Twede's** (137 W North Bend Way; burgers from $10.50; ⊘6:30am-8pm), the 'Double R Diner' in the TV show, proudly advertises its *Twin Peaks* credentials with cherry

pie and 'a damn fine cup o' coffee,' along with 50 – yes 50 – different types of burger. Down the road, the **Snoqualmie Valley Historical Museum** (www. snoqualmievalleymuseum. org; Bendigo Blvd; ⊘1-5pm Sat-Tue) charts the pre-Lynchian history of the valley with pioneer and Native American exhibits.

The Drive >> From North Bend take Bendigo Blvd, cross the South Fork of the Snoqualmie River and continue 3 miles into Snoqualmie.

TRIP HIGHLIGHT

8 Snoqualmie

Located a mile east of the famous falls, Snoqualmie is a diminutive town of esoteric shopfronts that ply hardware, organic coffee and Native American art. Across the tracks, the lovingly restored **Northwest Railway Museum** (www. trainmuseum.org; 38625 SE King St, North Bend; ⊘10am-5pm) is the largest of its

type in Washington. Its hook is its retro steam-train trips (adult/child $18/10), which chug (four times daily from April to October) 5 miles down the line to North Bend and another equally cute Thomas-the-Tank-Engine station.

Snoqualmie is also an ideal place to jump onto the **Snoqualmie Valley Trail**, the region's longest greenway (31 miles), which parallels the Snoqualmie River along the course of an old railway line. Access is best gained from the north end of Meadowbrook Way SE.

The Drive >> From Snoqualmie follow Railroad Ave northwest out of town and within a mile you'll be at Snoqualmie Falls.

---

9 Snoqualmie Falls

Come between April and June during the spring snow melt and you'll see why this 268ft mini-Niagara has been producing hydroelectric

---

HAY IS FOR HORSES

As you drive the rural roads around Ellensburg and then again as you descend into the Snoqualmie Valley, you're sure to see fields of timothy grass, a tall, rolled-form grass farmed for hay that's considered top-notch cattle and horse feed as well as tasty grub for rabbits and guinea pigs. Surprisingly, hay is the fourth highest-valued crop in Washington and around 35% of the harvest is shipped internationally, mostly to Asia. The grass is cut two times per year, usually in June and September.

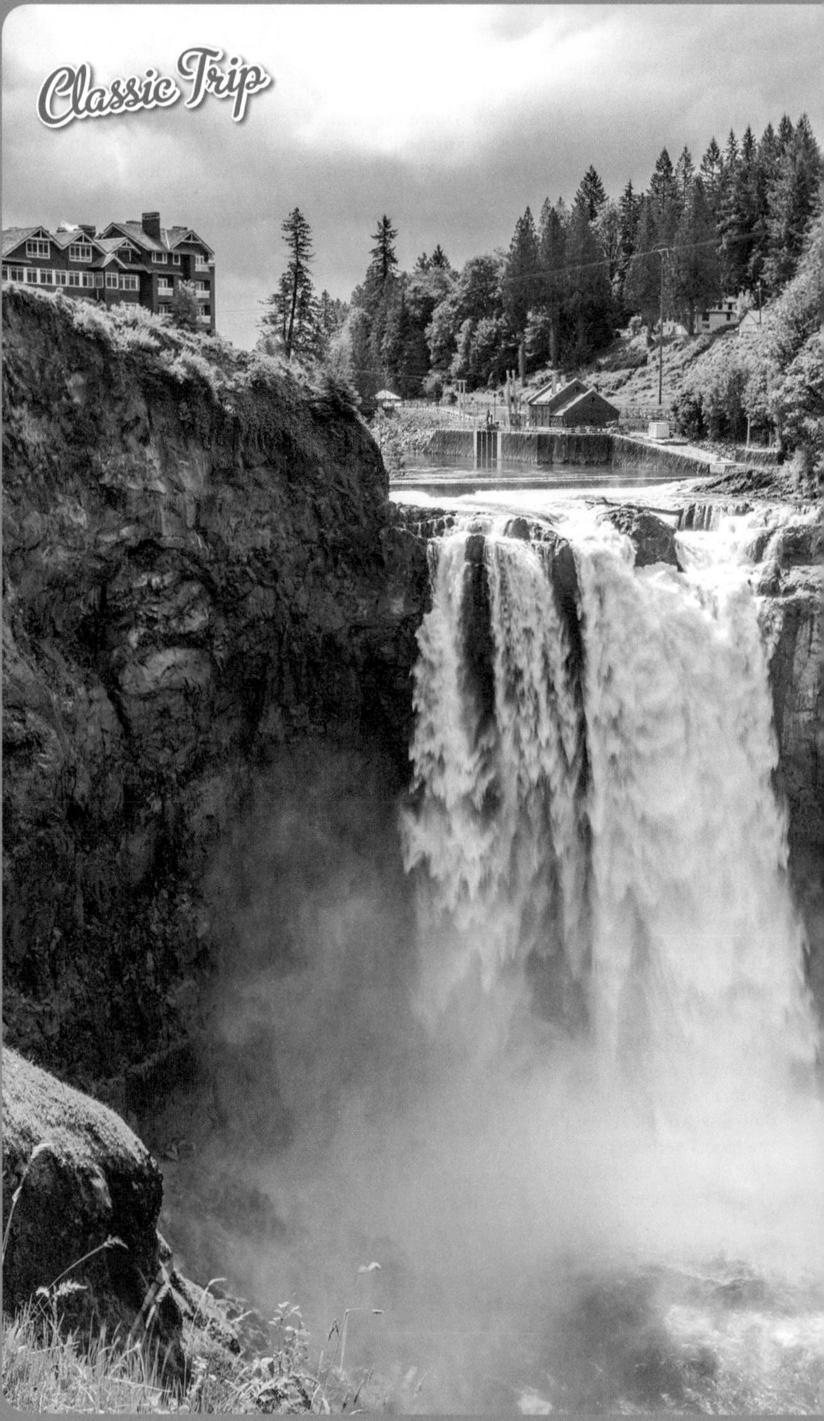
Classic Trip

WHY THIS IS A CLASSIC TRIP
CELESTE BRASH, WRITER

So near Seattle, this trip takes in several facets of Washington, from the snowy Cascade Mountains to real cowboy country, classic small towns and agricultural patchworks. The highlight for me is Snoqualmie Falls, which is sure to impress even the biggest waterfall aficionados. Make sure you get out of the car often for the spectacular wilderness walking opportunities all around you.

Left: Snoqualmie Falls

power since 1899. Observation decks and an overlook park stand face-on against the supersonic spray, while perched awfully close to the giant falls' rim is the luxurious **Salish Lodge & Spa** (p65), the second incarnation of a hotel that was first built here in 1918.

A half-mile trail drops down through spray-fed rain forest to the **Snoqualmie Falls Hydroelectric Museum** (SE 69th Pl, Snoqualmie; ☺10am-5pm Wed-Sun Jun-Sep), housed in the old train depot and chronicling the history of the power plant.

🛏 p65

The Drive » Take the Fall City–Snoqualmie Rd to Fall City, where you turn left onto the Preston–Fall City Rd opposite the Fall City Roadhouse and Inn. Merge west onto I-90 again at Preston (exit 22) to reach Mercer Island, 23 miles from Snoqualmie Falls.

⑩ Mercer Island

You don't have to get out of your car to experience Mercer Island's greatest engineering marvel. The community's two colossal parallel bridges that carry traffic over to metro Seattle are the second- and fifth-longest floating bridges in the world. An initial bridge, built here in 1939, was destroyed by a storm in 1990. Hence, the current structures, the **Homer M Hadley Memorial Bridge** (westbound traffic) and the **Lacey V Murrow Memorial Bridge** (eastbound) were built in 1989 and 1993 respectively.

The Drive » Coming off the floating bridges, traffic is directed through the Baker Tunnel before coming out with surprising suddenness in Seattle's downtown core close to King Street Station.

Classic Trip

TRIP HIGHLIGHT

⑪ Seattle

Put aside some time to enjoy Seattle at the end of this drive, which deposits you on the cusp of downtown and its cluster of craning skyscrapers (p152), great to explore on foot. For dazzling city views, ascend the **Columbia Center** (☎206-386-5564; www.skyview observatory.com; 701 5th Ave; adult/child $14.25/9; ☺10am-8pm; ⛉Pioneer Sq), which, at 932ft high, is the loftiest building in the Pacific Northwest and a lot cheaper than the Space Needle. Pioneer Square is Seattle's oldest quarter and home to the **Klondike Gold Rush National Historical Park** (☎206-553-3000; www.nps.gov/klse; 319 2nd Ave S; ☺10am-5pm; ⛉Occidental Mall), a shockingly good free museum about the 1897 Alaska gold rush. Another good family-orientated attraction is the **Seattle Aquarium** (☎206-386-4300; www.seattleaquarium.org; 1483 Alaskan Way, at Pier 59; adult/child 4-12yr $23/16; ☺9:30am-5pm; ♿; ⛉University St), the centerpiece of which is a glass-domed room where sharks, octopuses and other deepwater denizens lurk in the shadowy depths. For a post-drive picnic, decamp to **Pike Place Market** (www.pikeplacemarket.org; 85 Pike St; ☺9am-6pm Mon-Sat, 9am-5pm Sun; ⛉Westlake) for artisan cheeses, Russian pastries and Italian deli meats.

✕ 🛏 p65

TWIN PEAKS

Recognize that Snoqualmie Valley mountain, that waterfall, that cafe and that hotel? If you're under 40 and have never heard of Kyle MacLachlan or vexed over who murdered the unfortunate Laura Palmer, then *Twin Peaks* may need a bit of explaining. The TV drama series was conceived, written and directed by Mark Frost and legendary US film director David Lynch in the late 1980s. The latter's work (*Blue Velvet, Wild at Heart*) became so influential that he even had an adjective named after him: 'Lynchian' denotes anything that's surreal, dreamy, unsettling and – occasionally – freakishly funny.

Twin Peaks, which ran for 30 episodes over two series between 1990 and 1991, was set in a fictional Washington town of the same name (and filmed in North Bend and Snoqualmie). It starred Kyle MacLachlan as FBI agent Dale Cooper investigating the mysterious death of a pretty blonde homecoming queen. The series, with its complex plot and surreal, but suspenseful, story line, quickly gained a large audience and was heaped with critical praise earning numerous Golden Globes and Emmys. Time has done little to diminish its appeal. Like all great art, *Twin Peaks* proved to be powerfully influential and, over 25 years later, it still inspires obsessive geekdom with cult followers everywhere from Japan to Scandinavia.

As for those recognizable landmarks? The mountain (the fictional 'Twin Peaks') is Mt Si, the waterfall in the show's opening credits is Snoqualmie Falls, the cafe (where Kyle MacLachlan extolled the virtues of piping hot black coffee) is **Twede's** (p61) and the hotel (the Great Northern in the show) is the **Salish Lodge & Spa** (p65).

Eating & Sleeping

Ellensburg ❶

✖ Yellow Church Cafe   Fusion $$

(📞509-933-2233; www.theyellowchurchcafe.com; 111 S Pearl St; brunch mains $9-16, dinner $15-25; 🕑11am-9pm Mon-Thu, 8am-9pm Fri-Sun) This homey bright-yellow former church, built by the German Lutherans in 1923, is now an unconventional restaurant that serves urban-hipster-worthy food. The breakfast – including the aptly named St Benedict's – has won widespread fame, while the elegant dinner options include dishes such as sesame-crusted tuna and Thai green curry shrimp.

🛏 Rainbow Motel   Motel $

(📞509-933-7100; 1025 W University Way; 1-2-bedroom units from $62/72; 🛜) This place is so authentically and unintentionally retro, it's as if it's been in a plastic bubble since the '60s – you'll either love it or hate it. Rooms have a perfumed or smoky odor (even though they are all nonsmoking), original wood paneling, terrible landscape paintings and mid-Century furniture strait out of *Mad Men*. It's had the same friendly owner for 20 years. The two-bedroom units that sleep four people are a real bargain.

Snoqualmie Falls ❾

🛏 Salish Lodge & Spa   Hotel $$$

(📞800-826-6124, 425-888-2556; www.salishlodge.com; 6501 Railroad Ave; d from $195; 🛜🐾) Here is a beautiful resort that sits atop 268ft Snoqualmie Falls. *Twin Peaks* fans know the hotel as the Great Northern; the exterior of the lodge appeared in the opening credits, and an observation point near the parking lot offers the same view. Visitors can also see the falls from the lodge's dining room or hike to them.

Seattle ⓫

✖ Wild Ginger   Asian $$

(www.wildginger.net; 1401 3rd Ave; mains $17-33; 🕑11:30am-11pm Mon-Sat, 4-9pm Sun; 🚊University St) All around the Pacific Rim – via China, Indonesia, Malaysia, Vietnam and Seattle, of course – is the wide-ranging theme at this highly popular downtown fusion restaurant. The signature fragrant duck goes down nicely with a glass of Riesling. The restaurant also provides food for the swanky **Triple Door** (📞206-838-4333; www.thetripledoor.net; 216 Union St; 🚊University St) dinner club downstairs.

✖ Top Pot Hand-Forged Doughnuts   Cafe $

(www.toppotdoughnuts.com; 2124 5th Ave; doughnuts from $1.50; 🕑6am-7pm Mon-Fri, 7am-7pm Sat & Sun; 🚌13) Sitting pretty in a glass-fronted ex-car showroom with art-deco signage and immense book shelves, Top Pot's flagship cafe produces the Ferraris of the doughnut world. Top Pot might have morphed into a 20-outlet chain in recent years, but its hand-molded collection of sweet rings are still – arguably – worth visiting Seattle for alone. The coffee here is pretty potent too.

✖ Zeitgeist Coffee   Cafe $

(📞206-583-0497; www.zeitgeistcoffee.com; 171 S Jackson St; 🕑6am-7pm Mon-Fri, 7am-7pm Sat, 8am-6pm Sun; 🛜; 🚊Occidental Mall) Possibly Seattle's best indie coffee bar, Zeitgeist brews up smooth *doppio macchiatos* to go along with its sweet almond croissants and other luscious baked goods. The atmosphere is trendy industrial, with brick walls and large windows for people-watching. Soups, salads and sandwiches are also on offer.

🛏 Belltown Inn   Hotel $$

(📞206-529-3700; www.belltown-inn.com; 2301 3rd Ave; r from $159; ❄@🛜; 🚊Westlake) The reliable Belltown Inn is a popular midrange place to stow your suitcase – good on the basics, if a little light on embellishments. That said, there's a roof terrace, free bike rentals and some rooms have kitchenettes. Both Downtown and the Seattle Center are within easy walking distance.

Olympic Peninsula Loop

4

Freakishly wet, fantastically green and chillingly remote, the Olympic Peninsula looks like it's been resurrected from a wilder, precivilized era.

TRIP HIGHLIGHTS

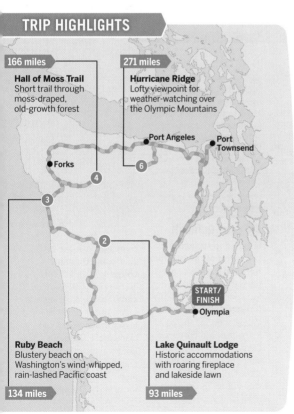

166 miles

Hall of Moss Trail
Short trail through moss-draped, old-growth forest

271 miles

Hurricane Ridge
Lofty viewpoint for weather-watching over the Olympic Mountains

Port Angeles

Port Townsend

Forks

START/FINISH

Olympia

Ruby Beach
Blustery beach on Washington's wind-whipped, rain-lashed Pacific coast

134 miles

Lake Quinault Lodge
Historic accommodations with roaring fireplace and lakeside lawn

93 miles

4 DAYS
435 MILES/700KM

GREAT FOR...

BEST TIME TO GO
June to September when deluges are slightly less likely.

ESSENTIAL PHOTO
Hoh Rainforest to see greens you've never imagined.

BEST FOR WILDLIFE
Roosevelt elk at the Hoh Rainforest.

4 Olympic Peninsula Loop

Imagine pine-clad beaches fused with an American Mt Olympus, with a slice of Stephenie Meyer's *Twilight* saga thrown in for good measure, and you've got an approximation of what a drive around the Olympic Peninsula looks like. This is wilderness of the highest order, where thick forest collides with an end-of-the-continent coastline that hasn't changed much since Juan de Fuca sailed by in 1592. Bring hiking boots – and rain gear!

1 Olympia

Welcome to Olympia, city of weird contrasts, where street-side buskers belt out acoustic grunge, and stiff bureaucrats answer their ringtones on the lawns of the expansive state legislature. A quick circuit of the **Washington State Capitol** (📞360-902-8880; 416 Sid Snyder Ave SW; ⏱7am-5:30pm Mon-Fri, 11am-4pm Sat & Sun), a huge Grecian temple of a building, will give you a last taste of civilization before you depart. Then load up the car and head swiftly for the exits.

🍴 p73

The Drive » Your basic route is due west, initially on Hwy 101, then (briefly) on SR-8 before joining US-12 in Elma. In Grays Harbor enter the twin cities of Aberdeen and Hoquiam, famous for producing William Boeing and the grunge group Nirvana. Here, you swing north on Hwy 101 (again!) to leafier climes at Lake Quinault, 93 miles from Olympia.

TRIP HIGHLIGHT

2 Lake Quinault

Situated in the extreme southwest of the **Olympic National Park** (www.nps.gov/olym; vehicle $20, pedestrian/cyclist $7), the thickly forested Quinault River Valley is one of the park's least-crowded corners. Clustered on the south shore of deep-blue glacial Lake Quinault is the tiny village of **Quinault**, complete with the luscious **Lake Quinault Lodge** (p73), a US Forest Service (USFS) office and a couple of stores.

A number of short **hiking trails** begin just below Lake Quinault Lodge; pick up a free map from the USFS office. The shortest of these is the **Quinault**

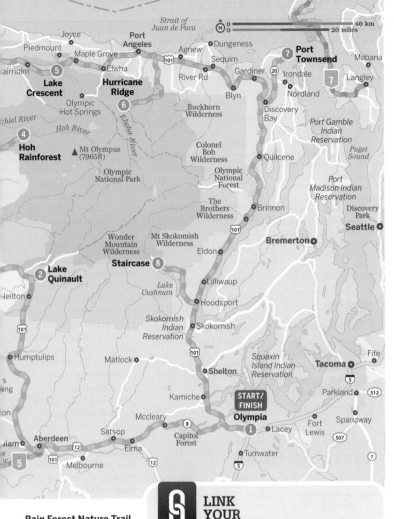

Rain Forest Nature Trail, a half-mile walk through 500-year-old Douglas firs. This brief trail adjoins the 3-mile Quinault Loop Trail, which meanders through the rain forests before circling back to the lake. The Quinault region is renowned for its huge trees. Close to the village is a 191ft Sitka

LINK YOUR TRIP

5 Graveyard of the Pacific Tour

Continue down the coast from Aberdeen, where you'll begin a coastal drive along a watery ship cemetery.

7 Chuckanut Drive & Whidbey Island

Across from Port Townsend, Whidbey is a gentler and – traditionally – dryer contrast to the Olympics.

spruce tree (supposedly over 1000 years old), and nearby are the world's largest red cedar, Douglas fir and mountain hemlock trees.

📖 p73

The Drive » West from Lake Quinault, Hwy 101 continues through the Quinault Indian Reservation before entering a thin strip of national park territory that protects the beaches around Kalaloch (*klay*-lock). This is some of the wildest US coastal scenery accessible by road; various pullovers allow for beach forays. After traveling for about 40 miles, you'll reach Ruby Beach.

TRIP HIGHLIGHT

❸ Ruby Beach

Inhabiting a thin coastal strip that was added to the national park in 1953, Ruby Beach is accessed via a short 0.2-mile path that

leads down to a large expanse of windswept coast embellished by polished black stones and wantonly strewn tree trunks. To the south toward Kalaloch, other accessible beachfronts are unimaginatively named **Beach One** through to **Beach Six**, all of which are popular with beachcombers. At low tide, rangers give talks on tidal-pool life at **Beach Four** and on the ecosystems of the Olympic coastal strip.

📖 p73

The Drive » North of Ruby Beach, Hwy 101 swings sharply northeast and inland, tracking the Hoh River. Turn right off 101 onto the Hoh River Rd to explore one of the national park's most popular inner sanctums, the Hoh Rainforest. Suspend your excitement as the trees eerily close in as you (re)enter the park.

TRIP HIGHLIGHT

❹ Hoh Rainforest

Count yourself lucky if you arrive on a day when it isn't raining! The most popular detour off Hwy 101 is the 19-mile paved road to the Hoh Valley, the densest, wettest, greenest and most intensely surreal temperate rain forest on planet earth. The essential hike here is the short but fascinating **Hall of Moss Trail**, an easy 0.75-mile loop through the kind of weird, ethereal scenery that even JRR Tolkien couldn't have invented. Old-man's beard drips from branches above you like corduroy fringe, while trailside licorice ferns and lettuce lichens overwhelm the massive fallen trunks of maple and Sitka spruce. Rangers lead interesting free guided walks here twice a day during summer and can help you spot some of the park's 5000-strong herd of **Roosevelt elk**.

The Drive » Rejoining Hwy 101, motor north to the small and relatively nondescript but handy settlement of Forks. Press on through as Hwy 101 bends north then east through a large logging area before plunging back into the national park on the shores of wondrous Lake Crescent, which is 66 miles from the Hoh Rainforest.

THE TWILIGHT ZONE

It would have been impossible to envisage a decade ago: diminutive Forks, a depressed lumber town full of hard-nosed loggers, reborn as a pilgrimage site for 'tweenage' girls following in the ghostly footsteps of two fictional sweethearts named Bella and Edward. The reason for this weird metamorphosis is the *Twilight* saga, a four-part book series by US author Stephenie Meyer about love and vampires on the foggy Olympic Peninsula that in seven short years has shifted over 100 million books and spawned three Hollywood movies. With Forks acting as the book's main setting, the town has catapulted to international stardom. Daily **Twilight Tours** (📞360-374-5634; www.forkswa.com; 130 S Spartan Ave) visit most of the places mentioned in Meyer's books.

CHECUBUS / SHUTTERSTOCK ©

Olympic National Park Ruby Beach

---

5 Lake Crescent

Before you've even had time to erase the horror of teenage vampires from your head, the scenery shifts again as the road winds along the glittering pine-scented shores of glacial-carved Lake Crescent. The lake looks best from water level, on a rental kayak, or from high above at its eastern edge on the **Storm King Mountain Trail** (named after the peak's wrathful spirit), accessible via a steep, 1.7-mile ascent that splits off the Barnes Creek Trail. For the less athletic, the **Marymere Falls Trail** is a 2-mile round trip to a 90ft cascade that drops down over a basalt cliff.

Both hikes leave from a parking lot to the right of SR 101 near the **Storm King Ranger Station** (☎360-928-3380; 343 Barnes Point Rd; ⊗May-Sep). The area is also the site of the **Lake Crescent Lodge** (p73), the oldest of the park's trio of celebrated lodges, which first opened in 1916.

🛏 p73

The Drive » From Lake Crescent take Hwy 101 22 miles east to the town of Port Angeles, a gateway to Victoria, Canada, which is reachable by ferry to the north. Starting in Race St, the 18-mile Hurricane Ridge Rd climbs up 5300ft toward extensive wildflower meadows and expansive mountain vistas often visible above the clouds.

TRIP HIGHLIGHT

6 Hurricane Ridge

Up above the clouds, stormy Hurricane Ridge lives up to its name with fickle weather and biting winds made slightly more bearable by the park's best high-altitude views. Its proximity to Port Angeles is another bonus; if you're heading up here, be sure to call into the museum-like **Olympic National Park Visitor Center** (360-565-3130; www.nps.gov/olym; 3002 Mt Angeles Rd; seasonal, but generally 9am-5pm) first. The smaller **Hurricane Ridge Visitor Center** (9:30am-5pm daily summer, Fri-Sun winter) has a snack bar, a gift shop and toilets and is the starting point of various hikes. **Hurricane Hill Trail** (which begins at the end of the road) and the **Meadow Loop Trails** network are popular and

moderately easy. The first half-mile of these trails is wheelchair accessible.

The Drive » Wind back down the Hurricane Ridge Rd, kiss the suburbs of Port Angeles and press east through the retirement community of Sequim (pronounced 'squwim'). Turn north on SR-20 to reach the more attractive Port Townsend.

----

7 Port Townsend

Leaving the park momentarily behind, ease back into civilization with the cultured Victorian comforts of Port Townsend, whose period charm dates from the railroad boom of the 1890s, when the town was earmarked to become the 'New York of the West.' That never happened, but you can pick up a historic walking tour map from the **visitor center** (www.ptmsc.org; 532 Battery Way; adult/child $5/3; 11am-5pm Wed-Mon Jun-Aug, reduced hours Sep-May) and wander the waterfront's collection of shops, galleries and antique malls. Don't miss the old-time **Belmont Saloon** (925 Water St; lunch $10-14, dinner $15-32; 10:30-2am Mon-Fri, 9am-2am Sat & Sun), the **Rose Theatre** (235 Taylor St), a gorgeously

renovated theater that's been showing movies since 1908, and the fine Victorian mansions on the bluff above town, where several charming residences have been turned into B&Bs.

✕ 🛏 p73

The Drive » From Port Townsend head back to the junction of Hwy 101, but this time head south passing Quilcene, Brinnon (p73), with its great diner, and the Dosewallips park entrance. You get more unbroken water views here on the park's eastern side courtesy of the Hood Canal. Track the watery beauty to Hoodsport where signs point west off Hwy 101 to Staircase, 67 miles from Port Townsend.

----

8 Staircase

It's drier on the park's eastern side and the mountains are closer. The Staircase park nexus, accessible via Hoodsport, has a ranger station, campground and a decent trail system that follows the drainage of the North Fork Skokomish River and is flanked by some of the most rugged peaks in the Olympics. Nearby **Lake Cushman** has a campground and water sports opportunities.

Eating & Sleeping

Olympia 1

🍴 Spar Cafe Bar
Pub, Diner $

(114 4th Ave E; breakfast $5-9, lunch $7-12; ⊙7am-midnight) A legendary local cafe and eating joint now owned by Portland's McMenamin brothers, who have maintained its authentic wood-panel interior. You could spend all morning here eating brunch, shooting pool, admiring the cigar collections and discussing the latest music trends. Come back later for some of the real thing – live.

Lake Quinault 2

🛏 Lake Quinault Lodge
Historic Hotel $$$

(☎360-288-2900; www.olympicnationalparks. com; 345 S Shore Rd; r $130- 412; ✳🤲🔉) Everything you could want in a historic national-park lodge and more, the suspended-in-time Quinault has a massive fireplace, a manicured cricket-pitch-quality lawn, huge, comfy leather sofas, a regal reception area, and a dignified lake-view restaurant serving upscale American cuisine. Trails into primeval forest leave from just outside the door.

Ruby Beach 3

🛏 Kalaloch Lodge
Historic Hotel $$$

(☎360-962-2271; www.thekalalochlodge. com; 157151 US 101; incl breakfast r $149- 400; ✳🤲🔉) The Kalaloch (built in 1953) makes up for a relatively unassuming facade with a spectacular setting perched on a bluff overlooking the crashing Pacific. In addition to rooms in the old lodge, there are log cabins and motel-style units. The family-friendly **Creekside Restaurant** (mains $13-33; ⊙8am-8pm Oct-Apr, 7am-9pm May-Sep) offers the best breakfasts on the coast and incomparable ocean views. Various trails lead down to the nearby beaches.

Lake Crescent 5

🛏 Lake Crescent Lodge
Lodge $$

(☎888-896-3818; www.olympicnationalparks. com; 416 Lake Crescent Rd; lodge r from $117, cabins from $299; P ✳🤲🔉) This turn-of-the-century lodge is handsomely furnished with antiques and surrounded by giant fir trees. There's a variety of lodgings, but the most popular (and the only ones open in winter – weekends only) are the cozy cottages. Sumptuous Northwestern-style food is served in the lodge's ecofriendly restaurant.

Port Townsend 7

🍴 Waterfront Pizza
Pizza $$

(☎360-379-9110; 951 Water St; slices $4, large pizzas $16-28; ⊙11am-8pm Sun-Thu, to 9pm Fri & Sat) If you're craving a quick snack, grab a delicious, crispy, thin-crust slice downstairs – just be prepared for lines in the walk-in-closet-sized dining room. For more relaxed, sit-down service, climb the stairs and sample the pies, topped with treats such as Cajun sausage, feta cheese, artichoke hearts and pesto.

🛏 Palace Hotel
Historic Hotel $$

(☎360-385-0773; www.palacehotelpt.com; 1004 Water St; r $109-229; 🤲🔉) Built in 1889, this beautiful Victorian building is a former brothel that was run by the locally notorious Madame Marie, who did business out of the 2nd-floor corner suite. It's been reincarnated as a character-filled period hotel. Pleasant common spaces; kitchenettes available. The cheapest rooms share a bathroom.

Brinnon 7

🍴 Halfway House
Diner $

(Hwy 101, Brinnon; mains from $10; ⊙7am-8pm) This is one of those 'great find' places that pepper the byways of rural America, with friendly staff and crusty fruit pies that taste like they were made by someone's treasured grandma. It sits aside Hwy 101 in Brinnon, halfway between Port Townsend and Staircase.

Graveyard of the Pacific

5

The wild Pacific Ocean turns positively fiendish where tide meets current at the mouth of the Columbia River. Explore shipwrecks and lighthouses in this landlubber's tour of the nautical Northwest.

TRIP HIGHLIGHTS

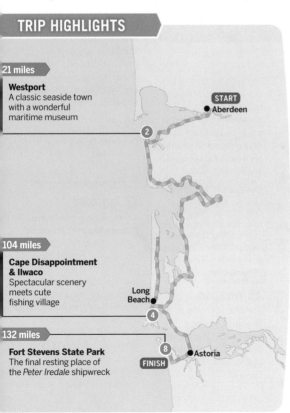

21 miles

Westport
A classic seaside town with a wonderful maritime museum

104 miles

Cape Disappointment & Ilwaco
Spectacular scenery meets cute fishing village

132 miles

Fort Stevens State Park
The final resting place of the *Peter Iredale* shipwreck

2 DAYS
132 MILES/212KM

GREAT FOR...

BEST TIME TO GO
April to September for the best weather.

 ESSENTIAL PHOTO

The wreckage of the *Peter Iredale*.

BEST SHIP SIGHTING

The tall ship *Lady Washington* docks along the coast.

5 Graveyard of the Pacific

They call it the Graveyard of the Pacific. The area from northern Oregon to Vancouver Island is known for its unpredictable weather, unforgiving coastline and bad habit of gobbling up ships. Thousands of vessels have been lost, from war ships to barges to countless smaller craft. Dive in to this area with its unique seafaring character and fascinating maritime history.

1 Aberdeen

Start your trip in Aberdeen's Grays Harbor, home port of the tall ship **Lady Washington** (http://historicalseaport.org), the Official Ship of the State of Washington. This impressive reproduction of a 1788 tall ship – featured in *Pirates of the Caribbean,* if that helps give you a visual – is available for dockside tours and adventure sails all along the state's coast. Check the website to find out where along the way you might catch her.

Fans of Nirvana front man Kurt Cobain might be interested in the self-guided **walking tour** (www.aberdeen-museum.org/kurt.htm) offered by the Aberdeen Museum of History. It includes the store where Kurt's uncle bought him his first guitar and several seen-better-days former residences.

The Drive » From Aberdeen, take Hwy 101 across the Chehalis River bridge, then follow Grays Harbor southwest on Hwy 105 for 21 miles to reach the coastal town of Westport.

TRIP HIGHLIGHT

2 Westport

The seaside town of Westport has two worthwhile stops. First, head to **Grays Harbor Lighthouse** (1020 West Ocean Ave; $5; 🕙10am-4pm May-Sep, noon-3pm Oct-Apr), the tallest lighthouse in Washington. It's always available for photo ops, and tours up the 135-step circular staircase (pant, wheeze) are available seasonally.

Next, head over to the **Westport Maritime Museum** (2201 Westhaven Dr; adult/child $5/2; 🕙10am-4pm Memorial Day-Labor Day, noon-4pm Thu-Mon Sep-May), a noteworthy Cape Cod–style building at the northern tip of town. It offers your typical array of nautical knickknacks, but most impressive is the authentic Fresnel lighthouse lens. It's a first-order lens, which is really impressive if you know about lens rankings; loosely translated, it's big enough to need its own separate building.

🍴 p81

The Drive » Continue on Hwy 105, following the coast 30 miles southeast to Raymond.

3 Raymond

Raymond is home to the **Willapa Seaport Museum** (📞360-589-3964; www.willapaseaportmuseum.org; 310 Alder St; $5; 🕙10am-4pm Tue-Sat or by appointment). It looks more like a cross between a fisherman's garage sale and Disney's Pirates of the Caribbean ride than a formal museum, but that's part of its charm, and it's a good leg-stretch on your way

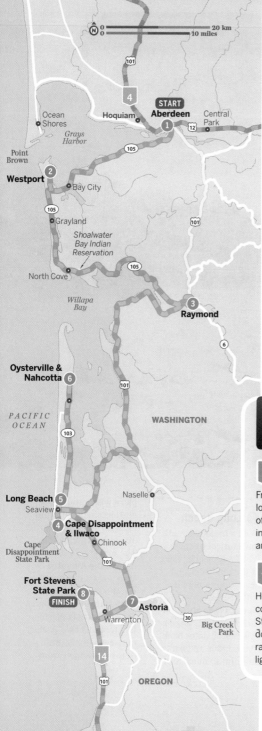

to your next stop. Let the salty ol' museum owner lead you around if you've got an hour or more.

Before you leave, though, you might want to stop to pay your respect to Willie Keils at **Willie Keils Grave State Park** (443 Hwy 6; ⊙ dawn-dusk), just south of town. Nineteen-year-old Willie died in 1855 right before his family left Missouri, but they couldn't bear leaving him; instead, they filled his coffin with whiskey and brought him along, turning their wagon train into a very slow funeral procession.

The Drive ❯❯ Pick up Hwy 101 west and head 45 miles south. When you get to Seaview, follow the signs for Cape Disappointment further south.

LINK YOUR TRIP

4 Olympic Peninsula Loop

From Aberdeen, pick up this loop that features the best of northwest Washington, including more coastline and Olympic National Park.

14 Highway 101 Oregon Coast

Hook up with the Oregon coast trip at Fort Stevens State Park, continuing down the coast for seafood, razor clams, tide pools and lighthouses.

77

TUSHARKOLEY / SHUTTERSTOCK ©

❹ Cape Disappointment & Ilwaco

Although little remains of the original Fort Canby that once stood in **Cape Disappointment State Park** (☎360-642-3078; Hwy 100; ☿dawn-dusk), 2 miles southwest of Ilwaco, the area does hold the excellent **Lewis & Clark Interpretive Center** (Hwy 100; adult/child $5/2.50; ☿10am-5pm Wed-Sun), wild beach, around 8 miles of coastal, forested hiking trails and two dramatic lighthouses. It's a short walk from the interpretive center to the small **Cape Disappointment Lighthouse**, perched on a particularly vertiginous cliff over crashing seas, or take a short trail on the other side of the park to **North Head Lighthouse**, which offers tours in summer and is the oldest lighthouse in use on the west coast.

Just north, you'll pass through the cute seaside village of Ilwaco, decorated with driftwood, glass floats and fishermen's nets. It's an excellent place to stop for fresh seafood.

🛏 p81

The Drive » Head back north on Hwy 101, which continues on to become SR-103; Long Beach is just 6 miles north of Cape Disappointment.

❺ Long Beach

Need a break from all the nautical history? Wee Long Beach packs in the roadside goodness and is a big hit with road-weary kids. **Marsh's Free Museum** (409 Pacific Ave S, Long Beach; ☿9am-6pm) dates back to the 1930s and isn't a museum so much as a place where souvenirs and sea shells intermingle with sideshow-worthy attractions and oddities. The real star of the show is **Jake the Alligator Man**, media darling of the *Weekly World News*. Half-alligator, half-man, his suspiciously plaster-like remains hold packs of tweens in his thrall. Across the street from

Cape Disappointment State Park

Marsh's is the **World's Largest Frying Pan**, over 18ft tall.

Want to find out just how long Long Beach is? Primary **beach access** points in Long Beach are off 10th St SW and at the end of Bolstad Ave; a 0.25-mile boardwalk links the two entryways.

✗ p81

The Drive ≫ Head north up the peninsula for 15 miles to find the quiet, undeveloped part of Willapa Bay.

- - - - - - - - -

❻ Oysterville & Nahcotta

Purists might prefer the Willapa Bay side of the peninsula, with its old towns, oyster beds and wildlife viewing.

The charm of these old communities – the only ones on the bay side of the Long Beach Peninsula – derives not just from their history but also from the absence of the beachfront towns' carnival atmosphere. Tiny Oysterville stands largely unchanged since its heyday in the 1870s,

79

TOP TIP:
WHICH WAY TO THE
PETER IREDALE?

As shipwrecks don't have street addresses, here's how to find the *Peter Iredale*. Go over the bridge from Astoria to Hammond and turn right on East Harbor Dr, which becomes Pacific Dr. Take a left at Lake Dr then a right at the KOA campground and go straight until you see the signs.

when the oyster boom was at its peak.

Oysterville is filled with well-preserved Victorian homes including the 1863 **Red Cottage** (Territory Rd, Oysterville), near Clay St, which served as the first Pacific County courthouse, and the **Big Red House** (cnr Division St & Territory Rd, Oysterville), built in 1871. Other historic buildings include a one-room schoolhouse and the 1892 **Oysterville Church** (cnr Clay St & Territory Rd, Oysterville); pick up a walking-tour brochure here.

✖ ⛺ p81

The Drive » Head back south down the Long Beach Peninsula, then take Hwy 101 south. After 9 miles you'll cross the Columbia River and arrive in Astoria.

- - - - - - - - - -

7 Astoria

Astoria sits at the mouth of the Columbia River, where you'll find some of the most treacherous

waters of the Pacific, thanks to river currents rushing out where ocean tide is trying to get in. The town has a long seafaring history and has seen its old harbor attract fancy hotels and restaurants in recent years, thanks in part to Astoria's popularity as a film location. *Kindergarten Cop, Free Willy* and *Into the Wild* were all filmed here, and fans of the cult hit *The Goonies* can seek out the house where Brandon and Mikey Walsh lived.

You can explore both flotsam and jetsam at **Columbia River Maritime Museum** (☎503-325-2323; www.crmm.org; 1792 Marine Dr; adult/child $14/5; ⊙9:30am-5pm). It sits right on the edge of the Columbia River, offering a look at everything from old boats to maritime mementos that have washed up in the area. A Coast Guard exhibit –

featuring a rescue boat plying dramatic, fake waves – makes you really appreciate the danger of their job.

✖ ⛺ p41, p81, p174

The Drive » Head west for the 10-mile drive to Hammond and Fort Stevens State Park.

- - - - - - - - - -

TRIP HIGHLIGHT

8 Fort Stevens State Park

Thousands of vessels have been lost in the Graveyard of the Pacific, from warships to barges to freighters, and those are just the ones on record. There are likely countless smaller craft littering the ocean floor. A few are still visible occasionally at low tide, but the easiest one to spot is the **Peter Iredale**, resting peacefully at Fort Stevens State Park. The ship was driven onto the shore by rough seas on October 25, 1906, and the wreckage has sat embedded in the sand for over a century. Today, kids have made a jungle gym out of the rusted skeleton and families picnic and build sandcastles on the nearby sand at low tide. (As a reassuring side note, no lives were lost in the shipwreck, so don't let the thought of ghostly sailors dampen your fun.)

Eating & Sleeping

Westport ❷

✖ Brady's Oysters   Seafood $

(☎800-572-3252; www.bradysoysters.com; 3714 Oyster Pl E, Aberdeen; ⊙9am-6pm) Stock your coolers with a sailor's snack of delicious bivalve mollusks at this family-owned institution just a few miles south of Westport (though its address is Aberdeen).

✖ Mermaid Deli   Deli $

(☎360-612-0435; 200 E Patterson St; sandwiches $7-15; ⊙11am-10pm) Hot and cold sandwiches (6in or foot-long), plus a mean clam chowder, make this dependable stop-off a favorite among locals and vacationers alike. Did we mention the full bar, mermaid mural and live music?

Cape Disappointment & Ilwaco ❹

🛏 Cape Disappointment
State Park Campground   Campground $

(☎360-642-3078; www.parks.state.wa.us; Hwy 100; tent/RV sites $25/45, yurts & cabins from $76) The campground has nearly 250 sites in two zones: by the beach and around a lake near the park entrance. Coin-operated hot showers and flush toilets are within easy reach. Yurts, cabins (sleeping up to six) and three former lightkeeper's residences provide further options.

🛏 Inn at Harbor Village   Hotel $$

(☎360-642-0087; www.innatharborvillage. com; 120 Williams Ave NE; r $129-199; 🛜) One of Washington's most improbable and creative accommodations is this gorgeously refurbished 1928 Presbyterian church, with sloped ceilings and nine exquisite rooms. A complimentary breakfast and wine is included. The inn is set in woodland, an easy walk from Ilwaco port.

Long Beach ❺

✖ Depot   Fusion $$$

(☎360-642-7880; http://depotrestaurantdining. com; 1208 38th Pl, Seaview; mains $23-30; ⊙from 5pm) Dine in Seaview's 1905 train

station. Dishes such as crab mac 'n' cheese, Parmesan chicken, pan-fried oysters and salads are created from local produce. It's consistently rated the top dining option in town.

Oysterville & Nahcotta ❻

✖ Bailey's Bakery & Café   Bakery, Cafe $

(www.baileysbakerycafe.com; 26910 Sandridge Rd, Nahcotta; snacks from $3; ⊙9am-3pm Thu-Sun) Sharing digs with Nahcotta post office, this small nook serves locally roasted Long Beach coffee and the lauded 'thunder buns': currants, pecans, honey-butter glaze and a whole lot of bun.

🛏 Moby Dick Hotel &
Oyster Farm   Hotel $$

(☎360-665-4543; www.mobydickhotel.com; 25814 Sandridge Rd, Nahcotta; d incl breakfast $90-150) Get intimate with the whale vertebrae that furnish the patio in this very rustic 1929 structure that once served as a Coast Guard barracks. There's a delicious three-course breakfast, but note that oysters are no longer served due to pesticides in the bay. Bold colors characterize the 10 rooms (two with private bath).

Astoria ❼

✖ Baked Alaska   Seafood $$$

(1 12th St; mains $22-32; ⊙11am-10pm) One of Astoria's finest restaurants, Baked Alaska sits right atop a pier on the water – views are excellent. Lunch means 0.5lb gourmet burgers and blackened sirloin salad, while dinner mains range from grilled wild salmon to the 10oz rib-eye steak.

🛏 Cannery Pier Hotel   Hotel $$$

(☎503-325-4996, 888-325-4996; www. cannerypierhotel.com; 10 Basin St; d from $309; 🍽🛜) Located on a pier at the west end of town, this luxurious hotel offers fine rooms right over the water, with balconies, bridge views, contemporary furnishings and bathtubs that open to the room. Perks include afternoon wine socials, continental breakfast and a free ride in a vintage car.

San Juan Islands Scenic Byway

6

More a float trip than a drive, this voyage will leave you swearing that you've dropped off the edge of the American continent and landed somewhere less clamorous.

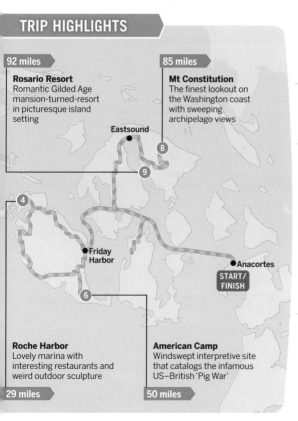

92 miles

Rosario Resort
Romantic Gilded Age mansion-turned-resort in picturesque island setting

85 miles

Mt Constitution
The finest lookout on the Washington coast with sweeping archipelago views

Eastsound

8

9

4

● Friday Harbor

● Anacortes

START/ FINISH

6

Roche Harbor
Lovely marina with interesting restaurants and weird outdoor sculpture

29 miles

American Camp
Windswept interpretive site that catalogs the infamous US–British 'Pig War'

50 miles

3 DAYS
136 MILES/219KM

GREAT FOR...

BEST TIME TO GO
April to September for calmer seas and common whale sightings.

ESSENTIAL PHOTO
View from atop Mt Constitution, Orcas Island.

BEST FOR WILDLIFE
Whale-watching trips.

6 San Juan Islands Scenic Byway

A thousand metaphoric miles from the urban disquiet of Puget Sound, the San Juan archipelago conjures up flashbacks from another era (the 1950s, perhaps?). Crime barely registers here, fast-food franchises are a nasty mainland apparition, and cars – those most essential US travel accessories – are an optional luxury on the three ferry-reachable islands of Orcas, Lopez and San Juan Island.

❶ Anacortes

This voyage starts at **Anacortes Ferry Terminal** (www.wsdot.wa.gov/ ferries; 2100 Ferry Terminal Rd; ⏰7am-9pm), where you'll board the ferry for Friday Harbor. Drivers might end up waiting for hours in the busy summer months (hint: reserve ferry tickets online). Two options are to spend the night in Anacortes and get to the ferry early; or park at the terminal and make the trip on foot or by bike.

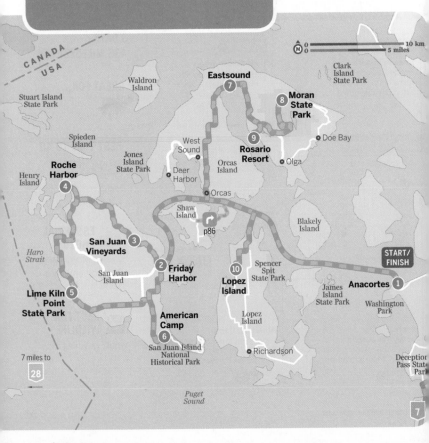

The Drive » If you're taking your car, today's drive is limited to sliding in slow motion onto the ferry where you'll be packed tightly in with several hundred others. Don't stay put; climb upstairs and enjoy the journey (and it is a great journey) from the passenger lounge.

---

❷ Friday Harbor

After an 80-minute ferry ride, you'll land at Friday Harbor, the San Juans' only real town and a blueprint for the archipelago as a whole, where the worst kind of hassle you're likely to face is a badly pitched baseball. Restaurants, shops and a couple of interesting museums

Chuckanut Drive & Whidbey Island

A short hop from Anacortes, this pastoral trip acts like a decompression chamber before re-entering metro Puget Sound.

28 Southern Vancouver Island Tour

Located a handful of watery miles from Vancouver Island, the San Juans provide an ideal opportunity to visit Canada by sea.

embellish the settlement's diminutive grid.

San Juan Island has the good fortune to be right in the migration path of three pods of orcas (aka killer whales), unimaginatively named the J, K and L pods. (Pod members' names aren't much better: 'K-17, meet L-9.') To learn more about the island's unofficial mascots, stop by the **Whale Museum** (📞360-378-4710; www.whale-museum.org; 62 1st St, Friday Harbor; adult/child $6/3; 🕙10am-5pm). To see the real thing – a regional highlight – hook up with **San Juan Excursions** (📞360-378-6636; www.watchwhales.com; Friday Harbor; whale-watching tours $99), which stands by its boast: 'see whales or come again free.'

✕ ⤵ p89

The Drive » Navigation on San Juan Island is a no-brainer. Take Roche Harbor Rd northwest out of Friday Harbor as far as Sportsman Lake.

---

❸ San Juan Vineyards

The isalnds' premier **vineyard** (📞844-243-6359; www.sanjuanvineyards.com; 3136 Roche Harbor Rd; tastings per glass $1; 🕙11am-5pm) has a tasting room adjacent to its on-site, 1896-vintage school-house, 3 miles northwest of Friday Harbor. The vineyard also has an outlet in town. For the

real homegrown stuff, you're looking at Sieg-errebe and Madeleine Angevine varietals with the occasional Pinot Noir thrown in. The vineyard also makes wines using grapes imported from East Washington.

The Drive » Continue northwest on Roche Harbor Rd. At the T-junction with West Valley Rd, 4.5 miles from the vineyard, turn right.

TRIP HIGHLIGHT

❹ Roche Harbor

A sublime rurally inclined 'resort,' Roche Harbor is a scenic mix of swanky yachts, historic houses and picnicking vacation-ers. At the entrance gate sits the eccentric **West-cott Bay Sculpture Park** (www.sjisculpturepark.com; cnr Westcott Dr & Roche Harbor Rd, Roche Harbor; 🕙dawn-dusk) where you can wander among more than 100 sculptures scattered over 19 acres. Half the fun is the sheer variety; each was made by a differ-ent artist, and materials range from aluminum to granite to recovered redwood.

Around the corner, Roche Harbor proper has a lovely marina packed with millionaire boats and backed by the historic buildings of the lime-mining McMillan clan, the oldest of which dates from 1886. Explore the manicured gardens, browse the plush shops or even play boules.

DETOUR: SHAW ISLAND

Start: ❼ Eastsound

The quietest and smallest of the four main San Juan Islands, tranquil Shaw is famous for its restrictive property laws and handsome Benedictine monastery. Ferries arrive here daily from Orcas Island (car and driver $28), but with only one campsite offering just 12 overnight berths, opportunities to linger are limited. For the curious, Shaw is worth a slow spin on a mountain bike or an afternoon of quiet contemplation on a pebbly beach. History buffs can break the reverie at the **Shaw Island Historical Museum** (Blind Bay Rd; by donation; ⊘2-4pm Tue, 11am-1pm Thu, 10am-noon & 2-4pm Sat), while perennial peace-seekers can find lazy solace on quiet South Beach in **Shaw Island County Park** (📞360-378-1842; http://sanjuanco.com/523/Shaw-Island; Squaw Bay Rd; tent sites $20), a stop and potential camping spot on the aquatic Cascadia Marine Trail, which starts in southern Puget Sound and is doable on nonmotorized boats and kayaks.

The Drive ≫ Heading back down the Roche Harbor Rd, take the West Valley Rd south at the first junction. Just past the alpaca farm, turn right on Mitchell Bay Rd and then left on West Side Rd, which skirts the lapping waters of Haro Strait.

❺ Lime Kiln Point State Park

Clinging to the island's rocky west coast, this beautiful park overlooks the deep Haro Strait and is one of the best places in the world to view whales from the shoreline. There is a small **interpretive center** in the park, open from Memorial Day to Labor Day along with trails, a restored lime kiln and the landmark **Lime Kiln Lighthouse** built in 1919. Orca and minke whale sightings are more common in summer after the June salmon run. Offering exceptional views of Vancouver Island and the Olympic Mountains, the park is best enjoyed at sunset, camera poised.

The Drive ≫ West Side Rd swings east and becomes Bailey Hill Rd and Little Rd before joining with Cattle Point Rd. Turn right here toward the island's wild treeless southern tip.

TRIP HIGHLIGHT

❻ American Camp

On the southern flank of the island, the American Camp hosts a small **visitor center** (⊘8:30am-5pm Jun-Aug, to 4:30pm Sep-May) and is a good place to learn about the islands' history and the infamous 'Pig War' with Britain in 1859, a military standoff ignited after an American settler shot a pig belonging to a homesteading Irishman on San Juan Island. The ensuing squabble led to a border dispute and near conflict between Britain

Orcas Island View from Mt Constitution

and the US. Among the remnants of an old fort are the officers' quarters and a laundress' house, while a series of interpretive trails lead to earthwork fortifications, a British farm from the dispute era and desolate **South Beach**. The 1.8-mile trail along the ridge of **Mt Finlayson** makes for a pleasant hike with splendid views and unlimited bird-watching potential.

The Drive » Head north on Cattle Point Rd back to Friday Harbor and catch an interisland ferry to Orcas Island, where you'll find a wilder, less manicured landscape than on San Juan Island. There's not a lot to see or do around the ferry landing so head straight down Orcas Rd for just over 8 miles to Eastsound.

------

⑦ Eastsound

Orcas Island is shaped like a pair of saddlebags, with the main town, Eastsound, diplomatically in the middle. This is where you'll find most of the dining options. The town shuts down early though, so don't wait till you're hungry to plan dinner.

Paddling around the island gives you an entirely different view of things, and **Shearwater Adventures** (360-376-4699; www.shearwater kayaks.com; 138 N Beach Rd, Eastsound; 3hr tours from $79) offers guided excursions from the north side of the island. Take anything from a quick, one-hour splash-about to an all-day outing in its handcrafted, Aleut-style kayaks.

p89

The Drive »» East of Eastsound, Olga Rd gives access to the island's eastern saddlebag dominated by Moran State Park, 4.5 miles from Eastsound.

TRIP HIGHLIGHT

8 Moran State Park

Ex-Seattle mayor, Robert Moran's generous gift to the island was **Moran State Park** (360-376-6173; 3572 Olga Rd; Discover Pass required at some parking lots $10; 6:30am-dusk Apr-Sep, 8am-dusk Oct-Mar), where over 5000 acres of forest lie draped over two mountains. On a clear day, the view from **Mt Constitution** is incomparable; you can see mountains, islands, even Vancouver. Sadly, on a

foggy day, you can only see the person standing next to you. Thirty miles of trails give you ample opportunity to explore on foot, but there's also a road straight to the top if you have a ferry to catch.

 p89

The Drive »» Just after exiting the park's northern gate a road turns left to the Rosario Resort.

TRIP HIGHLIGHT

9 Rosario Resort

Orcas' resort is a refined place unsullied by modern clamor, where seaplanes dock, kayaks launch and discerning vacationers bask in a heady kind of F Scott Fitzgerald–style romance. Its centerpiece is the seafront Rosario mansion built by former shipbuilding magnate Robert Moran in 1904 with 180 modern rooms sprawled across the surrounding grounds along with a swimming pool, tennis courts, a marina and elaborately tiled spa facilities. A **museum** (Rosario Way, Rosario; 9am-9pm) encased in the mansion tells the life and times of Moran, a former Seattle mayor who lived here from 1906

until 1938. Look out for the ship memorabilia and the huge custom-made organ.

p89

The Drive »» There's only one way back to the ferry terminal – the way you came! Interisland ferries leave five times daily for Shaw and Lopez Islands.

10 Lopez Island

Lopez, or 'Slow-pez' as it's sometimes known, is the ultimate friendly isle where local motorists give strangers the 'Lopezian wave' (two fingers raised from the steering wheel) and you can leave your bike outside the village store and it'll still have both wheels when you return several hours later. A leisurely pastoral spin can be tackled in a day, with good overnight digs available in the clustered settlement that passes for the main village. If you arrive bike-less, call up **Lopez Bicycle Works** (www.lopezbicycleworks.com; 2847 Fisherman Bay Rd; bikes per hour $7; 10am-6pm May-Sep), which can deliver a bicycle to the ferry terminal for you.

p89

Eating & Sleeping

Friday Harbor ❷

✗ Market Chef — Deli $
(☎360-378-4546; 225 A St, Friday Harbor; sandwiches $9; ⏱10am-4pm Mon-Fri) Super popular and famous for its delicious sandwiches, such as roast beef and rocket, and (its signature) curried-egg salad with roasted peanuts and chutney. Salads are also available; local ingredients used. If you're in town on a Saturday in summer, visit Market Chef at the San Juan Island Farmers Market (10am to 1pm).

🛏 Earthbox Inn & Spa — Motel $$
(☎360-378-4000; www.earthboxmotel.com; 410 Spring St, Friday Harbor; r from $169; 🛜🚭🐾) Earthbox is a hybrid of simplicity and sophistication as a former motor inn embellished with features more commonly associated with a deluxe hotel. The result: a variety of funky, cleverly designed rooms with comfy beds and colorful yet minimalist undercurrents. Other bonuses include a pool, spa, fitness room, bike rental and fine gardens.

Eastsound ❼

✗ Inn at Ship Bay — Seafood $$$
(☎877-276-7296; www.innatshipbay.com; 326 Olga Rd; mains $21-30; ⏱5:30-10pm Tue-Sat) Locals unanimously rate this place as the best fine-dining experience on the island. The chefs work overtime preparing everything from scratch using the freshest island ingredients. Seafood is the specialty and it's served in an attractive 1860s orchard house a couple of miles south of Eastsound. There's also an on-site 11-room hotel (doubles $175 to $195).

🛏 Outlook Inn — Hotel $$
(☎360-376-2200; www.outlookinn.com; 171 Main St, Eastsound; r with shared/private bath from $74/119; @🛜🐾) Eastsound's oldest and most eye-catching building, the Outlook Inn (1888) is an island institution. Rooms are cozy and neat (try for room 30), while the luxurious suites have fireplaces, Jacuzzis and stunning water views from the balconies. Excellent attached cafe.

Moran State Park ❽

✗ Cafe Olga — Cafe $
(18 Urner St, Eastsound; mains $9-12; ⏱7am-3pm Mon-Fri, to 8pm Sat & Sun, closed Wed Mar-Apr) Relocated to Eastsound after a fire in Olga in 2013, the Olga Cafe is still the definitive Orcas Island experience. Living up to the hype, the scones, cinnamon buns and pies here are stupendous – perfect if you've just busted a gut cycling up and down Mt Constitution.

Rosario Resort ❾

🛏 Rosario Resort & Spa — Resort $$$
(☎360-376-2222; www.rosario-resort.com; 1400 Rosario Rd, Eastsound; r $149-400; ❄🛜🚭) This magnificent seafront mansion built by former shipbuilding magnate Robert Moran in 1904 is now the centerpiece of an upscale resort, and the setting oozes F Scott Fitzgerald–style romance. The 180 modern rooms sprawl across the grounds, and the complex includes tennis courts, a swimming pool, a marina and a spa.

Lopez Island ❿

✗ Bay Cafe — Seafood $$
(☎360-468-3700; www.bay-cafe.com; 9 Old Post Rd, Lopez Village; mains $15-31; ⏱5-9pm Wed-Fri, noon-9pm Sat & Sun) Lopez' one and only attempt at fine dining offers romantic sunset views right on the water, with classic fish dishes, including chowder and crab cakes. You could also go bolder with specialties like truffled mac 'n' cheese or rack of lamb paired with wine from the local vineyard.

🛏 Lopez Islander Resort — Resort $$
(☎360-468-2233; www.lopezfun.com; 2864 Fisherman Bay Rd; r from $119; 🛜🚭) Equipped with a restaurant, swimming pool, Jacuzzi, gym and 'Tiki Lounge Bar,' this so-outdated-it's-kind-of-cool 'resort' sits alongside a marina in Fisherman Bay, where eagles glide. What it lacks in intimacy it makes up for in amiability and good service.

Chuckanut Drive & Whidbey Island

7

Veer off the congested interstate at Bellingham and you quickly enter a parallel universe of sinuous back roads, tulip fields and spectacular ribbons of coastal asphalt.

TRIP HIGHLIGHTS

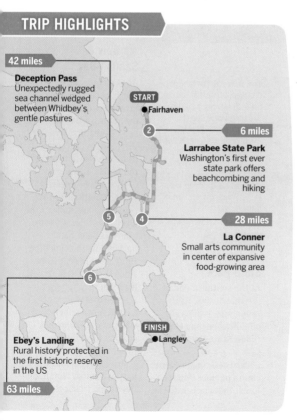

42 miles

Deception Pass
Unexpectedly rugged sea channel wedged between Whidbey's gentle pastures

START
● Fairhaven

2 **6 miles**

Larrabee State Park
Washington's first ever state park offers beachcombing and hiking

5 **4** **28 miles**

La Conner
Small arts community in center of expansive food-growing area

6

FINISH
● Langley

Ebey's Landing
Rural history protected in the first historic reserve in the US

63 miles

1–2 DAYS
89 MILES/143KM

GREAT FOR...

BEST TIME TO GO

March to June when spring flowers bloom.

 ESSENTIAL PHOTO

The daffodil and tulip fields around La Conner are the best this side of Holland.

 BEST FOR FOOD

La Conner – food from farm to plate in yards rather than miles.

ckanut Drive Coastal road near Bellingham

Chuckanut Drive & Whidbey Island

7

Short but sweet, this winding sojourn along Chuckanut Dr and through Whidbey Island is the kind of dreamy drive you see in car commercials: sunlight through trees, sparkling ocean and a dozen broccoli-colored islands shimmering in the middle distance. If you've got a convertible, it's roof-down time, weather permitting, as you glide between oyster restaurants, beaches and scenic state parks.

❶ Fairhaven

Of Bellingham's four original towns, Fairhaven is the best preserved; a four-square-block historic district of handsome redbrick Victorians testifies to a rich, if sometimes rambunctious, past. Today, the same buildings harbor bookstores, cafes and arty nooks – they're lovely to explore on foot (p154). Fairhaven is also an important transport nexus, and home of Bellingham's Amtrak station and ferry terminal, with regular ferries up the Inside Passage to Alaska.

✖ 🛏 p97

The Drive ❱❱ The thrill of Chuckanut Dr is that you don't have to wait long for its beauty to unfold. Vistas open out immediately south of Fairhaven, where homes hug million-dollar lots high above Puget Sound. Cut into the cliff, the road winds spectacularly through trees that frame island-speckled water views. Paralleling it on the right is the railway.

TRIP HIGHLIGHT

❷ Larrabee State Park

At the southern end of the Interurban Trail (p94), just 6 miles south of Fairhaven, sits **Larrabee State Park** (www.parks.wa.gov; Chuckanut Dr; ☺dawn-dusk; 🚶), a square chunk of emerald green forest that spills into the

bay at popular Clayton Beach and Wildcat Cove. Poking around in the tide pools or hiking up to **Fragrance Lake Trail** (5.1 miles return) are the most popular activities, though the trails can be crowded at weekends.

The Drive ❱❱ Chuckanut's precipitous topography continues for a few miles after Larrabee. Then, with dramatic suddenness, the landscape opens out into the flat agricultural pastures of the Skagit River Valley. Pass the Oyster Bar and Chuckanut Manor (both on the right) and you'll arrive at Bow Hill Rd, the first main intersection since Fairhaven.

❸ Bow & Samish Bay

As you continue the drive south, several pullouts lure you with fine views over Samish Bay as they explain the history of the road and its oyster industry. Oysters adore the brackish waters of the bay, and nearby **Taylor Shellfish Farms** (www.taylorshellfish.com; 2182 Chuckanut Dr, Bow; ☺9am-6pm) has been hand harvesting and shucking 1800 acres of seabed here since the 1880s. Staff can lead you through oyster etiquette as you learn to differentiate between a buttery Shigoku or a creamy Kumamoto.

Both Taylor and nearby Blau, across the bay on Samish Island, deliver their freshest catch

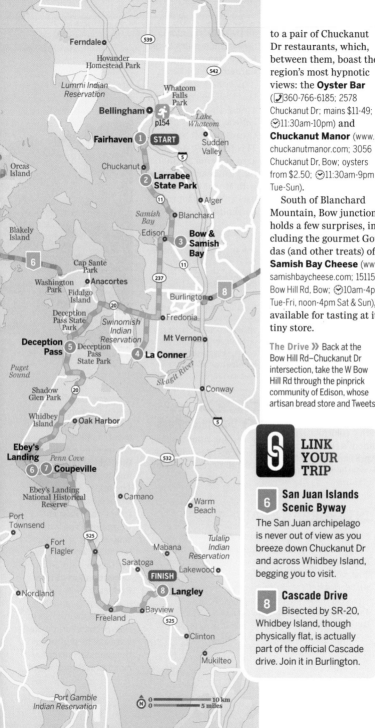

to a pair of Chuckanut Dr restaurants, which, between them, boast the region's most hypnotic views: the **Oyster Bar** (☏360-766-6185; 2578 Chuckanut Dr; mains $11-49; ⊙11:30am-10pm) and **Chuckanut Manor** (www.chuckanutmanor.com; 3056 Chuckanut Dr, Bow; oysters from $2.50; ⊙11:30am-9pm Tue-Sun).

South of Blanchard Mountain, Bow junction holds a few surprises, including the gourmet Goudas (and other treats) of **Samish Bay Cheese** (www.samishbaycheese.com; 15115 Bow Hill Rd, Bow; ⊙10am-4pm Tue-Fri, noon-4pm Sat & Sun), available for tasting at its tiny store.

The Drive » Back at the Bow Hill Rd–Chuckanut Dr intersection, take the W Bow Hill Rd through the pinprick community of Edison, whose artisan bread store and Tweets

🔗 LINK YOUR TRIP

6 San Juan Islands Scenic Byway

The San Juan archipelago is never out of view as you breeze down Chuckanut Dr and across Whidbey Island, begging you to visit.

8 Cascade Drive

Bisected by SR-20, Whidbey Island, though physically flat, is actually part of the official Cascade drive. Join it in Burlington.

93

Café merit a quick stopover. Continue south on the ruler-straight Farm to Market Rd to busy SR-20, which you join briefly heading west before turning left onto the La Conner–Whitney Rd.

TRIP HIGHLIGHT

④ La Conner

Celebrated for its tulips, wild turkeys, erudite writer's colony and (among other culinary treats) soccer-ball-sized cinnamon buns, La Conner's myriad attractions verge on the esoteric. Jammed with gift shops and classy B&Bs, it also has three decent museums; the best is the **Museum of Northwest Art** (www.monamuseum. org; 121 S 1st St; ⊙10am-5pm Tue-Sat, noon-5pm Sun & Mon). The zenith of La Conner's cultural calendar is the annual **Tulip Festival**, when the surrounding fields are embellished with a colorful carpet of daffodils (March), tulips (April) and irises (May). To see the flowers in

all their artistic glory, detour a few miles to the **Roozengaarde Display Garden** (www.tulips.com; 15867 Beaver Marsh Rd, Mt Vernon; $5; ⊙9am-6pm Mon-Sat, 11am-4pm Sun), halfway between La Conner and Mt Vernon. This renowned 3-acre garden plants 250,000 tulip bulbs annually and, with Mt Baker in the background, photo opportunities abound.

✕ 🏠 p97

The Drive » Retrace your tire tracks north to SR-20 and turn left with the Anacortes traffic toward the San Juan Islands ferry terminal. After crossing the Swinomish Channel turn left on SR-20 following signage to Whidbey Island. Although you probably don't realize it, you're now on Fidalgo Island, separated from the mainland by a narrow sea channel.

TRIP HIGHLIGHT

⑤ Deception Pass

Emerging from the flat pastures of Fidalgo Island, Deception Pass

leaps out like a mini Grand Canyon, its precipitous cliffs overlooked by a famous bridge made all the more dramatic by the sight of the churning, angry water below. The bridge consists of two steel arches that span Canoe Pass and Deception Pass, with a central support on Pass Island between the two. Visitors to the 5.5-sq-mile **Deception Pass State Park** (☎360-675-2417; 41229 N State Hwy 20) usually introduce themselves to the spectacular land and seascape by parking at the shoulders on either end and walking across

INTERURBAN TRAIL

For a break from the car, you can join Bellingham's fleece-wearing weekend warriors and savor a bit of Chuckanut Dr by bike along the 6-mile Interurban Trail, a deliciously flat former electric trolley bed that parallels the tarmac past deep forest and lovely views of Chuckanut Bay to Larrabee State Park. **Fairhaven Bike & Mountain Sports** (☎360-733-4433; www.fairhavenbike.com; 1103 11th St; rental per 4hr $25-37.50; ⊙9:30am-6pm Mon-Sat, 11am-5pm Sun) will set you up with a bike ($25 for four hours) for the easy two-hour ride.

Deception Pass State Park Bridge to Pass Island

the bridge. Built during the 1930s by the Civilian Conservation Corps, the bridge was considered an engineering feat in its day.

Besides the dramatic bridge overviews, the park's attractions include over 15 miles of saltwater shoreline and 27 miles of forest trails. **Deception Pass Tours** (www.deception passtours.com; 1hr Deception Pass tours adult/child $39/33) organizes jet boat tours through the turbulent waters daily.

The Drive » The rugged terrain of Deception Pass disappears almost as quickly as it materialized and you're soon in the pastoral fields that characterize Whidbey Island. After passing the entrance to the Naval Air station on your right, you'll skirt the rather ugly mall infestations of Oak Harbor. Traffic lights will slow your progress here. Keep on SR-20 to Ebey's Landing, 16 miles from Deception Pass.

- - - - - - - - - - - - -

TRIP HIGHLIGHT

⑥ Ebey's Landing

The nation's first national historic reserve, listed in 1978, was created in order to preserve Whidbey Island's historical heritage from the encroaching urbanization that had already partly engulfed Oak Harbor. Still 90% privately owned, **Ebey's Landing** (☎360-678-6084; www.nps.gov/ebla; 162 Cemetery Rd) comprises 17,400 acres encompassing working farms, four historic blockhouses, two state parks and the small historic town of Coupeville. A series of interpretive boards shows visitors how the patterns of croplands, woods and even roads reflect the activities of those who have peopled this scenic landscape, from its earliest indigenous inhabitants to 19th-century settlers.

The museum in Coupeville distributes a

brochure on suggested driving and cycling tours through the reserve. Highly recommended is the 3.6-mile **Bluff Trail**, which starts from a small parking area at the end of Ebey Rd. The energetic can walk or cycle here 2.5 miles from Coupeville, thus crossing the island at one of its narrowest points.

The Drive >> Veer off SR-20 just past Penn Cove to visit Coupeville.

- - - - - - - - - - - - -

7 Coupeville

Tiny Coupeville is Whidbey Island personified: fresh mussels and clams, old-world B&Bs, historic clapboard shop fronts, and instant access to a National Historical Reserve. Call in at the **Island County Historical Society Museum** (908 NW Alexander St; $4; ⊙10am-5pm May-Sep, to 4pm Fri-Mon Oct-Apr) for the lowdown on Washington state's second-oldest settlement (founded in 1852) and walking tour maps of the town's handsome vintage homes.

✗ ⚕ p97

The Drive >> SR-20 veers east at the southern end of Ebey's Landing toward the Keystone Ferry and Fort Casey State Park. The latter was once part of an early 1900s military defense system and is worth visiting for its old cement batteries, underground tunnels and lighthouse. Otherwise, continue south on SR-525 through Freeland to Bayview, where you take a left for Langley, 26 miles from Coupeville.

- - - - - - - - - - - - -

8 Langley

Langley, like Coupeville, is a small seafront community that is little changed since the late 19th century. Encased in an attractive historical center lie small cafes, antique furniture shops, funky clothes boutiques and a couple of decent B&Bs. While there's little to do here activity-wise, Langley provides a perfect antidote to the hustle and bustle of nearby Seattle and is a great place to relax and unwind, after numerous hours packed bumper to bumper on I-5.

Langley is 8 miles north of **Clinton** and the 20-minute ferry service from **Mukilteo** (www.wsdot.com/ferries; person/car free/$10.80), making this the closest of the Whidbey Island communities to the urban areas of northern Seattle.

✗ p97

Eating & Sleeping

Fairhaven ●

✕ Colophon Cafe   Cafe $

(1208 11th St; mains $8-13; ◷9am-8pm Sun-
Thu, to 9pm Fri & Sat) Linked with Fairhaven's
famous literary haven, **Village Books** (www.
villagebooks.com; 1210 11th St; ◷10am-9pm
Mon-Thu, to 10pm Fri & Sat, to 7pm Sun), the
Colophon is a multiethnic eatery for people who
like to follow their panini with Proust. Renowned
for its African peanut soup and chocolate
brandy cream pies, the cafe has indoor seating
along with an outside wine garden and is ever
popular with the local literati.

🛏 Fairhaven Village Inn   Hotel $$

(☏360-733-1311; www.fairhavenvillageinn.
com; 1200 10th St; r from $169; ❋🛜)
Downtown Bellingham lacks a decent number
of well-appointed independent hotels, but one
good alternative is this prime place in genteel
Fairhaven. Well in keeping with the vintage tone
of the historic district, the Village Inn is a class
above the standard motel fare, with prices
to match. In this instance, they're probably
justified.

La Conner ●

✕ Seeds
Bistro & Bar   Modern American $$

(☏360-466-3280; www.seedsbistro.com;
623 Morris St; mains $12-26; ◷11am-9pm;
🌿) Calling itself the 'seediest place in the
valley,' farm-to-table Seeds serves all the fresh
produce, fish and meats you'd hope for, all
in brunch-cafe-style friendliness. The menu
includes everything from creative salads to
Samish Bay oysters and charbroiled pork
tenderloin, and vegetarians and gluten-free
folks are well catered for. Finish your meal with a
slice of homemade berry pie.

The best time to visit is happy hour (3pm to
6pm daily) when you can sample several $8 to
$10 plates of the restaurant's specialties.

🛏 Heron Inn & Day Spa   B&B $$

(☏360-399-1074; www.theheroninn.com; 117
Maple Ave; r $105-185; ❋🛜🐾) Most rooms
here have a Jacuzzi, a fireplace and a view
(choose from the garden, the surrounding
farmlands or snow-capped Mt Baker). Above-
and-beyond service is propped up by the on-site
spa (massages, scrubs and more) and lovingly
home-cooked breakfasts.

Coupeville ●

✕ Christopher's   Seafood $$

(☏360-678-5480; www.christophersonwhidbey.
com; 103 NW Coveland St; mains $16-25;
◷11:30am-2pm & 5pm-close) The mussels
and clams are the best in town (no mean feat
in Coupeville), and the seafood alfredo pasta is
wonderfully rich.

🛏 Captain Whidbey Inn   Inn $$

(☏360-678-4097; www.captainwhidbey.com;
2072 W Captain Whidbey Inn Rd; r/cabins from
$103/210; 🛜) The beautifully forest-clad
Captain Whidbey is a 1907 inn with all the creaky
floors and enchantingly rustic log construction
that entails. With its low ceilings and cozy lounge
strewn with faded copies of *National Geographic*,
it feels more like something out of a medieval
forest than a 21st-century tourist island.

Lodging is in 12 sea-galleon-style guest
rooms (with shared bathrooms) in the main
lodge, as well as wood-heated cottages and a
more modern building with verandas facing a
lagoon. It's worth paying a little more for a view.

Langley ●

✕ Cafe Langley   Mediterranean $$

(www.cafelangley.com; 113 1st St; lunch
around $10, dinner $16-24; ◷11:30am-
2:30pm & 5-8:30pm Mon & Wed-Sat, to 3pm
Sun) Mediterranean cuisine, with a few deft
Northwestern seafood infusions (eg mussels)
thrown in for good measure.

Classic Trip

Cascade Drive

8

Rugged and inaccessible for half the year, this brawny mountain drive is etched with the kind of monumental, Alaskan-style beauty that once inspired Jack Kerouac.

TRIP HIGHLIGHTS

276 miles
Diablo Lake Overlook
Staggering natural view of a man-made reservoir

250 miles
Rainy Pass
Towering, seasonally accessible road amid saw-toothed Cascade peaks

FINISH Burlington

START Everett

Steven's Pass

Chelan

Leavenworth
Bavarian 'theme' town blessed with an authentic alpine backdrop

100 miles

Sun Mountain Lodge
One of the best places to stay in Washington state

215 miles

4–5 DAYS
350 MILES/563KM

GREAT FOR...

BEST TIME TO GO
June to September when roads are snow-free and passable.

 ESSENTIAL PHOTO
View from the Sun Mountain Lodge.

☑ **BEST FOR HIKING**
The Maple Pass Loop Trail from Rainy Pass.

rth Cascades National Park Diablo Lake

99

Classic Trip

8 Cascade Drive

Nature defies modern engineering in the North Cascades where high-altitude roads succumb to winter snow storms, and the names of the mountains – Mt Terror, Mt Fury, Forbidden Peak – whisper forebodingly. Less scary are the scattered settlements, small towns with esoteric distractions such as Bavarian Leavenworth and 'Wild West' Winthrop. Fill up the tank, put on your favorite Springsteen track and prepare for one of the rides of your life.

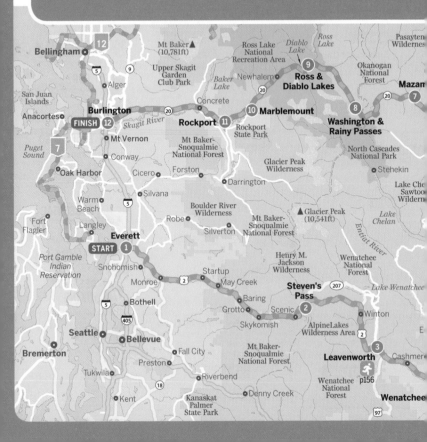

① Everett

This drive incorporates four-fifths of the popular 'Cascade Loop.' You can complete the other fifth by taking in the second half of the trip through Whidbey Island (p91). There's not much to detain you in Everett, the route's starting point 30 miles north of Seattle. It's known mainly for its Boeing connections and as the genesis for countless Seattle-region traffic jams. Head directly east and don't stop until Steven's Pass.

The Drive » The starting point of US-2, a 2579-mile cross-continental road that terminates in Maine, is in Everett. Crossing I-5, the route, which parallels the Great Northern Railway and Skykomish River for much of its journey, passes the towns of Startup, Sultan and Index, climbing toward Steven's Pass, 66 miles away. If you're thirsty, stop at one of the drive-through espresso huts en route.

② Steven's Pass

Accessible year-round thanks to its day-use **ski area** (www.stevenspass.com; day pass $64-69), Steven's Pass was only 'discovered' by white settlers as recently as 1890. Despite its lofty vantage – at 4045ft it is over 1000ft higher than Snoqualmie Pass – it was chosen for the Great Northern railroad's cross-Cascade route, but you won't see any train tracks here. Instead, the railway burrows underneath the pass via North America's longest rail tunnel (7.8 miles). The long-distance **Pacific Crest Trail** also crosses the highway here.

The Drive » From Steven's Pass the descent begins immediately with subtle changes in the vegetation; the cedars and hemlocks of the western slopes are gradually replaced with pine, larch and spruce. The road threads through the steep-sided Tumwater canyon alongside the turbulent Wenatchee River. Suddenly, German-style houses start to appear against an eerily familiar alpine backdrop.

TRIP HIGHLIGHT

③ Leavenworth

Blink hard and rub your eyes. This isn't some strange Germanic hallucination. This is Leavenworth, a former lumber town that underwent a Bavarian makeover in the 1960s after the re-routing of the cross-continental railway threatened to put it permanently out of business. Swapping loggers for tourists, Leavenworth today has successfully reinvented itself as a traditional *Romantische Strasse* village, right down to the beer and sausages. *The*

LINK YOUR TRIP

7 Chuckanut Drive & Whidbey Island

For a break from the mountain madness, veer north in Burlington to Bellingham and sample the coastal and pastoral joys of Puget Sound.

12 Mt Baker & Lummi Island

For more mountain madness, head north to Bellingham and then inland into another North Cascadian wilderness.

Classic Trip

Sound of Music–style setting helps, as does the fact that Leavenworth serves as the main activity center for sorties into the nearby **Alpine Lakes Wilderness** ($5 wilderness permit for certain areas) and **Wenatchee National Forest** (www.fs.usda.gov/okawen; 215 Melody Lane; ⊙ hours vary).

A surreal stroll (p156) through the gabled alpine houses of Leavenworth's Front St with its dirndl-wearing waitstaff, wandering accordionists and European cheese-mongers is one of Washington state's oddest, but most endearing experiences. For white-water rafting trips, call by **Osprey Rafting Co** (📞509-548-6800; www.ospreyrafting.com; 4342 Icicle Rd), which offers excursions from $79.

✕ 🛏 p107

The Drive ≫ The 22 miles between Leavenworth and Wenatchee highlight one of the most abrupt scenery changes in the state. One minute you're in quasi-Bavaria surrounded by crenellated alpine peaks, the next you're in a sprawled couldn't-be-anywhere-but-America town amid bald hills and a Nile-like river valley. East of Leavenworth US-2 shares the road briefly with US-97.

4 Wenatchee

Fruit stands start peppering the highway soon after you leave Leavenworth, paving your entry into Wenatchee, the self-proclaimed – and who's arguing? – Apple Capital of the World. Something of an ugly sister after cute Leavenworth, Wenatchee's a place to go local and taste the apples from the nearby orchards before swinging north. The best fruit stands enliven Hwy 2/97 on the way to Chelan. As an overture to your tasting experience, check out the **Washington Apple Com-**

mission Visitors Center (www.bestapples.com; 2900 Euclid Ave; ⊙8am-5pm Mon-Fri) on the way into town, where you can bone up on the relative merits of a Gala versus a Braeburn over a surprisingly interesting video.

The Drive ≫ Hwy 2/97 plies the east side of the Columbia River between Wenatchee and Chelan. This is one of the best places to 'shop' at impromptu seasonal fruit outlets run by enterprising local farmers who haul their freshly plucked produce from the nearby fields and orchards to sell roadside from semipermanent stores, carts or just plain old boxes.

5 Chelan

Lake Chelan shelters some of the nation's cleanest water and has consequently become one of Washington's premier water recreation areas. Not surprisingly, the place is cheek-to-jowl in summer, with all number of speedboats, Jet Skis and power-craft battling it out for their own private slice of water. To avoid any high-speed collisions, rent a kayak from **Lake Rider Sports** (www.lakeridersports.com; Lakeshore Waterfront Park; single/double kayaks per day $65/85; ⊙7am-6:30pm) and paddle up the lake to see some undiluted Cascadian nature firsthand.

There are public beaches at **Lakeside Park**, near the west side

KEROUAC AND THE VOID

A turnout at milepost 135 on US-20 offers the drive's only roadside views of **Desolation Peak**. The peak's lookout tower was famously home to Zen-influenced Beat writer Jack Kerouac who, in 1956, spent 63 days here in splendid isolation, honing his evolving Buddhist philosophy, raging at 'the Void' of nearby Hozomeen Mountain (also visible from the turnout) and penning drafts of *Desolation Angels*. It was the last time Kerouac would enjoy such anonymity; the following year saw the publication of *On the Road*, and his propulsion to the status of literary icon.

of Chelan town, and at **Lake Chelan State Park**, 9 miles west on S Lakeshore Rd.

If you have kids, don't even think they'll let you sneak past **Slidewaters Water Park** (www.slidewaters.com; 102 Waterslide Dr; day pass adult/child $22/17; ⏰10am-7pm May-Sep; 🚻), located on a hill above the *Lady of the Lake* boat dock.

The Drive ≫ Rejoin US-97 and follow it north through the grand coulees of the Columbia River Valley to the small town of Pateros. From here SR-153, aka the Methow Hwy, tracks the younger, faster-flowing Methow River north to Twisp. At a junction with US-20 turn left, and continue on the highway into Winthrop, 61 miles from Chelan.

- - - - - - - - - - - -

TRIP HIGHLIGHT

➏ Winthrop

Winthrop is, along with Leavenworth, one of two themed towns on this Cascade Drive. Once a struggling mining community, it avoided 'ghost town' status in the 1960s when it was made over to look like a cowboy settlement out of the Wild West. Although on paper it sounds more like corny Hollywood than *Gun Fight at the OK Corral*, the Gary Cooper touches are surprisingly authentic. Winthrop's *High Noon* shopfronts hide a genuine frontier spirit (in winter the road ends not far beyond

LOCAL KNOWLEDGE: METHOW VALLEY TRAILS

The Methow's combination of powdery winter snow and abundant summer sunshine has transformed the valley into one of Washington's primary recreation areas. You can bike, hike and fish in the summer, and cross-country ski on the second-biggest snow-trail network in the US during the winter. The 125 miles of trails are maintained by a nonprofit organization, the **Methow Valley Sport Trails Association** (MVSTA; ☎509-996-3287; www.methowtrails.org; 309 Riverside Ave, Winthrop; ⏰9:30am-3:30pm Mon-Fri), and in the winter it provides the most comprehensive network of hut-to-hut (and hotel-to-hotel) skiing in North America.

here), along with some fantastic eating places and accommodations.

The facades of downtown Winthrop are so realistic it's easy to miss the collection of homesteader cabins that make up the **Shafer Museum** (www.shafermuseum.com; 285 Castle Ave; admission by donation; ⏰10am-5pm Memorial Day–Labor Day). But best of all is the unmissable **Sun Mountain Lodge** (p107), a sporting and relaxation dreamscape 10 miles out of town overlooking the valley.

✕ ⛺ p107

The Drive ≫ Out of Winthrop, SR-20 enters the most bucolic and endearing stretch of the Methow Valley, whose broad valley floor, scattered with farms, gives little hint of the jagged wilderness that lies beyond. If you thought Winthrop was small, don't blink in Mazama, a small cluster of

wooden buildings reminiscent of a gunslinger movie.

- - - - - - - - - - - -

➐ Mazama

The last outpost before the raw, desolate, occasionally terrifying North Cascades, Mazama's half-dozen wooden abodes sit at the western end of the Methow Valley. Fuel up on brownies at the **Mazama Store** (50 Lost River Rd; ⏰7am-6pm Sun-Thu, to 7pm Fri & Sat), an espresso bar for outdoorsy locals, but also a great place to pick up trail tips.

The Drive ≫ You'll be working through your gears soon after leaving Mazama as the North Cascade Mountains start to close in. This part of US-20 is unlike any other trans-Cascade road. Not only is the scenery more spectacular, but the road itself is a major engineering feat. Only completed in 1972, it still remains closed November to May due to snow blockage.

WHY THIS IS A CLASSIC TRIP
CELESTE BRASH, WRITER

This route could well be called 'The Heart of the Cascades' because it takes you over, around and deep into the most glorious corners of some of the most astounding mountains in the Americas. It's difficult not to blurt out 'oohs' as you round corners and see vistas of blue lakes framed by sharp, white peaks and shaded by evergreens. Perfect for road-tripping, the highway scenery never falters.

Top: Cyclists on Washington Pass
Left: Leavenworth
Right: Gas station, Winthrop

DENISE LETT / SHUTTERSTOCK ©

TRIP HIGHLIGHT

❽ Washington & Rainy Passes

Venture less than 100yd from your car at the **Washington Pass overlook** (5477ft) and you'll be rewarded with fine views of the towering Liberty Bell and its Early Winter Spires, while the highway drops below you in ribbonlike loops. By the time the highway reaches **Rainy Pass** (5875ft) a couple of miles further west, the air has chilled and you're well into the high country, a hop and a skip from the drive's highest hiking trails. The 6.2-mile **Maple Pass Loop Trail** is a favorite, climbing 2150ft to aerial views over jewel-like Lake Ann. The epic **Pacific Crest Trail** also crosses Hwy 20 nearby, so keep an eye open for wide-eyed and bushy-bearded through-hikers popping out of the undergrowth. Perhaps the best choice for shaking the crowds is the excellent climb up to **Easy Pass** (7.4 miles return), hardly 'easy,' but offering spectacular views of Mt Logan and the Fisher Basin below.

The Drive » Surrounded by Gothic peaks, the North Cascades Scenic Hwy makes a big swing north, shadowing Granite Creek and then Ruby Creek, where it swings back west and enters the Ross Lake National Recreation Area near Ruby Arm.

TRIP HIGHLIGHT

9 Ross & Diablo Lakes

Much of the landscape on this trip is unnatural, born from the construction of three huge dams that still supply Seattle with much of its electricity. The wilderness that surrounds it, however, is the rawest you'll get outside Alaska. **Ross Lake** (Mile 134) was formed in the 1930s after the building of the eponymous dam. It stretches north 23 miles into Canada. Soon after the **Ross Lake overlook,** a path leads from the road to the dam. You'll see the unique **Ross Lake Resort** on the other side.

A classic photo op comes a couple of miles later at the **Diablo Lake overlook** (supply ferries adult/child 1 way $10/5). The turquoise lake is the most popular part of the park, offering beaches, gorgeous views and a boat launch at **Colonial Creek Campground** (206-386-4495; www.nps.gov; Hwy 20, Mile 130; campsites $16), with nearby hikes to Thunder Knob (3.6 miles return) and Thunder Creek (12 miles return).

📐 p107

The Drive » From Diablo head west alongside the sinuous Gorge Reservoir on US-20. Pass through Newhalem (where you can stop at the North Cascades National Park Visitor Center). As the valley opens out and the damp West Coast air drifts in from the Pacific, you'll enter Marblemount, 23 miles from Diablo Lake.

10 Marblemount

Blink and you'll miss the town of Marblemount, but the thought of buffalo burgers may entice you to pull over at the **Buffalo Run Restaurant** (60084 Hwy 20, Marblemount; mains $10-34; ⏲ lunch & dinner; 🚻), the first decent restaurant for miles, as long as you don't mind being greeted by the sight of several decoratively draped animal skins and a huge buffalo head mounted on the wall.

📐 p107

The Drive » The Skagit River remains your constant companion as you motor the 8 miles from Marblemount to equally diminutive Rockport. Look out for rafters, floaters and bald eagles.

11 Rockport

As the valley widens further you'll touchdown in Rockport where the miragelike appearance of an Indonesian-style Batak hut, aka the **Cascadian Home Farm** (360-853-8173; Hwy 20, Mile 100; ⏲10am-6pm May & Oct, 9am-7pm Jun-Sep; 🚻) begs you to stop for organic strawberries, delicious fruit shakes and lifesaving espresso, which you can slurp down on a short self-guided farm tour.

Nearby, a 10-mile stretch of the Skagit River is a wintering ground for over 600 bald eagles that come here from November to early March to feast on spawning salmon. January is the best time to view them, ideally on a winter float trip with **Skagit River Guide Service** (888-675-2448; www.skagitriverfishingguide.com; Mount Vernon), whose boats use propane heat and have comfy cushioned seats. Three-hour trips ($75) run early November to mid-February.

The Drive » From Rockport head west for 37 miles on US-20 through the Cascade Mountain foothills and the ever-broadening Skagit River Valley to the small city of Burlington, which sits just east of busy I-5.

12 Burlington

The drive's end, popularly known as the 'Hub City,' is not a 'sight' in itself (unless you like shopping malls), although the settlement's location in the heart of the Skagit River Valley means it acts as a hub for numerous nearby attractions, including the tulip fields of La Conner (p94), Chuckanut Dr (p91; which officially ends here) and the San Juan Islands (p83).

Eating & Sleeping

Leavenworth ③

✖ Pavs Cafe Bistro · French $$

(833 Front St; crepes $10-20; ⊙11:30am-9pm Mon-Fri, 9am-9pm Sat & Sun) Ah, *oui!* If another lick of accordion music will make you run screaming for the mountains, tuck into this wee French cafe serving delicious crepes, seafood and French-ified steaks and pastas. It's also one of the best choices in town for breakfast.

⌂ Enzian Inn · Hotel $$

(📞509-548-5269; www.enzianinn.com; 590 Hwy 2; d from $125; 🕸🖥) At this Leavenworth classic the day starts with a blast on an alpenhorn before breakfast. If this doesn't send you running for your lederhosen, cast an eye over the free putting green (with resident grass-trimming goats), the indoor and outdoor swimming pools, or the nightly pianist pounding out requests in the Bavarian lobby.

Winthrop ⑥

✖ Duck Brand Cantina · Mexican, Brunch $$

(www.methownet.com/duck; 248 Riverside Ave; mains $7-15; ⊙7am-9pm) No standard Mexican restaurant, the 'Duck' nonetheless serves quesadillas, enchiladas and tacos that could roast the socks off any authentic Monterey diner. The Wild West saloon-style cantina also churns out a mean American breakfast. In the winter the hearty porridge will keep you skiing all day.

⌂ Sun Mountain Lodge · Lodge $$$

(📞509-996-2211; www.sunmountainlodge.com; 604 Patterson Lake Rd, Winthrop; r from $300, cabins from $405; ⊙Dec-late Oct; 🕸🖥) Without a doubt one of the best places to stay in Washington, Sun Mountain Lodge has an incomparable natural setting, perched like an eagle's nest high above the Methow Valley. The 360-degree views from its highly lauded restaurant are awe-inspiring, and people travel from miles around just to enjoy breakfast here.

The lodge and its assorted cabins manage to provide luxury without pretension, while the outdoor attractions that are based around its extensive network of lakes and trails could keep a hyperactive hiker, cyclist or skier occupied for weeks. Not surprisingly, the Sun Mountain is pricey, but if you have just one splurge in the Washington wilderness east of Seattle, this should be the place; prices drop a bit from Sunday to Thursday nights.

Ross & Diablo Lakes ⑨

⌂ Ross Lake Resort · Historic Hotel $$

(📞206-386-4437; www.rosslakeresort.com; 503 Diablo St, Rockport; cabins $185-370; ⊙mid-Jun–late Oct) The floating cabins at this secluded resort, on the lake's west side, were built in the 1930s for loggers working in the valley soon to be flooded by Ross Dam. There's no road in – either hike the 2-mile trail from Hwy 20 or take the resort's supply boat from the parking area near Diablo Dam.

Cabins vary in size and facilities, but all feature electricity, plumbing and kitchenettes. Bedding and kitchen supplies are provided, but guests should bring food. The resort rents canoes, kayaks and motorboats, and operates a water-taxi service for hikers destined for trailheads around the lake. If you need to pick up some food, stop by the Skagit General Store in Newhalem, which has sandwiches and coffee. Note that there's no internet or phone reception out here, so this is a complete getaway.

Marblemount ⑩

⌂ Buffalo Run Inn · Motel $

(📞360-873-2103; www.buffaloruninn.com; 58179 Hwy 20, Marblemount; r $69-119; 🖥) Situated on a sharp bend on Hwy 20, the Buffalo doesn't look much from the outside. But within its wooden walls is a clean motel (kitchenettes, TVs and comfy beds) and backcountry cabin (kitschy bear and buffalo paraphernalia). Five of the 15 rooms share baths and a sitting area. There's an included microwavable breakfast 'buffet' stuffed in a communal fridge.

Mt Rainier Scenic Byways

9

Emblazoned on every Washington license plate and visible throughout the western state, Rainier is the contiguous USA's fifth-highest peak and, arguably, its most awe-inspiring.

TRIP HIGHLIGHTS

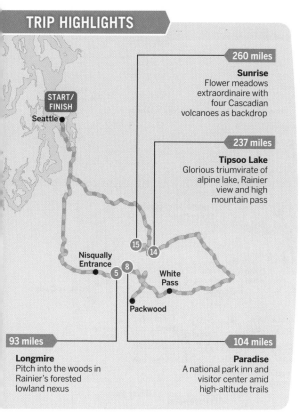

260 miles

Sunrise
Flower meadows extraordinaire with four Cascadian volcanoes as backdrop

237 miles

Tipsoo Lake
Glorious triumvirate of alpine lake, Rainier view and high mountain pass

START/FINISH
Seattle

15 14

Nisqually Entrance
5 8
White Pass
Packwood

93 miles

Longmire
Pitch into the woods in Rainier's forested lowland nexus

104 miles

Paradise
A national park inn and visitor center amid high-altitude trails

2–3 DAYS
354 MILES/570KM

GREAT FOR...

BEST TIME TO GO

June to October when alpine flowers bloom.

 ESSENTIAL PHOTO

Rainier's snow-topped summit reflected in Reflection Lakes.

☑ **BEST FOR ALPINE MEADOWS**

A toss-up between Paradise and Sunrise.

9 Mt Rainier Scenic Byways

Wrapped in a 368-sq-mile national park, and standing 2000ft higher than anything else in the Pacific Northwest, Rainier is a mountain of biblical proportions. Circumnavigate it by car and you'll quickly swap the urban melee of Seattle for forest-covered mountain foothills strafed with huge old-growth trees and imbued with Native American myth. Closer to Paradise (the inn), lucid flower meadows cower beneath its ice-encrusted summit during an intense summer season.

❶ Seattle

Seattle is an appropriate place to start this epic circuit around what locals refer to reverently as 'the Mountain.' Before heading off, take some time to walk (p152) around, seeking out the soul of the city at **Pike Place Market** (www.pikeplacemarket.org; 85 Pike St; 🕘9am-6pm Mon-Sat, 9am-5pm Sun; 🚇Westlake), for that's where it hides. On the days when Rainier reveals itself from the cloudy heavens (a minority, annually), you can

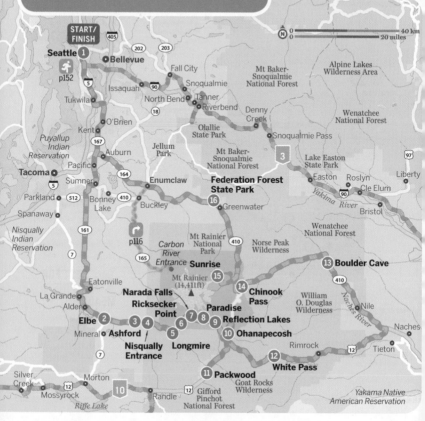

also wander down to the waterfront for a glimpse of the high-altitude glories to come.

 p65

The Drive » There is little to delay you out of Seattle until the tiny town of Elbe, 72 miles away. Drive south on I-5 to exit 154A, then east on I-405, and south again on SR-167 and SR-161. Just southwest of Eatonville, SR-161 merges with SR-7; follow this road into Elbe on the cusp of the national park.

➋ Elbe

The pinprick settlement of Elbe (population 29) has two claims to fame: its tiny white Lutheran **church** built by German immigrants in 1906 (and positively ancient by Pacific Northwest standards), and the heritage

LINK YOUR TRIP

 Mountains to Sound Greenway

Seattle is the finish point of this roller-coaster drive, which is equally spectacular if done in reverse.

 Mt St Helens Volcano Trail

A logical link and an easy one given the proximity of the two mountains – Packwood, near Rainier's Ohanapecosh entrance, serves both drives.

Mt Rainier Scenic Railroad (☏360-492-5588; www.mtrainierrailroad.com; 54124 Mountain Hwy E; adult/child $32/18) that runs summer steam trains between Elbe and Mineral (7 miles south). Trips depart three times daily from May to September. Aping the railway theme is the **Hobo Inn & Diner** (www.rrdiner.com; 54106 Mountain Hwy E; r from $115), whose restaurant, bar and rooms all inhabit vintage, but lovingly tended, cabooses (train carriages).

The Drive » From Elbe take SR-706 (the National Park Hwy) due east to Ashford.

➌ Ashford

Situated a couple of miles outside the busy Nisqually entrance, Ashford is the national park's main service center with some medium-ranking accommodations, an info center and **Whittaker's Motel & Bunkhouse** (p117), a hostel-cafe conceived by legendary local mountaineer Lou Whittaker in the early 1990s. It would be heresy to leave town without popping inside for an espresso before grabbing brunch (or lunch) down the road at the **Copper Creek Inn** (p117), where the wild blackberry pies have fuelled many a successful summit attempt.

 p117

The Drive » Just east of Ashford on SR-706 you'll find the park entrance gate.

➍ Nisqually Entrance

The southwestern Nisqually entrance (named for the nearby river, which in turn is named after a local Native American tribe) is the busiest in **Mt Rainier National Park** (www.nps.gov/mora; entry per car $25) and the only year-round entry gate. The simple entrance arch was built in 1922. Pay your park fee at the ticket window. As you drive through the entrance, you'll notice how, almost immediately, the trees appear denser and older. Many of these moss-covered behemoths date back over 700 years and measure up to 200ft in height.

The Drive » Follow the road alongside the Nisqually River for a couple of miles to Kautz Creek, where the summit of Rainier appears like a ghostly apparition.

TRIP HIGHLIGHT

➎ Longmire

Worth a stop to stretch your legs or gain an early glimpse of Rainier's mossy old-growth forest, Longmire is the brainchild of a certain James Longmire, who first came here in 1883 during a climbing trip, a noticed the hot mineral springs that bubbled up in a lovely meadow opposite

SUMMER WONDERLAND

You've circumnavigated it in a car; now how about walking it? Rainier is not only encircled by a road; you can also walk around it on foot via the long-distance **Wonderland Trail**. Laid out in 1915, the 93-mile precipitous path initially served as a patrol beat for park rangers and in the 1930s it was briefly earmarked as a paved ring road for cars. Fortunately, the plan never reached fruition and today the unbroken trail (which gains 21,000ft in cumulative elevation) is one of the most challenging and iconic hikes in the Pacific Northwest. You'll need food, camping gear, eight to 12 free days and a permit from the **Longmire Information Center** to do Wonderland. Longmire is a popular start point. There are 18 backcountry campgrounds en route; reservations ($20) are advisable in peak season (July and August). The official park page (www.nps.gov/mora) has more information.

the present-day **National Park Inn** (p117). He and his family returned the following year and established Longmire's Medicinal Springs, and in 1890 he built the Longmire Springs Hotel. Since 1917 the National Park Inn has stood on this site – built in classic 'parkitecture' style – and is complemented by a small store, the tiny **Longmire Information Center & Museum** (☎360-569-6575; ⊙9am-4:30pm May-Jul) and a number of important trailheads. For a laid-back look at some old-growth forest and pastoral meadows, try the **Trail of the Shadows** loop, a 0.8-mile circuit that begins across the road from the museum.

🛏 p117

The Drive » After Longmire the road slowly starts to climb, passing the Cougar Rock campground and Christine Falls, both on the left. A couple of miles after the falls, bear right onto a short stretch of summer-only one-way road (signposted 'Viewpoint') for a view stop at Ricksecker Point.

- - - - - - - - - - - - - - -

⑥ Ricksecker Point

One of the park's premier viewpoints beloved by photographers, professional or otherwise, Ricksecker Point is a fine place to study five of Rainier's 26 glaciers – Nisqually, Pyramid, Success, Kautz and Wilson. The summit you see here is actually a false one (Point Success); the obscured *true* summit is 257ft higher. Equally majestic to the

southeast is the saw-toothed Tatoosh range.

The Drive » Rejoin the main road and continue uphill.

- - - - - - - - - - - - - - -

⑦ Narada Falls

Eight miles east of Longmire, a parking area marks the starting point for a steep 0.2-mile trail that leads down through flowers and ferns to the misty 168ft Narada Falls. The falls, often embellished by brilliant rainbows, carry the Paradise River over a basalt cliff. In high season, expect to get a face-full of water spray and an earful of oohing and aahing as this is the park's most popular waterfall. In winter the falls freeze over and attract daring ice-climbers.

The Drive » Soon after the falls, the road forks; stay left for Paradise. Follow the winding asphalt for another 2 miles to the Upper Parking Lot, where you'll find the Paradise Inn and Henry M Jackson Visitor Center.

- - - - - - - - - - - - - - -

TRIP HIGHLIGHT

⑧ Paradise

The daughter of park pioneer James Longmire unintentionally named this high mountain nirvana, when she exclaimed what a paradise it was on visiting the spot for the first time in the 1880s. Suddenly, the area had a name, and a very apt one at that. One of the snowiest places on earth, 5400ft-high **Paradise** remains the park's most popular draw with its famous flower meadows backed by dramatic Rainier views on the days when the mountain decides to take its cloudy hat off. Aside from hiding numerous trailheads and being the starting point for most summit hikes, Paradise guards the iconic **Paradise Inn** (p117), built in 1916 and refurbished in 2008, and the informative **Henry M Jackson Visitor Center** (📞360-569-6571; Paradise; 🕐10am-7pm mid-Jun–Sep, to 5pm May & Oct, weekends only in winter), completely rebuilt and reopened in 2008. Park naturalists lead free interpretive hikes from the visitor center daily in summer, and snowshoe walks on winter weekends.

🛏 p117

The Drive ›› Drive out of the east end of the Paradise Upper Parking Lot, cross the Paradise River (looking out for marmots) and descend the one-way road for 2 miles to a junction. Turn left and rejoin the main two-way road heading toward Reflection Lakes and Steven's Canyon.

- - - - - - - - - - - - -

9 Reflection Lakes

Rainier eyes itself in the mirror on calm cloudless days at Reflection Lakes, formed during a violent volcanic eruption nearly 6000 years ago. You can pull over for double-vision photos of the mountain framed by tufts of precious wildflowers. The main lake used to have a boat concession, but now it's deliciously tranquil, bar the odd passing tour bus.

The Drive ›› Avalanche chutes plague the U-shaped Steven's Canyon Rd in the winter, ensuring it remains closed outside peak season (unlike Paradise on the western side). Seen from above, the canyon is rather spectacular. Stop for a bird's-eye view a mile or so after Reflection Lakes, before the trees close in. From here it's downhill all the way to Ohanapecosh.

- - - - - - - - - - - - -

10 Ohanapecosh

Ohanapecosh (o-*ha*-nuh-peh-*kosh* – the name means 'at the edge') in the park's southeastern corner is usually accessed by the small settlement of Packwood, which is 12 miles to the southwest on US 12, harbors a small number of eating and sleeping options. Shoehorned between Mt Rainier and its two southern neighbors, Mt St Helens and Mt Adams, this is a good base for travelers wanting to visit two or more of the mountains.

Just inside the Steven's Canyon gate, you'll find the 1.5-mile **Grove of the Patriarchs Trail**, one of the park's most popular short hikes. The trail explores a small island in the Ohanapecosh River replete with craning

Douglas fir, cedar and hemlock trees, some of which are over 1000 years old. To reach the **Ohanapecosh Visitors Center** (🕐9am-5pm May–mid-Oct), turn right at the Steven's Canyon entrance onto SR-123 and drive 1.5 miles south. Alternatively, you can hike down from the Grove of the Patriarchs.

The Drive ›› Go right at the Steven's Canyon entrance and follow SR-123 south past the visitor center to the intersection with US 12. For Packwood, bear right.

- - - - - - - - - - - - -

11 Packwood

A service center for Mt St Helens, Mt Rainier and the nearby ski area of White Pass, Packwood is what in the Old West they called a 'one-horse town.' A few low- to mid-ranking eating joints and accommodations glued to US 12 provide a good excuse to pull over and mingle with other road-trippers. Chin-waggers congregate at **Mountain Goat Coffee** (105 E Main St, Packwood; 🕐7am-5pm), where you may run into a park ranger or two.

🛏 p117

The Drive ›› Retrace your route to the intersection of US 12 and SR-123. The climb to White Pass begins here. Stop at a pullover soon after the intersection to appreciate the indelible sight of Mt Rainier as it appears briefly above the trees.

⑫ White Pass

Higher than Snoqualmie and Stevens Passes to the north, White Pass carries a quieter, open-year-round road that, at various points, offers glimpses of three Cascadian volcanoes: Mt Rainier, Mt Adams and Mt St Helens. The pass itself, perched at 4500ft, is home to an understated **ski area** (www.skiwhitepass.com; day passes adult/child $63/43), which has one condo complex for overnighters. Otherwise, people stay in nearby Packwood or drive up for the day from Yakima.

🛏 p117

The Drive » A classic east–west Washington scenery shift kicks in soon after White Pass as you follow US 12 amid increasingly scattered trees and bald, steep-sided river coulees. At the intersection with SR-410, swing north on the Chinook Scenic Byway just west of the town of Naches to reach Boulder Cave, 65 miles from White Pass.

CHECUBUS / SHUTTERSTOCK ©

⑬ Boulder Cave

Among the many excuses to pull over on this stretch of the Chinook Scenic Byway is **Boulder Cave** (☺May–Oct), a rarity in the relatively cave-free terrain of the Pacific Northwest and doubly unique due to its formation through a combination of volcanic and erosive processes. A 2-mile round-trip trail built by the Civilian Conservation Corp in 1935 leads into the cave's murky interior, formed when Devil's Creek cut a tunnel through soft sedimentary rock, leaving hard volcanic basalt on top. Up to 50 rare big-eared bats hibernate in the cave each winter, when it is closed to the public. Bring a flashlight.

The Drive » Continue west and uphill toward Chinook Pass, 25 miles from Boulder Cave, as the air cools and the snowdrifts pile up roadside.

TRIP HIGHLIGHT

⑭ Chinook Pass

Closed until May and infested with lingering snowdrifts well into July, Chinook Pass towers 5430ft on Rainier's

Mt Rainier National Park Views from Sunrise Point

eastern flank. The long-distance **Pacific Crest Trail** crosses the highway here on a pretty stone bridge, while nearby **Crystal Mountain** (☎360-663-2265; www.crystalmoun tainresort.com; 33914 Crystal Mountain Blvd, Hwy 410) comprises Washington's largest ski area and only bona fide overnight 'resort.' Rather than stop at the pass, cruise a few hundred yards further west to **Tipsoo Lake**, another reflective photographer's dream where a paved trail will return the blood to your legs.

The Drive » From Tipsoo Lake the road winds down to relatively 'low' Cayuse Pass (4694ft). Turn north here and descend a further 1000ft in 3 miles to the turning for Mt Rainier's White River entrance. This is the gateway to Sunrise, 16 miles uphill via a series of switchbacks.

— — — — — — — — — —

TRIP HIGHLIGHT

⓯ Sunrise

Sunrise, at 6400ft, marks the park's highest road. Thanks to the superior elevation, the summer season is particularly short and snow can linger into July. It is also noticeably drier than

115

DETOUR: CARBON RIVER ENTRANCE

Start: 16 Federation Forest State Park

The park's northwest entrance is its most isolated and undeveloped corner, with two unpaved (and unconnected) roads and little in the way of facilities, save a lone ranger station and the very basic **Ipsut Creek Campground** (📞360-829-5127; campsites with wilderness camping permit free; ⏰year-round, weather permitting). But while the tourist traffic might be thin on the ground, the landscape lacks nothing in magnificence or serendipity.

Named for its coal deposits, Carbon River is the park's wettest region and protects one of the few remaining examples of inland temperate rain forest in the contiguous USA. Dense, green and cloaked in moss, this verdant wilderness can be penetrated by a handful of interpretive trails that fan off the Carbon River Rd.

Getting here takes you part of the way back to Seattle. Take Hwy 410 W to 116 S (Carbon River Rd) then turn left. After about 15.5 miles you'll come to the Carbon River ranger station just before the entrance.

Paradise, resulting in an interesting variety of subalpine vegetation, including masses of wildflowers.

The views from Sunrise are famously spectacular and – aside from stunning close-ups of Rainier itself – you can also, quite literally, watch the weather roll in over the distant peaks of Mt Baker and Mt Adams. Similarly impressive is the glisten-ing Emmons Glacier, which, at 4 sq miles, is the largest glacier in the contiguous USA.

A trailhead directly across the parking lot from the **Sunrise Lodge Cafeteria** (snacks $6-9; ⏰10am-7pm Jul & Aug) provides access to **Emmons Vista**, with good views of Mt Rainier, Little Tahoma and the glacier. Nearby, the 1-mile **Sourdough Ridge Trail** leads to pristine subalpine meadows for stunning views over other volcanic giants.

The Drive » Coast downhill to the White River entrance and turn north onto the Mather Memorial Pkwy in order to exit the park. In the small community of Greenwater on SR-410 you can load up with gas and food.

- - - - - - - - - -

16 Federation Forest State Park

Just when you thought you'd left ancient nature behind, up springs Federation Forest State Park, created by a fore-sighted women's group in the 1940s in order to preserve a rapidly diminishing stock of local old-growth forest from logging interests. Today its fir, spruce, hemlock and cedar trees cluster around the lackadaisical White River, while the **Catherine Montgomery Interpretive Center** (Federation Forest State Park; ⏰8am-dusk) offers a run-down of the contrasting ecosystems of east–west Washington state. There's also a bookstore and 12 miles of trails, most of them family friendly.

Eating & Sleeping

Ashford ❸

✗ Copper Creek Inn   American $$

(www.coppercreekinn.com; 35707 SR 706 E, Ashford; breakfast from $8, burgers $10, dinner mains $12-29; ⏰7am-9pm) **Forget the historic inns.** This is one of the state's great rural restaurants, and breakfast is an absolute must if you're heading off for a lengthy hike. Situated just outside the Nisqually entrance, the Copper Creek has been knocking out pancakes, wild-blackberry pie and home-roasted coffee since 1946.

⌂ Whittaker's Motel & Bunkhouse   Hostel $

(☎360-569-2439; www.whittakersbunkhouse. com; 30205 SR 706 E; dm $35 d $65-120; 🛜) Part of Rainier's 'furniture', Whittaker's is the home base of legendary Northwestern climber Lou Whittaker, who first summited the mountain at the age of 19 and has guided countless adventurers to the top in the years since. Down-to-earth and comfortable, this place has a good old-fashioned youth-hostel feel, with cheap sleeps available in six-bed dorms.

The alluring on-site **Whittaker's Café & Espresso** (muffins $3; ⏰7am-9pm, weekends only winter) is a fine place to hunker down for breakfast.

⌂ Nisqually Lodge   Motel $

(☎360-569-8804; http://nisqually. whitepasstravel.com; 31609 SR 706 E; r from $110; ❄🛜♨) With an expansive lobby complete with crackling fireplace and huge well-stocked rooms, this lodge is far plusher than an average motel. The outdoor Jacuzzi, simple help-yourself breakfast and easy access to the park pretty much seal the deal in this price bracket.

Longmire ❺

⌂ National Park Inn   Inn $$

(☎360-569-2275; www.mtrainierguestservices. com; r with shared/private bath from $121/170; ❄) The National Park Inn, parts of which date from 1911, goes out of its way to be rustic, with no TVs or telephones and small yet cozy

facilities. But who needs cable when you've got fine service, fantastic surroundings and complimentary afternoon tea and scones? Reserve ahead in summer.

Paradise ❽

⌂ Paradise Inn   Historic Hotel $$

(☎360-569-2275; www.mtrainierguestservices. com; r with shared/private bath from $119/175; ⏰May-Oct; 🛜) Designed to blend in with the environment and constructed almost entirely of local materials, including exposed cedar logs in the Great Room, the historic Paradise Inn (1916) was an early blueprint for rustic National Park Service–style architecture.

Following a two-year, $30-million, earthquake-withstanding revamp, the smallish rooms (some with shared bath) retain their close-to-the-wilderness essence, while the communal areas are nothing short of regal.

Packwood ⓫

⌂ Cowlitz River Lodge   Motel $$

(☎360-494-4444; www.escapetothemountains. com; Hwy 12, at Skate Creek Rd, Packwood; r incl breakfast from $130; ❄🛜) Probably the most convenient accommodation for both Mt Rainier and Mt St Helens, the Cowlitz is the sister motel to Ashford's Nisqually Lodge and offers 32 above-average motel rooms along with the obligatory outdoor Jacuzzi.

White Pass ⓬

⌂ White Pass Village Inn   Condo $$$

(☎509-672-3131; www.whitepassvilageinn.com; 38933 US 12; studios $89-238, 1-bedroom condos $143-345; 🛜♨) Adjacent to the White Pass skiing area, this condo complex is open year-round, meaning it's also good for sorties into Mt Rainier National Park (12 miles away). Condo sizes range from studios to deluxe and all have kitchenettes and private bathrooms. The outdoor pool is heated to spa temperatures in the winter, and there's a store and laundry next door.

Mt St Helens Volcano Trail

10

Fiery infamy was made in 1980 when Mt St Helens blew megatons of molten ash into the atmosphere. Its devastated but recovering landscape looks like nothing else on earth.

TRIP HIGHLIGHTS

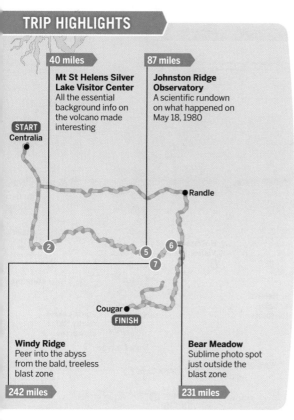

40 miles

Mt St Helens Silver Lake Visitor Center
All the essential background info on the volcano made interesting

87 miles

Johnston Ridge Observatory
A scientific rundown on what happened on May 18, 1980

START
Centralia

●Randle

②

⑤ ⑥

⑦

Cougar ●
FINISH

Windy Ridge
Peer into the abyss from the bald, treeless blast zone

242 miles

Bear Meadow
Sublime photo spot just outside the blast zone

231 miles

3 DAYS
366 MILES/589KM

GREAT FOR...

BEST TIME TO GO
July to October – the mountain's best sights and roads are open.

ESSENTIAL PHOTO
Mountain view from Bear Meadow.

BEST FOR FAMILIES
Silver Lake Visitor Center's interactive exhibits.

10 Mt St Helens Volcano Trail

The name Mt St Helens has a fearful resonance to anyone who was alive on May 18, 1980, when a massive volcanic eruption set off the largest landslide in human history. More than 30 years later, you can drive through the embattled but slowly recovering landscape, stopping at strategically placed interpretive centers that graphically document the erstwhile environmental carnage. It's a unique if sometimes disconcerting ride.

1 Centralia

The main reason to make this rather mundane mining and lumber town the starting point for your volcanic excursion is to stay at a converted brothel. The **Olympic Club Hotel** (p125), 'venue hotel' run by Portland's McMenamin brothers, dates from 1908 when it opened as a 'gentlemen's resort' designed to satisfy the various drinking, gambling and sexual vices of transient miners and loggers. In 1996

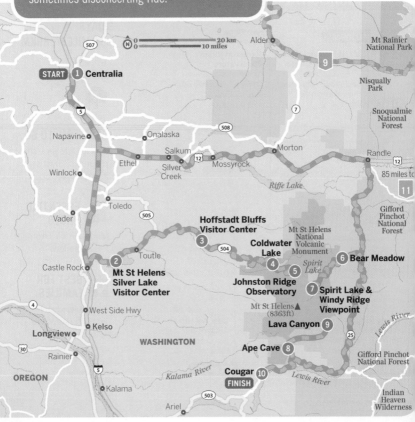

the turn-of-the-century building was taken over by the McMenamins, who restored the brothel to its former glory complete with creaking floorboards, Tiffany lamps and art-deco murals (but without the erstwhile nighttime shenanigans).

 p125

The Drive » Steer south out of Centralia on I-5 for 32 miles to exit 49, where you proceed east on SR-504, aka the Spirit Lake Memorial Hwy.

TRIP HIGHLIGHT

② Mt St Helens Silver Lake Visitor Center

Situated 5 miles east of Castle Rock on SR-504, the **Silver Lake Visitor Center** (www.parks.

LINK YOUR TRIP

9 Mt Rainier Scenic Byways

St Helens' taller, potentially more lethal mountain twin is easily accessible via its southeastern Ohanapecosh entrance.

11 Washington Wine Tour

Head east in Randle and continue on to Yakima on the cusp of a sunny valley full of grapes and wineries. Say no more.

wa.gov/245/Mount-St-Helens; 3029 Spirit Lake Hwy; adult/child $5/2.50; ☺9am-5pm mid-May–mid-Sep, to 4pm mid-Sep–mid-May; 🚹) is the best introduction to the monument. There's a classic film and various exhibits, including a mock-up of the volcano; duck beneath the cone for displays on the subterranean workings of the mountain. Outside is the mile-long **Silver Lake Wetlands Trail**.

 p125

The Drive » Take the road east along the Toutle River Valley toward the National Volcanic Monument and the blast zone.

③ Hoffstadt Bluffs Visitor Center

At milepost 27, the impressive wood-and-beam edifice that houses the **Hoffstadt Bluffs Visitor Center** (www.hoffstadtbluffs. com; 15000 Spirit Lake Hwy; ☺9am-6pm) has a good restaurant – the Fire Mountain Grill – and panoramic views of the Toutle River Valley. Exhibits inside focus on St Helens' ecology before the blast, plus there's an outdoor memorial to the 57 people who lost their lives. This is where you can organize **helicopter tours** ($199 per person) over the crater.

 p125

The Drive » Continue east on the Spirit Lake Memorial Hwy (504). At milepost 33, a

Forest Learning Center runs an interesting film about the eruption. Soon after, you enter the blast zone near the Elk Rock viewpoint.

④ Coldwater Lake

You're now categorically in the blast zone. Coldwater Lake, 43 miles east of Castle Rock, was created in 1980 when water backed up behind a dam caused by debris brought down by the eruption. The recreation area here (rest rooms, phone, boat launch) is the starting point of the 0.6-mile **Birth of a Lake Trail** (No 246), a paved interpretive hike that seeks to demonstrate the regrowth of vegetation in the area. Look out for beavers and their handiwork.

The Drive » Follow the increasingly winding Spirit Lake Memorial Hwy (SR-504) through the denuded landscape to the end of the road.

TRIP HIGHLIGHT

⑤ Johnston Ridge Observatory

Situated at the end of SR-504 and looking directly into the mouth of the crater, this famous **observatory** (☎360-274-2140; 24000 Spirit Lake Hwy; day use $8; ☺10am-6pm mid-May–Oct) has exhibits that take a more scientific angle than the Silver Lake Visitor Center, depicting the geological events surrounding the 1980 blast and how they

TUSHARKOLEY / SHUTTERSTOCK ©

MT ST HELENS NATIONAL VOLCANIC MONUMENT

Mt St Helens is one of only two National Volcanic Monuments in the nation. The unique park, which measures 110,000 acres, was set aside in 1982 and is mostly comprised of land in the so-called 'blast zone' – the plan being that anything inside the park boundary is to be left to recover as nature intends. The monument, which is closely monitored, acts like a massive outdoor scientific laboratory.

advanced the science of volcano forecasting and monitoring. The paved 1-mile round-trip **Eruption Trail** (No 201) offers once-in-a-lifetime views over toward the crater.

The Drive » Retrace your steps 52 miles to Castle Rock. Go north on I-5 and, at exit 68, east on US 12. In the tiny settlement of Randle, you can refuel with food and gas. Turn right off US 12 onto SR-131, which soon becomes USFS Rd 25. Just past Iron Creek Falls, amid old-growth forest, turn right onto USFS Rd 99.

- - - - - - - - - - - -

TRIP HIGHLIGHT

⑥ Bear Meadow

Bear Meadow, just outside the blast zone, is where Gary Rosenquist took his infamous photographs of Mt St Helens erupting on May 18, 1980. The four quick-succession shots that Rosenquist started snapping at 8:32am are reproduced on an interpretive board and show the mountain, 11 miles away, with its northern slopes literally sliding away. Rosenquist,

who was camping in the area at the time, was lucky and got out alive, driving north through thick ash. The blast zone stopped less than a mile away from the meadow, as the stands of still healthy trees in the foreground testify.

The Drive » Two miles further on, you'll enter the blast zone marked by eerie dead trees. Press on past various trailheads to the end of the road.

- - - - - - - - - - - -

TRIP HIGHLIGHT

⑦ Spirit Lake & Windy Ridge Viewpoint

More remote but less crowded than Johnston Ridge is the harder-to-reach **Windy Ridge viewpoint** on the mountain's eastern side, accessed via USFS Rd 99. Here visitors get a palpable, if eerie, sense of the destruction that the blast wrought, with felled forests, desolate mountain slopes and the rather surreal sight of lifeless **Spirit Lake**, once one of the premier

resorts in the South Cascades. There are toilets and a snack bar at the viewpoint parking lot, which is often closed until June. More than 350 steps ascend the hillside for close-up views of the crater 5 miles away. A stubbly green carpet covers the ridge slopes in summer as dwarf plants

St Helens National Monument SR-504 highway

struggle back to life more than 30 years later. A few miles down the road you can descend 600ft on the 1.5-mile **Harmony Trail** (No 224) that leads to Spirit Lake.

The Drive » Retrace your steps to USFS Rd 25; turn right (south) and drive over Elk Pass and past the Clearwater viewpoint to Pine Creek Work Center, a small information center. Turn west on USFS Rd 90 and drive along the north shore of Swift Reservoir before going right onto USFS Rd 83 and left onto USFS Rd 8303.

- - - - - - - - - - - - -

8 Ape Cave

Ape Cave, on the south flank of Mt St Helens, is a 2-mile-long lava tube formed 2000 years ago by a lava flow that followed a deep watercourse. It's the longest lava tube in the Western Hemisphere. Hikers can walk and scramble the length of Ape Cave on either the 0.8-mile **Lower Ape Cave Trail** or the 1.5-mile **Upper Ape Cave Trail**, which requires a certain amount of scrambling over rock piles and narrower passages. Bring

MT ST HELENS INSTITUTE

The not-for-profit **Mt St Helens Institute** (www.mshinstitute.org) is one of the most admired educational and conservation groups in the nation. Look out for the institute's expert volunteers at various interpretive sites around the mountain, where they organize hikes, talks, films and fundraisers, all related to the volcano and its geology.

your own light source. Free ranger-led explorations depart from **Apes' Headquarters** (☎360-449-7800; ☺10am-5pm Jul & Aug, 10am-5pm Sat & Sun Jun & Sep), located at the entrance to the caves, several times daily in summer.

The Drive » Retrace your route to USFS Rd 83. Turn left and drive to the road's terminus at Lava Canyon.

⑨ Lava Canyon

The geology class continues on Mt St Helens' southeast side. Although the mountain's 1980 lateral blast blew north, the heat of the massive explosion melted its eastern glaciers and created a huge mud flow. Water, boulders and trees came flooding down **Muddy Creek**, scouring it out and revealing much older lava basalt underneath. This fascinating geological demolition can be seen at Lava Canyon, where a short half-mile interpretive **trail** leads through new-growth trees to an overlook. To get closer, take a steeper path that zigzags down into the canyon, and can be crossed on a bouncy suspension bridge built in 1993. **Lava Canyon Falls** crashes below. The trail continues further along the Canyon (though it's

extremely exposed) to Smith Creek.

The Drive » Track back along USFS Rd 83 to the junction with USFS Rd 90. Turn right (west) and head into the small settlement of Cougar on Yale Lake.

⑩ Cougar

A 'town' with virtually no residents, lowly Cougar (population 120-ish), the nearest settlement to Mt St Helens, was mercifully spared the carnage of the 1980 eruption – though it was temporarily evacuated. Since 1953 it has sat on the shores of **Yale Lake**, a reservoir created after the construction of the Yale Dam on the Lewis River. It is a good pit stop courtesy of its **Lone Fir Resort & Café**, convenience store (with gas), grill restaurant and peaceful lakeside tranquility. Climbers making a St Helens summit bid often psyche up here.

✕ 🛏 p125

Eating & Sleeping

Centralia ●

✕ Berry Fields   American $

(201 S Pearl St; mains $10; ⊙7am-5pm) In
the culinary wasteland of Centralia stands an
exception to the rule. This formidable brunch
spot, situated in Centralia's biggest antiques
mall, offers formidable egg concoctions, and
cinnamon buns the size of soccer balls.

🛏 Olympic Club Hotel   Hotel $

(☎360-736-5164; 112 N Tower Ave; bunks/
queens/kings $55/70/80; 🛜) A 'venue hotel'
run by Portland's McMenamin brothers, where
you can eat, sleep, drink, shoot billiards, listen
to music and go to the cinema, all in the same
evening and – more to the point – all without
having to leave the hotel.

Mt St Helens Silver Lake Visitor Center ●

🛏 Blue Heron Chateau   Inn $$

(☎360-274-9595; www.blueheronchateau.com;
2846 Hwy 504; d/ste $240/280; 🛜) A welcome
B&B in an accommodation-lite area, the Blue
Heron offers seven rooms, including a Jacuzzi
suite, in a large house almost opposite the Silver
Lake Visitor Center on Hwy 504. Rooms are
clean if unspectacular, but the views of Silver
Lake and Mt St Helens – weather permitting –
are spellbinding.

Hoffstadt Bluffs Visitor Center ●

✕ Fire Mountain Grill   American $$

(15000 Spirit Lake Memorial Hwy, Toutle;
mains $13-22; ⊙11am-5pm) A not untypical
American grill menu is enhanced here by its
unexpectedness (there's nothing else for miles

around) and location (a fine outdoor patio offers
views of the Toutle River and that volcano). In
such circumstances those specialty burgers
and 10oz steaks start to taste a lot more –
well – fiery.

🛏 Eco Park Resort   Campground, Cabin $

(☎360-274-7007; www.ecoparkresort.com;
14000 Spirit Lake Hwy, Toutle; campsites $25,
yurts $75, cabins $135-145; 🐾) The closest
full-service accommodation to the blast zone
offers campsites and RV hookups, basic cabins
and rather incongruous yurts. Owned by the
family whose Spirit Lake Lodge was swept away
by the 1980 eruption, the resort also has a
cafe-restaurant.

Cougar ●

✕ Cougar Grill   American $

(16849 Lewis River Rd, Cougar; mains $8-12;
⊙8am-9pm) Zero competition hasn't left
the Cougar Grill resting on its laurels. On the
contrary, this little middle-of-nowhere abode
makes a heavy impression on passing travelers,
itinerants, summiteers and people who took the
wrong turning in Portland. After savoring the
burgers, beer, tacos and down-country service,
most swear they'll be back.

🛏 Lone Fir Resort & Café   Motel $

(☎360-238-5210; www.lonefirresort.com;
16806 Lewis River Rd; tent/RV sites $22/35, r
from $109, cabins from $129; ❄ 🐾) There's not
a lot to choose from on Mt St Helens' south side
in the noncamping genre, so thank your lucky
stars that this place, in the rather lonesome
settlement of Cougar, backs up its RV park
with a pleasantly sited motel, cafe (pizzas and
burgers, mainly) and swimming pool. Rustic's
the word.

Washington Wine Tour

11

From the mellow Bordeaux reds of the sunny Yakima Valley to the big, bold flavors of pastoral Walla Walla, Washington wines are as luscious as the landscapes surrounding them.

TRIP HIGHLIGHTS

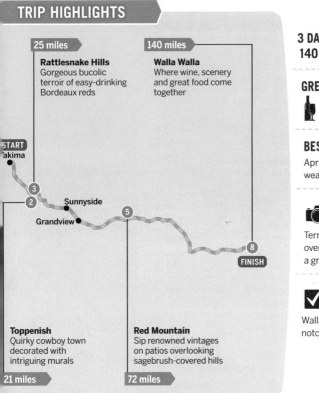

25 miles

Rattlesnake Hills
Gorgeous bucolic terroir of easy-drinking Bordeaux reds

140 miles

Walla Walla
Where wine, scenery and great food come together

START
Yakima

Sunnyside

Grandview

5

8

FINISH

Toppenish
Quirky cowboy town decorated with intriguing murals

21 miles

Red Mountain
Sip renowned vintages on patios overlooking sagebrush-covered hills

72 miles

**3 DAYS
140 MILES/225KM**

GREAT FOR...

BEST TIME TO GO
April to October for weather and flowers.

ESSENTIAL PHOTO

Terra Blanca – views over grapevines from a grand villa.

BEST FOR FOODIES

Walla Walla has top-notch restaurants.

Mountain Vineyards in harvest season

11 Washington Wine Tour

Napa? Too crowded. France? Too far away. Fortunately, the Yakima and Walla Walla valleys have emerged as major winemaking destinations. Learn about terroir and viticulture, or dedicate yourself to sampling lush reds and crisp whites in your search for your favorite appellation (you can always spit to manage consumption). For now this is still an unpretentious, small-town scene with bucolic views in all directions, but the wines are nothing less than extraordinary.

1 Yakima

The town of Yakima is a sprawling, flat mid-century-feeling city that doesn't have much allure, but it's a pleasant enough place to start your trip. The town is home to some of the only bubbles available in this region. Start the day at **Treveri Cellars** (www.trevericellars. com; 71 Gangl Rd, Wapato; ☺ noon-5pm Mon-Thu, to 6pm Fri & Sat, to 4pm Sun), whose sparkling wines are so good, they've been served at the White House.

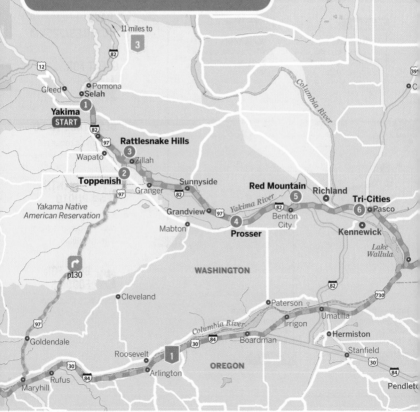

✕ ⊨ p134

The Drive » From I-82 E, take exit 50 toward Toppenish. Turn right on Buena Way off the exit and continue about 3 miles to 1st St, the main drag of downtown Toppenish.

TRIP HIGHLIGHT

2 Toppenish

Toppenish makes up for its lack of wineries with its kooky personality. The antique, distinctly Wild West brick-and-timber buildings are further beautified by some 70 **murals** within the downtown area.

Scenes include Native Americans, cowboys and early settlers as well as artistic hat-tipping to the majority Latino population. Country-and-western music is pumped via loudspeaker into the streets. While here, stop into the **American Hop Museum** (www.american hopmuseum.org; 22 S B St; $3; ◷10am-4pm Wed-Sat, 11am-4pm Sun May-Sep) to think about beer for awhile, and the **Yakama Nation Museum & Cultural Center** (www.yakama museum.com; 280 Buster Rd; adult/child $6/4; ◷8am-5pm Mon-Fri, 9am-5pm Sat & Sun) to see crafts from the area's original artists.

The Drive » Go back toward I-82 E, but instead of getting on the freeway, cross over it. Cross the Yakima Valley Hwy, then at the crossroads turn left (this is still Buena Way). Take the third right on Highland Rd, up a hill through orchards to Bonair Winery.

TRIP HIGHLIGHT

3 Rattlesnake Hills

Lazing next to the tiny town of Zillah, the warm, rolling Rattlesnake Hills grow thick with grapevines and apple orchards. Nary a rattlesnake has been found in recent memory but you will find plenty of smooth and delicious Bordeaux reds at any of the dozen or so wineries. Start at the wonderfully welcoming **Bonair Winery** (☎509-829-6027; www.bonairwine.com; 500 S Bonair Rd, Zillah; winery/vineyard tours $10/20; ◷10am-5pm), one of the oldest in the area, where you're heartily encouraged to picnic on the lawn overlooking the pond – or grab a table in front of the buttery-yellow chateau for tapas.

Just north of Bonair, **Silver Lake Winery** (www.silverlakewinery.com; 1500 Vintage Rd, Zillah; tasting fee $5; ◷11am-4pm, closed Tue & Wed Dec-Apr) sits at the top of a hill overlooking the whole valley, making it a prime location for weddings and fancy-schmancy events.

The Drive » You can choose to take I-82 E to exit 80 (about

West
alla Walla

Walla
Walla
p132

7 8

9 South
Walla Walla
FINISH

ureka

Waitsburg

12

12

n-Freewater

Athena

Umatilla
Indian
Reservation

Snake River

N 0 —————— 20 km
  0 —————— 10 miles

🔗 LINK YOUR TRIP

1 On the Trail of Lewis & Clark

From Pasco, you can head west through the Yakima Valley or east to Walla Walla.

3 Mountains to Sound Greenway

Drive 36 miles from Yakima to Ellensburg via the Yakima River Valley.

30 miles) to get to Prosser or take the Yakima Valley Hwy, which leads more slowly through scenic farmlands. With this second option, the Yakima Valley Hwy turns into Wine Country Rd at Grandview, which parallels I-82 and on to Prosser.

④ Prosser

The historic center of Prosser is a small grid of brick buildings worthy of a 1950s-era movie set – it's a choice stop for lunch or the night. Stop in at picture-book pretty **Chinook Wines** (www.chinookwines.com; Wine Country Rd, Prosser; tasting fee $5; ⊘ tastings noon-5pm Sat & Sun May-Oct), with a flower-filled yard and picnic area. The winery has been in operation since 1983 and is known for its classy Chardonnay and Sauvignon Blanc. It's just off Wine Country Rd to the east out of town.

Prosser sprawls less scenically across I-82, where you'll find **Vintner's Village**, a collection of excellent wineries in flat, housing-community-like surroundings. If you make one stop here, make it **Airfield Estates** (www.airfieldwines.com; 560 Merlot Dr, Prosser; tasting fee $5; ⊘ 11am-5pm), known for its esteemed whites including a zesty, easy-to-love unoaked Chardonnay.

Be sure to stop at the **Chukar Cherries** store. It has amazing chocolate-covered cherries – not like those gooey ones you get in a box at Christmas; these are really great. Some of them even have wine flavors.

 p134

The Drive » Back on I-82 East, another 17 miles of highway brings you to Benton City and the Red Mountain AVA. Take exit 96 then turn left on SR-224, veering left again when the road forks.

TRIP HIGHLIGHT

⑤ Red Mountain

Red Mountain, just next to Benton City, is the tiniest American Viticultural Area (AVA) in the state, coveted for its vintages brought to perfection on sun-drenched slopes. It's a California-esque landscape of hills covered in vineyards, golden grass and sagebrush. Meander up N Sunset Rd, making your first stop at humble **Cooper Wine Company** (www.cooperwinecompany.com; 35306 N Sunset Rd, Benton City; tasting fee $5; ⊘ 11am-5pm), whose L'Inizio Bordeaux blend is anything but boring. Next, sample the highly regarded Bordeaux blends at **Hedges Family Estate** (☑ 509-588-3105; www.hedgesfamilyestate.com; 53511 N Sunset Rd; tasting fee $5; ⊘ 11am-5pm Sat & Sun Apr-Nov) in a French-inspired mansion; then drive up further to **Taptiel Estate** (www.taptiel.com; 20206 E 583 PR NE, Benton City; tasting fee $5; ⊘ 11am-5pm Fri-Sun Apr-Nov), where you'll find delicious Syrah and Cabernet Sauvignons to sip over views of the valley.

Last, take a detour to the grandest estate on this trip, **Terra Blanca** (☑ 509-588-6082; www.terrablanca.com; 34715 N DeMoss Rd, Benton City; tasting fee $15; ⊘ 10am-6pm Apr-Oct, 11am-6pm Nov-Mar),

---

DETOUR: YAKAMA SCENIC BYWAY

Start: ❷ Toppenish (p129)

This byway leads 63 miles down Hwy 97 from Toppenish to Maryhill. You'll pass through native Yakama country and up through the desolate Simcoe Mountains. Highlights between them include the **Greek Orthodox St John the Forerunner Monastery** (www.stjohnmonastery.org; 5 Timmer Lane, Goldendale; ⊘ 9am-2pm & 4-6pm Mon-Sat) and **Goldendale Observatory State Park** (www.goldendaleobservatory.com; 1602 Observatory Dr, Goldendale; ⊘ Wed-Sun Apr-Sep, Fri-Sun Oct-Mar).

Terra Blanca winery, Red Mountain Barrel Caves

on N DeMoss Rd, which runs parallel to N Sunset Rd toward Benton. Try the reds and dessert wines in the castle-like tasting room or out on the terrace overlooking manicured gardens, a pond, the valley and the mountains.

The Drive » Go back out to your friend I-82, take the I-182 exit toward Richland then take exit 3. Turn right on Queensgate Dr and an immediate left onto Columbia Park Trail, then another left onto Tulip Lane.

- - - - - - - - - - - - - -

❻ Richland, Kennewick & Pasco

Next stop? The Tri-Cities: Richland, Kennewick and Pasco. Nicknamed the Tri-Windies for the pushy gusts of wind that scoot you into the tasting rooms, the trio of towns is home to another batch of wineries just off the freeway, among them **Barnard Griffin** (📞509-627-0266; www.barnardgriffin.com; 878 Tulip Lane, Richland; 🕙10am-5pm) in Richland. You don't have to ask if they've won any awards; the medals are practically used as decor.

🍴 🛏 p134

DETOUR:
DAYTON & WAITSBURG

Start: ❽ Walla Walla

Dayton (32 miles north of Walla Walla on US12) and Waitsburg (21 miles from Walla Walla on the same Hwy) have become the unlikely locations of a burgeoning restaurant and bar scene. Within the historic brick buildings of the few wide streets you'll find a handful of worth-the-drive restaurants, bars and cafes including Southern fare at **Whoopemup Hollow Cafe** (120 Main St; mains $18-35; ⊙5-10pm Thu-Sun, 11:30am-2pm Fri-Sun) in Waitsburg, and French country dining at **Patit Creek Restaurant** (☎509-382-2625; 725 E Dayton Ave, Dayton; mains $15-34; ⊙11:30am-2pm Wed-Fri & 5pm to close Wed-Sat) in Dayton.

INTI ST CLAIR / GETTY IMAGES ©

The Drive ❱❱ Get ready for a change of scenery and wine style. Take US 12 south then east about an hour to the Walla Walla Valley.

- - - - - - - - - -

❼ West Walla Walla

About 11 miles before you get to Walla Walla you'll find **L'Ecole No 41** (41 Lowden School Rd; ⊙10am-5pm). The building alone, an early-1900s schoolhouse, is worth a visit, but the Syrah and Bordeaux earn an easy 'A' among wine-lovers.

Back on the road about another mile toward Walla Walla is **Waterbrook Wine** (☎509-522-1262; www.waterbrook.com; 10518 W US 12; ⊙11am-6pm Sun-Thu, to 7pm Fri & Sat) with an afternoon-devouring outdoor patio by a pond and authentic, mouthwatering tacos available on Friday and

Saturday. Imbibe a long selection of wines in the fresh air.

The Drive ❱❱ Continue east on US 12 into central Walla Walla. The center of town is at Main St and 2nd Ave.

- - - - - - - - - -

TRIP HIGHLIGHT

❽ Walla Walla

Walla Walla, more than any Washington town, has fermented the ingredients to support a burgeoning wine culture, including a historic Main Street, a handsome college, a warm summer climate and a growing clutch of wine-loving restaurants. If it's time to let the pedal off the metal for a day or two, this is where to do it. The downtown area has lots of tasting rooms. A good one if you're on a stroll is **Otis Kenyan** (23 E Main St;

⊙11am-5pm Thu-Mon) – ask about their quirky story.

✗ 🛏 p135

The Drive ❱❱ Take Hwy 125 south out of town and turn right on Old Milton Hwy. You'll soon find yourself passing numerous orchards and wineries.

Walla Walla Wine tasting

9 South Walla Walla

The southern part of the Walla Walla wine-growing region is the most scenic, with wineries off the highway and tucked within apple orchards or within their own vineyards. Fabulous wines are served in a low-key garden patio and tasting room (actually a part of the owner's home) at **Dusted Valley Wines** (1248 Old Milton Hwy; ⊙noon-5pm Thu-Mon Apr-Nov). Just down the road is the not-to-miss **Amavi Cellars** (☏509-525-3541; www.amavicellars.com; 3796 Peppers Bridge Rd; ⊙10am-4pm), whose wines make headlines in the viticulture world. Indulge in their addictive Syrah and Cabernet Sauvignon on the classy yet comfortable outdoor patio, admire the view out to the Blue Mountains and toast to the end of your tour.

Eating & Sleeping

Yakima ❶

✖ Birchfield Manor Restaurant
Fusion $$$

(📞509-452-1960; www.birchfieldmanor.com; 2018 Birchfield Rd; mains from $22; ⏰6-9pm) The revered Birchfield is a dining experience offered in an intimate 1910 B&B. While the accommodations are considered top end, the food is even better. Reservations must be made in advance and seating is at set times, but everything from the bread to the after-dinner chocolates to the knowledgeable service is impeccable.

The highlights are the mains: salmon in puff pastry with Chardonnay sauce, steak Diane (in a brandy-cream sauce), all expertly paired with local wines (the place has its own cellar).

🛏 Birchfield Manor
B&B $$

(📞509-452-1960; www.birchfieldmanor.com; 2018 Birchfield Rd; manor r $149-159, cottage r $139-219; 📶) The Birchfield offers unusual and slightly fading antique-filled rooms in a park-like setting, two miles east of Yakima off Hwy 24. Five manor rooms are complemented by six guest cottages, some with double Jacuzzi. The manor, which makes a great alternative to the standard Yakima hotel chains, also serves as a first-class restaurant.

🛏 Ledgestone Hotel
Hotel $$

(📞509-453-3151; www.ledgestonehotel.com; 107 North Fair Ave; ste $89-149; ❄@📶) The Ledgestone looks like another roadside chain hotel, but it's not. All its rooms are one-bedroom suites with minikitchens, lounge areas, bathrooms and separate bedrooms. There's even a little office nook. Happily, the suites are sold at standard room prices and there's also a fitness room and laundry service.

Prosser ❹

✖ Bern's Tavern
Pub Food $

(618 6th St, Prosser; burgers from $8; ⏰9am-12am Mon-Thu, to 2am Fri & Sat, noon-12am Sun) In midcentury-movie-set-worthy Prosser, your best stop for lunch (and for a kitsch surprise), beer and burgers is Bern's Tavern.

✖ Wine O'Clock
Wine Bar $$

(548 Cabernet Ct, Vintner's Village; pizzatas from $11; ⏰noon-8pm Fri-Sat, 11am-6pm Sun) Chic wine bar with a patio serving *pizzatas*, cheese plates and light meals to nibble alongside wines from the Bunnel Family Cellar winery.

Richland, Kennewick & Pasco ❻

✖ Taverna
Fusion $$$

(📞509-628-0020; www.tagariswines.com; Tagaris Winery, 844 Tulip Lane, Richland; mains $19-45; ⏰noon-4pm daily, 5-10pm Mon-Sat) The sophisticated dining room is impressive, but on a pretty day the patio rules. The seasonal menu includes beautifully plated seafood and wood-fired pizzas.

🛏 Clover Island Inn
Hotel $

(📞509-586-0541; www.hotelkennewick.com; 435 Clover Island Dr, Kennewick; r/ste from $79/199; ❄📶📺📶) You won't have trouble finding an economical motel in the Tri-Cities but, if you want something a little plusher, hit the locally owned Clover Island Inn, which is situated on its own island on the Columbia River. This unique establishment boasts 152 rooms and suites, its own boat dock and panoramic views from the top-floor Crow's Nest Restaurant.

You can borrow bikes to use on the abundant paths for free.

Walla Walla ⑧

✖ Brasserie 4   French $$$

(📞509-529-2011; 4 E Main St; mains $15-26;
🕐5-9pm Tue-Thu, noon-10pm Fri & Sat) Sharing
a latitude with Bordeaux and a French passion
for growing grapes, it was only a matter of
time before Walla Walla got this *français*. Cool,
minimalist, the wait staff knows its wines and
the Gallic-inspired food is more than just a few
pretentious names on the menu. Try the *moules
frites* (mussels and fries), cheese plate or
excellent steaks.

✖ Saffron Mediterranean
Kitchen   Mediterranean $$$

(📞509-525-2112; www.saffronmediterranean
kitchen.com; 125 W Alder St; mains $28-40;
🕐2-10pm Tue-Sat, to 9pm Sun May-Oct, 2-9pm
Tue-Sun Nov-Apr) This place isn't about cooking,
it's about alchemy: Saffron takes seasonal, local
ingredients and turns them into pure gold. The
Med-inspired menu lists dishes such as bison
rib eye, nettle pappardelle with duck ragù,
and wild Burgundy snail flatbread. Then there
are the intelligently paired wines – and beers.
Reserve ahead.

🛏 Inn at Abeja   Inn $$$

(📞509-522-1234; www.abeja.net; 2014 Mill
Creek Rd; r from $295; 🛜🐾) If you have your
own transportation and approximately $300
to spare, you can spend a night at this historic
homestead and working winery set in the
foothills of the Blue Mountains 4 miles east
of Walla Walla. Luxury accommodation is in
unique self-contained houses that each played
a historical role at the farm (hayloft, mechanic's
shed etc).

🛏 Marcus Whitman Hotel   Hotel $$

(📞509-525-2200; www.marcuswhitmanhotel.
com; 6 W Rose St; r from $129; ❄🛜🐾) Walla
Walla's best-known landmark is also the town's
only tall building, impossible to miss with its
distinctive rooftop turret. In keeping with the
settlement's well-preserved image, the redbrick 1928 beauty has been elegantly renovated
and decorated, with ample rooms in rusts
and browns, embellished with Italian-crafted
furniture, huge beds and great views over the
nearby Blue Mountains.

The on-site restaurant, **Marc** (mains $15-40;
🕐from 5:30pm), is one of the town's fanciest
eating joints.

Mt Baker & Lummi Island

12

From seascape to snow in 84 miles, this journey takes you from a lesser-known Puget Sound island, to Mt Baker, the white sentinel that frames every northwest Washington vista.

TRIP HIGHLIGHTS

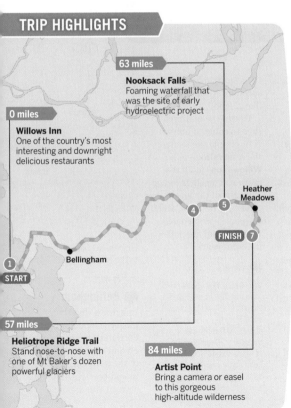

63 miles

Nooksack Falls
Foaming waterfall that was the site of early hydroelectric project

0 miles

Willows Inn
One of the country's most interesting and downright delicious restaurants

Heather Meadows

FINISH 7

Bellingham

1
START

57 miles

Heliotrope Ridge Trail
Stand nose-to-nose with one of Mt Baker's dozen powerful glaciers

84 miles

Artist Point
Bring a camera or easel to this gorgeous high-altitude wilderness

1–2 DAYS
84 MILES/135KM

- - - - - - - - - - - - - - -

GREAT FOR...

BEST TIME TO GO
Mid-July to September, when the whole road is open.

- - - - - - - - - - - - - - -

ESSENTIAL PHOTO
Mt Shuksan with Picture Lake in the foreground.

- - - - - - - - - - - - - - -

BEST FOR HIKING
Heliotrope Ridge Trail.

12 Mt Baker & Lummi Island

The 57-mile Mt Baker Scenic Byway that winds east from metropolitan Bellingham to the otherworldly flower meadows of Artist Point is one of the Northwest's most magic-inducing drives, replete with moss-draped forests and gurgling creeks. Affix Lummi Island onto the start of the trip with its slow-motion traffic and feisty insularity, and you have pretty much every facet the Pacific Northwest has to offer.

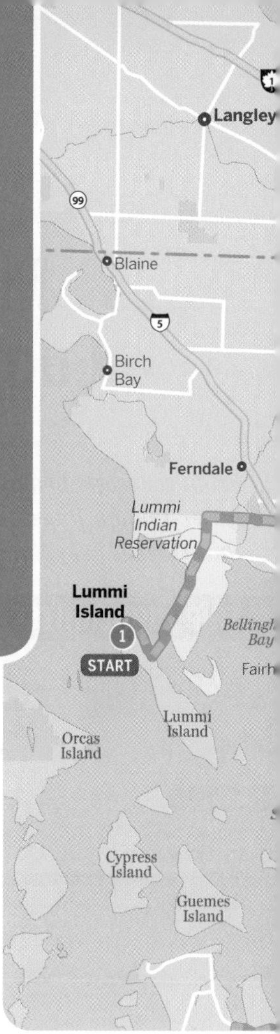

TRIP HIGHLIGHT

1 Lummi Island

Not technically one of the San Juan Islands but with them in spirit, Lummi acts as a bucolic buffer to the fast-spreading tentacles of American outlet-mall culture that plagues the I-5. A slender green finger of land measuring approximately 9 miles long by 2 miles wide, and supporting a population of just under 1000, this tranquil dose of rural realism is home to the world's only reef-net salmon fishing operation, a pioneering agritourism project and an unhurried tempo of life best epitomized by

the island's maximum speed limit – a tortoise-like 25mph.

One of the main reasons to come to Lummi is to sample the food at the reservations-only **Willows Inn** (p143) restaurant. The chefs forage for many of the locally grown ingredients, and the place has garnered international accolades in recent years.

🛏 p143

The Drive » If you're starting from the Willows Inn, take the Island's loop road to Lummi's small ferry terminal on the east shore. The five-minute crossing runs every 20 minutes (hourly at weekends) to Gooseberry Point on the mainland. From here, head north on Haxton Rd and right on Slater Rd to join I-5.

Forge several miles south and exit to Bellingham.

2 Bellingham

Imagine a slightly less-eccentric slice of Portland, Oregon, broken off and towed 250 miles to the north. Welcome to laid-back Bellingham, a green, liberal and

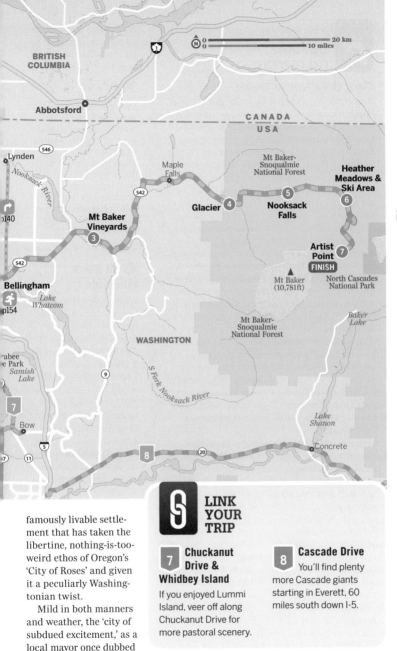

famously livable settlement that has taken the libertine, nothing-is-too-weird ethos of Oregon's 'City of Roses' and given it a peculiarly Washingtonian twist.

Mild in both manners and weather, the 'city of subdued excitement,' as a local mayor once dubbed it, is historically four

LINK YOUR TRIP

7 **Chuckanut Drive & Whidbey Island**

If you enjoyed Lummi Island, veer off along Chuckanut Drive for more pastoral scenery.

8 **Cascade Drive**

You'll find plenty more Cascade giants starting in Everett, 60 miles south down I-5.

DETOUR:
GO DUTCH

Start: ❷ Bellingham (p138)

Washington state has an interesting stash of small towns that harbor a palpable European influence. Leavenworth, in the Eastern Cascades, draws in thousands of tourists annually with an authentic Bavarian look (not to mention its beer and sausages); Poulsbo, near Seattle, has a detectable Norwegian flavor. Lynden, meanwhile, located a few miles north of the Mt Baker Scenic Byway in the agricultural lowlands of the Nooksack Valley, is unmistakably Dutch.

First settled in the 1850s, the area received its first wave of Dutch settlers in the early 1900s – a steady trickle of Calvinist farmers who arrived from the Netherlands via brief stopovers in the Midwest. United by raspberries (the town produces 60% of the US crop), they formed a Christian Reform Church and set up mixed farms on the kind of flat pastoral fields that would have had Van Gogh grasping for his paint palette.

As well as competing for the prize of 'cleanest town in the US,' Lynden also excels in historical preservation. Handsome Front St includes a 72ft windmill, a mall with a canal, various Dutch eateries and the inspired **Lynden Pioneer Museum** (www. lyndenpioneermuseum.com; 217 Front St; $7; ⏱10am-4pm Mon-Sat), which eloquently catalogs the pioneer experience.

Rumor has it that people from as far away as California plan pie sorties to **Lynden Dutch Bakery** (421 Front St; pie slices from $5; ⏱7am-4pm Mon-Thu, 7am-5pm Fri & Sat) a few doors down. Try the split-pea soup or humongous rhubarb and raspberry pie.

different towns – Fairhaven, Sehome, Whatcom and Bellingham – that amalgamated into a single metro area in the late 19th century. Despite vestiges of an ugly industrial past along the waterfront, and a flirtation with an out-of-town 1980s mall development directed mainly toward bargain-hunting Canadians, Bellingham's downtown has been revitalized in recent years with intra-urban trails, independent food coops, fine brunch spots and – in genteel Fairhaven – a rejuvenated historic district. It's an ideal place to stretch your legs (p154).

✕ ⫣ p143

The Drive » The Mt Baker Scenic Byway officially begins at exit 255 of I-5 on Sunset Dr, which, within a mile, becomes the Mt Baker Hwy. The road quickly escapes the scattered Bellingham suburbs and dips into the surprisingly pastoral landscape of the Baker foothills. At the Hannegan Rd intersection you can detour north to the town of Lynden.

- - - - - - - - - - - - - -

❸ Mt Baker Vineyards

Wrong side of the Cascade Mountains for grape-growing, you're thinking. Think again! The **Mt Baker Vineyards & Winery** (www.mount bakervineyards.com; 4298 Mt Baker Hwy; ⏱noon-5pm Thu-Sun) is a star player in the Puget Sound AVA (American Viticultural Area), where a cool, wet, year-round climate favors the sowing of mainly white grape varietals such as Siegerrebe and Madeleine Angevine. It's been in operation since 1982, longer than many of the trendy 'nouveau' Walla Walla places. Let curiosity get the better of you and hit its under-stated tasting room.

The Drive » The well-signposted Scenic Byway (SR-542) tracks the North Fork of the Nooksack River from

Mt Baker-Snoqualmie National Forest Hiking trails

where it splits near Denning. Ignore various turnoffs in the small settlements of Kendall and Maple Falls, and continue due east. Maple Falls is your last potential gas stop until you return (in 66 miles).

- - - - - - - - - - - - -

TRIP HIGHLIGHT

④ Glacier

A tiny service center and the last proper settle-ment before Mt Baker, Glacier is basically a ranger station, two restaurants, a ski shop and a small store. This is where SR-542 enters the **Mt Baker-Snoqualmie National Forest**. Consequently, many of Mt Baker's best trails start near here. A highlight is the 7.4-mile out-and-back **Heliotrope Ridge Trail**, which begins 8 miles down unpaved USFS Rd 39, 1 mile east of Glacier. The trail takes hikers from thick old-growth forest to flower-filled meadows and, ultimately, a breathtaking Coleman Glacier overlook. At the 2-mile point, the path for the Coleman Glacier ascent of Mt Baker branches to the left. Call into the excellent ranger station for maps, trail information and forest passes ($5).

✕ 🛏 p143

The Drive ›› You're now in the Mt Baker-Snoqualmie National Forest, where the trees tell a different story: tall moss-covered behemoths that look like ghostly old men sporting green beards. Keep straight on the highway for 6 miles to the Wells Creek Rd. Turn right here and follow the forest road for half a mile to a parking area and the Nooksack Falls viewpoint.

TRIP HIGHLIGHT

⑤ Nooksack Falls

Powerful Nooksack Falls drop 175ft into a deep gorge. This was the site of one of America's oldest hydropower facilities, built in 1906 and abandoned in 1997. Sharp-eyed movie nerds will recognize it as one of the hunting scenes in the 1978 film, *The Deer Hunter*.

The Drive ›› Rejoin the Scenic Byway and continue east paralleling the Nooksack River. Beyond milepost 48, the road leaves the river valley and starts to climb via a series of switchbacks. Mt Shuksan soon comes into view and at the road's 52 milepost you'll spy the Mt Baker Ski Area's White Salmon Day Lodge on the left.

⑥ Heather Meadows & Ski Area

Receiving record-breaking annual snowfall and enjoying one of the longest seasons in the US, the **Mt Baker Ski Area** (☎360-734-6771; www.mtbaker.us; lift tickets adult/child $58/30) prides itself on being the classic 'nonresort' ski area and a rustic antidote to Whistler in Canada. While luxury facilities are thin on the ground, the fast, adrenaline-fueled terrain has garnered many dedicated admirers. It was also one of the first North American ski locations to accommodate and encourage snowboarders.

There are two day lodges, both equipped with restaurants/cafeterias: the Cascadian-flavored **White Salmon Day Lodge** at milepost 52 and the **Heather Meadows Day Lodge**, 4 miles higher up.

In high summer, **Picture Lake** is the object of most people's affections. The view of Mt Shuksan reflected in its iridescent waters is a Facebook staple. You can wander for a half-mile around its shore taking follow-up snaps, or drive 1 mile further up to the **Heather Meadows Visitor Center** and plenty more trailheads.

The Drive ›› Stay right when the road forks at Picture Lake. The last 3 miles (mileposts 55 to 58) of the byway are only open from around mid-July to September and subject to a $5 fee. The road terminates at a parking lot at Artist Point (5140ft).

TRIP HIGHLIGHT

⑦ Artist Point

A picnic-spot extraordinaire surrounded by what is perhaps the best high-altitude wilderness area in the US that is accessible by road, Artist Point at 5140ft, is *high*, so high that in 2011 it remained snowed-in all year. Various hikes fan out from here overlooked by the dual seductresses of Mt Baker and Mt Shuksan. Some are appropriate for families and most are snow-free by mid-July.

The interpretive **Artist Ridge Trail** is an easy 1-mile loop through heather and berry fields with the craggy peaks of Baker and Shuksan scowling in the background. Another option is the half-mile **Fire and Ice Trail** adjacent to the Heather Meadows Visitors Center, which explores a valley punctuated by undersized mountain hemlock; or the 7.5-mile **Chain Lakes Loop** that starts at the Artist Point parking lot before dropping down to pass a half-dozen icy lakes surrounded by huckleberry meadows.

Eating & Sleeping

Lummi Island ❶

🛏 Willows Inn   Inn $$

(📞360-758-2620; www.willows-inn.com; 2579 West Shore Dr; r from $205; ❄🛜🏊) Of Lummi's two accommodations, this 100-year-old beauty reigns supreme with a variety of compact but cozy rooms poised above the Rosario Strait. It also has a creative and internationally lauded **restaurant** (tasting menu $175; 🕐dinner Wed & Thu), where pretty much all the ingredients are hauled from nearby **Nettles Farm** (📞360-758-7616; www.nettlesfarm.com; Matia View Rd; ste from $185) or the island's unique reef-net fishing operation.

Bellingham ❷

🍴 Mount Bakery   Breakfast $

(www.mountbakery.com; 308 W Champion St; brunch $6-16; 🕐8am-3:30pm) This is where you go on Sunday mornings with a Douglas fir–sized copy of the *New York Times* for Belgian waffles, crepes and organic eggs done any way you like. Plenty of gluten-free options. There's a second location in Fairhaven.

🍴 Pepper Sisters   Modern American $$

(📞360-671-3414; www.peppersisters.com; 1055 N State St; mains $10-18; 🕐4:30-9pm Tue-Sun; 👶) This cheerful, colorful restaurant serves innovative food that is hard to categorize – let's call it Mexican cuisine with a Northwestern twist. Try the grilled eggplant tostada, chipotle-and-pink-peppercorn enchilada or southwest pizza; there's even a chicken-strip-free kids' menu.

🛏 Hotel Bellwether   Boutique Hotel $$

(📞360-392-3100; www.hotelbellwether.com; 1 Bellwether Way; r from $179; ❄@🛜🏊) Bellingham's finest and most charismatic

hotel lies on the waterfront and offers views of Lummi Island. Standard rooms come with Italian furnishings and Hungarian-down duvets, but the finest stay is the 900-sq-ft lighthouse suite (from $500), an old converted three-story lighthouse with a wonderful private lookout. Spa and restaurant on premises.

Glacier ❹

🍴 Il Caffe Rifugio   Cafe $$$

(www.ilcafferifugio.com; 5415 Mt Baker Hwy; mains $12-28; 🕐4-8pm Thu-Sun) Just when you thought you were entering the wilderness, a little bit of Portland floats out to meet you. If you assumed your first glimpse of Baker was serendipitous, check out rural Deming where this Euro-centric cafe-restaurant offers big-city quality with field-to-plate freshness. Grass-fed burgers and tortellini Alfredo? Ease on those brakes!

🍴 Milano's
Restaurant & Deli   Italian $$

(9990 Mt Baker Hwy; dinner $16-22; 🕐noon-9pm) In common with much of the Mt Baker area, Milano's doesn't win any 'wows' for its fancy interior decor. But when the pasta's al dente, the bread's oven fresh and you've got an appetite that's been turned ravenous by successive bouts of white-knuckle snowboarding, who's complaining?

🛏 Winter Creek B&B   B&B $$

(📞360-599-2526; www.wintercreekbandb.com; 9253 Cornell Creek Rd, Glacier; r $135) This simply furnished cabin-in-the-woods, two-bedrooms-only place is as friendly and cozy as B&Bs come and is blessed with an outstanding view of Mt Baker. The 5-acre property holds horses and mules and you'll surely meet the resident dog and cat. Warm up in the dry sauna in the shared bathroom. Prices drop if you stay two nights or more.

International Selkirk Loop

13

Covering two American states and one Canadian province, and juxtaposing fabulous scenery with idiosyncratic towns, the Selkirk is the great unsung byway of the Pacific Northwest.

TRIP HIGHLIGHTS

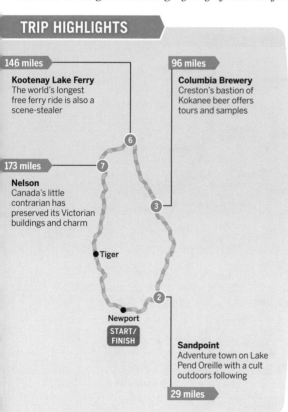

146 miles

Kootenay Lake Ferry
The world's longest free ferry ride is also a scene-stealer

173 miles

Nelson
Canada's little contrarian has preserved its Victorian buildings and charm

Tiger

Newport
START/ FINISH

96 miles

Columbia Brewery
Creston's bastion of Kokanee beer offers tours and samples

Sandpoint
Adventure town on Lake Pend Oreille with a cult outdoors following

29 miles

**3 DAYS
287 MILES/462KM**

GREAT FOR...

BEST TIME TO GO

May to October for sun-dappled lake views.

ESSENTIAL PHOTO

Anything with the sapphire waters of Kootenay Lake in it.

BEST FOR ROADSIDE ATTRACTIONS

The Glass House, an icon made completely out of glass bottles.

International Selkirk Loop

Borders are arbitrary in the Selkirks, a more remote and geologically older antidote to the Rockies, where curious roadside attractions verge on the esoteric and the word 'clamorous' means the occasional moose blocking your views of so-clear-you-can-drink-it Kootenay Lake. Pack your passport, shake the crowds and plunge into this wildly scenic two-national loop through the forgotten corners of Washington, Idaho and British Columbia.

❶ Newport

Newport, a Washington state lavender-growing and logging town, faces off against Oldtown (the town's original incarnation), which sits across the state line in Idaho. The visitor center is situated next to the **Pend Oreille County Historical Museum** (☎509-447-5388; www.pocmuseum.org; 402 S Washington Ave; donation accepted; ☺10am-4pm Fri & Sat May & Sep, daily Jun-Aug), housed in a 1908 train depot and filled with local farming and railway

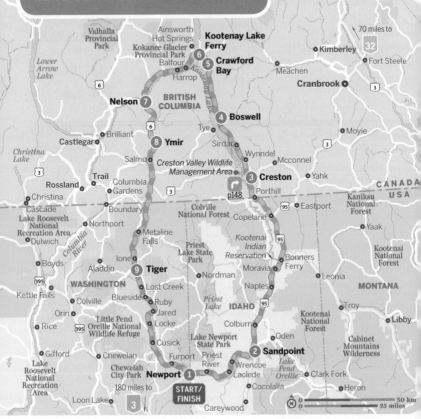

paraphernalia. Both look out onto carefully manicured Centennial Plaza, which sits majestically at the head of Washington Ave (US 2), your ticket out of town.

The Drive >> Follow US 2 east for 29 miles (47km) on the north bank of the Pend Oreille River through the town of Priest River to Sandpoint.

- - - - - - - - - - - - -

TRIP HIGHLIGHT

❷ Sandpoint

Within 45 minutes of leaving Washington at Newport you hit one of the Northwest's rarest jewels, Sandpoint, whose 7500 Idahoans make up the largest US town on this loop. Squeezed between the downhill runs

LINK YOUR TRIP

 Mountains to Sound Greenway

Drive west via Spokane and I-90 to the next spectacular mountain range, the volcano-punctuated, snow-enveloped Cascades. From Spokane it's 172 miles to Ellensburg, where this trip begins.

 Circling the Rockies

Since you brought your passport all this way, you might as well use it further north in what they call the real Rockies.

of Schweitzer Mountain and the deep waters of Lake Pend Oreille, Sandpoint is the most discovered 'undiscovered' town in the nation (countless magazines include it on their 'hidden jewel' lists). Budget a couple of hours to stroll the bars, restaurants and shops of 1st Ave.

Sandpoint is right on Lake Pend Oreille ('hanging from the ears,' pronounced *ponderay*), and the white sand and Jet Skis of City Beach are the closest the Idaho Panhandle ever gets to Miami. Bring a swimsuit and preferably some kind of boat.

The Drive >> Highway 95 heads to Bonners Ferry, originally built on stilts at the site of a goldrush river crossing, and continues north past ranches, Christmas-tree farms and the world's largest hop farm at Elk Mountain. Branch onto SR-1 and cross into Canada at the Porthill–Rykerts border crossing, where you join Canadian Hwy 21 to Creston for a total journey of 67 miles (108km).

- - - - - - - - - - - - -

TRIP HIGHLIGHT

❸ Creston

Creston advertises its premier business with a statue of a 7ft Sasquatch (Bigfoot) making off with a six-pack. Fear not; this is the home of the **Columbia Brewery** (p151), creators of the mass-market Kokanee and Kootenay brands. The brewery offers tours

(four to six daily) and visits to the sample room. These mild lagers are consumed by the barrel during hockey season.

Creston's other pulls are fruit (apples and cherries dominate) and murals (local artists have instituted an art walk and mural tour). The downtown's art-deco-heavy architecture is interrupted by two grain elevators – the only two city-center silos left in Canada.

✗ 🛏 p151

The Drive >> The long and shimmering fjord of Kootenay Lake bursts into view a few miles outside Creston. This 90-mile slice of sapphire framed by the peaks of the Selkirk and Purcell ranges has water pure enough to drink. This 30-mile (48km) Creston–Boswell section is the most stunning of the entire drive and is enjoyed by drivers and riders for its many curves.

- - - - - - - - - - - - -

❹ Boswell

The wackiest sight on Kootenay Lake's eastern shore is without doubt Boswell's **Glass House** (📞250-223-8372; 11341 Hwy 3A, Boswell, BC; adult/child $10/5; ⊙8am-8pm Jul & Aug, 9am-5pm May, Jun & Sep–mid-Oct). With a mortician's sense of humor, funeral director David H Brown decided to build his dream retirement home out of used embalming-fluid bottles, half a million of them in total (and, more incredibly, then persuaded his wife this

DETOUR:
CRESTON VALLEY WILDLIFE AREA

Start: ❸ Creston (p147)

Nature lovers and birders should detour 6 miles (9.7km) west of Creston to the **Creston Valley Wildlife Management Area** (☎250-402-6900; www. crestonwildlife.ca; 1760 West Creston Rd; ◷dawn-dusk), part of the region's most important wildlife corridor. Walk the boardwalks and spot osprey, tundra swans, pelicans or great blue herons from the two birding towers, or sign up for an hour-long guided canoe paddle through the wetlands. Dawn and dusk are the best times to spot wildlife, including the occasional moose chomping in the shadows. Don't miss the very sweet 'turtle crossing' road sign.

was a good idea). The result is a whimsy of turrets, towers, bridges and even a garden shed, all made from recycled bottles. Brown then topped this off with an interior decorated with fearless 1970s panache and a small army of garden gnomes.

The Drive » Keep on lake-hugging Hwy 3A for 17.4 miles (28km) to Crawford Bay.

❺ Crawford Bay

Wizards and muggles (nonwizards) with a penchant for Harry Potter will find empathy in Crawford Bay at **North Woven Broom** (☎250-227-9245; www.northwovenbroom. com; Hwy 3A, Crawford Bay, BC; ◷9am-5pm Mar–mid-Oct; ♿), maker of traditional brooms since 1975. One can only assume that orders have gone through the roof since the late

1990s when the word 'Quidditch' (a fictional sport in the Potter books that is played on broomsticks) entered the language. Numerous US colleges, including Harvard, now compete in real-life Quidditch cups and the workshop's owners once made 50 Nimbus 2000s (Harry Potter's prized broomstick) for a Vancouver book launch. The workshop's feathery golden hues and musky broomcorn fragrance are surprisingly beguiling, almost sensual, and there's something comforting about its almost total lack of modernity. While you're here, check out the glassblowers, blacksmith's forge and weavers' studio across the road.

The Drive » The highway runs out 3 miles west of Crawford Bay, and it's time for the ferry.

TRIP HIGHLIGHT

❻ Kootenay Lake Ferry

Bridges are overrated. Go slow on the world's longest free ferry ride, courtesy of the Canadian government and the Kootenay Lake Ferry. The scenic crossing departs every hour or so and offers 40 minutes of superb lake views before docking at Balfour, some 20 miles northeast of Nelson. If you have some time to kill before departure, drive south from the ferry terminal for 3 miles to a turnout that marks a section of Pilot Bay Provincial Park, a shoreline haven punctuated with walking trails and the charming white clapboard 1907 **Pilot Bay lighthouse**.

The Drive » At the ferry landing, take SR-31 alongside Kootenay Lake's West Arm for around 20 miles to Nelson.

TRIP HIGHLIGHT

❼ Nelson

Nelson has always flirted with contrarianism. It kept its early-20th-century boomtown buildings when everyone else was tearing theirs down, and it's happy to pursue anything outside of the mainstream.

Outdoorsy, alternative and organic, the historic former mining town has a tangible

Nelson Walking trail in Lakeside Park

Victorian air, and is considered by many to be the most interesting and creative hangout east of Vancouver. Pick up a free **architectural walking tour** pamphlet to track down the most interesting of the town's 360 heritage buildings and stroll the waterfront pathway 1.2 miles to the lovely beaches of Lake-side Park, returning on the restored century-old 'Streetcar No 23.'

Revel in the mélange of cultures on Baker St, enjoying sitar music and intriguing boutiques. Pause to absorb the lake and mountain views. Choose from cafes with superb coffee, browse a farmers market, try some creative seasonal cuisine and hear local talent at one of Nelson's bars (where you'll also find some fine microbrews).

✗ 🛏 p151

The Drive ›› Leaving Nelson in your rear-view mirror, the final day's drive takes you 18 miles (29km) south along Hwy 6 to Ymir, past remote, forested (and slightly odd) communities.

BORDER CROSSING

US citizens traveling between the US and Canada need a passport, enhanced driving license or NEXUS card. Returning to the US you can claim up to $800 of goods without duty after 48 hours.

- - - - - - - - - - -

⑧ Ymir

The oddest of the odd is historic Ymir (pronounced 'why-mur,' though grinning locals may well try to persuade you the name stands for 'Why Am I Here?'). It's weirdly named after a hermaphroditic giant from Norse mythology, though its history has more to do with gold mining than an Icelandic creature. Boomtown Ymir – founded as Quartz Creek in 1897 – once listed 10,000 inhabitants. Now there's little more than two hotels and a store. Connoisseurs of the unusual should pop into the **Hotel Ymir**, a 1916 flophouse that stands frozen in time. Try to imagine a Western saloon-style boarding house run by Bela Lugosi and you'll get an idea of the vibe here.

🛏 p151

The Drive » After completing your US border formalities at the low-key Nelway–Metaline border crossing, 23.5 miles (38km) from Ymir, continue straight down the Washington SR-31 for 26.5 miles (42.6km) through the town of Metaline Falls to the Tiger junction.

- - - - - - - - - - -

⑨ Tiger

The fiercely named ex-town of Tiger, four miles south of Ione, has been reduced to one last remnant, the 1912 clapboard **Tiger Historical Center and Museum** (Tiger Store; ☎509-442-4656; www.facebook.com/tigerhistorical; 390372 Hwy 20; ⏰10am-4pm Thu-Mon Jun-Sep), which functions as a gift shop, a cafe, an information center and a museum of the milling and railway town that once was. Glued to the junction of highways 31 and 20, it serves as a welcome apparition on this final part of the loop, aka the Pend Oreille Scenic Byway.

Eating & Sleeping

Creston ❸

✕ Retro Cafe
French $

(📞250-428-2726; www.retrocafe.ca; 1431 NW
Blvd, Creston; mains from CAN$6; 🕐7am-
5pm Mon-Fri, to 3pm Sat) A French mirage in
Creston, 'retro' will probably be the last thing
on your mind as you scour the hand-scrawled
blackboard and tuck into *très délicieux* crepes.

✕ Columbia Brewery
Brewery

(📞250-428-9344; www.columbiabrewery.
ca; 1220 Erikson St; tours CAN$5; 🕐9:30am-
2:30pm Mon-Fri mid-May–Jun & Sep–mid-Oct,
9:30am-3pm Jul & Aug) This is the home of the
Columbia Brewery, creators of the mass-market
Kokanee and Kootenay brands. The brewery
offers tours (four to six daily) and visits to the
sample room. These mild lagers are consumed
by the barrel during hockey season.

🛏 Valley View Motel
Motel $

(📞250-428-2336; www.valleyviewmotel.info;
216 Valley View Dr, Creston; r from CAN$90;
❄🛜) In the motel-ville of Creston, this could
be your best bet. On a view-splayed hillside. it's
clean, comfortable and quiet.

Nelson ❼

✕ All Seasons Cafe
Fusion $$$

(📞250-352-0101; www.allseasonscafe.com;
620 Herridge Lane; mains CAN$23-36; 🕐5-
10pm) Sitting on the patio here beneath little
lights twinkling in the huge maple above you
is a Nelson highlight; in winter, candles inside
provide the same romantic flair. The eclectic
menu changes with the seasons but always
celebrates BC foods. Presentations are artful;
service is gracious.

✕ Library Lounge
Lounge $$

(📞250-352-5331; 422 Vernon St, Hume Hotel;
🕐11am-late) This refined space in a classic
hotel has some good sidewalk tables from
where you can ponder the passing parade.
There's live jazz most nights. The adjoining
Mike's Place Pub bustles and has a great
beer selection. At both you can order good pub
food (mains from CAN$12).

🛏 Cloudside Inn
B&B $$

(📞250-352-3226; www.cloudside.ca; 408
Victoria St; r CAN$125-215; P❄🛜) Live like a
silver baron at this vintage mansion, where the
seven rooms are named after trees. Luxuries
abound, and a fine patio looks over the terraced
gardens and the town. Most rooms have private
bathrooms.

🛏 Hume Hotel
Hotel $$

(📞250-352-5331; www.humehotel.com; 422
Vernon St; r incl breakfast CAN$100-200;
P❄🛜) This 1898 classic hotel maintains its
period grandeur. The 43 rooms vary greatly in
shape and size; ask for the huge corner rooms
with views of the hills and lake. Rates include
a delicious breakfast. It has several appealing
nightlife venues.

Ymir ❽

🛏 Hotel Ymir
Historic Hotel $

(📞250-357-9611; www.hotelymir.com; 7104
1st Ave; r CAN$40-60) Connoisseurs of the
unusual should pop into the Hotel Ymir, a 1916
flophouse that stands frozen in time. Try to
imagine a Western saloon-style boarding house
run by Bela Lugosi and you'll get an idea of the
vibe here.

STRETCH YOUR LEGS
SEATTLE

Start/Finish: King Street Station/EMP Museum

Distance: 2 miles

Duration: 3½ hours

Successive mayors have tried hard to alleviate Seattle's car chaos, and – hills and drizzly rain aside – this is now a good city for walking. Strategically placed coffee bars provide liquid fuel for urban hikers.

Take this walk on Trips

King Street Station

The start/finish point of the *Empire Builder* train to Chicago and mid-point for the *Cascades* and *Coast Starlight* services, Seattle's **King Street Station** (303 S Jackson St; ☒ International District/Chinatown) was designed to imitate St Mark's bell tower in Venice. Now dwarfed by loftier towers, it was the tallest structure in Seattle upon its completion in 1906. It lay neglected until the late 2000s when restoration work revealed a once-grandiose interior.

The Walk >> From the station entrance just head around the corner onto S Jackson St.

Zeitgeist Coffee

Start this walk the way Seattleites start each day: with a latte. You'll find chain coffee shops on every corner, but **Zeitgeist Coffee** (p65), in a converted warehouse, is a great place to hang out with the hip crowd.

The Walk >> Go west on S Jackson St and right on 1st Ave S, admiring the historic redbrick buildings.

Pioneer Square

Seattle was born in the muddy shores of Elliott Bay and reborn here after the catastrophic 1889 fire. The handsome redbrick buildings remain, built in a style known as Richardson Romanesque in the 1890s. Yesler Way was America's original 'Skid Row,' so named as they used to skid logs down the thoroughfare toward the harbor.

The Walk >> Walk north on 1st Ave into the modern downtown core.

Seattle Art Museum

Seattle isn't just a meeting ground for Gore-Tex–wearing adventurers planning sorties into the surrounding mountains. There's culture here too. The **Seattle Art Museum** (SAM; ☎206-654-3210; www.seattleartmuseum.org; 1300 1st Ave; adult/student $19.95/12.95; ⊙10am-5pm Wed & Fri-Sun, 10am-9pm Thu; ☒University St) is the best place to start. The collections span modern Warhol to Northwestern totem poles.

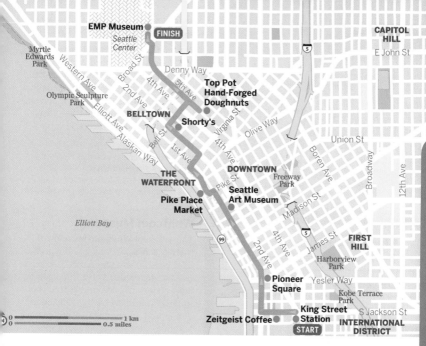

The Walk ›› Continue north on 1st Ave two blocks to Pike Place Market.

Pike Place Market

The soul of the city is encased in **Pike Place Market** (p110), first launched in 1907. Start early if you want to spend more time dodging flying fish and less time dodging hordes of people. Locals love it for its fresh flowers, produce and seafood; for out-of-towners, its big neon sign is a quintessential Seattle photo op.

The Walk ›› Exit the north end of Pike Pl and you're in Belltown.

Shorty's

An early pulpit for grunge music, Belltown, north of downtown, has gone upscale since the 1990s with new condo developments and huddles of restaurants. A relic of old Belltown is **Shorty's** (☎206-441-5449; www.shortydog.com; 2222 2nd Ave; ☺noon-2am; 🚌13), a cross between a pinball arcade and a dive bar.

The Walk ›› Turn right on Bell St and right again on 5th Ave.

Top Pot Hand-forged Doughnuts

Inhabiting an old car showroom, **Top Pot Hand-Forged Doughnuts** (p65) has done for doughnuts what Champagne did for wine. The coffee isn't bad either.

The Walk ›› Walk along 5th Ave to the intersection with Denny Way. Hang a left and you'll see the Seattle Center and Space Needle in front of you.

EMP Museum

It's hard to miss the huge, crazily colorful building at the foot of the Space Needle. That would be the **EMP Museum** (☎206-770-2700; www.empmuseum. org; 325 5th Ave N; adult/child $25/16; ☺10am-7pm Jun-Aug, to 5pm Sep-May; 🚊Seattle Center) and its on-site 'Icons of Science Fiction' exhibit, a fun place to immerse yourself in rock and roll and/or sci-fi for one admission price.

The Walk ›› To get back to the start simply catch bus 131 ($2.75) from Wall St and 3nd Ave, which drops you in S Jackson St near King Street Station.

STRETCH YOUR LEGS
BELLINGHAM

Start/Finish: Hotel Bellwether/Village Books

Distance: 4 miles

Duration: 3½ hours

Bellingham's all-American downtown is made for walking, with intra-urban trails, traffic-calmed streets and, in genteel Fairhaven, a rejuvenated historic district. Views of the gray or glittering sound and the San Juan Islands are highlighted with refreshing-to-icy sea breezes.

Take this walk on Trips

Hotel Bellwether

Kick off outside the **Hotel Bellwether** (p143), on a redeveloped part of the waterfront with water-hugging paths and views toward the whale-like hump of Lummi Island. The adjacent marina is a good place to ogle at other people's multimillion-dollar yachts.

The Walk » From the marina, walk down Bellwether Way onto Roeder Ave; turn right and then left, crossing the railway tracks onto W Holly St. Cut up through the Maritime Heritage Park toward the distinctive redbrick of Whatcom City Hall.

Whatcom Museum

The well-kept **Whatcom Museum of History & Art** (www.whatcommuseum.org; 121 Prospect St; adult/child $10/8; ⊙ noon-5pm Tue-Sun; ⊕) is spread over three buildings: historic Whatcom City Hall (built in 1892), the adjacent Syre Education Center and the innovative Lightcatcher building, which incorporates a spectacular 37ft glass wall. A rich array of exhibits includes historical material, Northwest art and Native American basket weaving.

The Walk » From the Lightcatcher building, head one block along Commercial St to the junction of W Champion St.

Mt Baker Theatre

With its minaret-like tower and elaborate interior, the grand **Mt Baker Theatre** (www.mountbakertheatre.com; 106 N Commercial St), built in 1925, harks back to an era when form was as important as function. Showcasing everything from live music to plays, the theater regularly draws in quirky national talent.

The Walk » Cross W Champion St and walk the half block to W Magnolia St. Turn left and continue two blocks to the corner of Railroad Ave, Bellingham's bike-friendly main thoroughfare. Numerous one-of-a-kind shops and cheap eating joints will detain you here.

Mallard

The start (or end) point of many a Bellingham date night, lurid **Mallard** (www.

mallardicecream.com; 1323 Railroad Ave; scoops from $2; ⊙11am-10pm Sun-Thu, to 11pm Fri & Sat) is a 1950s-style ice-cream parlor with a zillion flavors – many of them unusual. Stop in and try the vanilla-and-pepper or green-tea varieties – all organic!

The Walk » Continue southwest on Railroad Ave, stopping for a microbrew in the Boundary Bay Brewery & Bistro, if you wish. At the T-junction with E Maple St, hang right and proceed half a block to the South Bay Trail.

Boulevard Park

The epitome of Bellingham's waterside rejuvenation, this park – accessed via a footbridge over the railway line – is cherished by locals for its San Juan Island views and sunsets. There's an outdoor theater and chic outlet of **Woods Coffee**, the sustainable local roasters. The **South Bay Trail**, which bisects the park, travels out on a boardwalk over the water before swinging back to land on the cusp of Fairhaven.

The Walk » Cross the railway, go right on 10th St and you're quickly in Fairhaven.

Fairhaven

Bellingham's history is enshrined in the Fairhaven district, once a separate city founded in the 1880s but later amalgamated with its big brother to the north. These days Fairhaven's handsome cluster of redbrick buildings have been reincarnated as specialty shops, European-style cafes and offbeat art galleries. A map-brochure gives the rundown of every building.

The Walk » Make your way over to the corner of Mill Ave and 11th St.

Village Books

Bellingham has long nurtured bookish inclinations and sports almost a dozen bookstores. Ruling the roost is **Village Books** (p97), a sprawling community resource with the popular **Colophon Cafe** next door.

The Walk » To return to the start, take bus 401 from Fairhaven to Bellingham station (on Railroad Ave). Change here onto bus 4 and get off at the Holly St–Broadway St junction for Bellwether Way.

STRETCH YOUR LEGS
LEAVENWORTH

Start/Finish: München Haus

Distance: 2 miles

Duration: 1½ hours

Beer, sausages, nutcrackers, gabled Bavarian hotels and even some leafy forest – there aren't many places where you can enjoy such a condensed exposé of German culture in the US. Get out of your car and say *guten tag* to Leavenworth.

Take this walk on Trip

München Haus

Sizzling **München Haus** (☎509-548-1158; www.munchenhaus.com; 709 Front St; snacks from $6; ⏰11am-9pm) is 100% alfresco, meaning the hot German sausages and pretzels served up here are essential stomach-warmers in the winter, while the Bavarian brews and casual beer garden atmosphere do a good job of cooling you down in the summer.

The Walk » Exit München Haus, turn right and wander half a block down Front St.

Nutcracker Museum

If you have a penchant for obscure, highly specialized museums, stop by the **Nutcracker Museum** (www.nutcracker museum.com; 735 Front St; $5; ⏰1-5pm daily May-Dec, weekends only Jan-Apr; 🚻), which exhibits more than 6000 nutcrackers. There's a souvenir shop downstairs.

The Walk » Cross the road to the park.

Front Street Park

A feature sadly absent in most American small towns is the good old main square. Leavenworth likes to be different, furnishing the strip facing Front St with lawns, an elegant bandstand, elaborate flower displays and a maypole. Numerous festivals enliven the space year-round and it is the centerpiece of the Christmas Lights Festival.

The Walk » Keep straight on Front St to the intersection with 10th St.

Icicle Brewery

Ditch Bavaria for a moment at **Icicle Brewery** (935 Front St; snacks $1.50-10; ⏰11am-10pm Sun-Wed, to 11pm Thu-Sat), which has a funky outdoor patio and a distinctly Pacific Northwest–feeling modern-rustic interior (the tasting room) that's hard to resist. Pop in to sample the Khaos (the home-brewed beer, not the atmosphere, which is relaxed). Brewery tours are offered on Saturdays at noon.

The Walk » Cut down 10th St (Festhallen Strasse) for one block and turn right on Commercial St (Markt Strasse).

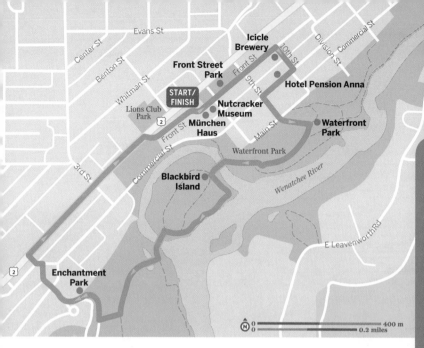

Hotel Pension Anna

For Leavenworth's most quintessen-
tially Bavarian architectural creation,
stop by to admire **Hotel Pension Anna**
(☎509-548-6273; www.pensionanna.com; 926
Commercial St; r from $175; ☎). Examine
the gabled roof, timbered balconies
and geranium-filled flower boxes,
and – should you decide to stay – slip
inside to see the hand-painted Austrian
furniture. The onion-domed St Joseph's
chapel is let out as a luxury hotel suite.

The Walk » Turn left on 9th St (Alpen Strasse)
and follow the slope down into the trees, lured
by the melodious tinkle of the Wenatchee River.
Suddenly this urban stroll has gone rural.

Waterfront Park

Tucked out of view but surprisingly
close, this green area provides access to
the Wenatchee River. Follow the leafy
domain from 9th St to catch a glimpse
of **Sleeping Lady Mountain**, ringed
by a border of green foliage. Interpretive signs furnish the route and help
explain the local plant and animal life.

In summer, people launch inner tubes
from the riverbanks. In winter, it's an
informal cross-country skiing park.

The Walk » Follow the path through the trees
and cross the footbridge onto Blackbird Island.

Blackbird Island

You're just as likely to spot an osprey
as a blackbird on this small bird-filled
nodule of land formed by a silt vacuum
from a mill pond in the 1930s.

The Walk » Take the left fork and follow
the main trail alongside the river to a second
footbridge. Cross it and proceed to the lawns and
sports grounds of Enchantment Park.

Enchantment Park

Connected by Enchantment Bridge to
Blackbird Island, this park has various
trailheads, a playground and rest rooms.
Take the steep path up the grassy knoll
and through the residential quarter to
return to the main drag (US 2).

The Walk » Turn right and stroll past the gabled
hotels to the start point.

Oregon

LAID-BACK OREGON CONCEDES ONLY ONE INTERSTATE HIGHWAY to those with a misplaced sense of urgency. The real joy in Oregon is lazily crisscrossing the state along back roads and scenic byways. And boy, are they scenic. The Cascades are dense with natural wonders, including mountains, waterfalls, forests and hot springs. The Oregon coast offers a completely different experience, with miles and miles of coastal highway stringing together charming seaside towns.

If sparsely populated Oregon still feels too busy for you, head to the remote eastern part of the state. In the land of fossils and pioneer relics, you can't help but think, 'Where am I, and what have they done with all the towns?'

John Day Fossil Beds Painted Hills Unit
ADAM HESTER / GETTY IMAGES ©

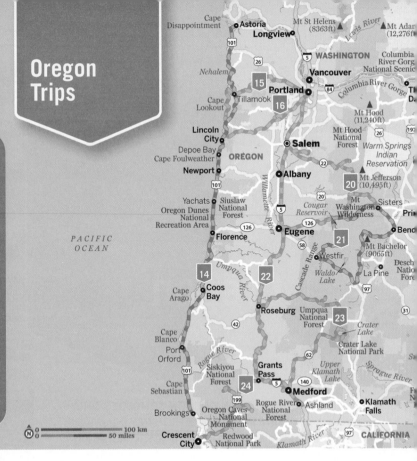

Oregon Trips

 DON'T MISS

Cape Perpetua

The best coast view isn't on the highway; drive to the top of Cape Perpetua for dizzying vistas on Trip 14

Kennedy School

Roam the halls of this former Portland school where you can spend the night, drink in the cafeteria and watch movies in the gym on Trip 22

Thomas Condon Paleontology Center

Get a fascinating lesson in history and paleontology on Trip 17

Golden State Heritage Site

Not all ghost towns are in remote locations. This abandoned mining town is amazingly located right off I-5 on Trip 23

Oregon Caves National Monument

After showing off with waterfalls and mountains, nature goes underground at the 'Marble Halls of Oregon.' Check them out on Trip 24

Classic Trip

Highway 101 Oregon Coast

14

Routes like Highway 101 are the reason the road trip was invented. It meanders the length of the Oregon coast past sandy beaches, colorful tide pools and nearly a dozen lighthouses.

TRIP HIGHLIGHTS

START

1 **0 miles**

Astoria
Cute Victorian town at the mouth of the Columbia

Tillamook

161 miles

Cape Perpetua
Hands-down the best views on the Oregon Coast

9 **134 miles**

Newport
Tide pools and two lighthouses make this a coastal favorite

11

Florence

283 miles

Port Orford
Hike Humbug Mountain and meet some prehistoric creatures

Coos Bay

17

Brookings

FINISH

7 DAYS
340 MILES/547KM

GREAT FOR...

BEST TIME TO GO

July to October, when the weather is more cooperative.

ESSENTIAL PHOTO

The life-size T-rex outside Prehistoric Gardens.

BEST HIKING

Cape Perpetua offers several breathtaking hikes.

Orford Humbug Mountain State Park

14 Highway 101 Oregon Coast

Scenic, two-lane Highway 101 follows hundreds of miles of shoreline punctuated by charming seaside towns, exhilarating hikes and ocean views that remind you you're on the edge of the continent. On this trip, it's not about getting from point A to point B. Instead, the route itself is the destination. And everyone from nature lovers to gourmets to families can find their dream vacation along this exceptional coastal route.

TRIP HIGHLIGHT

1 Astoria

We begin our coastal trek in the northwestern corner of the state, where the Columbia River meets the Pacific Ocean. Ever-so-slightly inland, Astoria doesn't rely on beach proximity for its character. It has a rich history, including being a stop on the Lewis and Clark trail. Because of its location, it also has a unique maritime history, which you can explore at the **Columbia River Maritime Museum** (☎503-325-2323; www.crmm.org; 1792 Marine Dr; adult/child $14/5; ☺9:30am-5pm).

Astoria has been the location of several Hollywood movies, making it a virtual Hollywood by the sea: it's best known as the setting for cult hit *The Goonies*. Fans can peek at the **Clatsop County Jail** (Oregon Film Museum; www.oregonfilm museum.com; 732 Duane St; adult/child $6/2; ☺11am-4pm Oct-Apr, 10am-5pm May-Sep).

✕ ⊨ p41, p81, p174

The Drive ›› Head south on Highway 101 14.5 miles to Gearhart.

2 Gearhart

Check your tide table and head to the beach; Gearhart is famous for its razor clamming at low tide. All you need are boots, a shovel or a clam gun, a cut-resistant glove, a license (available in Gearhart) and a bucket for your catch. Watch your fingers – the name razor clam is well earned. Boiling up a batch will likely result in the most memorable meal of your trip. For information on where, when and how to clam, visit the Oregon Department of Fish & Wildlife website; it's a maze of a site, so just Google 'ODFW clamming.'

The Drive ›› Don't get too comfortable yet: Seaside is just 2.4 miles further down the coast.

3 Seaside

Oregon's biggest and busiest resort town

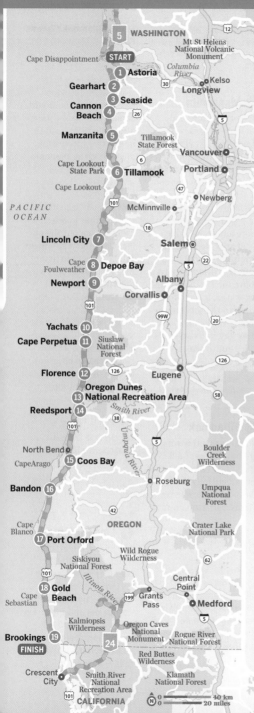

delivers exactly what you'd expect from a town called Seaside, which is wholesome, Coney Island-esque fun. The 2-mile boardwalk – known as 'the Prom' – is a kaleidoscope of seaside kitsch, with surrey rentals, video arcades, fudge, elephant ears, caramel apples, saltwater taffy and more. It's also where you'll find the **Seaside Aquarium** (☎503-738-6211; www.seasideaquarium.com; 200 N Promenade; adult/child $8/4; ☺9am-7pm, closes earlier winter; ♿). Open since 1937, the privately owned aquarium isn't much more than a few fish tanks, a touch pool and a small indoor seal tank where you can feed the splashy critters, but it's a fun stop for inquisitive kids.

✖ p174

🔗 LINK YOUR TRIP

5 Graveyard of the Pacific Tour

Continue your coastal adventure with this trip that starts in Astoria and heads north into Washington.

24 Caves of Highway 199

Pop down to Crescent City, California, for a short but lovely trip east that delivers you back to I-5.

The Drive » Leave the beach behind for a bit as you veer inland for the 8.8-mile drive to Cannon Beach.

④ Cannon Beach

Charming Cannon Beach is one of the most popular beach resorts on the Oregon coast. The wide sandy beach stretches for miles, and you'll find great photo opportunities and tide-pooling possibilities at glorious **Haystack Rock**, the third-tallest sea stack in the world. (What's a sea stack, you might ask? It's a vertical rock formation – in this case, one that's shaped like a haystack.) For the area's best coastal hiking, head immediately north of town to **Ecola State Park** (☎503-436-2844; www.oregonstateparks.org; day use $5), where you can hike to secluded beaches.

✕ 🛏 p174

The Drive » Follow the coast 14.4 miles through Oswald West State Park to reach your next stop.

⑤ Manzanita

One of the more laid-back beach resorts on Oregon's coast is the hamlet of Manzanita – much smaller and far less hyped than Cannon Beach. You can relax on the white-sand beaches, or, if you're feeling more ambitious, hike on nearby **Neahkahnie Mountain**, where high cliffs rise dramatically above the Pacific's pounding waves. It's a 3.8-mile climb to the top, but the views are worth it: on a clear day, you can see 50 miles out to sea.

The Drive » Drive 27 miles from Nehalem Bay to Tillamook Bay to reach inland Tillamook.

⑥ Tillamook

Not all coastal towns are built on seafood and sand. Tillamook has an entirely different claim to fame: cheese. Thousands stop annually at the **Tillamook Cheese Factory** (☎800-542-7290; www.tillamookcheese.com; 4175 N US 101; ☺8am-8pm mid-Jun–Labor Day, to 6pm Labor Day–mid-Jun) for free samples. You might choose to skip the dairy altogether and head to one of two interesting museums: the **Pioneer Museum** (☎503-842-4553; www.tcpm.org; 2106 2nd St; adult/child $4/1; ☺10am-4pm Tue-Sun) has antique toys, a great taxidermy room (check out the polar bear) and a basement full of pioneer artifacts. And just south of town, the **Tillamook Naval Air Museum** (☎503-842-1130; www.tillamookair.com; 6030 Hangar Rd; adult/child $9.50/5.50; ☺10am-4pm Mon-Fri, to 5pm Sat & Sun summer) has a large collection of fighter planes and a 7-acre blimp hangar.

✕ p183

The Drive » South of Tillamook, Hwy 101 follows the Nestucca River through pastureland and logged-off mountains 44 miles to Lincoln City.

⑦ Lincoln City

The sprawling modern beach resort of Lincoln City serves as the region's principal commercial center. In addition to gas and groceries, the town does offer a unique enticement to stop: from mid-October to late May volunteers

---

THREE CAPES LOOP

South of the town of Tillamook, Hwy 101 veers inland from the coast. An exhilarating alternative route is the slow, winding and sometimes bumpy Three Capes Loop, which hugs the shoreline for 30 miles and offers the chance to go clamming. En route you'll traverse Cape Meares, Cape Lookout and Cape Kiwanda – three stunning headlands that you'd otherwise miss entirely.

from the Visitor and Convention Bureau hide brightly colored glass floats – which have been hand-blown by local artisans – along the beaches, making a memorable souvenir for the resourceful and diligent vacationer.

 p174

The Drive » It's back to the coast for the 12-mile drive south to Depoe Bay.

---

8 Depoe Bay

Though edged by modern timeshare condominiums, Depoe Bay still retains some original coastal charm. It lays claim to having the 'world's smallest navigable harbor' and being the 'world's whale-watching capital' – pretty big talk for such a pint-sized town. Whale-watching and charter fishing are the main attractions in the area, though 5 miles south of town there is the **Devil's Punchbowl**, an impressive collapsed sea cave that churns with waves and offers good tide pools nearby.

The Drive » Another 12.8 miles brings you to the lively tourist city of Newport.

TRIP HIGHLIGHT

9 Newport

Don your marine-biologist cap and head to **Yaquina Head**

YAQUINA HEAD LIGHTHOUSE

If Yaquina Head Lighthouse in Newport, seems a little creepier than a lighthouse ought, that's because it was featured in the 2002 film starring Naomi Watts, *The Ring*. Built in 1873, it was originally called Cape Foulweather Lighthouse, but in the movie it was known as the Moesko Island Lighthouse. (The lighthouse was also in the 1977 masterpiece *Nancy Drew: Pirate's Cove*.)

Outstanding Natural Area (☎541-574-3100; 750 NW Lighthouse Dr; vehicle fee $7; ⏰8am-sunset, interpretive center 10am-6pm), a spit of land that protrudes nearly a mile into the ocean. This headland is home to some of the best touch pools on the Oregon coast. You'll also get a good look at the tallest lighthouse in Oregon, **Yaquina Head Lighthouse** (not to be confused with **Yaquina Bay Lighthouse**, 3 miles south).

Also worth a stop: the cutting-edge **Oregon Coast Aquarium** (☎541-867-3474; www.aquarium.org; 2820 SE Ferry Slip Rd; adult/child 3-12yr/child 13-17yr $22.95/14.95/19.95; ⏰10am-6pm Jun-Aug, to 5pm Sep-May; 🦽). The seals and sea otters are cute as can be, and the jellyfish room is a near psychedelic experience. But what really knocks this place off the charts is the deep-sea exhibit that lets you walk through a Plexiglas tunnel through sharks, rays and other fish.

✕ 🛏 p174

The Drive » It's another 24 miles to Yachats along the edge of the Siuslaw National Forest.

---

10 Yachats

One of the Oregon coast's best-kept secrets is the friendly little town of Yachats (ya-*hots*), which kicks off about 20 miles of spectacular shoreline. This entire area was once a series of volcanic intrusions that resisted the pummeling of the Pacific long enough to rise as oceanside peaks and promontories. Acres of tide pools are home to starfish, sea anemones and sea lions.

Fourteen miles south of town, picturesque **Heceta Head Lighthouse** (☎541-547-3416; heceta.h.lighthouse@oregon.gov; day-use fee $5; ⏰11am-3pm, to 2pm winter) is one of the most photographed lighthouses on the Oregon coast. You can't see it from the highway, but you can park at **Heceta Head State Park** for great views from afar, as well as a trail

WHY THIS IS A CLASSIC TRIP

Meandering your way down Oregon's coastline is the epitome of a carefree vacation. There are no major cities, no hustle, no bustle – just miles of ocean on one side of the road and miles of hiking on the other. The best part of the trip? Spending the night at Heceta Head Lighthouse and waking up to a seven-course breakfast, followed by hiking at Cape Perpetua.

Top: Cape Perpetua
Left: Spruce forest, Cape Perpetua
Right: Heceta Head Lighthouse, Yachats

leading past the former **lightkeeper's quarters** (now a B&B) and up to the lighthouse.

✕ 🛏 p175

The Drive » Just 3 miles down the coast is dramatic Cape Perpetua.

- - - - - - - - - - -

TRIP HIGHLIGHT

⑪ Cape Perpetua

Whatever you do, don't miss the spectacular scenery of the **Cape Perpetua Scenic Area** (Hwy 101; day-use fee $5), just 3 miles south of Yachats. You could easily spend a day or two exploring trails that take you through moss-laden, old-growth forests to rocky beaches, tide pools and blasting marine geysers.

At the very least, drive up to the **Cape Perpetua Overlook** for a colossal coastal view from 800ft above sea level – the highest point on the coast. While you're up there, check out the historic **West Shelter** observation point built by the Civilian Conservation Corps in 1933.

If you have more time to spend, stop at the **visitor center** (☎541-547-3289; www.fs.usda.gov/siuslaw; 2400 US 101; vehicle fee $5; ⏰9:30am-4:30pm Jun-Aug, reduced hours Sep-May) to plan your day. High points include **Devil's Churn**, where waves shoot up a 30ft inlet to explode against

Classic Trip

the narrowing sides of the channel, and the **Giant Spruce Trail**, which leads to a 500-year-old Sitka spruce with a 10ft diameter.

The Drive » It's 22 miles to Florence, but only 12 to the Sea Lion Caves.

⓬ Florence

Looking for a good, old-fashioned roadside attraction? North of Florence is the **Sea Lion Caves** (🕿541-547-3111; www.sealioncaves.com; 91560 US 101; adult/child $14/8; 🕙9am-5pm), an enormous sea grotto that's home to hundreds of groaning sea lions. Open to the public since the 1930s, the cave is accessed by an elevator that descends 208ft to the sea lions' stinky lair.

Here's the deal: it can be fascinating, but you might feel a little taken when you realize the view is exactly the same as what was on the monitor up in the gift shop – and there's not even free fudge samples down there. But if money's no object, you'll enjoy watching the sea lions cavort, especially if you have kids in tow.

✖ p175

The Drive » The Oregon Dunes start just south of Florence and continue for the next 50 miles.

⓭ Oregon Dunes National Recreation Area

As you drive south you start to notice something altogether different: sand. Lots of it. Stretching 50 miles, the **Oregon Dunes** are the largest expanse of oceanfront sand dunes in the USA. Sometimes topping heights of 500ft, these mountains of sand undulate inland up to 3 miles. Hikers and birdwatchers stick to the peaceful northern half of the dunes, and the southern half is dominated by dune buggies and dirt bikes.

At Mile 200.8, the **Oregon Dunes Overlook** is the easiest place to take a gander if you're just passing through. To learn more about trails and off-road vehicles, visit the **Oregon Dunes NRA Visitors Center** (🕿541-271-6000; www.fs.usda.gov/siuslaw; 855 Highway Ave, Reedsport; 🕙8am-4:30pm Mon-Sat Jun-Aug, Mon-Fri Sep-May). For the area's biggest dunes, the 6-mile **John Dellenbeck Trail** (at Mile 222.6) loops through a wilderness of massive sand peaks.

The Drive » Reedsport is about halfway into the dunes

area, about 22 miles south of Florence.

⓮ Reedsport

Reedsport's location in the middle of the Oregon Dunes makes it an ideal base for exploring the region. Check out the **Umpqua Lighthouse State Park**, offering summer tours of a local 1894 **lighthouse** (🕿541-271-4631; 1020 Lighthouse Rd; $5; 🕙10am-4:30pm May-Oct, hours vary rest of year). Opposite is a whale-watching platform, and a nearby nature trail rings freshwater **Lake Marie**, which is popular for swimming.

Want to see how Oregon's largest land mammal spends its free time? Three miles east of town on Hwy 38, you can spy a herd of about 120 Roosevelt elk meandering about at the **Dean Creek Elk Viewing Area**.

The Drive » Enjoy the sand for another 27.5 miles, as you reach Coos Bay and the end of the dunes.

⓯ Coos Bay

The no-nonsense city of Coos Bay and its modest neighbor North Bend make up the largest urban area on the Oregon coast. Coos Bay was once the largest timber port in the world. The logs are long gone, but tourists are slowly taking their place.

In a historic art-deco building downtown, the **Coos Art Museum** (☎541-267-3901; www. coosart.org; 235 Anderson Ave; adult/child $5/2; ◷10am-4pm Tue-Fri, from 1pm Sat) provides a hub for the region's art culture with rotating exhibits from the museum's permanent collection.

Cape Arago Hwy leads 14 miles southwest of town to **Cape Arago State Park** (☎800-551-6949; www.oregonstateparks. org; Cape Arago Hwy), where grassy picnic grounds make for great perches over a pounding sea. The park protects some of the best tide pools on the Oregon coast and is well worth the short detour.

The Drive » Highway 101 heads inland for a bit then gets back to the coast 24 miles later at Bandon.

----

⑯ Bandon

Optimistically touted as Bandon-by-the-Sea, this little town sits happily at the bay of the Coquille River, with an Old Town district that's been gentrified into a picturesque harborside shopping location that offers pleasant strolling and window-shopping.

Along the beach, ledges of stone rise out of the surf to provide shelter for seals, sea lions and myriad forms of life in tide pools. One

---

---

of the coast's most interesting rock formations is the much-photographed **Face Rock**, a huge monolith with some uncanny facial features that does indeed look like a woman with her head thrown back – giving rise to a requisite Native American legend.

The Drive » Follow the coastline another 24 miles south to Port Orford. This part of the drive isn't much to look at, but not to worry: there's more scenery to come.

TRIP HIGHLIGHT
⑰ Port Orford

Perched on a grassy headland, the hamlet of Port Orford is located in one of the most scenic stretches of coastal highway, and there are stellar views even from the center of town. If you're feeling ambitious, take the 3-mile trail up **Humbug Mountain** (38745 Hwy 101, ☎541-332-6774), which takes you up, up, up past streams and through prehistoric-looking landscapes to the top, where you'll be treated to dramatic

---

views of Cape Sebastian and the Pacific.

Speaking of prehistoric scenery: your kids will scream at the sight of a *Tyrannosaurus rex* 12 miles south of town in front of **Prehistoric Gardens** (☎541-332-4463; www.pre historicgardens.com; 36848 US 101; adult/child $12/8; ◷9am-6pm summer, shorter hours rest of year; ♿). Life-size replicas of the extinct beasties are set in a lush, first-growth temperate rain forest; the huge ferns and trees set the right mood for going back in time.

✕ ⌷ p175

The Drive » The scenery starts to pick up again, with unusual rock formations lining the 28-mile drive to Gold Beach.

----

⑱ Gold Beach

Next you'll pass through the tourist hub of Gold Beach, where you can take a jet boat excursion up the scenic **Rogue River**. But the real treat lies 13 miles south of town, when you enter the 12-mile stretch of

coastal splendor known as the **Samuel Boardman State Scenic Corridor**, featuring giant stands of Sitka spruce, natural rock bridges, tide pools and loads of hiking trails.

Along the highway are well over a dozen roadside turnouts and picnic areas, with short trails leading to secluded beaches and dramatic viewpoints. A 30-second walk from the parking area to the viewing platform at **Natural Bridge Viewpoint** (Mile 346, Hwy 101) offers a glorious photo op of rock arches – the remnants of collapsed sea caves – after which you can decide whether you want to commit to the hike down to **China Beach**.

🍴 🛏 p175

The Drive » It's just 34 miles to the California border, and 28 to Brookings.

- - - - - - - - - - -

⑲ Brookings

Your last stop on the Oregon coast is Brookings. With some of the warmest temperatures on the coast, Brookings is a leader in Easter lily-bulb production; in July, fields south of town are filled with bright colors and a heavy scent. In May and June you'll also find magnificent displays of flowers at the hilly, 30-acre **Azalea Park** (Azalea Park Rd).

History buffs take note: Brookings has the unique distinction of being the location of the only WWII aerial bombing on the US mainland. In 1942 a Japanese seaplane succeeded in bombing nearby forests with the intent to burn them, but they failed to ignite. The Japanese pilot, Nobuo Fujita, returned to Brookings 20 years later and presented the city with a peace offering: his family's 400-year-old samurai sword, which is now displayed at the **Chetco Community Public Library** (☎541-469-7738; chetcolibrary.org; 405 Alder St; ⏰10am-6pm Mon & Fri, to 7pm Tue & Thu, to 8pm Wed, to 5pm Sat).

🍴 🛏 p175

Eating & Sleeping

Astoria ❶

✖ Wet Dog Café   Brewpub $$

(☎503-325-6975; www.wetdogcafe.com; 144 11th St; mains $10-20; ⏱11am-9pm) For casual dining there's this large, quirky brewery-restaurant, with beers like Poop Deck Porter and Bitter Bitch IPA.

🛏 Hotel Elliott   Historic Hotel $$

(☎503-325-2222; www.hotelelliott.com; 357 12th St; d from $229, ste $240-328; ❀❄🐾🛜) Standard rooms have charming period elegance at this historic hotel. For more space, get a suite. There's also a rooftop terrace with great views, and a wine bar open Wednesday to Sunday. Breakfast included.

Seaside ❸

✖ Bell Buoy   Seafood $$

(☎503-738-6348; 1800 S Roosevelt Dr; mains $8-18; ⏱11:30am-7:30pm, closed Tue & Wed winter) Best known as a seafood store, this down-to-earth, family-run establishment has an attached seafood restaurant serving outstanding fish 'n' chips, chowder and more.

Cannon Beach ❹

✖ Irish Table   Irish $$$

(☎503-436-0708; www.theirishtablerestaurant. com; 1235 S Hemlock St; mains $20-30; ⏱5:30-9pm Fri-Tue) Excellent restaurant hidden at the back of a coffee shop, serving a fusion of Irish and Pacific Northwest cuisine made with local and seasonal ingredients.

🛏 Blue Gull Inn Motel   Motel $$

(☎800-507-2714; www.haystacklodgings.com; 487 S Hemlock St; d from $160; ❀🐾🛜) These are some of the more affordable rooms in town, with comfortable atmosphere and toned-down decor, except for the colorful Mexican headboards and serapes on the beds. Kitchenette and Jacuzzi units are available.

Lincoln City ❼

✖ Blackfish Cafe   Northwestern $$

(☎541-996-1007; www.blackfishcafe.com; 2733 NW US 101; mains $19-26; ⏱11:30am-3pm & 5-9pm, closed Tue) Blackfish Cafe specializes in cutting-edge cuisine highlighting fresh seafood and local, seasonal vegetables. Chef Rob Pounding is an accomplished master at creating his simple but delicious dishes; try his signature Northwest cioppino. Reserve in summer.

Newport ❾

✖ Rogue Ales Public House   Brewery

(☎541-265-3188; www.rogue.com; 748 SW Bay Blvd; ⏱11am-1am) Don't miss out on tasting some of the state's best-loved craft brews at the source. Sit at an outdoor table or inside at the big wooden bar. There's an expansive food menu, too.

🛏 Newport Belle   B&B $$

(☎541-867-6290; www.newportbelle.com; 2126 H Dock, SE Marine Science Dr, South Beach Marina; d $160-175; ⏱Feb-Oct; ❀🛜) For a unique stay there's no beating this sternwheeler B&B. The five small but lovely and shipshape rooms all have private baths and water views, while the common spaces are wonderful for relaxing.

🛏 Beverly Beach State Park   Campground $

(☎541-265-9278, 800-452-5687; www. oregonstateparks.org; tent/RV sites $21/29, yurts $44) This large campground, 7 miles north of town on US 101, has more than 250 sites, 21 yurts and hookups to cable TV. Also has showers and flush toilets.

Yachats 🔟

✕ Green Salmon Coffee House Cafe $

(☎541-547-3077; www.thegreensalmon.com; 220 US 101; mains $8-12; ⏰7:30am-2:30pm; 🖋) Organic and fair trade are big words at this eclectic cafe, where locals meet for tasty breakfast items (pastries, lox bagels, homemade oatmeal). Lunch means gourmet sandwiches, fancy salads and wraps, and there's a wide range of teas. Vegan menu available.

🛏 Heceta Head
Lighthouse B&B B&B $$$

(☎866-547-3696; www.hecetalighthouse. com; 92072 Hwy 101 S; d $235-355; 🖴🛜) This 1894 Queen Anne B&B can't help but attract passersby. Located near the lighthouse trail, it's 13 miles south of town on US 101. Inside there are six pretty rooms, all simply furnished with period antiques. Breakfast is a seven-course sensation.

Florence 🔟

✕ Waterfront Depot Northwestern $$

(☎541-902-9100; www.thewaterfrontdepot. com; 1252 Bay St; mains $12-18; ⏰4-10pm) This cozy, atmospheric joint is one of Florence's best restaurants. Come early to snag one of the few waterfront tables, then enjoy your jambalaya pasta or crab-encrusted halibut. There are excellent small plates, a great wine list and spectacular desserts. Reserve ahead.

Port Orford 🔟

✕ Redfish Seafood $$$

(☎541-336-2200; www.redfishportorford.com; Hawthorne Gallery, 517 Jefferson St; mains $18-34; ⏰11am-9pm Mon-Sat, 9am-9pm Sun) At first glance this slick, sea-view restaurant would seem better located in Portland's Pearl District – it's even attached to a highbrow art gallery. Redfish boasts the freshest seafood in town, so take advantage; the menu changes seasonally.

🛏 Wildspring Guest Habitat Cabin $$$

(☎866-333-9453; www.wildspring.com; 92978 Cemetery Loop; d $298-328; 🖴@🛜) A few acres of wooded serenity greet you at this quiet retreat. Five luxury cabin suites, all filled with elegant furniture and modern amenities such as radiant-floor heating and slate showers, make for a very comfortable and romantic getaway.

🛏 Cape Blanco
State Park Campground $

(☎541-332-6774, 800-551-6949; www. oregonstateparks.org; US 101; tent & RV sites/ cabins $22/40; 🐾) Located on US 101, 9 miles northeast of town on a high, sheltered rocky headland with great views of the lighthouse. Showers, flush toilets and boat ramp available.

Gold Beach 🔟

✕ Anna's by the Sea Northwestern $$

(☎541-247-2100; www.annasbythesea.com; 29672 Stewart St; mains $22-36; ⏰5-8:30pm Wed-Sat) One of Gold Beach's best restaurants, this homey spot serves up just a few key mains like black rock cod with sweet onions, oven-seared breast of duck and chicken thighs in chanterelle gravy.

🛏 Ireland's Rustic Lodges Lodge $$

(☎541-247-7718; www.irelandsrusticlodges. com; 29346 Ellensburg Ave; d $129-185; 🛜🐾) A wide variety of accommodations awaits you at this woodsy place. There are regular suites with kitchenette, rustic one- and two-bedroom cabins, beach houses or even RV sites. A glorious garden sits in front while beach views are out back.

Brookings 🔟

✕ Mattie's Pancake
& Omelette American $

(☎541-469-7211; www.mattiespancakehouse. com; 15975 US 101 S; mains $6-12.50; ⏰6am-1:45pm Mon-Sat) This casual breakfast and lunch spot offers 18 kinds of omelets (such as crab and Swiss cheese) along with pancakes (yes, chocolate chip!) and waffles.

🛏 Harris Beach
State Park Campground $

(☎541-469-2021; www.oregonstateparks.org; 1655 US 101 N; tent/RV sites $20/28; yurts $43; 🐾) Camp above the beach at one of 150 sites here. Six yurts, showers, flush toilets and coin laundry are among the amenities. Located about a mile north of town.

Three Capes Loop

15

Whether you're coming from Portland or detouring off Hwy 101, the dramatic, ever-changing scenery from forested Cape Meares to sandstone Cape Kiwanda is worth slowing down for.

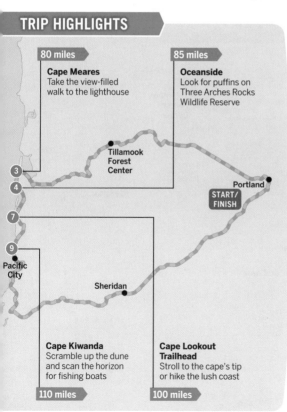

80 miles

Cape Meares
Take the view-filled walk to the lighthouse

85 miles

Oceanside
Look for puffins on Three Arches Rocks Wildlife Reserve

Tillamook Forest Center

3
4

Portland

START/ FINISH

7

9

Pacific City

Sheridan

Cape Kiwanda
Scramble up the dune and scan the horizon for fishing boats

110 miles

Cape Lookout Trailhead
Stroll to the cape's tip or hike the lush coast

100 miles

2 DAYS
176 MILES/283KM

GREAT FOR...

BEST TIME TO GO

May to October to avoid chilling wind and rain.

ESSENTIAL PHOTO

Capture the lens of the Cape Lookout Lighthouse contrasting with the steel sea.

BEST BEACH

Cape Kiwanda has endless sands and a dune to climb.

15 Three Capes Loop

Cape Meares, Cape Lookout and Cape Kiwanda are some of the coast's most stunning headlands, strung together on a slow, winding and sometimes bumpy 30-mile alternative to US 101. If you start from Portland you'll drive through towering forests and salmon-filled river country to complete a loop. But however you tackle this trip, strap on your boots for walks through spruce groves and over dunes to basalt and sandstone precipices.

❶ Tillamook Forest Center

Learn about the stretch of forest between Portland and the sea at the **Tillamook Forest Center** (☎866-930-4646; www.tillamookforestcenter.org; 45500 Wilson River Hwy; ⏱10am-5pm, closed late Nov-Feb), 51 miles from Portland. The interpretive center focuses on the history of wildfire in the region via hands-on exhibits, a 40ft replica fire tower to climb and a suspension bridge over an incredibly

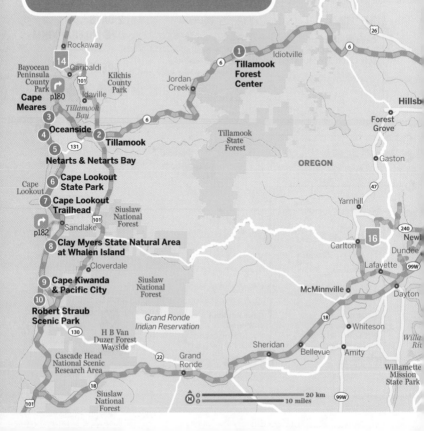

scenic part of the Wilson River; the film *Legacy of Fire* is worth watching. Also enjoy over 20 miles of hiking on the **Wilson River Trail** that wends along this powerful, Douglas fir- and maple-lined river renowned for its steelhead fishing. It's a 2-mile walk to **Wilson Falls** where you can splash through rapids moving around big boulders – look for signs of beavers and listen for kingfishers.

The Drive » Head 22 miles west to Tillamook through the scenic Tillamook State Forest.

② Tillamook

Best known for its huge cheese industry, Tillamook is a nondescript town that's worth a stop to down some dairy. Two miles north of town is the famed **Tillamook Cheese Factory** (☎800-542-7290; www.tillamookcheese.com; 4175 N US 101; ☺8am-8pm mid-Jun–Labor Day, to 6pm Labor Day–mid-Jun), which produces more than 100 million pounds of the product every year. Line up for free cheese samples, lick down an ice-cream cone or peek into the factory floor assembly line; there's a cafe, too. Aircraft lovers should stop at the gargantuan **Tillamook Naval Air Museum** (☎503-842-1130; www.tillamookair.com; 6030 Hangar Rd; adult/child $9.50/5.50; ☺10am-4pm Mon-Fri, to 5pm Sat & Sun summer), **2 miles** south of town on the way toward the next stop.

 p183

The Drive » Hwy 6 turns into Hwy 131 Scenic Route as it heads west. Shortly after the Tillamook Naval Air Museum take the right signposted for Cape Meares. Drive a mile around the Tillamook Estuary then uphill 2 miles to the cape.

TRIP HIGHLIGHT

③ Cape Meares

The first trailhead of Cape Meares has two trails through luxurious spruce forest: a 2.1-mile trail down to rocky **Meares Beach** or a quarter-mile stroll to **Big Spruce**, heralded as the largest Sitka spruce in Oregon (it's 144ft tall and 15.5ft in diameter). A half-mile further driving down Hwy 131 leads you to a second, much more developed parking area with paved paths to the perhaps-haunted 1889 **Cape Meares Lighthouse** (www.capemeareslighthouse.org; Bayshore Dr; ☺11am-4pm Apr-Oct) there are many viewpoints and information panels along the quarter-mile walk. A

LINK YOUR TRIP

14 **Highway 101 Oregon Coast**

Hwy 101 leads straight into Tillamook. Follow this trip's directions from there.

16 **Willamette Valley Wine Tour**

Follow the directions from Robert Straub Scenic Park toward Portland and you'll hit McMinnville. From here you can follow the Willamette Valley Wine Tour.

179

DETOUR:
BAYOCEAN PENINSULA COUNTY PARK

Start: ❷ Tillamook (p179)

At a humble fork in the road, where Hwy 131 veers left toward Cape Meares, turn right to Bayocean Peninsula County Park and follow the road about 2 miles. Today you'd hardly guess that this was once the site of a very swanky planned resort community built in 1906. In 1914 the town had 2000 residents, even though access was by steamship. The residents built a jetty in 1917 to ease the often-rough boat landings. Within a few years, shifting currents caused by the jetty made the beach begin to disappear; the townspeople extended the jetty and the problem amplified with more and more structures getting devoured by the ocean. By the late 1930s most of the remaining houses were abandoned and in 1953 the post office closed. In 1971 the last building, a car garage, crumbled into the sea. Today a commemorative sign is all that is left. It's a beautiful, isolated sandy stretch great for hiking along the beach and bird-watching.

shorter dirt path leads to the impressive **Octopus Tree**, a legendary eight-limbed spruce that mystifies science.

The Drive » Descend 3 miles down the cape then turn right to Oceanside.

TRIP HIGHLIGHT

❹ Oceanside

This tiny village of cozy beach houses perched over a long, flat white-sand beach is the most charming on this route and a great stop for lunch, dinner or overnight. The **Three Arches Rocks Wildlife Reserve** can be seen at the far right if you're facing the ocean. With binoculars you'll be able to see the orange beaks and yellow head tufts of tufted puffins, one of this coast's most recognizable birds, out on these towering rocks. Picnic or fly kites on the beach, search

for agates in the winter months or just chill out in the seaside vibe.

 p183

The Drive » Turn left onto Hwy 131 again and drive 2 miles to Netarts.

---

❺ Netarts & Netarts Bay

Take a sharp turn on Happy Camp Rd to reach a small parking lot for a pretty stretch of white beach protected by a wide, flat sandbar island. Or you can continue on Hwy 131 another quarter mile to Crab Ave on the left that goes into 'town,' which is a couple of ramshackle motels and deli markets. It's not the most scenic stop but it may be easier to park here than the more popular beaches on busy weekends.

p183

The Drive » Follow the Scenic Route signs that lead to a road veering left that winds along Netarts Bay, known for its clamming. After a few miles you'll rejoin Hwy 131 to Cape Lookout.

---

❻ Cape Lookout State Park

Besides great camping, there are several trails that fan out from this lovely, protected, white-sand beach area. Take the 2.3-mile (one-way) **North Trail** through lush forest and over cliffs to the summit of Cape Lookout, or the 2.4-mile (one-way) **Cape Trail** that goes through coastal rainforest to a panoramic lookout on the cape. Otherwise, try the easier 1.8-mile (one-way) **South Trail** over to a secluded beach off the cape.

p183

CHECUBUS / SHUTTERSTOCK ©

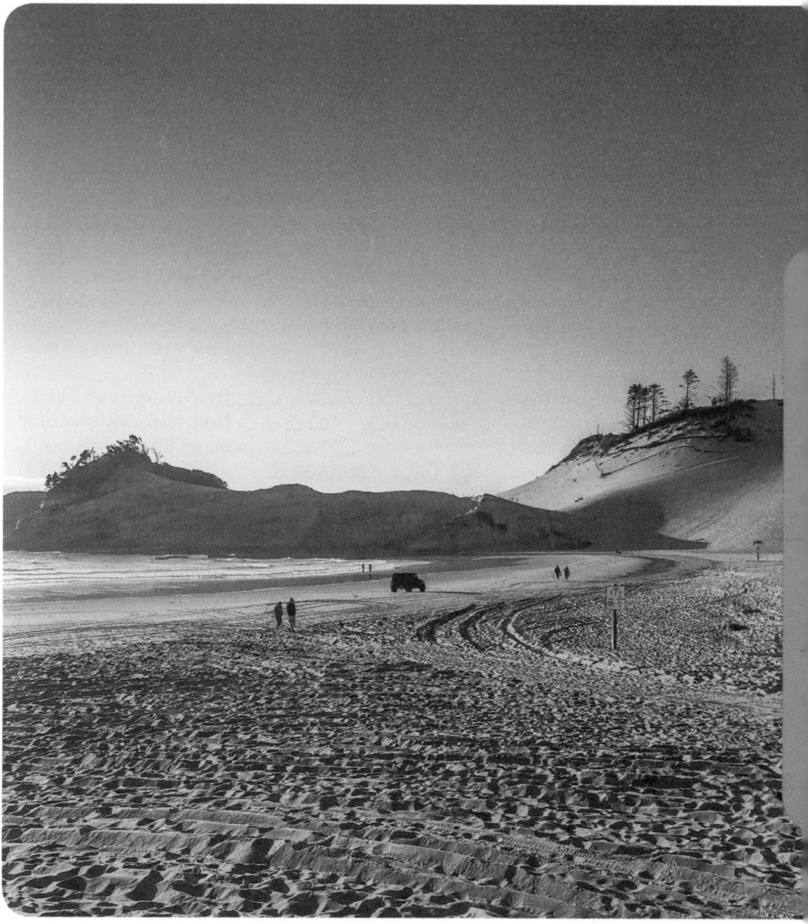

Cape Kiwanda Sand dunes

The Drive » Climb a little over a mile uphill then drive another 1.5 miles along the cape to the Cape Lookout Trailhead.

TRIP HIGHLIGHT

7 Cape Lookout Trailhead

You can access the same trails (at different points) that are found at **Cape Lookout State Park** from here. If you're after a short stroll, take the trail to the far left of the parking lot then walk straight at the first junction about 300ft along. In half a mile you'll be rewarded with a viewpoint – on a clear, sunny day you can see all the way to Cape Kiwanda.

The Drive » After descending about 5 miles from Cape Lookout you'll pass inland dunes on your right, a popular ATV spot. At the next junction turn right and continue about 4 miles.

8 Clay Myers State Natural Area at Whalen Island

Whalen Island is a virtually untouched, wildlife-filled, wooded island that's surrounded by the **Sand Creek Estuary**. A

CLAMMING

If you're around Netarts Bay at a low tide you're likely to see groups of rubber-booted, bucket-wielding foragers combing the beach. Want to get in on the clamming action? First, everyone 14 and older needs a $7 shellfish license; they're available at sporting good stores (there are a few in Tillamook) or get one at the Oregon Department of Fish & Wildlife website (www.dfw.state.or.us), where you can also check the regulations, limits and seasonal closures. Cockles, little necks, gaper clams and other species are all present, but razor clams are the real prize. In all cases, show up about an hour before the lowest tide with a bucket, shovel and/or a clam gun, look for small holes in the sand then dig fast!

trail makes a relatively flat but truly gorgeous 1.4-mile loop from the parking lot through low forest to fringing white-sand beaches. Wildlife that may be spotted here includes deer, otter, bear and (gulp!) cougar. It also has some of the best tent camping on this trip, but given the animal life you probably don't want to leave out any food.

 p183

The Drive » Go south 7 miles on Hwy 131 along the coast till the road veers inland at Cape Kiwanda.

TRIP HIGHLIGHT

⑨ Cape Kiwanda & Pacific City

The best beach of the Three Capes sits in front of tiny Pacific City, south of the towering sandstone, dune-covered Cape Kiwanda. Wide and lush with sand space to spare, you can hike the cape via the dune (under a quarter mile but straight up). Back on the beach, Dory fishermen haul their boats in or out from the beach around 6am and sunset when the weather

is calm. You can buy fish from them or order it at many local restaurants.

✖ ⊨ p183

The Drive » Head south through Pacific City then turn right at the first crossroads.

⑩ Robert Straub Scenic Park

You can access the wild and rugged part of Cape Kiwanda Beach via this little park at the Nestucca Sand Spit, where the legendary – and Chinook salmon–friendly – Little Nestucca River meets the sea. The beach here is less protected and thus is windier and has stronger surf and currents. You can find shelter from the elements in the grass-covered dunes.

> **DETOUR: SANDLAKE**
>
> **Start: ⑦ Cape Lookout Trailhead (p181)**
> About 2 miles before Whalen Island is a turnoff leading to Sandlake, a spit of land that's home to 1076 acres of sand dunes. Folks from all over the Pacific Northwest come here to camp, drink beer and tool around in their ATVs. You can join the fun watching the spills and thrills or, if that doesn't sound good, plug your ears and race back to the highway.

Eating & Sleeping

Tillamook ❷

✖ Pacific Seafood   Oyster Shucking $$

(☎503-377-2323; 5150 Oyster Dr; ⏱10am-8pm Jun-Sep, to 7pm Oct-May) To witness some of the fastest oyster shucking you'll ever see, head to Pacific Seafood in Bay City. The casual restaurant offers simple seafood dishes ($8 to $18) and a fish counter, but in the back is the assembly-line processing of oysters. Go early – the shuckers are sometimes done by noon.

Oceanside ❹

✖ Roseanna's Cafe   International $$

(☎503-842-7351; 1490 Pacific Ave; mains $7-30; ⏱9am-8pm Sun-Thu, to 9pm Fri & Sat) All round the best place to eat on this stretch of coastline is this little cafe in Oceanside. Choose from pastas, seafood and veggie options served in a sailor-shabby-chic seaside setting with a touch of elegance.

🛏 Oceanfront Cabins   Cabin $

(☎888-845-8475; www.oceanfrontcabins.com; 1610 Pacific Ave; cabins $70-140) Basic cabins, some with kitchens, just steps from the beach in the cute little hamlet of Oceanside.

Netarts & Netarts Bay ❺

✖ Schooner   Seafood $$

(2065 Netarts Boat Basin Rd; mains $13-32; ⏱11:30am-9pm Sun-Thu, 11.30am-10pm Fri & Sat) Wonderful views from the glass-enclosed eating area make the cocktails and locally sourced meals (oysters, fish, beef and more) even better.

Cape Lookout State Park ❻

🛏 Cape Lookout State Park Campground   Campground $

(☎800-452-5687; www.reserveamerica.com; Netarts; tent/RV sites $21/29, cabins $88) Thirty-eight full-hookups, 173 tent sites, 13 yurts ($44) and six cabins are available at this beachside beauty of a campground. Book early.

Clay Meyers State Natural Area at Whalen Island ❽

🛏 Whalen Island, Tillamook County Park   Campground $

(☎May-Oct 503-965-6085, Oct-Apr 503-322-3522; www.co.tillamook.or.us/gov/Parks/Campgrounds.htm; Sandlake Rd; sites $19-34) There are 34 adorable wooded campsites steps from the beach; there are no hookups but they do have a dump site.

Cape Kiwanda & Pacific City ❾

✖ Delicate Palate   Fusion $$$

(☎503-965-6464; 35280 Brooten Rd, Pacific City; mains $24-35; ⏱4-9pm Wed-Sun) The foodie's splurge for this stretch of coast. Dine on specialties like Asian seafood bouillabaisse and oven roasted rack of lamb in huckleberry red wine reduction sauce. It also has a bar with a more basic menu and outdoor seating.

✖ The Grateful Bread   Cafe $

(☎503-965-7337; 34805 Brooten Rd, Pacific City; mains $5-12; ⏱8am-3pm Thu-Mon) Start with heaping portions of fresh and delicious soups, salads, tacos, dory-caught fish, veggie and meat dishes then finish with fabulous fresh breads, cookies and desserts.

✖ Pelican Pub & Brewery   American $$

(☎503-965-7007; www.yourlittlebeachtown.com/pelican; 33180 Cape Kiwanda Dr, Pacific City; mains $12-32; ⏱8am-10pm Sun-Thu, to 11pm Fri & Sat) Offers decent pub grub and a good beer selection, but the setting – with tables inches from the sand – is the highlight.

🛏 Inn at Cape Kiwanda   Hotel $$$

(☎888-965-7001; www.yourlittlebeachtown.com/inn; 33105 Cape Kiwanda Dr, Pacific City; r from $229; 🛜) A classy and popular place that offers luxurious sea-view rooms, balconies and a location to die for.

Willamette Valley Wine Tour

16

Country roads lead through Pinot Noir–covered hills to small wineries with fresh, bucolic views and renowned vintages.

TRIP HIGHLIGHTS

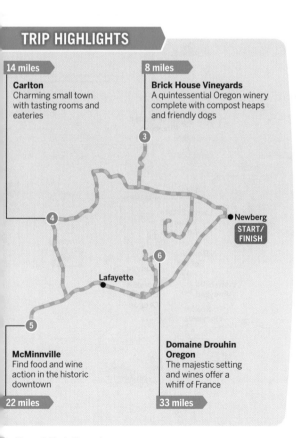

14 miles

Carlton
Charming small town with tasting rooms and eateries

8 miles

Brick House Vineyards
A quintessential Oregon winery complete with compost heaps and friendly dogs

3

4

● Newberg
START/ FINISH

6

Lafayette ●

5

McMinnville
Find food and wine action in the historic downtown

22 miles

Domaine Drouhin Oregon
The majestic setting and wines offer a whiff of France

33 miles

2 DAYS
50 MILES/80KM

GREAT FOR...

BEST TIME TO GO
April to August for sunshine on green hills.

ESSENTIAL PHOTO
Domaine Drouhin Oregon: take a picture of Pinot Noir vines with a view of the valley.

BEST SCENERY
Stop 6 through stop 8: take in the hillside beauty of the Dundee Hills appellation.

16 Willamette Valley Wine Tour

Oregon's Willamette Valley stretches over 100 miles from Eugene to Portland and more than 200 wineries lie within its six subappellations. Most of these are approachable, family-run operations dedicated to producing small quantities of high-quality Pinot Noir and sometimes other varietals. Organic, sustainable practices are the norm. This trip takes in the top half of the valley where you'll find the greatest concentration of wineries amid scenic farmlands.

❶ Newberg

The gateway to the Willamette Valley wine country was founded as a Quaker settlement and ironically was 'dry' for most of its early history. It's the biggest town in the area (population 23,312) and the one whose historic architecture has been most surrounded and overwhelmed by strip malls and fast-food joints. Still, it's a convenient place to stay and start your trip.

✕ ⨝ p191

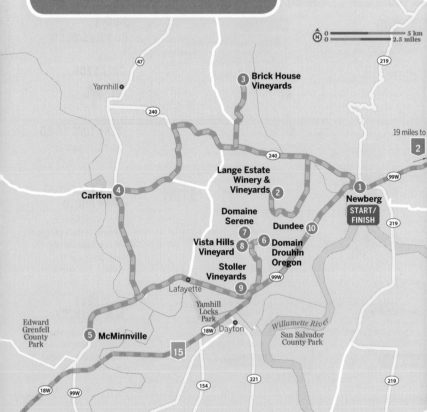

The Drive >> Take Hwy 240 west where the landscape quickly turns into the beautiful vineyard-covered countryside you came here for. Turn right on Red Hills Rd and follow the signs up to Lange, 3.5 miles from the turnoff. The last half is on a well-maintained gravel road.

- - - - - - - - - - -

❷ Lange Estate Winery & Vineyards

Your first tasting is at the **Lange Estate Winery & Vineyards** (☏503-538-6476; www.langewinery.com; 18380 NE Buena Vista Dr, Dundee; tastings from $15; ⊙11am-5pm), founded by one of the valley's earlier families. Here you'll find all the makings of an authentic Willamette Valley winery: gorgeous views, good wines and shaggy dogs. It's very much a family affair and they're known for their good-value Pinot Noir called Three Hills Cuvee.

LINK YOUR TRIP

2 **Columbia River Gorge & Mt Hood**

Head back through Portland and east on historic Hwy 30.

15 **Three Capes Loop**

Take the loop backwards by driving to Pacific City from Hwy 99W.

TOP TIP:
MARK YOUR CALENDAR

Many Willamette Valley wineries are open for tastings only on certain days of the week (usually Wednesday through Sunday or just the weekend), while others offer visits by appointment only. But on Memorial Day and Thanksgiving Day weekends, nearly all of the valley's wineries open their doors to the public – no reservations required. These are widely publicized and very busy weekends. Inside tip: most wineries also open their doors on the weekends prior to these...for those in the know.

The Drive >> Head back down to Hwy 240, turn left, drive about 3 miles and turn right at Ribbon Ridge Rd. After about 2.5 miles, turn right on Lewis Rogers Lane to Brick House Vineyards.

- - - - - - - - - - -

TRIP HIGHLIGHT

❸ Brick House Vineyards

Lying within the Ribbon Ridge appellation, **Brick House Vineyards** (☏503-538-5136; www.brickhousewines.com; 18200 Lewis Rogers Lane, Newberg; tasting fee $20; ⊙ by appointment only) is another classically Oregonian winery. Brick House's owner, Doug Tunnel, is a former CBS foreign correspondent and an Oregon native. He's also one of the state's pioneers in organic farming. And the winery is great. Drive up and dogs come out to greet you. Stand in the barn and look out over the vines and the compost piles and you'll get

a sense of the unpretentious charm that makes the Willamette Valley so special. The winery itself occupies a converted barn and the Pinot Noir, Chardonnay and Gamay Noir poured here are as fine as the experience is fresh.

The Drive >> Go back down Ribbon Ridge Rd and turn right on Hwy 240. After about 2 miles turn left onto Stag Hollow Rd, then right on Carlton–Chehalem Creek Rd, which eventually turns into Carlton's Main St.

- - - - - - - - - - -

TRIP HIGHLIGHT

❹ Carlton

It's hard to come up with a better descriptive word for Carlton than 'adorable.' Just a few streets wide, the town is made up almost entirely of pretty, historic buildings that house an impressive number of tasting rooms, great restaurants, antique shops, a jam maker and a fabulous French-style bakery. You won't find a better stop for lunch, and it's also a lovely place to stay overnight. If you're here on a Friday or Saturday, head to the particularly well-respected **Scott Paul Wines** (📞503-852-7300; www.scottpaul.com; 128 S Pine St; tasting fee $10; 🕑noon-5pm Wed-Sun), which only produces Pinot Noirs. Whenever you're here, be sure to wander around town aimlessly to turn up plenty of delicious surprises.

 p191

The Drive ›› Go south on Tualatin Valley Hwy 47. After about 4.5 miles turn right on Hwy 19, which goes right into downtown McMinnville.

TRIP HIGHLIGHT

⑤ McMinnville

At the heart of the region's wine industry lies McMinnville. Stay within its historic, red-brick downtown district and you'll find older buildings, art galleries, boutiques and fine restaurants, along with a small-town feel as kids play on sidewalks and tourists stroll up and down the main artery of 3rd St; head outside this area and this image is dimmed by modern housing communities and shopping areas. It's a great place to stay, eat

and end your tour of the wine region.

As you'd expect, there are also several wineries and tasting rooms that you can easily find by taking a stroll around downtown. The most special is **Eyrie Vineyards** (📞503-472-6315; www.eyrievineyards.com; 935 NE 10th Ave; tasting flights $10-20; 🕑noon-5pm). The owner here, David 'Papa Pinot' Lett, planted the region's first vines (including the first Pinot Gris in the USA) in 1965 and the first wines were produced in 1970. Today David's son, Jason, runs the operation.

 p191

The Drive ›› Head northeast on Hwy 99W. After 8 miles turn left at OR 18W/SE Dayton Bypass then take an immediate right onto NE MacDougall Rd. After half a mile turn left on NE Breyman Orchards Rd and follow the signs to Domaine Drouhin.

TRIP HIGHLIGHT

⑥ Domaine Drouhin Oregon

You may be on day two at this point and it's time for a little more glamour. Owned by renowned Burgundy producer Maison Joseph Drouhin, **Domaine Drouhin Oregon** (📞503-864-2700; www.domainedrouhin.com; 6750 Breymen Orchards Rd, Dayton; flights $10-20; 🕑11am-4pm Wed-Sun) is famed as much for its

history as it is for its Pinot Noir. The winery owes its existence in part to the 1979 Gault Millau 'Wine Olympics,' a blind tasting held in France. In the competition, McMinnville's Eyrie Vineyards placed in the top 10, holding its own against France's most esteemed Pinots, including one from the respected Maison Joseph Drouhin. This stoked Drouhin's already existing interest in the Willamette Valley (Drouhin first visited the valley in 1961), and he soon decided it was time to extend the family's operation. In 1988 he opened Domaine Drouhin Oregon under the management of his daughter, winemaker Véronique Drouhin. She still makes the wine and the top picks are named after her three children. Today the winery is one of the most elegant and scenically located in the valley and the wines, which are made from grapes planted in the French style with vines close together, have a distinct old-world touch.

The Drive ›› Go straight out the driveway across Breyman Orchards Rd (don't turn) and follow the signs for Domaine Serene.

⑦ Domaine Serene

Domaine Serene (📞503-864-4600; www.domaine serene.com; 6555 NE Hilltop

Dundee Hills Vineyards

TOP TIP:
SPIT & DRIVE

Some words of advice: when tasting wine, learn to spit. That bucket is there for a reason. Spitting will actually mark you as a pro rather than an amateur.

Lane, Dayton; tasting fee $15; ⏱tasting room 11am-4pm Mon-Thu, 11am-5pm Fri-Sun) is one of the Willamette Valley's best-known wineries heralded, as would be expected, for its Pinot Noir. It's a grand, modern place with a stunning wine cellar and lovely views over the rolling hills and vineyards that sweep across the valley. Along with Pinot Noir, the winery produces highly regarded Chardonnays and a Syrah, which it makes from grapes grown in Washington State's Walla Walla region. You can go with the standard tasting-room-only wine tasting or tour the entire winery, including the cellar, as part of the VIP tour – that, however, will cost you extra.

The Drive » Turn right out of the driveway and don't blink or you'll miss Vista Hills Vineyard, your next stop.

- - - - - - - - - - -

⑧ Vista Hills Vineyard

A short hop down the road is **Vista Hills Vineyard** (☎503-864-3200; www.vistahillsvineyard.com;

6475 Hilltop Lane, Dayton; tasting flights $15; ⏱11am-5pm) with wonderful views from the cozy Treehouse Tasting Room that's literally up in the trees. This unpretentious place offers a unique approach to wine making: Vista Hills' wines (Pinot Noir and a delicious fruity Pinot Gris) are made in several different facilities around the valley using Vista Hills grapes. The subtleties of vintages, in other words, are determined by more than just the weather. Another unique trait: 10% of its profits go to a foundation created by the owners to offer financial support to students pursuing higher education. It should come as no surprise that sustainability is one of the winery's core values.

The Drive » Go back down Breyman Orchards Rd and turn right at NE MacDougall Rd. Stoller Vineyards is about a mile along.

- - - - - - - - - - -

⑨ Stoller Vineyards

On the site of what was once the biggest turkey farm in Oregon, **Stoller Vineyards** (☎503-864-

3404; www.stollervineyards.com; 16161 NE McDougall Rd, Dayton; tasting flights $15; ⏱11am-5pm) is one of the most ecologically sustainable wineries in the country, if not the world. The winery building holds the US Green Building Council's gold-level certification for Leadership in Energy and Environmental Design, plus the architecture (that looks like a cross between a grain elevator and a barn – but prettier) is true to the site's history. It produces well-heralded Pinot Noirs and Chardonnays.

The Drive » Backtrack east on NE MacDougall Rd, drive a little over a mile then turn right onto Hwy 99W. You'll be in central Dundee in under 4 miles.

- - - - - - - - - - -

⑩ Dundee

Dundee is the hub of the Dundee Hills, the Willamette Valley's preeminent subappellation, where you've already visited three superb wineries. Now it's time to see what the region can produce for lunch and chances are you won't be disappointed. Although Dundee isn't the most scenic of the region's towns, it's pleasant enough with a few parks and early 20th-century homes. The real draw, however, is that it's teeming with fabulous restaurants.

🍴 🛏 p191

Eating & Sleeping

Newberg ❶

✕ Painted Lady Northwestern $$$
(☎503-538-3850; www.thepaintedlady restaurant.com; 201 S College St; prix fixe $85-125; ⏱5-10pm Wed-Sun) Accomplished chefs Allen Routt and Jessica Bagley use their wide travel and culinary experiences at this restaurant in a renovated 1890s Victorian house.

🛏 Allison Inn & Spa Resort $$$
(☎503-554-2525, 877-294-2525; www. theallison.com; 2525 Allison Ln; d from $405; ⊛✿🛜🏊🐾) Spacious, plush rooms, relaxing soaking tubs, excellent restaurant and great services (including a spa). The place has its own vineyard nearby, and it's ecofriendly, too.

Carlton ❹

✕ Horse Radish American $$
(☎503-852-6656; www.thehorseradish.com; 211 W Main St; small-plate combos $12-18; ⏱noon-3pm Sun-Thu, noon-10pm Fri & Sat) Gourmet meals, cheese plates and a wine bar. On Friday and Saturday nights there are dinner specials (6pm to 8pm) and live music.

🛏 Brookside Inn On Abbey Road B&B $$$
(☎503-852-4433; www.brooksideinn-oregon. com; 8243 NE Abbey Rd; r $225-325; 🛜) This luxurious nine-room guesthouse sits on 21 acres in the heart of wine country. There's fishing, walking trails and a farm-to-table kitchen.

McMinnville ❺

✕ Nick's Italian Cafe Italian $$
(☎503-434-4471; www.nicksitaliancafe.com; 521 NE 3rd St; pizzas $14-16, mains $22-28, prix fixe from $45; ⏱5-9pm Sun-Thu, to 11pm Fri & Sat) Going strong for over 30 years, Nick's was named one of 'America's Classics' by the James Beard Foundation in 2014 for its timeless Italian cuisine.

✕ Joel Palmer House Northwestern $$$
(☎503-864-2995; www.joelpalmerhouse.com; 600 Ferry St, Dayton; prix-fixe menus from $65; ⏱4:30-9:30pm Tue-Sat) Renowned for its dishes laced with wild mushrooms, this highly lauded restaurant is just northwest of McMinnville.

✕ Thistle Northwestern $$$
(☎503-472-9623; www.thistlerestaurant.com; 228 NE Evans St; mains $24-27; ⏱5:30-9pm Tue-Sat) Small but top-drawer restaurant run by Eric Bechard, an award-winning chef who fiercely believes in using local, organic ingredients whenever possible.

🛏 McMenamins Hotel Oregon Hotel $$
(☎503-472-8427; www.mcmenamins.com; 310 NE Evans St; d $65-125; ⊛✿🛜🐾) Expect the typical McMenamins eccentricities, such as eclectic artwork, at this cool hotel; there's also an unbeatable rooftop restaurant-pub, mandatory for drinks on warm summer nights.

🛏 Joseph Mattey House B&B B&B $$
(☎503-434-5058; www.josephmatteyhouse. com; 10221 NE Mattey Lane; d $170-185; ⊛✿🛜) This 1892 Queen Anne Victorian farmhouse features country-style atmosphere, charming old details and four comfortable rooms with quilts, lace and private bathrooms.

Dundee ❿

✕ Recipe Mediterranean $$
(☎503-487-6853; www.recipenewbergor.com; 115 N Washington St; lunch $11-21, dinner $21-33; ⏱11am-3pm & 5-10pm Tue-Sat) Adorably cozy space serving perfectly house French- and Italian-inspired stews, steaks and pastas, as well as their house-made charcuterie.

🛏 Black Walnut Inn & Vineyard Inn $$$
(☎866-429-4114, 503-429-4114; www.black walnut-inn.com; 9600 NE Worden Hill Rd; r $295-529; 🛜) One of the Willamette Valley's most luxurious lodgings, the Black Walnut Inn has beautiful suites each with its own individual charms – a vineyard view, antique French furniture, private gardens, whatever your fancy.

Journey Through Time Scenic Byway

17

An epic drive across windswept plains, desolate badlands and forested mountain passes. Visit ghost towns and fossil beds, gold-mining sites and small-town museums.

TRIP HIGHLIGHTS

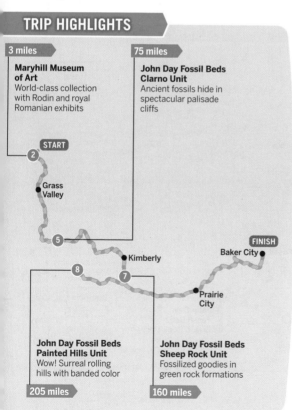

3 miles

Maryhill Museum of Art
World-class collection with Rodin and royal Romanian exhibits

START
2

Grass Valley

5

8

75 miles

John Day Fossil Beds Clarno Unit
Ancient fossils hide in spectacular palisade cliffs

● Kimberly

7

FINISH
Baker City ●

● Prairie City

John Day Fossil Beds Painted Hills Unit
Wow! Surreal rolling hills with banded color

205 miles

John Day Fossil Beds Sheep Rock Unit
Fossilized goodies in green rock formations

160 miles

3 DAYS
363 MILES/584KM

GREAT FOR...

BEST TIME TO GO
June to September for warm temperatures and less rain.

 ESSENTIAL PHOTO
John Day Fossil Beds Painted Hills Unit: the love-child of a National Geographic spread and a Mark Rothko painting.

 BEST FOR HISTORY
The Thomas Condon Paleontology Center.

17 Journey Through Time Scenic Byway

Unless you count the futuristic-looking windmills around the town of Wasco, a more precise name for this state scenic byway would be Journey Back in Time Scenic Byway. From the moment you leave Hwy 84 it's truly a time warp: ghost towns lie off the roadside, fossils expose millions of years of history, and even the restaurants and hotels make you feel you've driven into decades past.

① Stonehenge

Although it's not part of the official byway, the perfect place to kick off your time travel is at the full-scale replica of **Stonehenge** (US Hwy 97), on the Washington side of the Columbia River, just east of Hwy 97. Built by eccentric businessman Sam Hill as a memorial to the 13 men in Klickitat County killed in WWI, the site is a completed version of the Salisbury Plain monument, although its detractors argue that

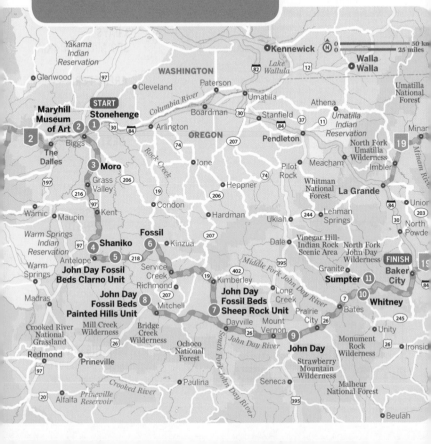

the keystone is incorrectly aligned with the stars.

The Drive ›› Turn left on Hwy 14 and drive about three miles to the Maryhill Museum of Art.

TRIP HIGHLIGHT

❷ Maryhill Museum of Art

The spectacular **Maryhill Museum of Art** (☎509-773-3733; www.maryhill museum.org; 35 Maryhill Museum Dr, WA; adult/child $9/3; ☺10am-5pm mid-Mar–mid-Nov), set in a mansion on a bluff above the Columbia River, was another Sam Hill project. Among its eclectic exhibits is a noteworthy collection of Rodin sculptures, a room full of decadent objects once belonging to Queen Marie of Romania

LINK YOUR TRIP

2 Columbia River Gorge & Mt Hood

From the Dalles it's only about 30 miles east along Hwy 84 and the Columbia River Gorge to Maryhill.

19 Hells Canyon Scenic Byway

The Hells Canyon Scenic Byway begins in Baker City right where this trip ends so they link up perfectly.

and Native American artifacts.

The Drive ›› Make a right on Hwy 14 then another right two miles later onto Hwy 97, which takes you over the Columbia River via the Sam Hill Memorial Bridge. The scenic byway officially begins in the town of Biggs. From here it's about 20 miles to the next stop past grassy hills, wind farms and homesteads.

❸ Moro

In Moro you'll find **Sherman County Historical Museum** (www.sherman museum.org; 200 Dewey St, Moro; adult/student $5/1; ☺10am-5pm May 1-Oct 31;). For a small-town museum it has some surprisingly interesting exhibits, including on the history of wheat production, Native Americans and rural living in the days of old. The town is also home to a handful of antique shops that are worth a browse.

The Drive ›› South on Hwy 97 you'll be treated to breathtaking views of several volcanoes in the distance, including Mt Hood, Mt Jefferson and Mt Adams. Continue on 35 miles through the near-deserted towns of Grass Valley and Kent.

❹ Shaniko

This wee ghost town (population 26) was once the wool-shipping center of the USA. Its decrepit old buildings make for exceptional

photo ops, and its architectural grand dame, the Shaniko Hotel, is one of the finer historic buildings in eastern Oregon. (It was recently refurbished but was closed and up for sale when we passed.) A few shops and a tiny museum are open through summer.

The Drive ›› Continue south on Hwy 218. About a mile out the road narrows and winds as it descends through sagebrush-covered hills to the minuscule settlement of Antelope. Turn east here onto Hwy 218 and drive about 16 miles to the next stop.

TRIP HIGHLIGHT

❺ John Day Fossil Beds Clarno Unit

Dramatically eroded Palisade Cliffs mark your arrival at the **John Day Fossil Beds Clarno Unit** (www.nps.gov/joda; Hwy 218), your first stop in the John Day Fossil Beds National Monument trilogy. The short trails and fossil remains plunge you into a time more than 40 million years ago, when the region was subtropical forest. Wander the half-mile **Geologic Time Trail** to the **Trail of Fossils,** and you'll see boulder-sized fossils of logs, seeds and other remains from the ancient forest. The quarter-mile **Arch Trail** leads to a natural arch in the striking Palisade Cliffs.

The Drive ›› Continue 18 miles northeast to Fossil.

WITOLD SKRYPCZAK / GETTY IMAGES ©

⑥ Fossil

The town of Fossil (population 370) is aptly named given that it's in the middle of paleontology heaven. It's a good stop for lunch and you can browse the town's very small **Fossil Museum** (☎541-763-2113; 1st St; admission by donation; ⊗1-4pm Wed-Mon) or dig for fossils in the town's **public digging area** (☎541-763-4303; 404 Main St; per person $5; ⊗May-Oct). You're pretty much guaranteed to find something and there's usually someone around to help explain the things you've dug up.

The Drive » Head 20 miles southeast on Hwy 19 to the tiny Service Creek (population 2), an old stagecoach stop that today consists of a recommended inn and a rafting-launch-cum-campground on the John Day River. It's exceptionally scenic along the river valley for the next 40 miles to the next stop.

TRIP HIGHLIGHT

⑦ John Day Fossil Beds Sheep Rock Unit

The rust-colored walls of the river canyon narrow and then open up again before reaching the spectacular John Day Fossil Beds Sheep Rock Unit. Continue 3 miles south to the **Thomas Condon Paleontology Center** (☎541-987-2333; www.nps.gov/joda; 32651 Hwy 19, Kimberly; ⊗10am-5pm). This is where everything comes together. With giant murals and exhibits of fossilized skulls, skeletons, leaves, nuts and branches, the center brings to life the region's history.

After filling your head with paleontology, drive across the highway to the historic **Cant Ranch House** (www.nps.gov/joda; ⊗9am-4pm Mon-Fri),

Shaniko Former wool-shipping town

perfect for a picnic or snack on the wooden tables overlooking the John Day River. Then backtrack the 3 miles (north) to the **Blue Basin Area** parking lot at the Sheep Rock Unit. Hike the 0.6-mile **Island in Time Trail** and/or the 3-mile **Blue Basin Overlook Trail**. The former passes replicas of large mammal fossils and ends in a massive amphitheater of towering greenish pinnacles. The latter leads around and above the amphitheater.

The Drive >> From Hwy 19 turn west onto Hwy 26, from where it's 36 miles to Mitchell.

At 25 miles check out the tree on the north side of the road covered with shoes. It's been there as long as anyone can remember – string a pair up for good luck. From Mitchell it's another 10 miles to the Painted Hills Unit.

- - - - - - - - - - - -

TRIP HIGHLIGHT

8 John Day Fossil Beds Painted Hills Unit

This is a detour off the official byway, but it's arguably the most striking unit of the John Day Fossil Beds, so you won't want to miss it. The goal is to see the low-slung, colorfully banded

Painted Hills (www.nps.gov/joda; Burnt Ranch Rd) at sunset, when the evening light emphasizes the ochres, blacks, beiges and yellows of the eroded hillsides; an honorable reason to stay overnight in Mitchell. At the site, choose from four trails including the 0.5-mile **Painted Hills Overlook and Trail** (the most picturesque of the area) and the **Painted Cove Trail** that takes you via boardwalk around a hill (5 to 10 minutes) to see the area's popcorn-textured claystone up close.

✗ ⊨ p199

The Drive » Backtrack east along Hwy 26 and pass the Hwy 19 junction to Picture Gorge, a canyon hemmed in by stone pillars known as Picture Gorge Basalts. Two miles along is the Mascall Formation Overlook, where you'll get spectacular views of the John Day River, Strawberry Mountains, Picture Gorge, and Mascall and Rattlesnake formations. It's another 36 miles to John Day.

❾ John Day

After so many small towns, the one-stoplight town of John Day (population 1821) feels like a metropolis. Make your way to the outstanding **Kam Wah Chung State Heritage Site** (☎541-575-2800; http://oregonstateparks.org; 125 NW Canton St; ⏰9am-5pm May-Oct), which served as an apothecary, community center, temple and general store for Chinese gold miners and settlers from the late 19th century until the 1940s. Today it's a widely acclaimed museum featuring the history of the

TOP TIP: SHORT CUT TO MITCHELL

Taking Hwy 207 from Service Creek 30 miles to Mitchell will shave about 50 miles off your route and also saves you from having to backtrack east along Hwy 26 – but you'll miss some exceptional scenery along the John Day River.

building and the region's Chinese past.

✖ 🛏 p199

The Drive » Drive east past stop-for-the-night-worthy Prairie City (see p199) into the lush, conifer-clad Blue Mountains. Up the first grade, pull off at the Strawberry Mountain Overlook for views of the John Day River Valley and the Strawberry Mountains. Continue northeast over Dixie Pass (elevation 5280ft), swing left onto Hwy 7, cross Tipton Summit (elevation 5124ft) and you'll drop into a lovely valley.

❿ Whitney

This isolated and unsignposted prairie settlement, a ghost town in the best sense of the

word, was once a busy logging town and the primary stop on the Sumpter Valley Railroad. Its sagging wooden buildings, which lie on either side of a short dirt road that branches south from Hwy 7, are certainly worth a stop. Find it between mile marker 15 and 16.

The Drive » About 9 miles east turn left on Sumpter Valley Hwy, then drive another 3 miles or so to Sumpter.

⓫ Sumpter

Once home to 3500 people, the town today is a sleepy cluster of Old West buildings huddled along a dusty main drag. The official attraction is the **Sumpter Valley Dredge**, a massive relic of gold-mining engineering sitting beside the river. The dredge's 72-bucket 'digging ladder' extracted some 9 tons of gold. Once you return from here to Hwy 7, it's 26 miles to the Eastern Oregon hub of Baker City.

ROCK ART

If you're heading east through Picture Gorge (on Hwy 26), at the far end you'll see a sign on the left and a gravel parking area big enough for about two cars. There's a little footpath from the pullout. Walk down the footpath and then hang onto the rock wall on your left, lean around and you'll see some red pictographs. They're really cool. And you can't hurt them because you can't reach them.

Eating & Sleeping

John Day Fossil Beds Painted Hills Unit (Mitchell) 8

✖ Bridge Creek Cafe — American $

(☎541-462-3434; 208 Hwy 26, Mitchell; mains $6-12; ⏰8am-7pm Fri-Wed; 🖱) Petite diner in tiny Mitchell with homemade pie and the usual country cooking.

✖ Mitchell Stage Stop — American $

(☎541-462-3532; http://mitchellstagestop. com; 100 E Main St, Mitchell; mains $8-16; ⏰7:30am-7:30pm Tue-Fri, 11am-8pm Sat; 🖱) Fabulous country diner with pizzas, burgers, sandwiches, soups and a tater-tot breakfast scramble.

🛏 Historic Oregon Hotel — Hotel $

(☎541-462-3027; www.theoregonhotel.net; 104 E Main St, Mitchell; dm $20, d $50-110; 🛜) This homey old-fashioned hotel is in the little town of Mitchell, about 10 miles southeast of the Painted Hills Unit. Plain but comfy rooms mostly have shared bathrooms and no TV. There's one dorm, plus a kitchenette room for $110. It's popular with cyclists. Call ahead December to March to make sure it's open.

John Day 9

✖ Snaffle Bit — American $$

(☎541-575-2426; 830 S Canyon City Blvd; steaks $13-32, mains $10-19; ⏰4-9pm Tue, 7am-9pm Wed-Thu, 7am-9.30pm Fri & Sat) Some of the county's best steaks are at this no-nonsense, friendly restaurant with a nice fountain patio. Also on the menu are salads, pasta, hamburgers and Mexican specialties. Large portions. Reservations are a good idea.

✖ Outpost — American $$

(☎541-575-0250; www.outpostpizzapubgrill. com; 201 W Main St; breakfast $6-11, dinner mains $13-20; ⏰5:30am-9pm Mon-Sat, to 8pm Sun) There's something for everyone at this Western-style joint: soups, salads, sandwiches, pizzas, burgers and steaks, pasta and fajitas; and homemade cinnamon rolls for breakfast. There's a good atmosphere with upscale rustic decor.

🛏 Dreamers Lodge — Motel $

(☎800-654-2849; www.dreamerslodge.com; 144 N Canyon Blvd; d from $69; 🐾❄🛜🖥) One of John Day's better-value places, this decent motel offers good-sized rooms with nice touches – comfy old armchairs, in-room coffee, mini-fridge and microwave – and it's off the main drag. Rates plunge if there are lots of vacancies.

Prairie City 9

✖ Chuck's Little Diner — American $

(☎541-820-4353; 142 Front St; mains $6-12; ⏰6am-2pm Wed-Sun) With its Formica-top bar, tarnished chrome bar stools, friendly staff and greasy breakfast classics, this is a diner par excellence.

🛏 Hotel Prairie — Hotel $$

(☎541-820-4800; www.hotelprairie.com; 112 Front St; d $84-144; 🐾❄🛜) This historic 1905 hotel with nine suites (one with kitchenette) caters especially to bicyclists. There's a subdued, classy atmosphere – rooms are simple and not at all fancy, but comfortable; out back is a nice modern patio for hanging out. Cafe on premises, and breakfast included.

Blue Mountains Loop

18

From Oregon Trail wagon stops to million-acre forests and rodeo towns, this loop shows off Eastern Oregon's rural variety.

TRIP HIGHLIGHTS

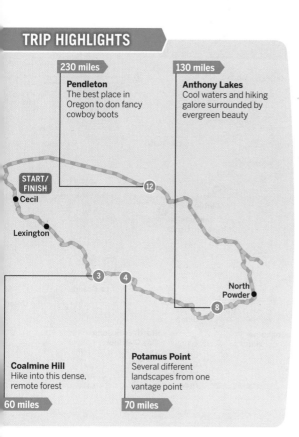

230 miles

Pendleton
The best place in Oregon to don fancy cowboy boots

130 miles

Anthony Lakes
Cool waters and hiking galore surrounded by evergreen beauty

START/FINISH
● Cecil

Lexington

North Powder ●

Coalmine Hill
Hike into this dense, remote forest

60 miles

Potamus Point
Several different landscapes from one vantage point

70 miles

3 DAYS
230 MILES/370KM

GREAT FOR...

BEST TIME TO GO
June to September, the only time all the roads are open!

 ESSENTIAL PHOTO
Potamus Point.

 BEST FOR HISTORY
Capture a panorama of a Wild West quilt of color.

18

Blue Mountains Loop

This trip takes you way off the beaten path through country that feels as if the pioneer days never ended. Start in the grain kingdoms of Morrow County before heading up and up into deep, remote, wildlife-filled forests. Just as you start craving a real cup of coffee you'll descend back to civilization via the good ole cow-poking towns of Union and La Grande to lively, Western-chic Pendleton.

① Cecil

Turn onto Hwy 74 from the Columbia River Gorge and stratified river country is quickly replaced by grassy fields and hillside tracts of space-age windmills. The first town you come to is the sheep- and grain-farming hamlet of Cecil, which was founded in the late 1800s when William Cecil stopped here on the Oregon Trail to fix his wagon and ended up opening a wagon repair shop. Take Cecil's

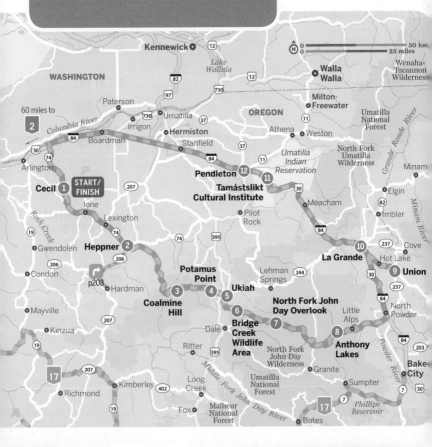

one road to the left off Hwy 74 to check out the ancient **Cecil Store**, a photogenic Old West–style building with a ghost town feel to it.

The Drive » Continue 32 miles down Hwy 74 through the grain elevator–dominated towns of Morgan (a ghost town), Ione and Lexington. The scenery here is the highlight: picture-perfect homesteads and grazing horses along a meandering creek bed.

----

2 Heppner

Welcome to the big smoke (although perhaps 'spoke' may be more fitting) of Morrow County. Heppner has a massive grain elevator, a small grid of wide streets and a few stately brick buildings. The town's pride and joy is the

LINK YOUR TRIP

2 Columbia River Gorge & Mt Hood

It's about 60 miles east along Hwy 84 from The Dalles to the turnoff for Hwy 74.

17 Journey Through Time Scenic Byway

From Baker City take the mountainous half of this route via Ukiah or I-84 to Pendleton to create a loop.

majestic **Historic Morrow County Courthouse** (✆541-676-9061; 100 Court St; ⊙8am-5pm Mon-Fri), built in 1903 and still in use, making it one of the oldest continuously used courthouses in the state. It's also said to be haunted, perhaps by the 275 people who lost their lives in the 1903 Heppner Flood. Call if you want a tour.

Another worthwhile stop is the **Morrow County Museum** (444 N Main St; $3; ⊙1-5pm Tue-Fri & 11am-3pm Sat Mar-Oct), where you'll find a collection of pioneer and rural artifacts. Then, before you hit the road again, check in at the **US Forest Service Ranger Station** (✆541-676-9187; 117 S Main St; ⊙7.45am-4.30pm Mon-Fri) for maps, trail and road information.

✕ ⊨ p207

The Drive » Main St leads into Hwy 206/207. After about a mile turn left toward

DETOUR:
HARDMAN

Start: 2 Heppner

Once a stagecoach stop named 'Rawdog,' Hardman's demise began in the late 1880s when Heppner was chosen as the location for the train stop. The town's last business closed in 1968 and today it's one of the region's most scenic ghost towns. The most attractive building is the renovated dance hall.

It's a 40-mile round-trip drive south from Heppner along Hwy 207.

Willow Creek Reservoir on Hwy 53. From here it's 24 miles to Cutsforth Park, where the Umatilla National Forest officially starts. It's another 2 miles from here to Coalmine Hill.

TRIP HIGHLIGHT

3 Coalmine Hill

The best way to explore the pine and fir tree loveliness of the 1.4-million-acre **Umatilla National Forest** is on foot. Stop at the **Coalmine Hill Trailhead** to tackle the 2.5-mile one-way **Bald Mountain Trail**, where you'll be rewarded with a view over Butter Creek. At about 1.25 miles you'll pass **Gibson Cave**, which provided shelter to Native American families long ago. During the 1930s Great Depression, a man named Gibson lived here and became known as a modern caveman.

The Drive » Head south on NF-270 a little over a mile then turn right on NF-021/Western Raite Lane/Western

Rt Rd. Continue 6 miles before hanging a right on Arbuckle Mt Rd/NF-180. Continue to follow Arbuckle Mt Rd for about 2.5 miles. Turn right on NF-030 then right onto NF-5316 5 miles on, then right 1.5 miles later on NF-360.

TRIP HIGHLIGHT

④ Potamus Point

This is the best viewpoint of the trip, looking over North Fork John Day River. In winter herds of elk can be seen from here, but unfortunately the road is closed at this time. In the summer months, enjoy the vistas of mountain ponds and unusual rock formations.

The Drive » Backtrack to NF-030 then take a quick right onto NF-5316. After around 6 miles turn right on NF-053. After 10 miles this turns into OR-244 E/Ukiah-Hilgard Hwy and a little over a mile later you'll be back to civilization in Ukiah.

⑤ Ukiah

Nestled within the Camas Prairie, this tiny town is surrounded by rolling grasslands and cut by clear Camas Creek. It's the low, flat heart of the Blue Mountains and a pleasant place for a leg stretch, but there's not much on offer besides the small supply shop.

The Drive » Travel west on OR-244 W/Main St/Ukiah-Hilgard Hwy for a little over a mile, then turn right at

Granite/Ukiah Rd 52 and travel 4 miles. The entrance to the wildlife area is on the right side of the road.

⑥ Bridge Creek Wildlife Area

This protected area is known mostly as a wintering ground for elk, but in summer (the only time of year it's accessible without specialty equipment – plus you need a permit to enter between December 1 and April 30) you'll see plenty of birdlife, including mountain bluebirds and horned larks. For a bit of exercise, take the 0.2-mile-long **Ron Bridges Memorial Trail** for views over Bridge Creek Flats. The trailhead is on the right, 1 mile after the wilderness area on Granite/Ukiah Rd 52.

The Drive » Drive 9 miles east on Granite-Ukiah Rd 52.

⑦ North Fork John Day Overlook

Pull over for spectacular views (when it's clear) over the patchwork of color of the John Day Wilderness to the north, the majestic Strawberry Mountains to the south and the river-filled Bridge Creek Flats to the southeast. If it's early or late in season you may be able to spot elk.

The Drive » Continue east on Granite-Ukiah Rd 52 then turn left on NF-73. Drive around

16 miles then turn right toward NF-300/172 and follow the signs to Anthony Lakes.

TRIP HIGHLIGHT

⑧ Anthony Lakes

Known for its powdery winter skiing, Anthony Lakes is also a trove of excellent hiking in summer with alpine landscapes, five lakes and craggy granite peaks. **Anthony Lake** is the only lake accessible by car, and it's also the biggest and most crowded. Better, take the 1-mile hike to **Black Lake**, which is smaller and just as beautiful, to find serious tranquility. Find the trailhead at the Anthony Lakes Campground.

🛏 p207

The Drive » Head back to NF-73 and turn right into Anthony Lake Rd, which eventually turns into Anthony Lakes Hwy. After about 9 miles of winding downhill through pines, turn left on Ellis Rd/Ermey Davis Rd then take the first right on River Lane. This will lead you onto OR-237 N/La Grande-Baker Hwy toward Union. Total distance: 36 miles.

⑨ Union

One of Eastern Oregon's most likeable, unpretentious towns, Victorianera, brick-solid Union is like a smaller, cuter version of La Grande and is a quieter place to spend the night if you're ready for a stop. While you're here, learn more

John Day Wilderness Painted Hills Unit

TOP TIP: NAVIGATING FOREST ROADS

It's easy to get lost in this tangle of forest roads, so make sure you fill up your tank in Heppner, bring plenty of water, snacks and emergency supplies, let the Ranger Station know where you're going and keep meticulous track of the route you've taken so that in a worst case scenario you can at least backtrack. Cell phone reception and GPS coverage are iffy at best so don't expect to rely on anything besides your wits.

about cowboys then and now at the **Union County Museum** (📞541-562-6003; 333 South Main St; adult/child $5/free; 🕙10am-4pm Mon-Sat).

🛏 p207

The Drive » Get back on the La Grande-Baker Hwy. In about 13 miles you'll see the first exit for La Grande.

- - - - - - - - - -

⑩ La Grande

Apart from its pleasant historic area downtown, La Grande is really just a stop for food, gas and lodging. Thirteen miles west of town, however, is the **Oregon Trail Interpretive Park** (📞541-963-7186; I-84 exit 248; day-use fee $5; 🕙9am-7pm Tue-Sun Memorial Day-Labor Day), a great place for a visceral feeling of what it was like for Oregon pioneers crossing the Blue Mountains. Paths wind through the forest to ruts left by pioneer

wagons – still visible after 150 years. Find the park on well-marked roads from freeway exit 248.

🍴 p207, p216

The Drive » Continue on I-84 toward Pendleton. About 25 miles along you'll find yourself descending Emigrant Hill on a 6% downgrade. Stop at the Cabbage Hill Viewpoint to experience something akin to looking down from the heavens. Just before Pendleton, take exit 216 to the Tamástslikt Cultural Institute. Total distance: 50 miles.

- - - - - - - - - -

⑪ Tamástslikt Cultural Institute

You've learned all about the pioneers so now it's time to delve into the cultures that were here long before covered wagons. State-of-the-art exhibits weave voices, memories and artifacts through an evolving history of the region at this

grand **cultural center** (📞541-429-7700; www.tamastslikt.org; 47106 Wild Horse Blvd; adult/child $10/6; 🕙10am-5pm Mon-Sat).

The Drive » Get back onto I-84 W. In about 2.5 miles you'll see the first exit for Pendleton.

- - - - - - - - - -

TRIP HIGHLIGHT

⑫ Pendleton

Eastern Oregon's largest city, 'wild and woolly' Pendleton is a handsome old town famous for its wool shirts and rowdy, big-name rodeo, the **Pendleton Round-Up** (📞800-457-6336; www.pendletonroundup.com; 1205 SW Court Ave; tickets $15-28; 🕙mid-Sep). The town has managed to retain a glint of its cow-poking past, though in the past few years at least one small boutique winery has popped up, not to mention art galleries and antique shops.

Take a free tour of **Pendleton Woolen Mills** (📞541-276-6911; www.pendleton-usa.com; 1307 SE Court Pl; 🕙8am-6pm Mon-Sat, 9am-5pm Sun), which has been weaving blankets for more than 100 years, and is especially known for Native American designs.

🍴🛏 p207

The Drive » From here it's about 70 miles to the Hwy 74 turnoff to Cecil where the loop began.

Eating & Sleeping

Heppner ②

✗ Howe's About Pizza
Pizza $$

(☎541-676-5210; 111 Court St; pizzas from $12; ⏰10am-8pm Mon-Sat) Get delicious handmade pizzas and homemade ice cream at this little hole-in-the-wall near the courthouse. Take-out orders welcome.

🛏 Northwestern Motel & RV Park
Motel $

(☎541-676-9167; www.heppnerlodging.com; 389 N Main St; r from $60, campsites $10-18; ❄🛜🐾) Kitschy outside with red-and-white paint and garden gnomes a go-go, this motel's clean, stylish rooms are a big surprise: each one has a theme, from cowboy to Caribbean. Tent and RV camping across the street.

Anthony Lakes ⑧

🛏 Anthony Lakes Campground
Campground $

(☎541-894-2393; 47500 Anthony Lakes Hwy; campsites $10-14; ⏰Jul-Sep) Though it's 35 miles from town, this rustic but splendid campground is worth the drive (bring mosquito repellent!). It's opens only after the snow melts, so call first.

Union ⑨

🛏 Union Hotel
Hotel $$

(☎541-562-1200; www.thehistoricunionhotel. com; 326 N Main St; d $99-125, RV sites from $27; ❄❄🛜🐾) Fifteen miles southeast of La Grande, in the town of Union, is this very atmospheric old hotel. All 16 rooms are decorated individually, and none has a TV or telephone, though three come with kitchenette (there are common rooms with a TV and library).

La Grande ⑩

✗ Ten Depot Street
American $$

(☎541-963-8766; www.tendepotstreet.com; 10 Depot St; mains $12-35; ⏰5-10pm Mon-Sat; 🖊) This longtime local favorite offers some classics such as prime rib and seafood fettuccini, along with a few surprises like the Thai salad and lentil-pecan vegan burger.

Pendleton ⑫

✗ Hamley's Steakhouse
American $$

(☎541-278-1100; www.hamleysteakhouse.com; 8 SE Court Ave; steaks $34-54, dinner mains $16-26; ⏰5-8.30pm Sun-Thu, to 9pm Fri & Sat) This 150-seat steakhouse has been gorgeously done up with wood floors, stone accents and tin ceilings. There's a bar with sports on TV and the bathrooms have 'interesting' art work. Food is decent, with large portions.

✗ Prodigal Son Brewery
Pub $

(☎541-276-6090; www.prodigalsonbrewery.com; 230 SE Court Ave; mains $8-14; ⏰11am-10pm Tue-Sat, noon-9pm Sun; 👶) Pendleton's award-winning brewery is a popular place, even with families (there are two kids' rooms). It has a great atmosphere and 10 beers on tap, plus a pub menu that includes burgers, various salads and some surprises like Scotch egg and onion tarts.

🛏 Working Girls Old Hotel
Hotel $

(☎541-276-0730; www.pendletonunderground tours.org; 17 SW Emigrant Ave; d $75-95; ❄❄🛜) Run by **Pendleton Underground Tours** (☎800-226-6398; 37 SW Emigrant Ave; per person $15; ⏰dates vary), this former bordello offers five large, beautiful and antique-filled rooms. Only one is en suite; two have private hallway bathrooms. There's a guest kitchen and parlor. Best for those who don't need much service (there's no reception). Reserve ahead.

🛏 Pendleton House B&B
B&B $$

(☎541-276-8581; www.pendletonhousebnb. com; 311 N Main St; d $135-165; ❄❄🛜🐾) Near downtown is this pink 1917 Italian Renaissance mansion with its original furniture, wallpaper and drapes. The home's details are amazing (especially the communal shower), and there's a relaxing front patio with wicker furniture. Three of the five beautiful rooms (one with half-bath) share a bathroom.

Hells Canyon Loop

19

North America's deepest river gorge is more than just scorching temperatures and desolate landscapes. You'll find both, but you'll also find forested ridge tops, peaceful river valleys and hamlets.

TRIP HIGHLIGHTS

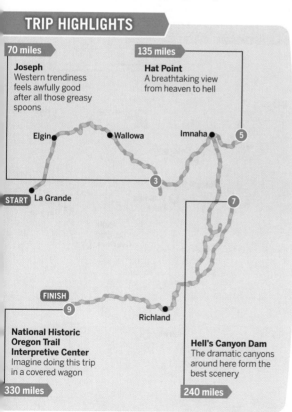

70 miles

Joseph
Western trendiness feels awfully good after all those greasy spoons

135 miles

Hat Point
A breathtaking view from heaven to hell

Elgin • • Wallowa

Imnaha •

START La Grande

7

FINISH
9

Richland

National Historic Oregon Trail Interpretive Center
Imagine doing this trip in a covered wagon

330 miles

Hell's Canyon Dam
The dramatic canyons around here form the best scenery

240 miles

4 DAYS
330 MILES/531KM

GREAT FOR...

BEST TIME TO GO
June to September – the road from Imnaha to Halfway is closed at other times.

 ESSENTIAL PHOTO

Capture the majesty of an 8000ft rise from river to peak at Hat Point.

BEST DAY
Exploring the vistas and valleys of Hells Canyon, stops 6 to 9.

19 | Hells Canyon Loop

In this remote corner of Oregon, at the foot of the Seven Devils Mountains, lies one of the Pacific Northwest's most spectacular sights: Hells Canyon, measuring 8043ft deep from peak to river. The few roads that access the canyon and the mountains above offer spectacular vistas but are only open in summer months, once the snows have melted and temperatures soar.

❶ La Grande

The Oregon Trail crossed this valley, and pioneers rested here before traversing the challenging Blue Mountains. La Grande is the best place in the region to stock up on provisions (trail mix? sunscreen? water?) before driving into the boondocks. Despite the number of services and the few blocks of historical brick architecture, the city isn't that memorable.

✕ ⮕ p207, p216

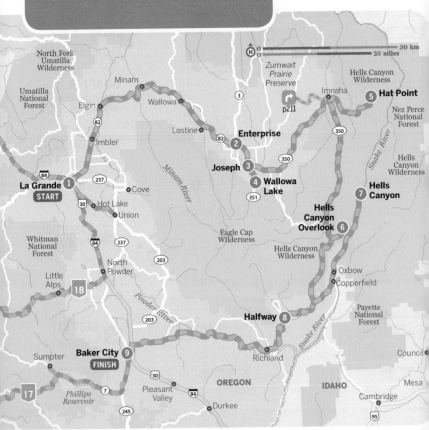

The Drive ❯❯ Take I-82 east and you'll soon be in farmlands hemmed in by mountains. After the tiny town of Minam, the road veers right to run along the Minam River through a beautiful, slim valley with pine-covered hillsides. You'll eventually drive through the small settlements of Wallowa and Lostine.

---

❷ Enterprise

Unlike nearby Joseph (which has arguably become *too* cute), Enterprise maintains its good old small-town atmosphere. In fact its downtown – two blocks of handsome buildings – is lonesome at times. It's a good, economical place to rest for the night and get any gear you may realize you need after all (fish hooks? bug spray?).

LINK YOUR TRIP

 17 Journey Through Time Scenic Byway

It's a seamless link: start in Baker City, where the Journey Through Time Scenic Byway ends.

18 Blue Mountains Loop

From La Grande, drive south 25 miles on Hwy 84 to North Powder or northwest toward Pendleton to hook up with this varied circuit.

DETOUR: ZUMWAIT PRAIRIE PRESERVE

Start: ❺ Hat Point (p212)

If you have a high-clearance vehicle and three to five hours to spare, detour up to Zumwait Prairie Preserve. Owned by the Nature Conservancy, this 51-sq-mile preserve is the largest remaining grassland of its kind in the USA. Several trails meander through the prairie, which is home to a vast number of hawks and eagles. To get there, take the dirt Camp Creek Rd, which departs Little Sheep Creek Hwy about 1 mile south of Imnaha.

The Wallowa Mountains Visitor Center is an invaluable place to stock up on information about Hells Canyon and its surrounding areas. Since it burned down in 2010, the center has been temporarily relocated to the **Wallowa County Chamber of Commerce** (📞541-426-4622, 800-585-4121; www.wallowacounty chamber.com; 309 S River St; ⏰8am-5pm Mon-Sat), but it will probably reopen at its previous highwayside location at some point in future.

🍴 🛏 p216

The Drive ❯❯ Joseph is only 6 miles down I-62.

TRIP HIGHLIGHT

❸ Joseph

If ever there was a trendy eastern Oregon town, it's Joseph. You can see its wealth right on the brick sidewalks, where well-groomed planter boxes and huge bronze

statues sit proudly on every downtown corner. In fact, Joseph is noted for its cast-bronze sculptures, thanks in part to **Valley Bronze** (📞541-432-7445; www.valleybronze.com; 18 S Main St; adult/child $15/free; ⏰tours 11am). Foundry tours are $15 per person. You can also visit the **Wallowa County Museum** (📞541-432-6095; 110 S Main St; adult/child $4/2; ⏰10am-4pm Memorial Day-late Sep), housed in an 1888 bank building and notable for its displays on pioneer and Nez Percé histories.

🍴 🛏 p216

The Drive ❯❯ Drive 6 miles south on Wallowa Lake Rd (Hwy 351).

---

❹ Wallowa Lake

Over 5 miles long and glacially formed, Wallowa Lake sits at the foot of the Wallowa Mountains, dominated at its southern end by 9617ft

DANNY WARREN / SHUTTERSTOCK ©

Chief Joseph Mountain. Giant old-growth conifers tower over a grassy beach area here, and families lounge in the sun, fish and otherwise frolic away the summer afternoons. A major trailhead starts at the south end of Wallowa Lake Rd. One popular trail from here is the 6-mile one-way jaunt to the gorgeous **Aneroid Lake**.

 p216

The Drive » Backtrack to Joseph then take Hwy 350 east. After leaving Joseph, the road passes a highway sign that tellingly reads 'Open Range Next 23 Miles,' then meets up with Little Sheep Creek, which it follows all the way to Imnaha. It's 30 miles to Imnaha, then another 24 miles to Hat Point.

TRIP HIGHLIGHT

❺ Hat Point

Now it's time to leave civilization. Get an early start for the 30-mile drive to **Imnaha** (p217), one of the most isolated towns in the USA. You may want to stay the night here (if you didn't in Joseph or Enterprise) before tackling the road ahead.

The area around Imnaha has some of the most dramatic scenery of the trip. A 24-mile gravel road leads to Hat Point (elevation 6982ft) from Imnaha. The good news: only the first 5 or 6 miles are steep. The road follows a spec-

tacular forested ridge, offering stunning views along the way. Be sure to stop at the **Granny View Vista** pullout. By the time you get to Hat Point, you'll wonder if the views could get any better. They do. Atop Hat Point stands the 82ft **Hat Point lookout tower**, a fire lookout offering dizzying 360-degree views of the Seven Devils, the Wallowas and Hells Canyon itself. And, yes, you can climb to the top. Without a doubt, this is one of the grandest views in the Pacific Northwest. In summer the road is

usually passable for all passenger cars.

The Drive » Head 24 miles back to Imnaha (p217) and follow the gravel Upper Imnaha Rd south for 30 miles to USFS Rd 39 (also called Wallowa Mountain Loop Rd). This is a dusty, scenic drive along the Imnaha River Valley. If you wish to avoid the dust, backtrack along Little Sheep Creek Hwy to USFS Rd 39 and swing left.

❻ Hells Canyon Overlook

Whichever route you take, after joining USFS Rd 39 continue southeast until the turnoff for the Hells Canyon

Hells Canyon Hikers look across the canyon

Overlook. This is the *only* overlook into Hells Canyon that's accessible by paved road, so take advantage of it. Although you don't get the same 360-degree views as from Hat Point, it's a marvelous vista nonetheless.

The Drive » This southern end of USFS Rd 39 is bucolic, with meadows and old farmhouses flanking the river. When you reach Hwy 86, turn left toward Copperfield and Oxbow.

- - - - - - - - - - -

TRIP HIGHLIGHT

⑦ Hells Canyon

At Copperfield you'll reach the Snake River and officially be at the very bottom of Hells Canyon. Down here, it's hot, hot, hot, and the canyon has absolutely no problem living up to its name. Cross the Snake River into Idaho and turn onto Idaho's Forest Rd 454 (also called Hells Canyon Dam Rd), which eventually dead-ends at Hells Canyon Dam. Here you will find the **Hells Canyon Visitor Center** (Idaho Power Rd, Hells Canyon Dam; ⊙8am-4pm May-Oct), which is a must if you need hiking trail information. The **Stud Creek Trail** begins immediately below the visitors center and passes some great spots to relax above the river and ponder the immensity of your surroundings.

North of Hells Canyon Dam and the visitors center, the Snake River returns to its natural flowing self, descending through epic scenery and roaring rapids. You can float those rapids by signing on with **Hells Canyon Adventures** (📞800-422-3568; www.hellscanyonadventures.com; jet-boat tours adult/child from $75/38; ⊙May-Sep), which offers rafting and jet-boat trips into an otherwise inaccessible area.

213

TOP TIP:
OLLOKOT
CAMPGROUND

One of our favorite spots to go is Ollokot Campground, not simply for camping but because it's so beautiful in there with the river and the trees. It's just off the Wallowa Mountain Loop Rd (USFS Rd 39), about an hour or so from Imnaha.

If there's time for a hike, tackle the 4.5-mile (out and back) **Allison Creek Trail**, which you'll pass about 12 miles north of Oxbow (10 miles before the dam); it has a total elevation gain of about 1200ft up Allison Creek Canyon.

🛏 p217

The Drive » From Hells Canyon, return by way of Hwy 86 to Halfway.

8 Halfway

Halfway is an idyllic little town lying on the southern edge of the Wallowa Mountains and surrounded by beautiful meadows dotted with old barns and hay fields. It's also a friendly spot with just enough tourist services to make it a decent base to explore the Hells Canyon Dam area. The **Pine Ranger Station** (📞541-742-7511; 38470 Pine Town Lane; ⏰7.45am-4.30pm Mon-Fri) is 1 mile south of Halfway and acts as the region's tourist information.

The **Pine Valley Museum** (admission by donation; ⏰10am-4pm Fri, Sat & Sun Memorial Day-Labor Day) is located right in the middle of town and has a few of the region's old photos and relics. It's open on weekdays and by request for a $5 suggested donation.

🛏 p217

The Drive » You're way more than halfway there! It's 54 miles through pastoral countryside to the end of the trail at Baker City.

TRIP HIGHLIGHT

9 Baker City

In the gold-rush days, Baker City was the largest metropolis between Salt Lake City and Portland, and a heady mix of miners, cowboys, shopkeepers and loggers kept the city's many saloons, brothels and gaming halls boisterously alive. Today the city's wide downtown streets and historical architecture recall its rich bygone days.

To remind yourself how easy your modern road trip is, stop in at the evocative **National Historic Oregon Trail Interpretive Center** (📞541-523-1843; www.oregontrail.blm.gov; 22267 Hwy 86; adult/child $8/free; ⏰9am-6pm Apr-Oct, to 4pm Thu-Sun Nov-Mar), one of the best museums in the state. Lying atop a hill 7 miles east of town along Hwy 86, the center contains interactive displays, artifacts and films that brilliantly illustrate the day-to-day realities of the pioneers who crossed this region in the 1800s. Outside you can stroll on the 4-mile interpretive path and spot the actual Oregon Trail.

🛏 p217

Hells Canyon White-water rafting

Eating & Sleeping

La Grande ❶

✗ Nells-N-Out   American $

(📞541-963-5733; 1704 Adams Ave; mains $3-8;
🕙10:30am-10pm) Long-running drive-thru
burger joint offering some of Eastern Oregon's
best fast food. Choose from a huge menu of
burgers (including specials), plus hotdogs,
sandwiches, wraps, salads and sides like
battered green beans and jalapeño poppers.
The milkshakes are legendary. A few shady
picnic tables are available.

🛏 Hot Lake Springs   Hotel $$

(📞541-963-4685; www.hotlakesprings.com;
66172 Hwy 203; d from $169, hot springs per
hour $25; 😊 ❄ 🛜) Eight miles southeast of
La Grande is this grand, restored hotel in a
historic building that was once a hospital. (If you
wander the halls, you may stumble across old
hospital equipment – not recommended late
at night, unless you're into that.) There's also
a spa, restaurant, museum, art gallery, bronze
foundry (tours available) and several hot spring
pools.

Enterprise ❷

✗ Terminal Gravity
Brewing   Pub Food $

(📞541-426-0158; www.terminalgravitybrewing.
com; 803 SE School St; mains $8-14; 🕙11am-
9pm Sun-Tue, to 10pm Wed-Sat) One of Oregon's
best breweries. There's limited inside seating,
but on a warm day you'll want to be at a picnic
table outside with a tasty IPA and buffalo burger
anyway. Sandwiches and salads dominate the
menu, with a few specials such as beer mac 'n'
cheese.

🛏 Ponderosa Motel   Motel $

(📞541-426-3186; 102 E Greenwood St; d from
$75; ❄ 🛜 🐾) Right downtown is this well-run

motel with attractive wood-and-stone facade.
The excellent rooms are clean and comfortable,
with lodge-like furniture. Prices skyrocket
during special events and drop in the off season.

Joseph ❸

✗ Embers Brewhouse   Brewpub $$

(www.embersbrewhouse.com; 206 N Main St;
mains $9-20; 🕙11am-9pm) Pizza, sandwiches,
salads and microbrews all go down easy in this
relaxed pub. On summer evenings the place to
be is on the front deck, with people-watching
opportunities and views of the Wallowas.

🛏 Bronze Antler B&B   B&B $$

(📞541-432-0230, 866-520-9769; www.
bronzeantler.com; 309 S Main St; d $145-238;
😊 ❄ 🛜) This restored arts-and-crafts home
offers three elegant rooms, each with private
bathroom, plus one luxurious suite with steam
shower and jets in the tub. There's also a bocce
court in the yard, and your friendly hosts know
the area well. A cat roams the premises.

Wallowa Lake ❹

✗ Vali's Alpine
Restaurant   Hungarian $$

(📞541-432-5691; www.valisrestaurant.com;
59811 Wallowa Lake Hwy; mains $14-21; 🕙5pm &
7pm seatings Wed-Sun Memorial Day-Labor Day)
Hungarian specialties such as cabbage rolls,
chicken paprika, beef kabobs and schnitzel are
all excellent here; there's a set menu item each
night (with a mix of options on Fridays). Do not
miss dessert. Credit cards are not accepted,
and reservations are required.

🛏 Wallowa Lake
State Park   Campground $

(📞541-432-4185, 800-551-6949; www.
oregonstateparks.org; 72214 Marina Lane; tent/

RV sites $20/30, yurts $42; 🐾) This popular lakeside state park offers more than 200 campsites, along with two yurts. Flush toilets, showers and firewood are available.

Imnaha ⑤

✖ Imnaha Store & Tavern
Tavern $

(☎541-577-3111; 102 Hat Point Rd; mains $6-18; ⌚9am-9pm) This store, restaurant and tavern is pretty much Imnaha's only option. It stocks minimal supplies but has a reliable bar menu (notable item: frog legs) and offers tent sites ($5).

🛏 Imnaha River Inn
Inn $$

(☎541-577-6002; www.imnahariverinn. com; 73946 Rimrock Rd; s/d from $70/130) A beautiful inn 5 miles north of Imnaha, with individually decorated cabin-like rooms, a games room with pool table, and lunch or dinner available (added fee). Two-night minimum.

Hells Canyon ⑦

🛏 Hells Canyon B&B
B&B $

(☎541-785-3373; www.hcbb.us; 49922 Homestead Rd; s/d $80/90; 😊❄🛜) Simple but great-value B&B in the Oxbow area, with low-slung simple rooms and an awesome deck.

Halfway ⑧

🛏 Pine Valley Lodge
Lodge $$

(☎541-742-2027; www.pvlodge.com; 163 N Main St; r $80-150; 😊❄🛜🐾) Halfway's fanciest accommodations, with 14 lovely and very comfortable rooms in four buildings, all surrounded by flowery gardens. There's a great porch with wicker rocking chairs, and tiny rooms that can be added to regular doubles (from $20); one cabin is also available. Some rooms have kitchenette; breakfast included.

Baker City ⑨

🛏 Geiser Grand Hotel
Hotel $$

(☎888-434-7374, 541-523-1889; www. geisergrand.com; 1996 Main St; d $99-189, ste $139-299; 😊❄🛜🐾) Baker City's downtown landmark and fanciest lodging is this meticulously restored Italian Renaissance Revival building, designed by John Bennes, an architect with his fingerprints all over Oregon's coolest buildings. The elegant rooms are spacious and decorated with old-style furniture, while the restaurant offers fine food and has a stunning stained-glass ceiling. There's a great old saloon, too.

To Bend & Back

20

You may be tempted to make a beeline for Bend – with its sunshine, microbrews and amazing array of outdoor activities – but take time to enjoy the spectacular stop-offs along the way.

TRIP HIGHLIGHTS

25 miles

Silver Falls State Park
Hike to 10 waterfalls in one beautiful state park

START
Salem

2

Sisters

FINISH
Eugene

7

5

260 miles

Terwilliger Hot Springs
Take a soak at one of Oregon's most stunning springs

175 miles

Bend
Outdoor activities galore (followed by a cold microbrew)

5 DAYS
310 MILES/500KM

GREAT FOR...

BEST TIME TO GO
April to October, though there's always something to do.

 ### ESSENTIAL PHOTO
South Falls in Silver Falls State Park.

 ### BEST MUSEUM
Bend's High Desert Museum offers great insight into the area.

20

To Bend & Back

Pack your snowshoes, swimsuit, hiking boots, daypack and kayak: you'll need them all in Bend. This high desert town enjoys glorious weather and blue skies 250 days a year – not to mention microbreweries and a quirky character for when you're ready to have fun. Along the drive to Bend, you'll experience waterfalls, hot springs and miles and miles of forest, making this an ideal trip for the outdoor adventurer.

1 Salem

Your trip begins in the state capital, just an hour south of Portland. Before setting off on your journey, stop for a little pioneer history at the **Willamette Heritage Center** (☎503-585-7012; www.willametteheritage.org; 1313 Mill St SE; adult/child $7/3; ◷10am-5pm Mon-Sat), which includes two homes, a parsonage, a Presbyterian church and a mill, all looking much like they did in the 1840s and '50s.

If you've got kids in tow, thrill them with a stop in the **Enchanted Forest** (☎503-371-4242; www.enchantedforest. com; 8462 Enchanted Way SE, Turner; adult/child $11.75/10.50; ◷10am-4pm, longer hours in summer), 7 miles south of Salem. This theme park is a fun fantasyland offering rides (extra charge), a haunted house, a European village and a Western town, among other things. Opening hours vary, so check the website.

✖ ⊨ p225

The Drive » Head 10 miles southeast on Hwy 22, then take Hwy 214 10 miles west to Silver Falls.

TRIP HIGHLIGHT

2 Silver Falls State Park

Hoping to glimpse a waterfall or two on your trip? How about 10? Oregon's largest state park packs in 10 waterfalls ranging in height from 27ft to 177ft, and you can see each and every one of them by hiking an 8-mile loop trail known as the **Trail of Ten Falls**. The best place to start the hike is the South Falls parking lot,

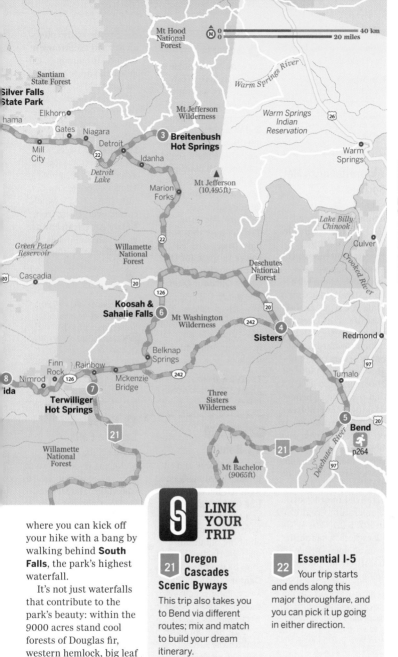

where you can kick off your hike with a bang by walking behind **South Falls**, the park's highest waterfall.

It's not just waterfalls that contribute to the park's beauty: within the 9000 acres stand cool forests of Douglas fir, western hemlock, big leaf maples and cedars, with

LINK YOUR TRIP

21 Oregon Cascades Scenic Byways

This trip also takes you to Bend via different routes; mix and match to build your dream itinerary.

22 Essential I-5

Your trip starts and ends along this major thoroughfare, and you can pick it up going in either direction.

ferns, Oregon grape and salmonberry covering the forest floor.

The Drive ›› Head back to Santiam Hwy/Hwy 22 and continue west for 40 miles, then strike north for 10 miles on Breitenbush Rd, just past Detroit Lake.

❸ Breitenbush Hot Springs

Set above the Breitenbush River on a 154-acre reserve inside Willamette National Forest, Breitenbush Hot Springs is as Oregon as it gets. Along with a fantastically relaxing soak, you'll get a solid dose of earthy Oregonian mellowness. Hot mineral water burbles out of several springs at a scorching 180°F to 200°F (82°C to 93°C) and is cooled to prime soaking temperatures with water from the river. There are seven pools in all. Three overlook a pretty meadow and one of these is a silent pool. Another four pools are arranged in order of temperature, from 100°F to 107°F (37°C to 41°C). Elsewhere, a sauna sits over an open spring and is entirely heated by the steam.

The Drive ›› Head back to Hwy 22 and drive south for 31 miles. This scenic stretch of road will meet up with Hwy 20, and then it's 26 more miles to Sisters.

❹ Sisters

Looking like a movie set for a spaghetti Western, Sisters was once a stagecoach stop and trade town for loggers and ranchers. Today it's a bustling tourist destination whose main street is lined with boutiques, art galleries and eateries housed in Western-facade buildings.

There's nothing specific here that you have to see – unless you're in town for the Sisters Rodeo in June or the **Outdoor Quilt Show** (☑541-549-0989; www.sistersoutdoorquiltshow.org; ⏱2nd Sat in Jul) – but it's still a cute town to mosey around in for a while.

The Drive ›› From Sisters it's a quick 20-minute hop down to Bend.

TRIP HIGHLIGHT

❺ Bend

Hip, outdoorsy and enjoying ridiculously good weather, Bend is the darling of the high desert. You could spend a week here hiking, paddling, climbing, mountain biking – the list goes on. Stop by the **Bend Visitor Center** (☑541-382-8048; www.visitbend.com; 750 NW Lava Rd; ⏱9am-5pm Mon-Fri, 10am-4pm Sat & Sun) to explore your options.

With the lovely Deschutes River carving its way through the heart of the city, Bend also offers an attractive downtown: explore its boutiques, galleries and dining options on foot (p264).

To learn more about the area, don't miss the superb – and rather extensive – **High Desert Museum** (☑541-382-4754; www.highdesertmuseum.org; 59800 S US 97; adult/child $15/9; ⏱9am-5pm May-Oct, 10am-4pm Nov-Apr), which covers everything from Native American culture to live animal displays on 135 acres of pine forest.

✕ 🛏 p225, p235

The Drive ›› Take Hwy 20 north, curving back through Sisters, then go south where Hwy 126/McKenzie Hwy splits off. Look for the turnoff to the Koosah & Sahalie Falls about 5 miles later. Total distance: 57 miles.

❻ Koosah & Sahalie Falls

Right off the roadside of McKenzie Hwy are two of Oregon's most impressive waterfalls. The McKenzie River plunges 120ft over Sahalie Falls – the more dramatic of the two – and after a good snowmelt it drenches everything around it in mist as it roars into the frothy pool below.

Only 0.3 miles downstream, Koosah Falls measures 90ft and is wider and easier going than its upstream neighbor. The stretch

MARILYN D. LAMBERTZ / SHUTTERSTOCK ©

Silver Falls State Park South Falls

of the McKenzie River between the falls is utterly spectacular, with roaring cascades that tumble over basalt boulders, through massive logjams and into deep, dark pools.

The Drive >> Keep following Hwy 126 another 24 miles and turn left on Aufderheide Rd. Continue on for 8 miles more.

TRIP HIGHLIGHT

❼ Terwilliger Hot Springs

Also known as Cougar Hot Springs for its proximity to Cougar Reservoir, this wildly popular hot springs near Terwilliger Reservoir has a beautiful setting among the trees in the Willamette National Forest.

The Drive >> Keep following Hwy 126 another 19 miles to the town of Vida.

❽ Vida

Oregon is known for its wooden bridges, and in Vida is the state's second-longest, **Goodpasture Bridge**. A wooden truss bridge, it's painted white and looks almost like a small-town church – albeit a 237ft-long church that straddles a river. It's right on the highway, so you can stop for a picture (it is a rather good-looking bridge) or just point and say, 'Oooooh,' as you whiz past. Look for it on the left after Mile 26.

The Drive >> You're on the home stretch: it's just under 30 miles to Eugene.

❾ Eugene

It's back to civilization in dynamic and liberal Eugene, full of energetic college students, pretty riverside parks and a plethora of restaurant choices.

Where to start? For great fun and a quintessential introduction to Eugene's peculiar vitality, try to time your visit with the **Saturday Market** (☎541-686-8885; www.eugenesaturdaymarket. org; 8th & Oak St; ⏱10am-5pm Sat Apr–mid-Nov), held each Saturday from April through mid-November. Otherwise, wander the **5th St Public Market** (☎541-484-0383; www.5stmarket.com; cnr 5th Ave & High St; ⏱shops 10am-7pm Mon-Sat, 11am-6pm Sun), an old mill that now anchors several dozen restaurants, cafes and boutique stores.

To wrap up your trip with a bit of culture, stop by the **Jordan Schnitzer Museum of Art** (☎541-346-3027; http://jsma.uoregon.edu; 1430 Johnson Lane; adult/child $5/free; ⏱11am-5pm Tue-Sun, to 8pm Wed). This renowned museum offers a 13,000-piece rotating permanent collection with an Asian art specialty. Highlights include a 10-panel Korean folding screen and a standing Thai Buddha in gold leaf.

✕ 🛏 p225, p243

FIRE ON MT WASHINGTON

About a mile after you join Hwy 20, the lush greenery dwindles and the trees start to look like a weird art project involving charred toothpicks. This is the handiwork of a pair of wildfires – the Bear Butte Fire and the Booth Fire – that joined together in the summer of 2003 to become the B&B Complex Fire, burning over 90,000 acres of the Cascades.

It's hard not to want to stare at the devastation. But keep your eyes on the road for now, because you can pull over at the **Mt Washington Viewpoint,** between Miles 84 and 85. Here you'll find dramatic views of the mountains and seven interpretive signs that give you the full picture.

Eating & Sleeping

Salem ①

✗ Word of Mouth Bistro Bistro $
(☎503-930-4285; www.wordofsalem.com; 140 17th St NE; mains $7-14; ⊙7am-3pm Wed-Sun) If crème brûlée French toast sounds good, then make a beeline to this friendly and excellent bistro. Other tasty (and unusual) treats include the blueberry pancakes, asparagus and brie omelette and prime rib Benedict. Gourmet sandwiches, salads and burgers rule the lunch menu.

✗ Wild Pear Deli $
(☎503-378-7515; www.wildpearcatering. com; 372 State St; mains $11-14, pizzas $7-11; ⊙10:30am-6:30pm Mon-Sat) Popular modern deli serving up tasty soups, sandwiches and salads, along with fancier options like a lobster melt. There's also a Greek wrap, artichoke fritters, pizzas, homemade pastries and even a surprisingly good *pho* (Vietnamese noodle soup) – all combined with good, efficient service.

🛏 Grand Hotel Hotel $$
(☎877-540-7800; www.grandhotelsalem.com; 201 Liberty St SE; r from $159; ❄@🌐🏊) This upscale hotel is next to the city's conference center. Most standard rooms have sitting areas, and all are stylish, modern and elegant. It's geared toward business travelers, with amenities like indoor pool, spa, gym, restaurant and lounge; a breakfast buffet is also included.

Bend ⑤

✗ Victorian Café Cafe $
(1404 NW Galveston Ave; mains $8-15; ⊙7am-2pm) One of Bend's best breakfast spots, Victorian Café is especially awesome for its eggs Benedict (nine kinds). It's also good for sandwiches, burgers and salads. There's really nice outdoor seating in summer. Be ready to wait for a table, especially on weekends.

✗ Pine Tavern American $$
(www.pinetavern.com; 967 NW Brooks St; mains $14-35; ⊙11.30am-9pm Sun-Thu, to 10pm Fri & Sat; 👶) Long-running, popular and traditional family-friendly restaurant near the river. Everyone should find something to like here, from the great half-pound burger to smoked-salmon salad to house meat loaf to rib-eye steak. Awesome back patio.

🛏 Mill Inn Inn $
(☎541-389-9198; www.millinn.com; 642 NW Colorado Ave; d incl breakfast $100-170; ⊖🌐) A 10-room boutique hotel with small, classy rooms decked out with velvet drapes and comforters; four share outside bathrooms. Full breakfast and hot-tub use is included, and there are nice small patios on which to hang out.

Eugene ⑨

✗ 5th Street Public Market Fast Food $
(www.5stmarket.com; 296 E 5th Ave; ⊙8am-7pm Mon-Sat, 11am-6pm Sun) Italian? Mexican? Burgers? Options abound in this cheery market that anchors several dozen restaurants, cafes and stores around a pretty central courtyard.

✗ Beppe & Gianni's Trattoria Italian $$
(☎541-683-6661; www.beppeandgiannis. net; 1646 E 19th Ave; mains $19-24; ⊙5-9pm Sun-Thu, to 10pm Fri & Sat) One of Eugene's most beloved restaurants and its favorite Italian food is at Beppe & Gianni's. Homemade pastas are the real deal here, and the desserts are excellent. Expect a wait, especially on weekends.

🛏 Campbell House Inn $$$
(☎541-343-1119, 800-264-2519; www. campbellhouse.com; 252 Pearl St; r $129-349; ⊖❄@🌐🏊) A large inn with 18 rooms and lovely common spaces, Campbell House also has a lush garden, popular for weddings. Choose from small, cozy rooms, spacious suites with Jacuzzi and fireplace, or a two-bedroom suite. Well located on a hill in an upscale neighborhood; hot breakfast included.

Oregon Cascades Scenic Byways

21

Oregon's Central Cascades are a bonanza of natural wonder. Scenic byways pack in lush forests, thundering waterfalls, snow-capped mountains, high desert and lakes galore.

TRIP HIGHLIGHTS

178 miles

Terwilliger Hot Springs
A series of hot pools in a gorgeous natural setting

139 miles

Dee Wright Observatory
A Civilian Conservation Corps project offering spectacular views

Sisters

⑧

⑨

⑫

Bend

Mt Bachelor

START/ FINISH
Westfir

④

Salt Creek Falls
Right off the road is the second-highest waterfall in Oregon

26 miles

152 miles

Proxy Falls
Sheer veils of water tumble over columnar basalt

4 DAYS
228 MILES/367KM

GREAT FOR...

BEST TIME TO GO
Go June through September to avoid seasonal road closures.

ESSENTIAL PHOTO
Salt Creek Falls, the second-highest waterfall in Oregon.

✓ **BEST HOT SPRINGS**
Terwilliger Hot Springs at Cougar Reservoir.

Classic Trip

21 Oregon Cascades Scenic Byways

The region around Oregon's Central Cascades is, without a doubt, some of the most spectacular terrain in the entire state. But one scenic byway just isn't enough to see it all. Here you have our version of an Oregon sampler platter: a loop that brings together several of the best roads to create a majestic route full of the state's best features.

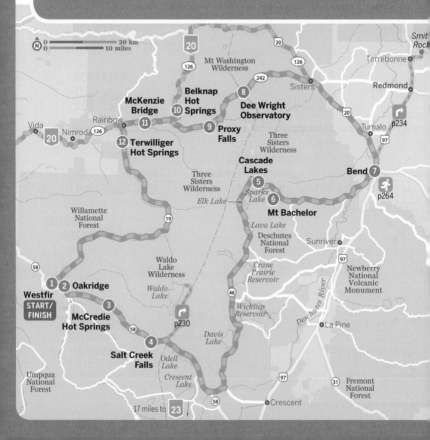

1 Westfir

Before you spend several days enjoying abundant natural wonders, start with a quick photo op of an entirely man-made one: Oregon's longest covered bridge, the 180ft **Office Bridge**. Built in 1944, the bridge features a covered walkway to enable pedestrians to share the way with logging trucks crossing the Willamette River.

If you plan to do some exploring or mountain biking in the area, pick up a map of the Willamette National Forest at the **Middle Fork Ranger District** (☎541-782-2283; 46375 Hwy 58, Westfir; ☻8am-4:30pm Mon-Fri, plus Sat in summer).

🛏 p235

LINK YOUR TRIP

20 **To Bend & Back** One trip isn't enough to cover the Cascades; this complementary route offers alternate paths through the same countryside.

23 **Crater Lake Circuit** Crater Lake is a must-see, and it's just south of the Cascades. Take Hwy 97 south from Bend to join this route.

The Drive ≫ Oakridge is just a few miles to the east on either Hwy 58 or Westfir–Oakridge Rd.

2 Oakridge

Oakridge is one of Oregon's mountain-biking meccas. There are hundreds of miles of trails around town, ranging from short, easy loops to challenging single-track routes. For novice riders, the **Warrior Fitness Trail** is a mostly flat 12-mile loop. The **Larison Creek Trail** is a challenging ride through old-growth forests, and the 16-mile **Alpine Trail** is considered the 'crown jewel' of the local trails for its 7-mile downhill stretch. **Oregon Adventures** (☎541-968-5397; www.oregon-adventures.com; 47921 Hwy 58; day trips from $30, 3-day tour $649; ☻Jul-Sep) offers shuttles to the top so you can skip the climb; it also offers bike-tour packages.

🛏 p235

The Drive ≫ From Oakridge Hwy 58 climbs steadily up the Cascade Range's densely forested western slope. Your next stop is about 10 miles east of Oakridge; park on the right just past Mile Marker 45.

3 McCredie Hot Springs

Because **McCredie Hot Springs** (☎541-782-4146; Hwy 58, Oakridge; per person $6; ☻dawn-dusk) lies just off the highway, it's a very popular spot for everyone from mountain bikers fresh off the trails near Oakridge to truckers plying Hwy 58. Despite this, it's worth a stop if only because it's the site of one of the largest – and hottest – thermal pools in Oregon. If you can hit it early in the morning or late in the evening midweek, you could have the place to yourself.

There are five pools in all: two upper pools that are often dangerously hot (as in don't-even-dip-your-foot-in hot), two warm riverside pools and one smaller, murkier but usually perfectly heated pool tucked back into the trees. **Salt Creek** rushes past only steps from the springs and is ideal for splashing down with icy water.

The Drive ≫ Keep heading east another 12 miles and pull off the highway at the signed parking lot.

TRIP HIGHLIGHT

4 Salt Creek Falls

At 286ft, this monster of a waterfall is Oregon's second highest. After a good snowmelt, this aqueous behemoth really roars, making for one of the most spectacular sights on the trip. Walk from the parking lot to the viewpoint and there below, in a massive basalt amphitheater hidden by the towering

trees, 50,000 gallons of water pour every minute over a cliff into a giant, dark, tumultuous pool. Be sure to hike the short trail downhill toward the bottom of the falls. It's lined with rhododendrons that put on a colorful show in springtime, and the views of the falls on the way down are stunning.

Salt Creek Falls is also the starting point for some excellent short hikes, including a 1.5-mile jaunt to **Diamond Creek Falls** and a 4.75-mile hike to **Vivian Lake**.

The Drive >> Continue 19 miles along Hwy 58 until you reach the Cascade Lakes Scenic Byway (Hwy 46), which winds its way north through numerous tiny lakes and up to Mt Bachelor. This road is closed from November to May; as an alternative, follow Hwy 97 to Bend.

---

⑤ Cascade Lakes

We could get all scientific and explain how lava from nearby volcanoes created the lakes around this area, or we could just tell you that Hwy 46 isn't called the Cascade Lakes Scenic Byway for nothing. The road winds past lake after beautiful lake – **Davis Lake**, **Crane Prairie Reservoir**, **Lava Lake**, **Elk Lake** – all worth a stop. Most have outstanding camping, trout fishing, boating and invigorating swimming ('invigorating' being a euphemism for *cold*).

We love **Sparks Lake** for its scenic beauty set against the backdrop of Mt Bachelor, and it's perfect for peaceful paddling. If you find yourself without a boat, **Wanderlust Tours** (☑800-862-2862; www.wanderlusttours.com; Suite 13, 61535 S Hwy 97, Bend; canoe & kayak day tour adult/child $75/55) can hook you up with a guided canoe or kayak tour.

🛏 p235

The Drive >> Mt Bachelor is just a few miles past Sparks Lake. If Hwy 46 is closed for the season, you can backtrack from Bend to reach Mt Bachelor.

---

⑥ Mt Bachelor

Glorious Mt Bachelor (9065ft) provides Oregon's best skiing. Here Central Oregon's cold, continental air meets up with the warm, wet Pacific air. The result is tons of fairly dry snow and plenty of sunshine, and with 370in of snow a year, the season begins in November and can last until May.

At **Mount Bachelor Ski Resort** (☑800-829-2442; www.mtbachelor.com; lift tickets adult/child $69/42, cross-country day pass $15/8) rentals are available at the base of the lifts. Mt Bachelor grooms about 35 miles of cross-country trails, though the day

DETOUR:
WALDO LAKE

Start: ❹ Salt Creek Falls (p229)

There's no shortage of lakes in the area, but lovely Waldo Lake stands out for its amazing clarity. Because it's at the crest of the Cascades, water doesn't flow into it from other sources; the only water that enters it is rainfall and snowfall, making it one of the purest bodies of water in the world. In fact, it's so clear that objects in the water are visible 100ft below the surface. You can swim in the summer months (it's too cold in the winter), and if you're feeling ambitious after playing 'I Spy' on the lakebed, you can hike the **Waldo Lake Trail**, a 22-mile loop that circumnavigates the lake.

To get there, head 2 miles east of Salt Creek Falls on Hwy 58, and turn left at the Waldo Lake Sno-Park; follow the signs for 8 more miles to the lake.

Proxy Falls

pass (weekends and holidays $17, weekdays $14) may prompt skiers to check out the free trails at **Dutchman Flat Sno-Park**, just past the turnoff for Mt Bachelor on Hwy 46.

The Drive » Ready to add a little civilization to your rugged outdoor adventure? Head east to Bend, which is just 22 miles away.

❼ Bend

Sporting gear is de rigueur in a town where you can go rock-climbing in the morning, hike through lava caves in the afternoon, and stand-up paddleboard yourself into the sunset. Plus you'll probably be enjoying all that activity in great weather, as the area gets more than 250 days of sunshine each year (don't forget the sunscreen!).

Explore downtown on foot (p264), and be sure to check out the excellent **High Desert Museum** (☎541-382-4754; www.high desertmuseum.org; 59800 S US 97; adult/child $15/9; ⊙9am-5pm May-Oct, 10am-4pm Nov-Apr). It charts the exploration and settlement of the West, but it's no slog through history. The fascinating Native American exhibit shows off several wigwams' worth of impressive artifacts, and live animal exhibits and living history are sure to be hits with the kids.

✕ 🛏 p225, p235

The Drive » Head 22 miles north to Sisters, then drive northwest along Hwy 242. This is part of the McKenzie Pass–Santiam Pass Scenic Byway – closed during the winter months. Your next stop is 15 miles from Sisters.

TRIP HIGHLIGHT

❽ Dee Wright Observatory

Perched on a giant mound of lava rock, built entirely of lava rock, in the middle of a field of lava rock, stands the historic Dee Wright Observatory. The structure, built in 1935 by Franklin D Roosevelt's Civilian Conservation Corps, offers spectacular views in all directions. The observatory windows, called 'lava tubes,' were placed to highlight all the prominent Cascade peaks that can be seen from the summit, including Mt Washington, Mt Jefferson, North Sister, Middle Sister and a host of others.

The Drive » Head west on Hwy 242 for 13 miles to Mile

Classic Trip

WHY THIS IS A CLASSIC TRIP
BECKY OHLSEN,
WRITER

This trip is all about the best of Oregon's outdoor pleasures. The Central Cascades offer hours' worth of hiking trails that lead you to crisp, refreshing lake swims and gorgeous waterfalls, or – if you're more into relaxing after a long drive – a variety of natural hot springs, from rustic to relatively fancy.

Top: McKenzie River
Left: Dee Wright Observatory
Right: Salt Creek Falls

CHRISTIAN HEEB / GETTY IMAGES ©

ZEB ANDREWS / GETTY IMAGES ©

LOREN L MASSETH / SHUTTERSTOCK ©

Marker 64 and look for the well-signed Proxy Falls trailhead.

TRIP HIGHLIGHT

9 Proxy Falls

With all the waterfalls around the Central Cascades – hundreds of them in Oregon alone – it's easy to feel like, 'You've seen one, you've seen 'em all.' Not so fast. Grab your camera and see if you're not at least a little impressed by photogenic Proxy Falls. If there were a beauty contest for waterfalls, Proxy would certainly be in the running, scattering into sheer veils down a mossy wall of columnar basalt. It's not even like the falls make you work for it: it's an easy 1.3-mile loop from the parking area. If you want to save the best for last, take the path in the opposite direction from what the sign suggests so you hit Upper Proxy Falls first and you can build up to the even better Lower Proxy Falls.

The Drive >> Nine miles from the falls, turn right on Hwy 126 (McKenzie Hwy); Belknap is just 1.4 miles away.

10 Belknap Hot Springs

Although nudity is the norm at most hot springs, Belknap is the sort of hot spring resort you can take your grandmother to and neither of you will feel out of place.

233

Classic Trip

Two giant swimming pools filled with 103°F (40°C) mineral water provide optimum soaking conditions in a family environment. The McKenzie River rushes by below, trees tower over everything, and everyone still has a good time. An excellent alternative to camping, the resort has rooms for nearly all budgets.

🛏 p235

The Drive » Head southwest on Hwy 126 for 6 miles to get to your next stop.

---

⑪ McKenzie Bridge

Although from the road it looks like there is nothing but trees, there's actually plenty to do around here, including fishing on the McKenzie River and hiking on the nearby **McKenzie**

VOLCANO SIGHTS

The Cascades are a region of immense volcanic importance. Lava fields can be seen from McKenzie Pass and along Hwy 46. Road cuts expose gray ash flows. Stratovolcanoes like South Sister and Mt Bachelor and shield volcanoes like Mt Washington tower over the landscape. Although it's not obvious when you drive to the center of **Newberry National Volcanic Monument** (39 miles south of Bend), you're actually inside the caldera of an active, 500-sq-mile volcano. What could be stranger than that?

↱ DETOUR: SMITH ROCK

Start: ⑦ Bend (p231)

Best known for its glorious rock climbing, **Smith Rock State Park** (☎800-551-6949; www.oregonstateparks.org; 9241 NE Crooked River Dr; day use $5) boasts rust-colored 800ft cliffs that tower over the pretty Crooked River, just 25 miles north of Bend. Nonclimbers can enjoy miles of hiking trails, some of which involve a little rock scrambling.

River National Recreation Trail. To learn more about all your recreational options, stop at the **McKenzie Ranger Station** (☎541-822-3381; www.fs.fed.us/r6/willamette; 57600 McKenzie Hwy; ⏰8am-4:30pm Mon-Sat), about 2 miles east of town. The rangers are founts of information, plus you can find anything you ever wanted to know about the McKenzie River trail, including maps and books.

🛏 p235

The Drive » About 6 miles west of McKenzie Bridge, turn left on Hwy 19 (aka Aufderheide Memorial Drive) just past Rainbow. After almost 8 miles, you'll come to the parking lot from which you'll take a 0.25-mile trail through old-growth forest.

TRIP HIGHLIGHT

⑫ Terwilliger Hot Springs

In a picturesque canyon in the Willamette National Forest is one of the state's most stunning hot springs. From a fern-shrouded hole, scorching water spills into a pool that maintains a steady minimum temperature of 108°F (42°C). The water then cascades into three successive pools, each one cooler than the one above it. Sitting there staring up at the trees is an utterly sublime experience. After hiking back to the car, you can even jump into Cougar Reservoir from the rocky shore below the parking lot.

The Drive » From Terwilliger Hot Springs, take Aufderheide/Hwy 19 south 41 miles to return to Westfir.

Eating & Sleeping

Westfir ❶

🛏 Westfir Lodge · Lodge $
(📞541-782-3103; www.westfirlodge.com; 47365 1st St; d $90-140; 😄 ❄ 🛜) A stone's throw from Oregon's longest covered bridge is this B&B lodge with eight homey guest rooms. Some rooms share bathrooms down the hall. Check out the central vault, left over from when this building used to be a lumber company office.

Oakridge ❷

🛏 Oakridge Motel · Motel $
(📞541-782-2432; www.theoakridgemotel.com; 48197 Hwy 58; r $45-60; 😄 ❄ 🛜🐾) With a log exterior and wooden walls inside, this otherwise run-of-the-mill motel is slightly more interesting than some others.

Cascade Lakes ❺

🛏 Cultus Lake Resort · Cabin $$
(📞541-408-1560; www.cultuslakeresort.com; Hwy 46; cabins $85-175; 😊 mid-May–Sep; 🐾) This pleasant lakeside resort offers several homey cabins with a two-night minimum; from July 4 to Labor Day they rent by the week only. There's a restaurant and marina, too.

🛏 Sparks Lake Campground · Campground
(Hwy 46; campsites free; 😊 Jul-Sep) One of the most scenically situated campgrounds on the Cascade Lakes Scenic Byway, with views of Mt Bachelor. Pit toilets available; no water.

Bend ❼

🍴 Blacksmith · American $$$
(📞541-318-0588; www.bendblacksmith.com; 211 NW Greenwood Ave; mains $25-42; 😊 4-10pm Mon-Thu, to midnight Fri & Sat, 4-9pm Sun) This upscale restaurant offers cowboy comfort food with a twist, such as cider-brined pork chop with Brussels sprouts, Cajun beef medallions and grilled shrimp with house-made grits.

🍴 Deschutes Brewery & Public House · Brewpub $$
(📞541-382-9242; www.deschutesbrewery. com; 1044 NW Bond St; 😊 11am-10pm Sun-Thu, to 10pm Fri & Sat) Bend's first microbrewery serves up plenty of food at its beautiful two-story restaurant with balcony seating. Handcrafted beers include Mirror Pond Pale Ale, Black Butte Porter and Obsidian Stout; its Red Chair NWPA was voted 'world's best beer' in 2012 by the World Beer Awards. Free tours are given every hour from 1pm to 4pm at its plant at 901 SW Simpson Ave.

🛏 McMenamins Old St Francis School · Hotel $$
(📞541-382-5174; www.mcmenamins.com; 700 NW Bond St; d $155-245; 😄 ❄ 🛜) One of McMenamins' best venues, this schoolhouse has been remodeled into a classy 19-room hotel – two rooms even have side-by-side clawfoot tubs. An addition will add 40 new rooms. The fabulous tiled saltwater Turkish bath is worth the stay alone, though nonguests can soak for $5. A restaurant-pub, three bars, a movie theater and creative artwork complete the picture.

Belknap Hot Springs ❿

🛏 Belknap Hot Springs Resort · Resort $$
(📞541-822-3512; www.belknaphotsprings.com; Hwy 126, nr Hwy 242, McKenzie Bridge; campsites $35, r $100-185, cabins $60-400, day use only $7-12) In addition to soaking, the resort boasts an 18-room lodge, 14 private cabins and 15 tent sites, so it's affordable for nearly all budgets.

McKenzie Bridge ⓫

🛏 Cedarwood Lodge · Cabin $$
(📞541-822-3351; www.cedarwoodlodge.com; 56535 McKenzie Hwy; cabins $115-185; 😊 closed Nov–mid-Apr; 🛜) Ensconce yourself in one of eight rustic, comfortable, fully equipped cabins set above the McKenzie River.

Essential I-5

22

Taking the direct route? That doesn't mean you have to miss out on Oregon's road-trip staples. Right off the I-5 lie pioneer history, covered bridges, even a little Shakespeare.

TRIP HIGHLIGHTS

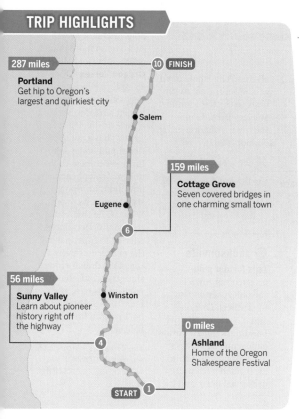

287 miles

Portland
Get hip to Oregon's largest and quirkiest city

● Salem

159 miles

Cottage Grove
Seven covered bridges in one charming small town

Eugene ●

6

56 miles

Sunny Valley
Learn about pioneer history right off the highway

● Winston

4

0 miles

Ashland
Home of the Oregon Shakespeare Festival

START 1

10 FINISH

1–2 DAYS
287 MILES/462KM

GREAT FOR...

BEST TIME TO GO
March through October, when everything is open.

ESSENTIAL PHOTO
Any of the covered bridges of Cottage Grove.

BEST FOR CULTURE
A night of theater at Ashland's Shakespeare Festival.

22 Essential I-5

The word 'interstate' seldom evokes a road-tripper's dream itinerary, but I-5 will dash those preconceived notions. Oregon's major thoroughfare takes you through mountains, farmland and forests, and there's plenty to see and do along the way — provided you know which exits to take. Just off the highway, you'll find historical sites, roadside attractions and more. It's also the jumping-off place for many of Oregon's backroad gems.

TRIP HIGHLIGHT

1 Ashland

Prithee, fair traveler, begin thy trip in Ashland, and get thee to the box office, for the players of the **Oregon Shakespeare Festival** (OSF; ☎541-482-4331; www.osfashland.org; Main & Pioneer Sts; tickets $30-119) do strut and fret upon three stages each year from February through October. Back in the Victorian era, Ashland was known for its sulfurous mineral springs that smell not unlike rotten eggs. But now the festival's 10 productions are Ashland's primary claim to fame and draw visitors from all over. The whole town gets in on the act, with nods to the bard found at every turn. Explore the town's historic heart on foot (p262).

✕ ⌂ p243, p251

The Drive ›› From Ashland, head 11 miles north on I-5 and take exit 30, then go west on OR-238 for 6 miles.

2 Jacksonville

This former gold-prospecting town is the oldest settlement in southern Oregon and a National Historic Landmark. Small but endearing, the town's main drag, California St, is lined with well-preserved brick-and-wood buildings dating from the 1880s. But the best place to get in touch with local history is to wander the 32-acre **Jacksonville Cemetery**, at the top of Cemetery Rd, which you access at East E St and N Oregon St, where historic pioneer gravesites chronicle wars, epidemics and other untimely deaths.

The Drive ›› Take Oregon St north and it will meet up with I-5 in Gold Hill. The well-signed Vortex is a bit over 4 miles north of Gold Hill on Sardine Creek Rd.

3 Gold Hill

Some attractions will suck you in more than others, but Gold Hill's **Oregon Vortex** (☎541-855-1543; www.oregonvortex.com; 4303 Sardine Creek L Fork Rd; adult/child $12.50/9; ◷9am-4pm Mar-Oct, to 5pm Jun-Aug) has gravitational pull on its side, luring visitors with its unexplained phenomena: how did that broom stand up on its own? What made that water run uphill? Detractors will try to explain away the mysterious events that have drawn crowds since the 1930s, but it just sounds like, 'Blah, blah, physics, blah.' Isn't it more fun to just believe?

The Drive ›› Backtrack to I-5 and go north 27 miles to exit 71. Sunny Valley is right off the highway.

TRIP HIGHLIGHT

4 Sunny Valley

Sunny Valley serves as a quick, convenient stop for a little Oregon pioneer history. Visible from the highway, you could mistake it for a Western-themed rest stop, thanks mostly to the **Applegate Trail Interpretive Center** (📞541-472-8545; www.rogueweb.com/interpretive; I-5 exit 71; admission $5.95; ⏰10am-5pm Fri-Sun late May-Sep), an excellent little museum gussied up like a spaghetti-Western storefront, where history is revived with taxidermy and sound effects.

If the museum's closed, you can still check out the **covered bridge** that crosses **Grave Creek** and the namesake grave itself, belonging to one Martha Crowley, a pioneer girl who died of typhoid fever

LINK YOUR TRIP

21 Oregon Cascades Scenic Byways

From Eugene, drive 42 miles east to Westfir to kick off a tour of some of the state's most beautiful scenery.

23 Crater Lake Circuit

Hop off at Medford for an inland loop that includes the serene and mysterious Crater Lake.

on the Applegate wagon train.

The Drive ⟫ Get back on I-5 and travel 71 miles to exit 112. Take Hwy 99 N for just under 9 miles.

----

⑤ Winston

Tiny Winston itself isn't much of a drawcard, but 10 miles southwest is where you'll find the **Wildlife Safari** (☎541-679-6761; www.wildlifesafari. net; 1790 Safari Rd, I-5 exit 119; adult/child $18/12; ⊙10am-4pm mid-Nov–mid-Mar, 9am-5pm mid-Mar–mid-Nov; ♿), an animal attraction you don't even

have to get out of your car for. Here you can drive around a 600-acre park dotted with inquisitive ostriches, camels, giraffes, lions, tigers and bears (oh, my!) among other exotic animals, then hop right back on the highway and keep driving.

The Drive ⟫ Follow OR-42 north to I-5, then travel 48 miles north to get to Cottage Grove. To get to the Mosby Creek bridges, go east on Main St, pass under I-5, then continue 2.5 miles on Mosby Creek Rd and turn left on Layng Rd to access parking.

TRIP HIGHLIGHT

⑥ Cottage Grove

With seven covered bridges around town, Cottage Grove has rightfully earned its nickname of the Covered Bridge Capital of Oregon. But the most famous bridge here is a small, open-top railroad trestle that had a cameo at the beginning of the movie *Stand By Me,* when the four pre-teen boys set off on their journey into the woods. The rails have been paved over, and

Winston Elk

the **Mosby Creek Trestle Bridge** is now part of the **Row River Trail**, easily accessible for hikers, bikers and film buffs. It's also kind of a two-fer, as it crosses the creek just a couple hundred feet from Lane County's oldest covered bridge, the photogenic **Mosby Creek Bridge**, built in 1920.

The Drive » Take Mosby Creek Rd back to I-5, then travel north 17.5 miles and take exit 192 for Eugene.

- - - - - - - - - - - - - -

7 Eugene

Fun-loving Eugene is full of youthful energy, liberal politics and alternative lifestylers, making it a vibrant stop along your I-5 travels. Here you'll find a great art scene, exceptionally fine restaurants, boisterous festivals, miles of riverside paths and several lovely parks. A hike up wooded **Skinner Butte**, directly north of downtown, provides good orientation and a bit of exercise (though you can drive up if you're feeling lazy).

If you want to get a dose of history while you're at it, stop at the **Museum of Natural and Cultural History** (☏541-346-3024; http://natural-history.uoregon.edu; 1680 E 15th Ave; adult/child $5/3; ⊙11am-5pm Tue-Sun). Housed in a replica of a Native American longhouse, this museum contains good displays on Native American artifacts and fossils.

🍴 🛏 p225, p243

The Drive » Get back on I-5 and travel north 66 miles to the capital of Oregon.

- - - - - - - - - - - - - -

8 Salem

As long as you're driving across the Beaver State,

241

DETOUR: SILVER FALLS STATE PARK

Start: 🔵 **Salem (p241)**

Sure, most of Oregon's 100-plus waterfalls are tucked away in the mountains, but that doesn't mean you have to take a whole separate trip. You can see 10 of them just 22 miles east of Salem at **Silver Falls State Park** (📞503-873-8681; day-use fee $5, tent sites/RV sites/cabins $19/26/40). Take an 8-mile loop to see them all, or skip straight to the tallest, 177ft **South Falls**.

be sure to stop by and pay homage – perhaps even sing a few bars of 'Oregon, My Oregon' – at the **Oregon State Capitol** (📞503-986-1388; www.oregonlegislature.gov; 900 Court St NE; ⊗8am-5pm Mon-Fri). The third Oregon capitol building (the first two burned down) is a sleek, deco-style structure faced with gray Vermont marble. The most notable features of the capitol are four Works Progress Administration–era murals lining the rotunda. Check the schedule – you might be able to catch a free tour.

✗ 🛏 p225

The Drive >> Take I-5 north another 20 miles, then take exit 278 toward Aurora.

🟤 Aurora

Originally built as a religious commune, the town of Aurora still has a com-

mon purpose, but now it's antique shops galore (rather than the Golden Rule–based teachings of founder Wilhelm Keil). Dozens of shops line the main streets with offerings that range from rustic to quirky to garage-sale-esque.

If you like your antiques big and chunky instead of dainty and fragile, then make your way immediately to the awesome **Aurora Mills Agricultural Salvage Yard** (www.auroramills.com; 14971 First St NE; ⊗10am-5pm Tue-Sun). An enormous, two-story building houses a cornucopia of vintage signs, architectural elements and dazzling miscellany that has the ability to both inspire and overwhelm.

The Drive >> Aurora is practically a suburb of Portland, so hop back on I-5 and drive 25 miles to reach downtown and your final destination.

TRIP HIGHLIGHT

🔟 Portland

Stay for more than 10 minutes and you're bound to feel like you've ended up in an episode of *Portlandia* at some point. Quirky, friendly, laid-back – but with a slightly disproportionate number of hipsters sporting bushy beards and skinny jeans – Portland is a must-do on any I-5 itinerary. Stop a while to experience some of the best food, art, beer and music the Pacific Northwest has to offer.

If you didn't book a room at the McMenamin brothers' Kennedy Schoo, you should at least pop into this former elementary school that's now a hotel, brewpub and movie theater. Wander the halls to check out its colorful collection of mosaics, collages and other cool artworks.

Be sure to poke around the hip boutiques, cafes, bars, bike shops and bookstores along three eastside streets: N Mississippi Ave, NE Alberta St and SE Hawthorne Blvd. Then head downtown and explore some of its best stop-offs (p260).

✗ 🛏 p243

Eating & Sleeping

Ashland ❶

✗ Standing Stone
Brewery International $$

(📞541-482-2448; www.standingstonebrewing.
com; 101 Oak St; mains $9-25, small plates
$5-10; 🕙11am-midnight) Popular and friendly
brewery-restaurant with a confusing but good
menu offering everything from burgers and
pizzas to BBQ ribs to tacos and enchiladas.
Wash it all down with some microbrews or a
cocktail. There's a great back patio, too.

🛏 Palm Boutique Hotel $$

(📞541-482-2636; www.palmcottages.com;
1065 Siskiyou Blvd; d $169-249; 🐕❄🛜🏊👶)
Fabulous small motel remodeled into 16 charming
cottage rooms and suites (some with kitchens.)
It's an oasis of green on a busy avenue, complete
with lawns and a saltwater pool. A house nearby
harbors three large suites (from $249).

🛏 Country Willows B&B $$

(📞541-488-1590; www.countrywillowsinn.
com; 1313 Clay St; d $120-210, ste $165-295;
🐕❄@🛜🏊) Only minutes from downtown is
this luxurious B&B on 5 acres in the 'countryside'.
The nine rooms, suites and a cottage sport a mix
of antiques and contemporary furniture; some
suites are as big as small apartments and have a
kitchenette or private deck.

Eugene ❼

✗ McMenamins
North Bank American $$

(📞541-343-5622; www.mcmenamins.com; 22
Club Rd; mains $12-25; 🕙11am-11pm Sun-Thu,
to midnight Fri & Sat) Gloriously located on the
banks of the mighty Willamette, this relatively
modest (for a McMenamins) pub-restaurant
boasts some of the best views in Eugene. Grab
a riverside patio table on a warm, sunny day and
order a cheeseburger with the Hammerhead ale.

🛏 C'est La Vie Inn B&B $$

(📞541-302-3014; www.cestlavieinn.com; 1006
Taylor St; r $175-279; 🐕❄@🛜) This gorgeous

Victorian house, run by a friendly French woman
and her American husband, is a neighborhood
showstopper. Beautiful antique furniture fills the
living and dining areas, while the three tastefully
appointed rooms offer comfort and luxury. Also
available is an amazing suite with kitchenette.

Portland ❿

✗ Little Big Burger Burgers $

(📞503-274-9008; www.littlebigburger.com; 122
NW 10th Ave; burgers $4-4.25; 🕙11am-10pm)
It's now owned by the same folks who own
Hooters, but this burger chainlet keeps things
appealingly simple, with a six-item menu of mini
burgers made from prime ingredients. Try a
beef burger topped with cheddar, Swiss, chèvre
(goat cheese) or blue cheese, with a side of
truffled fries – then wash it down with a root-
beer float. Several locations around town.

🛏 Ace Hotel Boutique Hotel $$

(📞503-228-2277; www.acehotel.com; 1022
SW Stark St; d with shared/private bath from
$195/285; 🅿❄@🛜👶) By now a well-
established brand, the Ace fuses industrial,
minimalist and retro styles to great effect.
From the photo booth in its lobby to the
recycled fabrics and salvaged-wood furniture
in its rooms, the hotel feels very chic and
very Portland. There's a Stumptown coffee
shop and underground bar on site, and
Clyde Common (📞503-228-3333; www.
clydecommon.com; 1014 SW Stark St; mains $9-
29; 🕙11:30am-midnight Mon-Fri, 3pm-midnight
Sat, 3pm-11pm Sun) adjoins the lobby. The
location can't be beat.

🛏 Kennedy School Hotel $$

(📞503-249-3983; www.mcmenamins.com/
KennedySchool; 5736 NE 33rd Ave; d from
$185; 🛜) This former elementary school is
now home to a hotel (sleep in old classrooms!),
a restaurant with a great garden courtyard,
several bars, a microbrewery and a movie
theater. Guests can use the soaking pool for
free, and the whole school is decorated in
McMenamins' cool art style – mosaics, fantasy
paintings and historical photographs.

Crater Lake Circuit

23

Make it a (big) day trip or stay a week – serene, mystical Crater Lake is one of Oregon's most enticing destinations. The best route takes you on a heavily forested, waterfall-studded loop.

TRIP HIGHLIGHTS

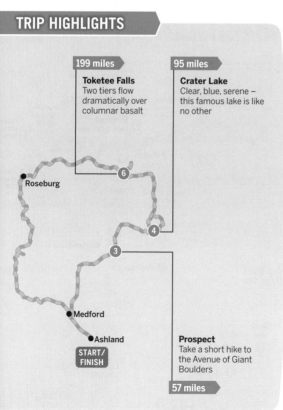

199 miles

Toketee Falls
Two tiers flow dramatically over columnar basalt

95 miles

Crater Lake
Clear, blue, serene – this famous lake is like no other

Roseburg

Medford

Ashland

START/ FINISH

Prospect
Take a short hike to the Avenue of Giant Boulders

57 miles

2–3 DAYS
365 MILES/587KM

GREAT FOR...

BEST TIME TO GO

Late May to mid-October when all the roads are open.

 ESSENTIAL PHOTO

No surprise here: Crater Lake.

 BEST WATERFALL

Two-tiered Toketee Falls is our favorite.

23 Crater Lake Circuit

The star attraction of this trip is Crater Lake, considered by many to be the most beautiful spot in all of Oregon. The sight of the still, clear and ridiculously blue water that fills an ancient volcanic caldera is worth the trip alone, but the drive there is lined with beautiful hikes, dramatic waterfalls and natural hot springs, all right off the highway.

1 Ashland

A favorite base for day trips to Crater Lake, Ashland is bursting at the seams with lovely places to sleep and eat (though you'll want to book your hotel room far in advance during the busy summer months). Home of the **Oregon Shakespeare Festival** (OSF; ☎541-482-4331; www.osfashland.org; Main & Pioneer Sts; tickets $30-119), it has more culture than most towns its size, and is just far enough off the highway to resist becoming a chain-motel mecca.

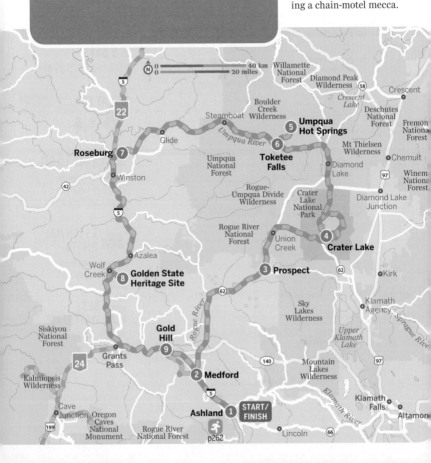

Crater Lake Crater Lake Lodge

It's not just Shakespeare that makes Ashland the cultural heart of southern Oregon. If you like contemporary art, check out the **Schneider Museum of Art** (☏541-552-6245; www.sou.edu/sma; 1250 Siskiyou Blvd; suggested donation $5; ☉10am-4pm Mon-Sat).

Ashland's historic downtown and lovely **Lithia Park** (59 Winburn Way) make it a dandy place to go for a walk (p262) before or after your journey to Crater Lake.

✗ 🛏 p243, p251

The Drive » Medford is 13 miles north of Ashland on I-5.

❷ Medford

Southern Oregon's largest metropolis is where you hop off I-5 for your trek out to Crater Lake, and it can also serve as a suitable base of operations if you want a cheap, convenient place to bunk down for the night.

On your way out, check out the **Table Rocks**, impressive 800ft mesas that speak of the area's volcanic past and are home to unique plant and animal species. Flowery spring is the best time for hiking to the flat tops, which were revered Native American sites. After **TouVelle State Park** (Table Rock Rd), fork either left to reach the trailhead to **Lower Table Rock** (3.5-mile round-trip hike) or right for **Upper Table Rock** (2.5-mile round-trip hike).

✗ p251

The Drive » The drive along Hwy 62 isn't much until after Shady Cove, when urban sprawl stops and forest begins. Your next stop is 45 miles northeast in Prospect.

TRIP HIGHLIGHT

❸ Prospect

No wonder they changed the name of Mill Creek Falls Scenic Area – that implies you're just going

---

LINK YOUR TRIP

22 **Essential I-5**
Join up with this tour of Oregon's major thoroughfare at Ashland, Medford or Roseburg.

24 **Caves of Highway 199**
Go from forest to caves to beach with this trip that starts in Grants Pass, between Medford and Roseburg.

to see another waterfall (not that there's anything wrong with that). But the real treat at **Prospect State Scenic Viewpoint** is hiking down to the **Avenue of Giant Boulders**, where the Rogue River crashes dramatically through huge chunks of rock and a little bit of scrambling offers the most rewarding views.

Take the trail from the southernmost of two parking lots on Mill Creek Dr. Keep left to get to the boulders or right for a short hike to two viewpoints for **Mill Creek Falls** and **Barr Creek Falls**. If you've got one more falls-sighting left in you, take the short hike from the upper parking lot to the lovely **Pearsony Falls**.

The Drive » Follow Hwy 62 for another 28 miles to get to the Crater Lake National Park turnoff at Munson Valley Rd.

- - - - - - - - - - -

TRIP HIGHLIGHT

4 Crater Lake

This is it: the main highlight and reason for being of this entire

trip is Oregon's most beautiful body of water, **Crater Lake** (☎541-594-3000; www.nps.gov/crla; 7-day vehicle pass $15). This amazingly blue lake is filled with some of the clearest, purest water you can imagine – you can easily peer 100ft down – and sits inside a 6-mile-wide caldera created when Mt Mazama erupted nearly 8000 years ago. Protruding from the water and adding to the drama of the landscape is **Wizard Island**, a volcanic cinder cone topped by its own mini crater called Witches Cauldron.

Get the overview with the 33-mile **Rim Drive** (⏱Jun–mid-Oct), which offers over 30 viewpoints as it winds around the edge of Crater Lake. The gloriously still waters reflect surrounding mountain peaks like a giant dark-blue mirror, making for spectacular photographs and breathtaking panoramas.

You can also camp, ski or hike in the surrounding old-growth forests. The popular and steep

mile-long **Cleetwood Cove Trail**, at the north end of the crater, provides the only water access at the cove. Or get up close with a two-hour **boat tour** (☎888-774-2728; www.craterlakelodges.com/activities/volcano-boat-cruises; Cleetwood Cove boat dock; adult/child $40/27; ⏱late Jun–mid-Aug).

 p251

The Drive » Head north on Hwy 138 for 41 miles and turn right on Rd 34.

- - - - - - - - - - -

5 Umpqua Hot Springs

Set on a mountainside overlooking the North Umpqua River, Umpqua Hot Springs is one of Oregon's most splendid hot springs, with a little bit of height-induced adrenaline thanks to its position atop a rocky bluff.

Springs are known for soothing weary muscles, so earn your soak at Umpqua by starting with a hike – it is in a national forest, after all – where you'll be treated to lush, old-growth forest and waterfalls punctuating the landscape. Half a mile from the parking lot is the scenic **North Umpqua Trail**.

The Drive » The turnout for Toketee Falls is right on Hwy 138, 2 miles past the Umpqua turnoff.

TOP TIP:
VISITING CRATER LAKE

Crater Lake's popular south entrance is open year-round. In winter you can only go up to the lake's rim and back down the same way; no other roads are plowed. The north entrance is only open from early June to late October, depending on snowfall.

Toketee Falls

6 Toketee Falls

More than half a dozen waterfalls line this section of the Rogue-Umpqua Scenic Byway, but the one that truly demands a stop is the stunning, two-tiered **Toketee Falls** (USFS Rd 34). The falls' first tier drops 40ft into an upper pool behind a cliff of columnar basalt, then crashes another 80ft down the rock columns into yet another gorgeous, green-blue pool below. One tiny disclaimer: although the hike is just 0.4 miles, there's a staircase of 200 steps down to the viewpoint, so climbing back up to your car is a bit of a workout.

The Drive » From here, the scenery tapers back down to only moderately spectacular as you leave the Umpqua National Forest. It's just one hour to Roseburg.

7 Roseburg

Sprawling Roseburg lies in a valley near the confluence of the South and North Umpqua Rivers. The city is mostly a cheap, modern sleepover for travelers headed elsewhere (such as Crater Lake), but it does have a cute, historic downtown area and is surrounded by award-winning wineries.

Don't miss the excellent **Douglas County Museum** (☏541-957-7007; www.umpquavalleymuseums.org; 123 Museum Dr, I-5 exit 123; adult/child $8/2; ☺10am-5pm Tue-Sat; ♿), which displays the area's cultural and natural histories. Especially interesting are the railroad derailment photos and History of Wine exhibit. Kids have an interactive area and live snakes to look at.

✖ p251

The Drive » Go south on I-5 for 47 miles and take the Wolf Creek exit. Follow Old State Hwy 99 to curve back under the interstate. Golden is 3.2 miles east on Coyote Creek Rd.

8 Golden State Heritage Site

Not ready to return to civilization quite yet? Stop off in the ghost town of **Golden**, population zero. A former mining town that had over 100 residents in the mid-1800s, Golden was built on the banks of Coyote Creek when gold was discovered there.

A handful of structures remains, as well as some newfangled interpretive signs that tell the tale of a curiously devout community that eschewed drinking and dancing, all giving a fascinating glimpse of what life was like back then. The weathered wooden buildings include a residence, the general store/post office, and a classic country church. Fun fact: the town was once used as a location for the long-running Western TV series *Gunsmoke*.

The Drive » Go south another 45 miles on I-5 and take exit 43. The Oregon Vortex is 4.2 miles north of the access road.

9 Gold Hill

Just outside the town of Gold Hill lies the **Oregon Vortex** (☏541-855-1543; www.oregonvortex.com; 4303 Sardine Creek L Fork Rd, Gold Hill; adult/child $12.50/9; ☺9am-4pm Mar-Oct, to 5pm Jun-Aug), where the laws of physics don't seem to apply – or is it all just an optical illusion created by skewed buildings on steep hillsides? However you see it, the place is definitely bizarre: objects roll uphill, a person's height changes depending on where they stand, and brooms stand up on their own...or so it seems.

Eating & Sleeping

Ashland ❶

🍴 Morning Glory　　　　　　Cafe $
(📞541-488-8636; 1149 Siskiyou Blvd; mains $9-15; ⏰8am-1:30pm) This colorful, casual cafe is one of Ashland's best breakfast joints. Creative dishes include the Alaskan crab omelet, vegetarian hash with roasted chilis, and shrimp cakes with poached eggs. For lunch there's gourmet salad and sandwiches. Go early or late to avoid a wait.

🍴 Agave　　　　　　　　Mexican $
(📞541-488-1770; www.agavetaco.net; 5 Granite St; tacos $3.75-5; ⏰11am-10pm Sun-Thu, to 11pm Fri & Sat) Tasty and creative tacos are cooked up at this popular restaurant. There's the regular stuff such as *carnitas* (little meats) and grilled chicken, but for something more exotic go for the shredded duck or sautéed lobster ($9.95).

🛏 Columbia Hotel　　　　Hotel $$
(📞541-482-3726; www.columbiahotel.com; 262 1/2 E Main St; d $95-189; 🐾❄🛜) Awesomely located 'European-style' hotel – which means most rooms share outside bathrooms. It's an especially great deal for downtown Ashland, with 24 quaint vintage rooms (no TVs), a nice lobby and a historic feel.

Medford ❷

🍴 Organic Natural Café　　Cafe $
(📞541-245-9802; 226 E Main St; mains $6-12; ⏰9am-3pm, closed Sun; 🍴) Step up to the cafeteria here and order a panini-style sandwich or burger (choose from vegetarian/buffalo/organic beef). There's a salad bar, along with fresh juices and fruit smoothies. The theme – in case you haven't guessed yet – is all about local, organic, vegan and gluten-free.

🍴 Porters　　　　　　American $$
(📞541-857-1910; www.porterstrainstation.com; 147 N Front St; mains $11-32; ⏰5pm-close, bar from 4pm) This gorgeous, arts-and-crafts-style restaurant is decked out in dark-wood booths and boasts an awesome patio next to the train tracks.

Steak, seafood and pasta dishes dominate the menu, though the food won't blow you away.

Crater Lake ❹

🍴 Crater Lake Lodge Dining Room　　　　Northwestern $$$
(📞541-594-2255; www.craterlakelodges.com; dinner mains $24-43; ⏰7-10am, 11.30am-2.30pm & 5-10pm mid-May–mid-Oct) Crater Lake's finest dining is at the lodge, where you can feast on Northwestern cuisine from a changing menu that includes dishes like bison meatloaf and elk chops with huckleberry sauce. Dinner reservations are recommended.

🛏 Crater Lake Lodge　　Lodge $$
(📞888-774-2728; www.craterlakelodges.com; r $179-245; ⏰late May–mid-Oct; 🐾🛜) This grand old lodge has 71 simple but comfortable rooms (no TV or telephone), but it's the common areas that are most impressive. Large stone fireplaces, leather sofas and a spectacular view of Crater Lake from the outside patio make this place special.

🛏 Cabins at Mazama Village　Cabin $$
(📞888-774-2728; www.craterlakelodges.com; d $152; ⏰late May–mid-Oct; 🐾) These 40 pleasant rooms (no TV or telephone) are located in attractive four-plex buildings. They're 7 miles from Crater Lake, with a small grocery store and gas pump nearby. Reserve as early as possible.

Roseburg ❼

🍴 McMenamins Roseburg Station Pub　　　American $$
(www.mcmenamins.com/286-roseburg-station-pub-brewery-home; 700 SE Sheridan St; mains $9-21; ⏰11am-11pm Mon-Thu, to midnight Fri & Sat, to 10pm Sun) This is a beautiful, cozy pub-restaurant in subdued McMenamins style – dark-wood paneling and lots of antique chandeliers. Typical burgers, sandwiches and salads dominate the menu. It's in an old train depot; sit and order a microbrew on the sunny patio in summer, or cozy up in the little dark bar on a bleak day.

Caves of
Highway 199

24

Short but scenic, Hwy 199 strings together a hit parade of natural wonders, from wildflower-covered mountain trails to marble caves and redwood forests, culminating in the Pacific Coast.

TRIP HIGHLIGHTS

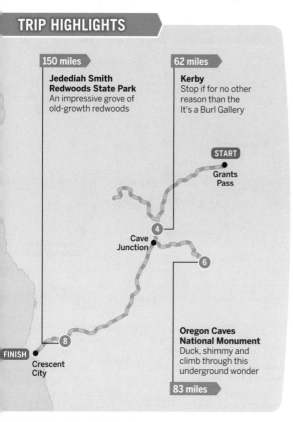

150 miles

Jedediah Smith Redwoods State Park
An impressive grove of old-growth redwoods

62 miles

Kerby
Stop if for no other reason than the It's a Burl Gallery

START
Grants Pass

4

Cave Junction

6

FINISH
Crescent City

8

Oregon Caves National Monument
Duck, shimmy and climb through this underground wonder

83 miles

2 DAYS
159 MILES/255KM

GREAT FOR...

BEST TIME TO GO

April through October, when the caves are open.

ESSENTIAL PHOTO

You, on the banks of the scenic Smith River.

BEST BOTANY LESSON

Check out the carnivorous Darlingtonia plant.

24 Caves of Highway 199

Think Hwy 199 is just a convenient connector from the interstate to the coast and Hwy 101? Well, you could buzz through it in a couple of hours and think, 'My, what pretty trees we passed.' But take your time and you'll discover an amazing amount of natural diversity all conveniently packaged into one compact area. Prepare to picnic, hike, climb, swim and explore all along the Redwood Hwy.

① Grants Pass

As a modern and not particularly scenic city, Grants Pass isn't a huge tourist destination, but its location on the banks of the Rogue River makes it a portal to adventure. White-water rafting, fine fishing and jet-boat excursions are the biggest attractions, and there's also good camping and hiking in the area. If you're here on a Saturday between mid-March and Thanksgiving, be sure to check out the **Outdoors Growers' Market** (4th &

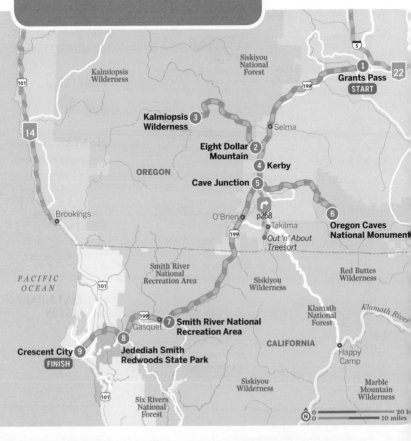

F Sts; ⊙9am-1pm Sat), a farmers and craft market that draws the city together.

Since the theme of this trip is caves, be sure to stop by the **visitor center** (☑541-476-5510; 1995 NW Vine St) and snap a picture with the local caveman statue for posterity.

 ⊨ p259

The Drive » Take Hwy 199 24 miles southwest and turn right on Eight Dollar Rd, just 3.5 miles past Selma. The trailheads mentioned in the next stop are less than a mile from the turnout.

- - - - - - - - - - - - - -

❷ Eight Dollar Mountain

If you think seeing some rare, carnivorous plants would just about make your trip, you've come to

LINK YOUR TRIP

14 **Highway 101 Oregon Coast**

From Crescent City, drive 26 miles north to Brookings to kick off your Oregon coastal adventure.

22 **Essential I-5**

Grants Pass is right on this major thoroughfare that gets you where you're going and has some fun along the way.

the right place. This area is one of the only places on earth where you'll find the *Darlingtonia californica* (also called the Pitcher Plant, the Cobra Lily and 'that little plant that eats bugs'). Beautiful and deadly (but not to us), this lily-like plant gobbles up insects and digests them. The **Eight Dollar Mountain Boardwalk Trail** offers easy viewing of the *Darlingtonia* with a gentle stroll on a boardwalk trail – or if you refuse to be coddled, opt for the still-not-that-strenuous one-mile hike that overlooks the Illinois River.

The Drive » Continue west on USFS Rd 4201 (Eight Dollar Rd). The next stop is 16 long, winding miles from the boardwalk, taking a little over an hour to navigate.

- - - - - - - - - - - - - -

❸ Kalmiopsis Wilderness

One of Oregon's largest wilderness areas, the remote Kalmiopsis Wilderness is famous for its rare plant life. About 150 million years ago, the area was separated from North America by a wide gulf and vegetation evolved on its own, so by the time the mountains fused to the continent the plant life was very different from that of the mainland. These unique plant species are showcased on the steep,

0.75-mile hike to **Babyfoot Lake**. In addition to the carnivorous *Darlingtonia,* the pink-flowered *Kalmiopsis leachiana* and rare Port Orford cedar are found almost nowhere else on earth.

The Drive » Backtrack to US 199. Turn right and go 2.7 miles south to Kerby.

- - - - - - - - - - - - - -

TRIP HIGHLIGHT

❹ Kerby

With a population of just 400 – and sometimes listed as a ghost town – tiny Kerby still has a surprising amount going for it. First of all, there's the **Kerbyville Museum** (☑541-592-5252; 24195 Redwood Hwy; adult/child $5/2; ⊙11am-3pm Tue-Sat, noon-3pm Sun Apr-Oct), which is located in an 1880s pioneer home and offers insight into pioneer life and Native American history.

And for real roadside fun, try the whimsical **It's a Burl Gallery** (☑800-548-7064; www.itsaburl.com; 24025 US 199; ⊙8am-5pm), which looks like a hobbit home right on the highway. Part gallery, part attraction, it features fantastical carvings, driftwood sculptures and elaborate tree houses. At the very least, stop by and admire the garden gallery.

 ⊨ p259

The Drive » Go 2.4 short miles south on US 199 to the town of Cave Junction.

⑤ Cave Junction

Relatively bustling among towns along US 199, Cave Junction is the jumping-off point for the Oregon Caves National Monument. The local terroir – taking advantage of both coastal and inland climates – lends itself nicely to Pinot Noir and Chardonnay, which you can sample at several local wineries.

While you're out here in the middle of nowhere, be on the lookout for lions, leopards, tigers and jaguars – you can actually spot all of those and more at **Great Cats World Park** (☎541-592-2957; www.greatcatsworld park.com; 27919 Redwood Hwy; adult/child $14/10; ⏰10am-6pm Jun-Aug, varies rest of year). Especially popular among kids and cat lovers, this interactive, 10-acre park features more than 30 trained cats, which, although big enough to eat your head, will merely lick their chops at you.

✕ 🛏 p259

The Drive ≫ Drive southeast on OR-46 for 19 miles.

TRIP HIGHLIGHT

⑥ Oregon Caves National Monument

The 'Marble Halls of Oregon' are the highlight of any US 199 trip. During your adventure at **Oregon Caves National**

Monument (☎541-592-2100; www.nps.gov/orca; 19000 Caves Hwy, Hwy 46; tours adult/child $10/7; ⏰tours 9am-6pm Jun-Aug, closed Dec-Feb, varies rest of year), expect to climb, twist, duck and wriggle your way through the 3 miles of passages and stairs during the 90-minute tour. Your reward is myriad cave formations such as cave popcorn, pearls, moonmilk, classic pipe organs and stalactites.

Guided tours run at least hourly – half-hourly in July and August. Dress warmly, wear good shoes and be prepared to get dripped on. For safety reasons, children less than 42in tall are not allowed.

A handful of short nature trails surround the area, such as the 0.75-mile **Cliff Nature Trail** and the 3.3-mile **Big Tree Trail**, which loops through old-growth forest to a huge Douglas fir.

🛏 p259

The Drive ≫ Backtrack to US 199 and head south. After about 15 minutes you'll cross the state line into California. The Smith River Information Center is 34 miles southwest of Cave Junction.

⑦ Smith River National Recreational Area

For about 16 miles, Smith River weaves back and forth alongside the Redwood Hwy, making this stretch of the **Six Rivers National Forest** the prettiest part of the drive. In summer you can stop off for a swim in the clear, emerald waters; in winter you can try to land a trophy-sized salmon or steelhead (or at least something modest for dinner).

Short, easy and right off the highway, the 2-mile **Myrtle Creek Trail** (US 199 & South Fork Rd, California) is a popular hike that's lush and green. As you traipse through wildflowers, ferns, cedars and red alder, look for unusual species that will bring out the botany enthusiast in you.

To learn more about the area, stop by the **Smith River Information Center** (☎707-457-3131; 10600 US 199, Gasquet, California; ⏰8am-4:30pm Mon-Fri).

The Drive ≫ Drive 9.2 miles west on US 199 to get to the Jedediah Smith Redwoods State Park visitor center.

TRIP HIGHLIGHT

⑧ Jedediah Smith Redwoods State Park

Tree-huggers can find plenty to hug in this forest filled with centuries-old redwoods, spruce, hemlock and Douglas firs – and with 20 miles of hiking and

FDASTUDILLO / GETTY IMAGES ©

Oregon Caves National Monument

257

DETOUR:
TREETOP TREK

Start: ❺ Cave Junction (p256)

Why settle for a motel when you can sleep in a tree house? The **Out 'n' About Treesort** (☎541-592-2208; www.treehouses.com; 300 Page Creek Rd, Takilma; tree houses $140-320; 🐾), near Cave Junction in Takilma, offers 16 kinds of tree houses that sleep between two and six guests. If your fear of heights or the booked-up rooms (reservations are crucial) are keeping you from a treetop sleepover, consider stopping by for a ride on a **zip-line** (☎541-592-2207) or a horseback trail ride.

nature trails, there's a lot to explore, even if you choose not to canoodle. **Jedediah Smith Redwoods State Park** (☎707-465-7335; www.parks.ca.gov; Hwy 199, Hiouchi; per car $8; ⏰sunrise-sunset; 🅿 🚻) is a blissfully undeveloped spot full of old-growth redwoods, which can grow up to 300ft tall. The park's best scenery can be found at **Stout Grove**. To get there, go south on South Fork Rd. After half a mile, turn right on Douglas Park Rd then continue onto the narrow, unpaved Howland Hill Rd for one of the best redwood routes anywhere.

The Drive >> Go 4.5 miles west to the junction of Hwy 101, then take 101 south 4.5 more miles into Crescent City.

- - - - - - - - - - - -

❾ Crescent City

You've made it! After nonstop trees, mountains and rivers, you get a change of pace when US 199 ends at the Pacific Ocean. Slightly scruffy Crescent City is hardly the crown jewel of the Pacific Coast, but **Beachfront Park** (Howe Dr; 🚻) is a great harborside beach for families, with picnic tables, a bicycle trail and no waves.

The **Battery Point Lighthouse** (☎707-467-3089; www.delnortehistory.org; adult/child $3/1; ⏰10am-4pm Wed-Sun Apr-Oct) offers tours, but only at low tide, and only April through October. But if you luck out (call first) you'll see the keeper's quarters and over 150 years of artifacts, plus a spectacular ocean view from the top.

Nearby, you can hike through the wetlands at the 5000-acre **Tolowa Dunes State Park** to find sand dunes, beaches strewn with driftwood, two lakes and more than 250 species of birds.

✗ 🛏 p259

Eating & Sleeping

Grants Pass ❶

✘ Laughing Clam
Pub Food $$

(☎541-479-1110; http://laughingclam.com; 121 SW G St; mains $8-25; ⏱11am-9pm Mon-Sat) Exotic dishes like the cosmic Cajun catfish sandwich and magic mushroom burger are served at this neon-lit, brick-walled eatery. More standard things like fish 'n' chips, pasta and of course clams are also available, along with a few rotating microbrews.

✘ Taprock
American $$

(☎541-476-2501; www.taprock.com; 971 SE 6th St; mains $12-25; ⏱8am-10pm) A gorgeous, multimillion-dollar restaurant perched above the Rogue River. The menu has something for everyone – steaks, burgers, seafood, sandwiches and salads. There's also breakfast, and awesome deck seating with water views.

🛏 Buona Sera Inn
Motel $

(☎541-476-4260; www.buonaserainn.com; 1001 NE 6th St; s/d from $66/72; ❄🏠🐾) A lovingly renovated motel with 14 comfortable, and even slightly luxurious, country-style rooms. All have quality linens and boast a fridge and microwave; some come with kitchenette.

Kerby ❹

🛏 Kerbyville Inn
B&B $

(☎541-592-4689; www.bridgeviewwine.com/ kerbyville-inn; 24304 Redwood Hwy; r $64-110) There's one queen room and four suites, two of which have spa tubs and all of which include continental breakfast. The owners are super-friendly and, since they also own Bridgeview Vineyards, free wine tasting is included.

Cave Junction ❺

✘ Wild River Brewing & Pizza Co
Pizza $$

(☎541-592-3556; www.wildriverbrewing.com; 249 N Redwood Hwy; pizzas $10-29, sandwiches $5-8; ⏱11am-9pm Mon-Thu, 11am-10pm Fri & Sat, noon-9pm Sun) This is a link in a small but good restaurant-brewery chain. There are large family tables inside, but if it's sunny, the back deck (overlooking a creek) is the place to be.

🛏 Country Hills Resort
Campground $

(☎541-592-3406; www.countryhillsresort.com; 7901 Caves Hwy; tent/RV sites $18/26, d $65, cabins from $80) This rustic resort has five country-style motel rooms and six cabins that come with kitchenettes. It also offers creekside camping and full-hookup RV sites. It's 8 miles from Cave Junction, on the way to the Oregon Caves (p256); reserve in summer.

Oregon Caves National Monument ❻

🛏 Oregon Caves Chateau
Lodge $$

(☎541-592-3400; www.oregoncaveschateau. com; 20000 Caves Hwy; r $109-199; ⏱May-Oct; 🐾) Situated near the entrance to Oregon Cave (p256), this impressive, historic lodge has huge windows facing the forest, 23 simple, vintage rooms, and a fine restaurant (5:30pm to 8pm) overlooking a plunging ravine.

Crescent City ❾

✘ Good Harvest Cafe
American $

(☎707-465-6028; 575 Hwy 101 S; mains $7-16; ⏱7:30am-9pm Mon-Sat, from 8am Sun; 🖉🦽) This popular local cafe is in a spacious location across from the harbor. It's got a bit of everything, from soups and sandwiches to full meals and smoothies. Good beers, a crackling fire and loads of vegetarian options make this the best dining spot in town.

🛏 Curly Redwood Lodge
Motel $

(☎707-464-2137; www.curlyredwoodlodge. com; 701 Hwy 101 S; r $70-105; 🅿❄✳🛜) The motel is a marvel: it's entirely built and paneled from a single curly redwood tree that measured over 18ft in diameter. Progressively restored and polished into a gem of mid-20th-century kitsch, the inn is a delight for retro junkies. Rooms are clean, large and comfortable (request one away from the road).

STRETCH YOUR LEGS
PORTLAND

Start/Finish: Stumptown Coffee Roasters

Distance: 2 miles

Duration: 3 hours

With green spaces galore, the world's largest independent bookstore, art, handcrafted beer, a vibrant food culture and a livability rating that's off the charts, Portland is made for walking. This route takes you to the highlights of downtown.

Take this walk on Trips

Coffee & Doughnuts

Start with coffee at **Stumptown Coffee Roasters** (www.stumptowncoffee.com; 128 SW 3rd Ave; ⏰6am-7pm Mon-Fri, 7am-7pm Sat & Sun; 📶), which has been roasting its own beans since 1999. A minute's walk away is **Voodoo Doughnut** (📞503-241-4704; www.voodoodoughnut.com; 22 SW 3rd Ave; donuts from $2; ⏰24hr), which bakes quirky treats – go for the bacon maple bar or the 'voodoo doll' filled with raspberry jelly 'blood.'

The Walk » Head toward the waterfront on pedestrian-only SW Ankeny St.

Saturday Market & Tom McCall Waterfront Park

Victorian-era architecture and the lovely **Skidmore Fountain** give the area beneath the Burnside Bridge near-European flair. Hit it on a weekend to catch the chaotic **Saturday Market** (📞503-222-6072; www.portlandsaturday market.com; 2 SW Naito Pkwy; ⏰10am-5pm Sat, 11am-4:30pm Sun Mar-Dec), an outdoor crafts fair with food carts. From here you can explore the **Tom McCall Waterfront Park** (Naito Pkwy) along the Willamette River.

The Walk » Walk north under the Burnside Bridge through the park, then turn left on NW Couch St and right into NW 3rd Ave.

Chinatown

The ornate **Chinatown Gates** (cnr W Burnside St & NW 4th Ave) define the southern edge of Portland's so-called Chinatown – but you'll be lucky to find any Chinese people here at all. The main attraction is the **Lan Su Chinese Garden** (📞503-228-8131; www.lansugarden. org; 239 NW Everett St; adult/child $9.50/7; ⏰10am-6pm mid-Apr–mid-Oct, to 5pm mid-Oct–mid-Apr), a one-block haven of tranquility, ponds and manicured greenery.

The Walk » Make your way west on NW Davis St to NW 8th Ave.

Art Galleries

Several top-notch galleries can be found on this block. They're open late

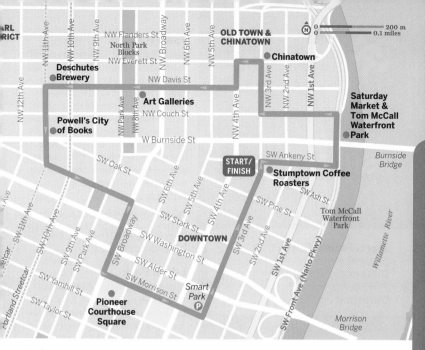

the first Thursday of each month, when new exhibits open and crowds of appreciative gawpers stroll through the area.

The Walk » Continue up NW Davis St to NW 11th Ave.

Deschutes Brewery

Walking makes you thirsty and you're in Beervana (a group is lobbying to make this Portland's official name), so it's time for a pint and lunch. Grab a table under the arches framing the restaurant at **Deschutes Brewery** (☎503-296-4906; www.deschutesbrewery.com; 210 NW 11th Ave; ⏰11am-10pm, to midnight Fri & Sat).

The Walk » Walk south on NW 11th Ave one block to find yourself in the Pearl District's upmarket shopping area.

Powell's City of Books

Powell's City of Books (☎800-878-7323; www.powells.com; 1005 W Burnside St; ⏰9am-11pm) is, until someone proves otherwise, the world's largest independent bookstore. Find a whole, awe-inspiring

city block of new and used titles and prepare to get lost.

The Walk » Cross W Burnside St then turn left on SW Stark St and right on SW Broadway to SW Morrison St.

Pioneer Courthouse Square

End your walk in the heart of downtown Portland. This brick plaza is nicknamed 'Portland's living room' and is the most visited public space in the city. When it isn't full of hacky-sack players, sunbathers or office workers lunching, the square hosts concerts, festivals, rallies, farmers markets – and even summer Friday-night movies, **Flicks on the Bricks** (https://thesquarepdx.org/events; Pioneer Courthouse Square; ⏰7pm Fri Jul-Aug). Around the square is a seemingly endless array of shopping, restaurants and food carts.

The Walk » Head east three blocks down SW Morrison St, turn left on SW 3rd Ave and in six blocks you'll be back at Stumptown Coffee Roasters.

STRETCH YOUR LEGS
ASHLAND

Start/Finish: Town Plaza

Distance: 2 miles

Duration: 2 hours

With a historic downtown right on the edges of a beautifully designed park, Ashland's best assets are all within easy walking distance of each other – including the ever-popular Oregon Shakespeare Festival.

Take this walk on Trips

Town Plaza

People have been 'taking the waters' in Ashland ever since a lithia-water spring was discovered in 1907; early visitors flocked here to enjoy its supposed health benefits. Sample the coveted mineral water at the **Lithia Fountain** on the Town Plaza, or just enjoy watching unsuspecting tourists take a drink and quickly spit it out: the water tastes and smells like rotten eggs, and just to enhance the experience, it's also carbonated.

The Walk » Right behind the plaza is the northern tip of Lithia Park. Head south to explore the 1.4-mile stretch of greenery; because it's so narrow, it's hard to get lost.

Lithia Park

Listed on the National Register of Historic Places, fetching Lithia Park has been around since 1892. The 93-acre park got a dramatic upgrade in 1914, thanks to the hiring of Golden Gate Park's John McLaren as landscape architect. Today the park includes fountains, a Japanese garden, tennis courts, a duck pond and a band shell – not to mention miles of tree-lined trails. Enjoy colorful blossoms in spring, lush greenery in summer and dazzling, changing colors in fall.

The Walk » When you're done exploring the park, head back to the plaza and turn right on E Main St. One short block later, turn right on Pioneer St.

Shakespeare Theatres

Even if you don't have tickets to the **Oregon Shakespeare Festival** (p246) you can still join the fun during festival season. Plan ahead to catch a **backstage tour** that takes you behind the scenes of the three stages, including the outdoor Elizabethan stage. For something more spur-of-the-moment, there are free, half-hour **Green Shows** (www.osfashland.org; 15 S Pioneer St; ⏰6.45pm Tue-Sun Jun–mid-Oct) in the

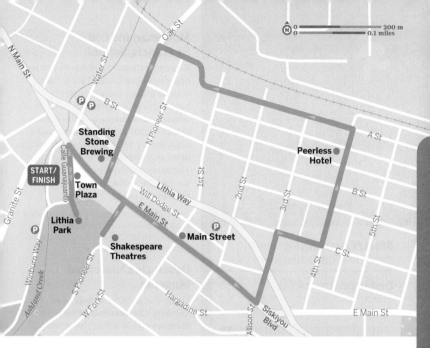

festival courtyard before each night's performance.

The Walk » Make your way back to Main St and turn right again to explore the historic downtown.

Main Street

The few blocks of Main St between Oak St and N 3rd St are the heart of town, and they're lined with historical buildings that have been turned into shops, cafes and boutiques. The 1910 **Columbia Hotel** (p251) is Ashland's oldest hotel and it contains the oldest phone booth in Oregon, complete with pressed-tin ceiling.

The Walk » Keep heading east until you reach N 3rd St, then turn left. Turn right on C St, then left on N 4th St. You'll pass a mishmash of commercial buildings as you head toward the old railyard area.

Peerless Hotel

Built in 1900, the **Peerless Hotel** (📞800-460-8758, 541-488-1082; www. peerlesshotel.com; 243 4th St; d $229-285; 🖙❄🛜) started as a modest board-

ing house for railroad workers with 10 rooms and one bath. The building was restored (and baths added) in 1994, and part of the process included uncovering and restoring the photogenic, 10ft-tall Coca-Cola sign painted on the exterior brick walls back in 1915.

The Walk » Head west along A St to make your way through the historic railroad district. Turn left on Oak St and get ready for refreshments.

Standing Stone Brewery

Sure, there's the craft microbrew made right on the premises. And, yes, there's the sampler tray that lets you try six at once. But **Standing Stone Brewery** (p243) is about more than just beer: the varied menu offers everything from nachos to Thai curry to wild salmon, and there's a kids' menu with lots of non-beer drink options. There's even live music on the back patio during the summer.

The Walk » Just south is the Town Plaza where you began the walk.

STRETCH YOUR LEGS
BEND

Start/Finish: McMenamins Old St Francis School

Distance: 2 miles

Duration: 2 hours

Pretty, compact and occasionally even a little sleepy, downtown Bend has a friendly, laid-back vibe and a small-town feel. Discover public art, quirky businesses, bustling brewpubs and local history in this 2-mile tour of downtown.

Take this walk on Trips

McMenamins Old St Francis School

Former students would hardly recognize their old parochial school today, with its quirky murals, fantastical light fixtures and pronounced sense of whimsy. McMenamins Old St Francis School (p235) has been repurposed as a fun-loving hotel, but you don't have to be an overnight guest to enjoy recess. The movie theater, brewpub, outdoor bar and Turkish soaking pool are all open to the public.

The Walk ≫ From the front doors of the school, go left and follow Bond St two short blocks southwest to Idaho Ave, where you'll find the next stop between Bond St and Wall St.

Deschutes Historical Museum

Located in another former grade-school building, the **Deschutes Historical Museum** (📞541-389-1813; www.deschutes history.org; 129 NW Idaho Ave; adult/child $5/2; ⏰10am-4:30pm Tue-Sat) has plenty to teach you about local history, showing off historical photos and artifacts that illuminate the lives of pioneers, Native Americans, loggers and everyday citizens.

The Walk ≫ Cross Wall St to admire the historic Trinity Episcopal Church. Head northeast on Wall St then go left on Louisiana Ave to Drake Park.

Drake Park

Nature's never far away in Bend; if you can't hit the trails, slopes or river, Drake Park provides a quick fix right downtown. The Deschutes River flows through the park, slowing briefly to form scenic **Mirror Pond**. Grab a bench, spread a picnic, feed the geese or stroll the paths of this pretty, tree-lined park surrounded by some of Bend's nicest Craftsman homes. If you're lucky, you might catch a performance of **Shakespeare in the Park** (www.shakespearebend. com; Drake Park; tickets $22-75; ⏰late Aug).

The Walk ≫ Cross the pedestrian bridge and continue on Nashville Ave for three blocks.

Public Art

In the roundabout at the intersection of Newport Ave and Nashville Ave is a metal horse sculpture called *Bueno Homage to the Buckaroo*. It's all part of the **Roundabout Art Route** (www.round aboutartroute.com), which has beautified 20 local roundabouts with large-scale sculptures. This is the only one that's walking distance from downtown, but it might inspire you to jump in your car and visit them all.

The Walk » Double back across the river over the pedestrian bridge, turning left on the path that follows Riverside Blvd. When the path ends, continue onto Franklin Ave and turn left on Wall St one block later.

Wall Street

Bend's charming downtown is epito-mized in the stretch of Wall St between Franklin Ave and Oregon Ave. Wander in and out of stores and boutiques and check out the historic **Tower Theatre** (541-317-0700; www.towertheatre.org; 835

NW Wall St), built in 1940. Be sure to stop and indulge your sweet tooth (as well as those of any children you have in tow) at **Powell's Sweet Shoppe** (www. powellsss.com; 818 NW Wall St; 10am-9pm Mon-Sat, to 8pm Sun;).

The Walk » Go right on Oregon Ave and left on Bond St, another street with lots of shops to explore; the brewery is half a block down on your right.

Deschutes Brewery & Public House

The Deschutes Brewery & Public House (p235) is just one stop on the 'Bend Ale Trail,' a group of several local microbreweries that will help you reach 'beervana.' The best way to experience its extensive beer menu? The six-beer sampler – though even choosing just six can be difficult. The food is no afterthought: the brewery serves a wide range of way-better-than-pub grub.

The Walk » Follow Bond St southwest to return to your starting point.

British Columbia

FOLLOW WINDING ROADS INTO THE DEEP FORESTS of northern Vancouver Island, where bald eagles soar and black bears munch dandelions, or point your wheels north toward Whistler, where dramatic glazed mountaintops scrape the sky. Then coast back down to explore dynamic Vancouver or quaint Victoria. Healthy living reaches its zenith in British Columbia (BC). You'll eat well, drink well and play well. From islands to glaciers to world-class vineyards, this region beckons for road trips and doesn't disappoint.

Banff National Park Moraine Lake
BJOERN ALBERTS / SHUTTERSTOCK ©

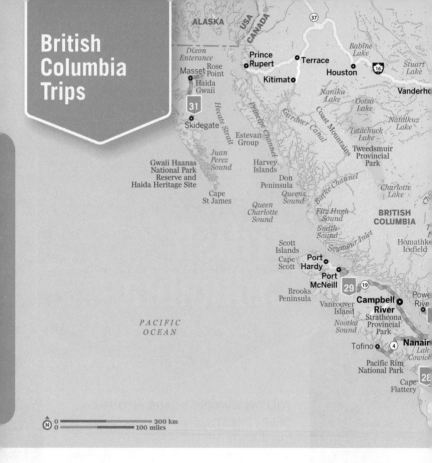

British Columbia Trips

ALASKA

USA
CANADA

Dixon
Enterance
Prince
Rupert   Terrace   Babine
Masset Rose   Lake
        Point   Kitimat   Houston   Stuart
        Haida   Lake
        Gwaii
                Nanika   Vanderho
        Lake   Ootsa
31   Lake
Skidegate   Natalkuz
        Hecate Strait   Lake
        Estevan Principe Channel Tetachuck
        Group   Lake
Juan   Tweedsmuir
Perez   Harvey   Provincial
Sound   Islands   Park
Gwaii Haanas   Don
National Park   Peninsula Coast Mountains
Reserve and   Queens
Haida Heritage Site   Sound   Charlotte
        Cape   Lake
        St James Queen   Fitz Hugh
                Charlotte Sound   BRITISH
                Sound   Burke Channel COLUMBIA
                Smith
                Sound
        Scott   Seymour Inlet   Homathk
        Islands   Icefield
        Cape   Port
        Scott Hardy
                Port
                McNeill   29 19
        Brooks   Powe
        Peninsula   Campbell Rive
                Vancouver   River
                Island   Strathcona
                Nootka   Provincial
                Sound   Park   Nanair
                Tofino 4   Lak
                                       Cowich
        PACIFIC   Pacific Rim
        OCEAN   National Park
                                       Cape 28
                                       Flattery

N 0   200 km
   0   100 miles

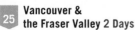

Okanagan Valley Wine Tour 2 Days
30 Overflowing fruit stands, award-winning vineyards and amazing cuisine next to a shimmering lake. (p315)

31 **Haida Gwaii Adventure 2 Days**
Experience remote wilderness and fascinating First Nations culture on these edge-of-the-earth islands. (p325)

32 **Circling the Rockies 3 Days**
See iconic mountain scenery and wildlife at its greatest. (p333)

DON'T MISS

First Nations Culture
With state-of-the-art museums, art galleries, totem poles and modern communities, Native culture is accessible on Trips 28 29 31

Local Refreshments
In-house roasted coffee, local breweries, countless wineries and unique cideries will tempt your taste buds on Trips 27 28 30

Dramatic Beaches
Long Beach with its endless sand, remote Botanical Beach and forested China Beach await on Trips 27 28 29

Ancient Forests
Looking up at the towering old-growth trees in Cathedral Grove, Goldstream Provincial Park and Capilano will leave you dizzy on Trips 25 27 29

Wildlife
While never a sure bet, you have a chance to spot a bear, a bald eagle or a pod of whales on Trips 28 29 32

Vancouver & the Fraser Valley

25

This tour has something for everyone – parks, beaches, mountains, vineyards, hot springs and a big dollop of history, starting with an exploration of the coveted seaside city of Vancouver.

TRIP HIGHLIGHTS

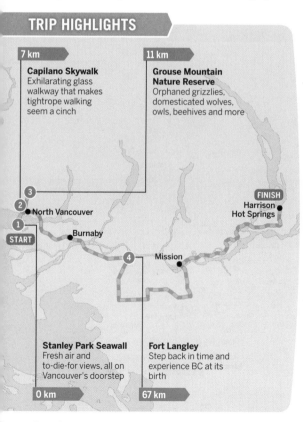

7 km

Capilano Skywalk
Exhilarating glass walkway that makes tightrope walking seem a cinch

11 km

Grouse Mountain Nature Reserve
Orphaned grizzlies, domesticated wolves, owls, beehives and more

3 **2** **1** START
North Vancouver
Burnaby
4 Mission

FINISH
Harrison Hot Springs

Stanley Park Seawall
Fresh air and to-die-for views, all on Vancouver's doorstep

0 km

Fort Langley
Step back in time and experience BC at its birth

67 km

---

2 DAYS
186KM/116 MILES

GREAT FOR...

BEST TIME TO GO
June to September for warm days and ripened fruit.

 ESSENTIAL PHOTO
Wobbling over the Capilano Suspension Bridge.

 BEST FOR FAMILIES
Fort Langley offers family fun for all ages. And you might strike it rich panning for gold!

Vancouver & the Fraser Valley

As you step out onto the swinging Capilano Suspension Bridge, get eyed up by a grizzly bear atop Grouse Mountain or watch your children practicing their bartering skills for wolverine skins at Fort Langley, you might wonder what happened to the promised pretty valley drive. But don't worry – it's there. With dramatic mountains rising up on either side, a tour along the Fraser River is as action-packed as it is scenic.

TRIP HIGHLIGHT

❶ Stanley Park

Just steps from downtown Vancouver (also worth a walk (p340) around), but seemingly worlds away, **Stanley Park** (P 👤: 🚌19) is an urban oasis, covered in a quarter of a million trees that tower as high as 249ft. Bigger than New York's Central Park, this 1000-acre peninsula is a favorite hangout for locals, who walk, run or cycle around the 9km (5.5-mile) super-scenic

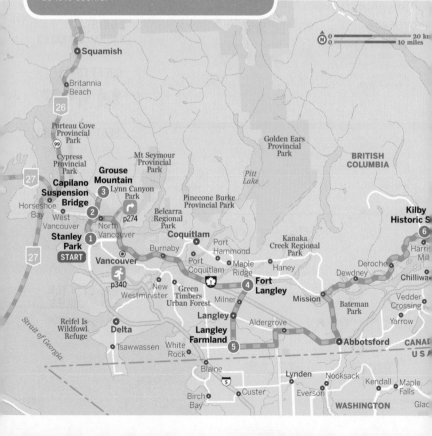

seawall that circles the outer edge of the park. The path offers amazing views of Burrard Inlet and passes impressive **totem poles**, squat **Brockton Point Lighthouse** and log-strewn **Third Beach**, where you can take a dip. Also watch for **Siwash Rock** standing sentry off the western shore. Meaning 'he is standing up,' it was named after a traditional legend that purports it's a man transformed into stone; the hole in the rock is where he kept his fishing tackle.

Looking out across palm-tree-fringed English Bay, Second Beach has a heated outdoor **swimming pool** (open May to September) that is suitable for families. From here, a long sandy beach stretches south along Beach Ave. On the park's eastern shore you'll find a fantastic **water park** (Lumberman's Arch; ⏱10am-6pm Jun-Sep; 👶) that will keep your kids happily squealing for hours.

Also in the park is the popular **Vancouver Aquarium** (📞604-659-3400; www.vanaqua.org; 845 Avison Way; adult/child CAN$31/22; ⏱9:30am-6pm Jul & Aug, 10am-5pm Sep-Jun; 👶; 🚌19), a nonprofit conservation center home to penguins, beluga whales, dolphins, reef sharks and other aquatic life.

🛏 p277

The Drive » Head north over Stanley Park Causeway and the beautiful Lions Gate Bridge to North Vancouver. Head east on Marine Dr for a block and turn left onto Capilano Rd, heading north for 2.4km (1.5 miles).

TRIP HIGHLIGHT

2 Capilano Suspension Bridge

Not for the faint of heart, **Capilano Suspension Bridge** (📞604-985-7474; www.capbridge.com; 3735 Capilano Rd, North Vancouver; adult/child CAN$40/12, reduced off-season; ⏱8:30am-8pm Jun-Aug, reduced off-season; P 👶; 🚌236) is the world's longest (460ft) and highest (230ft) suspension bridge, swaying gently over the roiling waters of Capilano Canyon. As you cross, try to remember that the steel cables you are gripping are embedded in huge concrete blocks on either side. This is the region's most popular attraction – hence the summertime crowds. The grounds here include rain forest walks, totem poles and some smaller bridges strung between the trees that offer a lovely squirrel's-eye forest walk. You can also test your bravery on the **Skywalk**, a 20in-wide glass walkway secured with horizontal

LINK YOUR TRIP

26 Sea to Sky Highway

Head northwest from Vancouver, rather than east, and wind your way up into the mountains.

27 A Strait Hop

Hop on the ferry at Horseshoe Bay, just west of North Vancouver.

DETOUR:
LYNN CANYON PARK

Start: ② Capilano Suspension Bridge (p273)

A free alternative to Capilano, **Lynn Canyon** (www. lynncanyon.ca; Park Rd, North Vancouver; ⏰7am-9pm; ⏸; 🚌229) is a verdant park with its own slightly smaller suspension bridge. There are also plenty of excellent hiking trails and some great tree-hugging picnic spots. Check out the park's **Ecology Centre** (www. lynncanyonecologycentre.ca; 3663 Park Rd, North Vancouver; entry by suggested CAN$2 donation; ⏰10am-5pm Jun-Sep, 10am-5pm Mon-Fri & noon-4pm Sat & Sun Oct-May; ⏸; 🚌227) for displays on the area's rich biodiversity. To find the park, head east on Hwy 1 from Capilano Rd and turn left on Lynn Valley Rd.

bars to a granite cliff face and suspended 300ft over the canyon floor. Deep breath...

The Drive » Continue north on Capilano Rd. This turns into Nancy Greene Way, which ends at the next stop.

TRIP HIGHLIGHT

❸ Grouse Mountain

One of the region's most popular outdoor hangouts, **Grouse Mountain** (☎604-980-9311; www. grousemountain.com; 6400 Nancy Greene Way, North Vancouver; Skyride adult/child CAN$44/15; ⏰9am-10pm; 🅿 ⏸; 🚌236) rises 4039ft against North Vancouver's skyline. In summer, Skyride gondola tickets to the top include access to lumberjack shows, alpine hiking trails and a **nature reserve** that's home to orphaned grizzly bears and timber wolves.

A couple of extra dollars gets you a ticket onto an open chairlift that takes you up to 4100ft above sea level (children must be 3.3ft tall). You can also brave the two-hour, five-line circuit **zip-line course** (CAN$115, incl Skyride) or the 'Eye of the Wind' tour, which takes you to the top of a 20-story wind turbine tower for spectacular 360-degree views. In winter, Grouse is also a magnet for skiers and snowboarders.

The Drive » Return south down Nancy Greene Way and Capilano Rd, taking a left onto Edgemont Blvd, which leads to Hwy 1. Head east, following the highway through Burnaby, crossing the Second Narrows Bridge and then the impressive, 10-lane Port Mann Bridge. Continue on Hwy 1, exiting at 88 Ave East and following the signs to Fort Langley. This drive takes around an hour.

TRIP HIGHLIGHT

❹ Fort Langley

Little Fort Langley's tree-lined streets and 19th-century storefronts make it one of the Lower Mainland's most picturesque historic villages. Its main historic highlight is the evocative **Fort Langley National Historic Site** (☎604-513-4777; www.parkscanada. gc.ca/fortlangley; adult/child CAN$7.80/3.90; ⏰10am-5pm; ⏸), perhaps the region's most important old-school landmark.

A fortified trading post since 1827, this is where James Douglas announced the creation of British Columbia in 1858, giving the site a legitimate claim to being the province's birthplace. Chat with costumed re-enactors knitting, working on beaver pelts or sweeping their pioneer home. Also open to explore are re-created artisan workshops and a **gold-panning area** that's very popular with kids. And when you need a rest, sample baking and lunchtime meals from the 1800s in the **Lelam' Café**.

Be sure to check the fort's website before you arrive: there's a wide array of events that bring the past back to life, including a summertime evening campfire program that will take you

Capilano Suspension Bridge

right back to the pioneer days of the 1800s.

 p277

The Drive » Head south out of the village on Glover Rd, crossing Hwy 1 and then taking a slight left so that you're traveling south on 216th St. The next stop is just past 16th Ave.

- - - - - - - - - -

5 Langley Farmland

The vine-covered grounds of **Chaberton Estate Winery** (📞604-530-1736; www.chabertonwinery.com; 1064 216 St; 🕙10am-6pm Mon-Wed, 10am-8pm Thu-Sat, 11am-6pm Sun) are the Fraser Valley's oldest winery operation, here

since 1991. The French-influenced, 55-acre vineyard specializes in cool-climate whites: its subtle, Riesling-style Bacchus is dangerously easy to drink too much of. There's also a handy bistro here if you need to soak up your overindulgence with a hearty meal.

From here, head south and right on 4th St to the charming **Vista D'oro** (📞604-514-3539; www.vistadoro.com; 346 208th St; 🕙11am-5pm Thu-Sun), a working farm and winery where you can load up on fresh pears, plums, apples and stripy heirloom tomatoes. Sample preserves

TOP TIP: TRAFFIC REPORTS

Traffic over the Lions Gate Bridge and along Hwy 1 can be heavy enough to bring you to a standstill at times. Check the website of DriveBC (www.drivebc.ca) for traffic, construction and incident reports.

DETOUR:
HOPE

Start: ❼ Harrison Hot Springs

Hope's nickname is the 'Chainsaw Capital' and this rather unusual moniker certainly draws attention. The name was earned by the wooden sculptures peppered throughout the town. Hope is a small community at the eastern edge of the Fraser Valley, set beneath the shadow of the Cascade Mountains. Created with (you guessed it) chainsaws, the 70-plus sculptures are the products of both local and visiting artists. Most depict wildlife, including the Sasquatch who is believed to live in the nearby woods.

If Hope looks oddly familiar to you, you may be dating yourself. The original *Rambo* movie was filmed here in 1982. For a self-guided tour map of the sculptures and *Rambo* locations, drop into the visitor center on the edge of town. Hope is 40km (25 miles) east of Harrison Hot Springs on Hwy 7.

such as piquant mango lime salsa and sweet rhubarb and vanilla jam. Also pick up a bottle of the unusual fig wine or the port-style walnut wine made from nuts grown just outside the shop.

The Fraser Valley is home to countless farms, producing everything from tulips to cheese. Many accept visitors, give tours and sell their wares in farm shops. If you're keen to visit some more, go to www.circlefarm tour.com for details.

The Drive ❯❯ Return north up 216th St and hang a right on North Bluff Rd. Continue east

for four blocks and turn left onto 248th St, which takes you to the Fraser Hwy. Head east toward Abbotsford, and then north on the Abbotsford Mission Hwy over the Fraser River to Hwy 7. Turn right and follow the road along the river. This drive takes approximately 1½ hours.

- - - - - - - - - -

❻ Kilby Historic Site

To get to **Kilby Historic Site** (📞604-796-9576; www. kilby.ca; 215 Kilby Rd; adult/ child CAN$10/8; 🕐11am-4pm Jul & Aug, reduced hours off-season), **turn right onto School Rd and then right again onto Kilby Rd. The clocks turn back to the 1920s when you enter**

this site, all that remains of the once thriving Harrison Mills community. Join a tour led by costumed interpreters as you explore the general store, hotel, post office and working farm, complete with friendly farm animals. Save time for treats made with traditional ice cream.

The Drive ❯❯ Return to Hwy 7 and carry on east, passing through farmland and hazelnut orchards. Turn left on Hwy 9, which takes you to Harrison Hot Springs, for a total drive of 21km (13 miles).

- - - - - - - - - -

❼ Harrison Hot Springs

Set on the edge of Harrison Lake with views to forest-carpeted mountains, Harrison Hot Springs (www. tourismharrison.com) is a resort town that draws both locals and visitors to its sandy beach, warm lagoon and lakeside promenade. While the lake itself is glacier-fed, two hot springs bubble at the southern end of the lake and the warm water can be enjoyed year-round at the town's upscale resort and the indoor public pool.

🛏 p277

Eating & Sleeping

Stanley Park ❶

🛏 Listel Hotel — Boutique Hotel $$

(☎604-684-8461; www.thelistelhotel.com;
1300 Robson St; d CAN$265; ⊜ ❋ @ ☎;
🖥5) A sophisticated, self-described 'art
hotel,' the Listel attracts grown-ups through
its on-site installations and package deals with
local galleries. Many rooms display original
artworks and all have a relaxing, mood-lit West
Coast feel. Artsy types should check out the
lobby sculptures for selfie opportunities, while
the property's on-site bar and restaurant are
arguably the best hotel drink and dine options
in the city.

Check the hotel's website for an ever-
changing roster of art-themed package deals. And don't worry about finding
the shops on your visit: you're steps away from
Robson St's retailing center. Overnight parking
is $29.

🛏 Sylvia Hotel — Hotel $$

(☎604-681-9321; www.sylviahotel.com; 1154
Gilford St; d CAN$199; P ⊜ ☎❋; 🖥5) This
ivy-covered 1912 charmer enjoys a prime
location overlooking English Bay. Generations
of guests keep coming back – many requesting
the same room every year – for a dollop of
old-world ambiance, plus a side order of first-
name service. The rooms, some with older
furnishings, have a wide array of comfortable
configurations, but the best are the large suites,
which have kitchens and waterfront views.
If you don't have a room with a view, decamp to
the lobby-level lounge to nurse a beer and watch
the sun set over the beach. Overnight parking
costs $18.

Fort Langley ❹

🍴 Veggie Bob's Kitchen — Vegetarian $

(☎604-888-1223; http://veggiebobs.ca; 9044
Glover Rd; mains CAN$8-11; ⊙11am-8pm Tue-
Sun; 🍴) This cafe and organic produce shop is
overflowing in a wonderful way. Tidy checkered
tablecloths and barrels of apples greet you, along
with a hearty menu of sandwiches, burgers and
soups. Try the Mexi Burger or go for the simple
(but amazingly tasty) aged cheddar, fresh basil
and vine tomato sandwich. It's all organic.

🍴 Wendel's Bookstore & Cafe — Cafe $

(☎604-513-2238; www.wendelsonline.com;
9233 Glove Rd; CAN$8-14; ⊙7:30am-10pm;
☎🍴) Arrive early to avoid the line-ups at
this clapboard corner gem that's been luring
the locals for years. They keep coming back
for the great breakfasts and hearty array of
well-prepared comfort dishes from quesadillas
to mac 'n' cheese. Our favorite is the vegetarian
coconut curry bowl. Save time to browse the
well-curated bookstore section, too.

Harrison Hot Springs ❼

🛏 Harrison Hot Springs Resort — Hotel $$

(☎866-626-8822; www.harrisonresort.com;
100 Esplanade Ave; r CAN$150-180) This fabled
resort exudes peace. Open since 1886, it
has an art-deco flair and offers good service.
The five hot-spring pools are set in an inner
courtyard complete with trees and fairy lights.
There is also a divine-smelling spa, numerous
restaurants and a concierge who can arrange
everything from fishing trips to golf.

Sea to Sky Highway

26

The coastal scenery here is magnificent – as are the deep forests, crashing waterfalls and lofty mountains. When you can see it all in a day, it's almost too good to be true.

TRIP HIGHLIGHTS

1–2 DAYS
132KM/82 MILES

132 km ──── ⑩ **FINISH**

Audain Art Museum
Dramatic art gallery housing historic and contemporary BC art

⑨ ──── **84 km**
Brandywine Falls
Your knees will turn to jelly as you look over the plummeting water

56 km ──── ⑤

Brackendale Eagles
Soaring, hunting and hanging out in their hundreds

● Squamish

③ ──── **35 km**
Britannia Mine Museum
Grab your hard hat for a look into a mining community

Horseshoe Bay ●
START

GREAT FOR...

BEST TIME TO GO

November to March has the best snow; June to September offers sunny hiking, plus driving without chains.

📷 ESSENTIAL PHOTO

Get the ultimate snowy-peak picture from Tantalus Lookout.

✓ BEST FOR OUTDOORS

Ski Olympic-style down Whistler Mountain.

Classic Trip

26 Sea to Sky Highway

Drive out of North Vancouver and straight onto the wild west coast. This short excursion reveals the essence of British Columbia's shoreline with majestic sea and mountain vistas, outdoor activity opportunities, wildlife-watching possibilities and a peek into the regional First Nations culture and pioneer history that's woven along the route. There's even freshly roasted, organic coffee along the way. How much more 'BC' can you get?

1 Horseshoe Bay

As clouds and mist drift in across the snow-capped mountains of Howe Sound, standing at the foot of Horseshoe Bay may well make you feel like you've stepped into Middle Earth. Green-forested hills tumble down around the village, which has a small-town vibe that doesn't attest to its proximity to Vancouver. Grab a coffee and some fish 'n' chips from one of the many waterfront cafes and watch the bobbling boats from the seaside park. This first stop is all about slowing down and taking it all in.

Have a wander through the **Spirit Gallery** (☏604-921-8972; www.spirit-gallery.com; 6408 Bay St; ⏰10am-6pm, with seasonal variations; 🚌257), which is filled with classic and contemporary First Nations art and design from the region. You'll find everything from eye glasses to animal hand-puppets, prints, pewter and carvings.

🍴 p287

The Drive » Head north on Hwy 99, which curves around the coast and follows Howe Sound. You'll be traveling between steep mountainsides, down which waterfalls plummet, and the often misty ocean where islands are perched like sleeping giants. Watch out for Tunnel Point Lookout on the western side of the highway for a vantage point across the sound.

TOP TIP:
GAS STATION?

There is nowhere to fill your tank between North Vancouver and Squamish, a distance of around 46.7km (29 miles). This is mountain driving so make sure you've got at least half a tank when you set out.

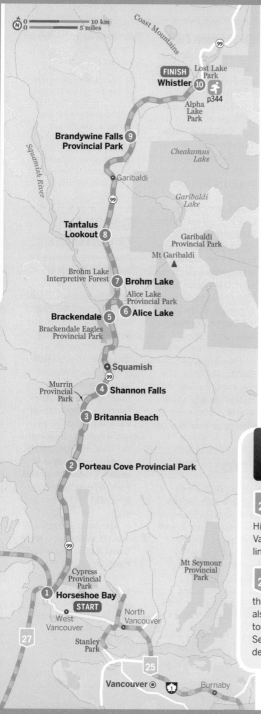

❷ Porteau Cove Provincial Park

Once popular with regional First Nations communities for sturgeon fishing, Porteau Cove is one of the oldest archaeological sites on the Northwest coast. These days it's a haven for divers, with reefs that support countless species of marine life, such as octopus and wolf eels. The rocky beach is good for exploring, with plenty of logs to clamber on, and in summer the water is just about warm enough for a very quick dip.

The Drive » From here, the sound narrows and as you continue north on Hwy 99, the mountains from the opposite shore begin to loom over you.

 LINK YOUR TRIP

25 Vancouver & the Fraser Valley

Highway 99 begins in North Vancouver, so it's easy to link these tours.

27 A Strait Hop

A Strait Hop goes through Horseshoe Bay, also the first stop on this tour, so you could do the Sea to Sky Highway as a detour.

Classic Trip

TRIP HIGHLIGHT

❸ Britannia Beach

Today you can don a hard hat and hop on a bone-shaking train that trundles you through a floodlit mine tunnel. With hands-on exhibits, gold panning, an engaging film and entry into the dizzying 20-story mill, the **Britannia Mine Museum** (📞604-896-2260; www.britanniaminemuseum. ca; Hwy 99; adult/child CAN$29/18.50; ⏰9am-5pm; 👪) has plenty to keep you (and any kids in tow) busy. You'll need a couple of hours here.

🍴 p287

The Drive ›› Continue north on Hwy 99, through the lush green Murrin Provincial Park.

❹ Shannon Falls

Torpedoing 1100ft over the mountaintop, Shannon Falls (p286) are the third largest in the province. Historically, the medicine people of the Squamish First Nation trained alongside these falls. A short, picturesque walk through the woods leads to a viewing platform.

You can also hike from here to the peak of the **Stawamus Chief** (2300ft), but an even better way to check out the region's breathtaking vistas is to hop back in your car and continue another minute or two along Hwy 99 to the **Sea to Sky Gondola** (📞604-892-2551; www. seatoskygondola.com; 36800 Hwy 99, Squamish; adult/child CAN$40/14; ⏰10am-6pm daily May-Oct, to 8pm Fri & Sat May-Sep, reduced hours in winter). Start snapping photos on your ride up the mountain, but save plenty of battery juice for the awesome panoramic views up top.

The Drive ›› Continue north on Hwy 99, past the Stawamus Chief and through Squamish (p287), where you can stop for road snacks, gas and supplies. Carry on along the highway, taking a left on Depot Rd and then another left onto Government Rd. The next stop is a few minutes up the road on your right.

TRIP HIGHLIGHT

❺ Brackendale

Brackendale is home to one of the largest populations of wintering bald eagles in North America. Visit between November and February to see an almost overwhelming number of these massive, magnificent birds feasting on salmon in the Squamish River. A path running alongside the riverbank offers a short walk and plenty of easy eagle-spotting opportunities. Across the river are the tall trees of **Brackendale Eagles Provincial Park**, where the beady-eyed birds perch in the night.

Also in this neighborhood is the historic **West Coast Railway Heritage Park** (📞604-898-9336; www.wcra.org; 39645 Government Rd, Squamish; adult/child CAN$18/13; ⏰10am-5pm; 👪). This large, mostly outdoor museum is the final resting place of British Columbia's

THE STAWAMUS CHIEF

This guy is hard to miss. Towering 2300ft above the waters of Howe Sound, it's the world's second-largest freestanding granite monolith. The Stawamus Chief and its three peaks have long been considered a sacred place to the Squamish people; they once came here seeking spiritual renewal. It's also the nesting grounds of peregrine falcons, who have increasingly returned to the area.

The views from the top are unbelievable, but getting up here is a challenge. The sheer face of the monolith has become a magnet for rock climbers, while hikers take trails from the eastern side. If you plan to scale the Chief, pick up a map and any supplies in nearby Squamish.

legendary *Royal Hudson* steam engine and has dozens of other historic railcars, including working engines and cabooses, sumptuous sleepers and a cool vintage mail car. Check out the handsome Roundhouse building, home to the park's most precious trains and artifacts.

The Drive ≫ North from Brackendale, Hwy 99 leaves the Squamish River and heads into the trees. The next stop is on the right.

---

6 Alice Lake

Delve into an old-growth hemlock forest for hiking and biking trails as well as lakeside picnic opportunities. Surrounded by a ring of towering mountains and offering two sandy beaches fringed by relatively warm water in summer, **Alice Lake Provincial Park** (www.discovercamping.ca; Hwy 99, Brackendale; campsites CAN$35) is a popular spot for a dip, a walk and an alfresco lunch.

If you want to stretch your legs, the 6km (3.75-mile) **Four Lakes Trail** is a fairly easy hike that does a loop around all four lakes in the park, passing through stands of Douglas fir and western red cedar. Keep your eyes (and your ears) peeled for warblers, Steller's jays and chickadees as well as for the box turtles that sometimes sun

THE STORY BEGINS

As you enter the **Squamish Lil'wat Cultural Centre** (604-964-0990; www.slcc.ca; 4584 Blackcomb Way; adult/child CAN$18/8; 9:30am-5pm Apr-Sep, 10am-5pm Tue-Sun Oct-Mar), take a look at the carved cedar doors you're passing through. According to the center's guide map, the door on the left shows a grizzly bear – protector of the Lil'wat – with a salmon in its mouth, representing sharing. The carving references a mother bear and cub that walked into the centre during construction. The door on the right, depicting a human face and hands up, symbolizes the Squamish welcoming all visitors.

themselves on the logs at Stump Lake.

The Drive ≫ Continue north along Hwy 99 for around 6.4km (4 miles) to Brohm Lake.

---

7 Brohm Lake

Less developed than Alice Lake Provincial Park, **Brohm Lake Interpretive Forest** (Hwy 99) has 10km (6.25 miles) of walking trails, many of them easy and flat. The lake is warm enough for summer swimming as the sun filters down onto the tree-studded shoreline.

Archaeological digs from this area have unearthed arrowheads and tools from early First Nations communities that date back 10,000 years. The area was later the scene of a logging mill and today is home to **Tenderfoot Fish Hatchery** (604-898-3657; 1000 Midnight Way, Brackendale; 9am-3pm), a facility

aimed at replenishing depleted salmon stocks, which fell from around 25,000 in the 1960s to around 1500 in the early 1980s. You can visit the hatchery and take a self-guided tour by following a 3.2km (2-mile) trail from Brohm Lake.

The Drive ≫ Continue up Hwy 99 just over 3.2km (2-mile) to the next stop.

---

8 Tantalus Lookout

This viewpoint looks out across the Tantalus Mountain Range. Tantalus was a character in Greek mythology who gave us the word 'tantalize'; apparently the mountains were named by an explorer who was tempted to climb the range's snowy peaks, but was stuck on the other side of the turbulent Squamish River. In addition to Mt Tantalus, the Greek hero's entire family is here – his wife,

WHY THIS IS A CLASSIC TRIP
JOHN LEE, WRITER

From mountains to ocean to
regional history and culture, this
is a grand tour of breathtaking BC features without
having to venture too far from the big city. I like
taking my sweet time on a weave like this, allowing
plenty of opportunities to stop, snap photos of the
life-affirming views and visit Whistler's sparkling
Audain Art Museum, the best gallery to open in BC
in years.

Left: Garibaldi Lake under Mt Garibaldi
Right: Whistler village

Mt Dione, his daughter,
Mt Niobe, his son, Mt
Pelops, and his grandson,
Mt Thyestes.

The Squamish people
once used this area to
train in hunting and
believe that, long ago,
hunters and their dogs
were immortalized here,
becoming the soaring
mountain range. Those
stone hunters must be

GALYNA ANDRUSHKO / SHUTTERSTOCK ©

ROLF HICKER / GETTY IMAGES ©

rather tantalized themselves; the forested slopes of the mountains are home to grizzly bears, elk, wolverines, wolves and cougars.

The Drive » Follow Hwy 99 22.5km (14 miles) north through the woods, skirting the edge of Daisy Lake before reaching the next stop on your right.

TRIP HIGHLIGHT

⑨ Brandywine Falls Provincial Park

Surging powerfully over the edge of a volcanic escarpment, **Brandywine Falls** (www.bcparks.ca; Hwy 99) plunge a dramatic 230ft – a straight shot into the pool below. Follow the easy 10-minute trail through the woods and step out onto the viewing platform, directly over the falls.

From here you can also see **Mt Garibaldi**, the most easily recognizable mountain in the Coast Range. Its distinctive jagged top and color has earned it the name Black Tusk. This mountain is of particular significance to local First Nations

285

Classic Trip

groups who believe the great Thunderbird landed here. With its supernatural ways, it shot bolts of lightning from its eyes, creating the color and shape of the mountaintop.

A 7km (4.3-mile) looped trail leads further through the park's dense forest and ancient lava beds to **Cal-Cheak Suspension Bridge**.

The Drive » Continue north along Hwy 99, passing Creekside Village and carrying on to the main Whistler village entrance (it's well signposted and obvious once you see it).

TRIP HIGHLIGHT

⑩ Whistler

Nestled in the shade of the formidable Whistler and Blackcomb Mountains, Whistler has long been BC's golden child. Popular in winter for its world-class ski slopes and in summer for everything from hiking to scream-inducing zip-line runs, it draws fans from around the world. It was named for the furry marmots that fill the area with their loud whistle, but there are also plenty of berry-snuffling black bears about.

The site of many of the outdoor events at the 2010 Winter Olympic and Paralympic Games, Whistler village is well worth a stroll (p344) and is filled with an eclectic mix of stores – everything from hip chains to Lululemon and Billabong. You'll also find flash hotels and seemingly countless cafes and restaurants.

Crisscrossed with over 200 runs, the **Whistler-Blackcomb** (☎604-967-8950; www.whistlerblackcomb.com; 2-day winter lift ticket adult/child CAN$258/129) sister mountains are linked by a 4.4km (2.75-mile) gondola that includes the world's longest unsupported span. Ski season runs late November to April on Whistler and June on Blackcomb. **Ziptrek Ecotours** (☎604-935-0001; www.ziptrek.com; Carleton Lodge, 4280 Mountain Sq; adult/child from CAN$119/99; ⚹) offers zip-line courses that will have you screaming with gut-quivering pleasure.

While you're here, be sure to take in the wood-beamed Squamish Lil'wat Cultural Centre (p283), built to resemble a traditional longhouse. It's filled with impressive art, images and displays that illuminate the tradiional and contemporary cultures of the Squamish and Lil'wat Nations.

A short stroll away, you'll find the **Audain Art Museum** (☎604-962-0413; www.audainartmuseum.com; 4350 Blackcomb Way; adult/child CAN$18/free; ⊙10am-5pm Sat-Mon & Wed, 10am-9pm Thu & Fri), a dramatic angular building nestled among the trees. One of the best new galleries to open in BC in years, it's home to an exciting array of paintings from BC icons, including Emily Carr and EJ Hughes, plus a shimmering collection of historic and contemporary First Nations works. Give yourself at least an hour here.

✗ ⊨ p287

LOOK FAMILIAR?

The mine complex (p282) at Britannia Beach has been used as a filming location for more than 50 movies and TV shows. *The X-Files, Smallville, Dark Angel* and *Insomnia* are just a few of the names on its list of appearances.

If you carry on to **Shannon Falls** (www.bcparks.ca; Hwy 99, Squamish) and have any teens with you, they may experience severe déjà vu. These falls featured in the *Twilight* film *Breaking Dawn*.

Eating & Sleeping

Horseshoe Bay ❶

🍴 The Boathouse   Canadian $$

(📞604-921-8188; www.boathouserestaurants. ca; 6695 Nelson Ave; mains CAN$16-40; ⏱11:30am-9pm Mon-Thu, 11am-9:30pm Fri, 10am-9:30pm Sat, 10am-9pm Sun) With a big, open sea view that's a necessity in Horseshoe Bay, the Boathouse is casual in a sophisticated kind of way. Crisp white tablecloths await diners, as does a contemporary menu heavy on the seafood but with steaks and some burger options for the less aquatically inclined. There's also a good wine list to wash it all down.

Britannia Beach ❸

🍴 Galileo Coffee Company   Cafe $

(📞604-896-0272; www.galileocoffee.com; 173 Hwy 99; baked goods from CAN$4; ⏱6am-3pm Mon-Fri, 7am-3pm Sat & Sun) Across from the entrance to Britannia Mine Museum (p282), Galileo Coffee is everyone's favorite java pit stop en route to Whistler.

Squamish ❹

🍴 Howe Sound Pub & Brewing Company   Pub Food $$

(📞778-654-3358; www.howesound.com; 37801 Cleveland Ave; mains CAN$12-22; ⏱11am-midnight Mon-Thu, 11am-1am Fri, 8am-1am Sat, 8am-midnight Sun; 🛜) This wood-beamed, ever-popular brewpub has a deck with views of the 'Chief' (Stawamus Chief Provincial Park's 652m-high granite rock face), where you can get comfortable and partake of some irresistible yam fries and delicious Devil's Elbow IPA. Or head inside for handmade pizzas, eclectic burgers and sandwiches, and elevated pub classics including cod 'n' chips (beer-battered, of course, with housemade honey pale ale).

Whistler ❿

🍴 21 Steps Kitchen & Bar   Canadian $$

(📞604-966-2121; www.21steps.ca; 4433 Sundial Pl; mains CAN$18-36; ⏱5:30pm-midnight) With small plates (CAN$8-14) for nibblers, the main dishes at this cozy spot all have a high-end comfort-food approach. The Thai curry is recommended for vegetarians while there are lots of gluten-free options for those who require it. Check out the great attic bar, a Whistlerite favorite.

🛏 Adara Hotel   Boutique Hotel $$

(📞604-905-4009; www.adarahotel.com; 4122 Village Green; r from CAN$209; 🛜 ♨ 🐾) Unlike all those lodges now claiming to be boutique hotels, the sophisticated and very centrally located Adara is the real deal. Studded with designer details, including a mod circular sofa in the lobby, accommodations have spa-like bathrooms and fireplaces that look like TVs. Despite the ultra-cool aesthetics, service is warm and relaxed. Check ahead for packages and off-season deals.

🛏 HI Whistler Hostel   Hostel $

(📞604-962-0025; www.hihostels.ca/whistler; 1035 Legacy Way; dm/r CAN$37/97; @ 🛜) Built as athlete accommodation for the 2010 Winter Olympics, this sparkling hostel is 7km south of the village near Function Junction. Transit buses to/from town stop right outside. Book ahead for private rooms (with en-suite bathrooms and TVs) or save by staying in a small dorm. Eschewing the sometimes institutionalized HI hostel feel, this one has IKEA-style furnishings, art-lined walls and a licensed cafe.

There's also a great TV room for rainy-day hunkering. If it's fine, hit the nearby biking and hiking trails or barbecue on one of the two mountain-view decks. When it's time to hit the village, the bus will have you there in around 15 minutes.

A Straight Hop

27

BC's forested, multi-fjorded coastline stretches for at least 24,000km (15,000 miles). But you don't have to drive that far for a taste of the region's salty, character-packed waterfront communities.

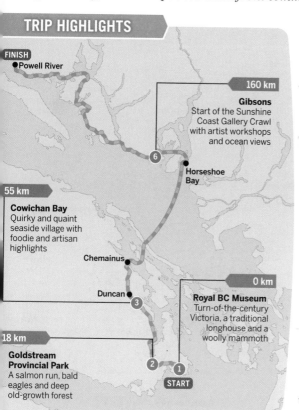

TRIP HIGHLIGHTS

FINISH
● Powell River

160 km

Gibsons
Start of the Sunshine Coast Gallery Crawl with artist workshops and ocean views

6

Horseshoe Bay

55 km

Cowichan Bay
Quirky and quaint seaside village with foodie and artisan highlights

Chemainus ●

0 km

Royal BC Museum
Turn-of-the-century Victoria, a traditional longhouse and a woolly mammoth

Duncan ●
3

18 km

Goldstream Provincial Park
A salmon run, bald eagles and deep old-growth forest

2 **1**
START

2–3 DAYS
351KM/218 MILES

GREAT FOR...

BEST TIME TO GO
June to September offers the most sunshine and least rain.

ESSENTIAL PHOTO
Clouds draped across mountaintops from the deck of a Horseshoe Bay ferry.

BEST FOR FOODIES
Dive into some delightful regional flavors in Cowichan Bay.

ichan Bay Marina at sunset

27 A Straight Hop

Perhaps it's the way sunlight reflects across the ever-shifting ocean, or the forest walks and beachcombing that seem an essential part of coastal life. Whatever the reason, the towns and villages snuggled next to the Pacific draw artistic folk from around the world to settle here and create strong communities and beautiful art. Take this leisurely tour for a slice of life on both the mainland and Vancouver Island.

TRIP HIGHLIGHT

1 Victoria

British Columbia's lovely, walkable (p342) seaside capital is dripping with colonial architecture and has enough museums, attractions, hotels and restaurants – many showcasing lip-smacking regional ingredients – to keep many visitors enthralled for an extra night or two.

Must-see attractions include the excellent **Royal BC Museum** (☎250-356-7226; www.

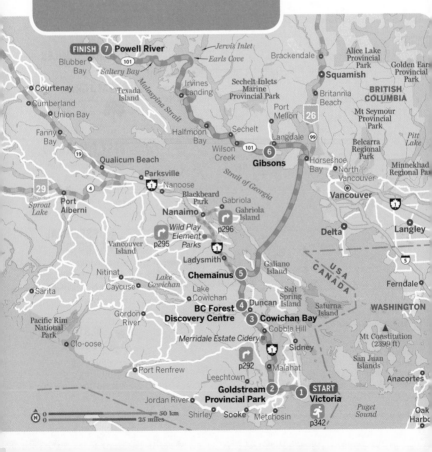

royalbcmuseum.bc.ca; 675 Belleville St; adult/child from CAN$16/11; ⏰10am-5pm daily, to 10pm Fri & Sat mid-May–Sep; ; 🚍70). Come eye to beady eye with a woolly mammoth and look out for cougars and grizzlies peeking from behind the trees. Step aboard Captain Vancouver's ship, enter a First Nations cedar longhouse, and explore a re-created early colonial street complete with shops, a movie house and an evocative replica Chinatown. A few minutes' stroll away, you'll also find the hidden gem **Miniature World** (☎250-385-9731; www.miniatureworld.com; 649 Humboldt St; adult/child CAN$15/10; ⏰9am-9pm mid-May–mid-Sep, 9am-5pm mid-

LINK YOUR TRIP

26 Sea to Sky Highway

Join this trip at Horseshoe Bay, making a return trip to Whistler and then carrying on to Gibsons.

29 Vancouver Island's Remote North

From Nanaimo on Vancouver Island, head north to Parksville or catch the ferry between Powell River on the mainland and Courtenay on the island.

RULE OF THE ROAD

Bone-shaking automobiles began increasingly popping up on the roads of British Columbia in the early years of the 20th century, often the toys of rich playboys with too much time on their hands. But for many years, BC had few regulations governing the trundling procession of cars around the region: vehicles could drive on either side of the road in some communities, although the left-hand side (echoing the country's British colonial overlords) gradually became the accepted practice.

Aiming to match driving rules in the USA (and in much of the rest of the world), yet managing to confuse the local issue still further, BC began legislating drivers over to the right-hand side of the road in the 1920s. One of the last areas to make the switch official was Vancouver Island. During the transition period, some minor accidents were reported around the region as forgetful drivers tootled toward each other before veering across at the last minute.

Sep–mid-May; ; 🚍70), an immaculate, old-school attraction crammed with 80 diminutive dioramas themed on everything from Arthurian Britain to a futuristic sci-fi realm.

Also worth visiting is the **Art Gallery of Greater Victoria** (☎250-384-4171; www.aggv.ca; 1040 Moss St; adult/child CAN$13/2.50; ⏰10am-5pm Mon-Sat, noon-5pm Sun, closed Mon mid-Sep–mid-May; 🚍14), home to one of Canada's best Emily Carr collections. Aside from Carr's swirling nature canvases, you'll find an ever-changing array of temporary exhibitions.

And save time to hop on a not-much-bigger-than-a-bathtub-sized **Victoria Harbour Ferry**

(☎250-708-0201; www.victoriaharbourferry.com; fares from CAN$6). This colorful armada of tiny tugboats stop at numerous docks along the waterfront, including the Inner Harbour, Songhees Park and Fisherman's Wharf (where alfresco fish 'n' chips is heartily recommended.)

🍴 🛏 p297, p305

The Drive » Follow Hwy 1 (which begins its cross-country journey in Victoria) west onto the sometimes narrow, heavily forested Malahat Dr section, also known as the Malahat Hwy.

TRIP HIGHLIGHT

② Goldstream Provincial Park

Alongside the Malahat, the abundantly scenic

DETOUR:
MERRIDALE ESTATE CIDERY

Start: ❷ Goldstream (p291)

After leaving Goldstream, head west off the highway onto Cobble Hill Rd. This weaves through bucolic farmland and wine-growing country. Watch for asparagus farms, beady-eyed llamas, blueberry stalls and verdant vineyards. Stop in at charming **Merridale Estate Cidery** (📞250-743-4293; www.merridalecider.com; 1230 Merridale Rd, Cobble Hill; ⊙11am-5pm, reduced hours off-season), an inviting apple-cider producer offering many varieties, as well as artisan gin and vodka.

Cobble Hill Rd crosses over the highway and loops east to Cowichan Bay.

Goldstream Provincial Park (📞250-478-9414; www.goldstreampark.com; 2930 Trans Canada Hwy; 🅿) drips with ancient, moss-covered cedar trees and a moist carpet of plant life. The short walk through the woods to the **Free-man King Visitors Centre** (📞250-478-9414; 2390 Trans-Canada Hwy; ⊙9am-4:30pm) is beautiful; once you're there, take in the center's hands-on exhibits about natural history.

The park is known for its chum salmon spawning season (from late October to December), when the water literally bubbles with thousands of struggling fish. Hungry bald eagles also swoop in at this time to feast on the full-grown salmon.

You'll also find great **hiking** here: marked trails range from tough to easy and some are wheelchair accessible. The visitor center can advise. If you do head off down the trail, remember this is bear and cougar country.

The Drive ›› From Goldstream, the Malahat climbs north to its summit with a number of gorgeous viewpoints over Brentwood Bay. Continue on Hwy 1, following signs east off the highway for Cowichan Bay.

- - - - - - - - - -

TRIP HIGHLIGHT

❸ Cowichan Bay

With a colorful string of wooden buildings perched on stilts over a mountain-shadowed ocean inlet, Cowichan Bay – Cow Bay to locals – is well worth a stop. Wander along the pier of the **Maritime Centre** (📞250-746-4955; www.classicboats.org; 1761 Cowichan Bay Rd; admission by suggested donation CAN$5; ⊙dawn-dusk May-Sep,

reduced hours in winter) to peruse some salty boat-building exhibits and intricate models, and get your camera out to shoot the handsome panoramic views of the harbor. Duck into the galleries and studios lining the water-front or stretch your legs on a five-minute stroll to the **Cowichan Estuary Nature Centre** (📞250-597-2288; www.cowichan estuary.ca; 1845 Cowichan Bay Rd; admission by suggested CAN$2 donation; ♿), where area birdlife and marine critters are profiled.

Art-wise, drop into the **Mud Room** (📞250-710-7329; www.cowbaymudroom.com; 1725 Cowichan Bay Rd; ⊙9am-6pm Jun-Sep, reduced hours in winter) to see potters at work making usable objects like cups and plates. Look for seaside-themed mugs and the popular yellow-glazed dragonfly motif pieces.

The artisans are also at work in Cow Bay's kitchens. This is a great place to gather the mak-ings of a great picnic at **True Grain Bread** (p297). Alternatively drop in for succulent, fresh-made fish 'n' chips at the locally loved **Rock Cod Cafe** (📞250-746-1550; www.rockcodcafe.com; 1759 Cowichan Bay Rd; mains CAN$10-18; ⊙11am-9pm Jul & Aug, 11am-7pm Sun-Thu, to 8pm Fri & Sat Sep-Jun; ♿).

✕ ⊨ p297

The Drive » Return to Hwy 1 and head north a further 12km (7.5 miles).

❹ BC Forest Discovery Centre

You won't find Tigger in this 100-acre wood, but if you want to know more about those giants swaying overhead, stop in at the **BC Forest Discovery Centre** (☏250-715-1113; www.bcforestdiscovery centre.com; 2892 Drinkwater Rd; adult/child CAN$16/11; ☺10am-4:30pm Jun-Aug, reduced hours off-season; 🅿). Woodland paths lead you among western yews, Garry oaks and 400-year-old fir trees with nesting bald eagles in their branches. Visit a 1920s sawmill and a 1905 wooden schoolhouse, and climb to the top of a wildfire lookout tower. Hop on a historical train for a ride around the grounds and check out some cool logging trucks from the early 1900s. Visit the indoor exhibits for the lowdown on contemporary forest management.

The Drive » It's a 20km (12.5-mile) journey to the next stop. Continue north on Hwy 1, turning right onto Henry Rd and then left onto Chemainus Rd.

❺ Chemainus

The residents of this tree-ringed settlement – a former resource community that almost became a ghost town – began commissioning **murals** on its walls in the 1980s, part of a forward-thinking revitalization project. The paintings – there are now almost 50 dotted around the community – soon became visitor attractions, stoking the town's rebirth. Among the best are the 54ft-long pioneer-town painting of Chemainus c 1891 on Mill St; the 50ft-long depiction of First Nations faces and totems on Chemainus Rd; and the evocative Maple St mural showing the waterfront community as it was in 1948.

Pick up a walking tour map of the murals from the **visitor center** next to Waterwheel Park (where there's also a parking lot). In the same building, the town's small **museum** is bristling with yesteryear reminders of the old town. Be sure to chat with the friendly volunteers: they'll regale you with real-life stories of the area's colorful past.

The lower part of the town is rather quiet but the southern end of Willow St has many cafes,

COUGAR!

Weighing in at up to 150lb (68kg), cougars are extremely stealthy and can, on their own, hunt and kill a 600lb (272kg) moose. While they're rarely seen, they can (and do) occasionally attack humans so it pays to be prepared – especially as the majority of the large cats in this region reside on the southern third of Vancouver Island.

Cougars are most active at dusk and dawn and most encounters take place in late spring and summer; however, cougars roam and hunt at any time of the day or night and in all seasons. Almost all human-based cougar attacks are on children, so keep your young ones close when you're outside and pick them up immediately if you see a cougar. Hike in groups of two or more and make enough noise to prevent surprising a cougar.

If you come across a cougar, always give it an avenue of escape. Talk to the cougar in a confident voice, face it and remain upright. Do not turn your back on the cougar. Do not run. Try to back away from the cougar slowly. If the cougar appears aggressive, do all you can to enlarge your image. Don't crouch down or try to hide. Pick up sticks or branches and wave them about. Convince the cougar that you are a threat, not prey. And if a cougar does attack, fight back!

restaurants and boutique galleries to keep you and your wallet occupied.

The impressive **Chemainus Theatre Festival** (☎800-565-7738, 250-246-9820; www.chemainustheatre festival.ca; 9737 Chemainus Rd; tickets from CAN$25) is also popular. Its large auditorium stages shows for much of the year. Check the website to see what's playing.

The Drive › Head north on Hwy 1 toward Nanaimo. Follow the signs to Departure Bay and catch a BC Ferries vessel to mainland Horseshoe Bay. From there, hop a second 40-minute ferry ride to Langdale on the Sunshine Coast (there are many restaurants in Horseshoe Bay if you're waiting between ferries). From Langdale it's a short drive along Hwy 101 to Gibsons.

TRIP HIGHLIGHT

⑥ Gibsons

Gibsons *feels* cozy. If you didn't know better, you'd think you were on an island – such is the strong community and almost isolated feel this town exudes. Head straight for the waterfront area – known as **Gibsons Landing** – where you can take in the many bright-painted clapboard buildings that back on to the water's edge, as well as intriguing artisan stores.

A walk along the town's main wooden jetty leads you past a colorful array of houseboats and

ANDROVER / SHUTTERSTOCK ©

floating garden plots. You'll also come to the sun-dappled gallery of **Sa Boothroyd** (☎604-886-7072; www.saboothroyd. com; Government Wharf; ◷10am-5pm). The artist is typically on hand to illuminate her browse-worthy and often humorous works. Although her bigger canvases are suitably pricey, there are

lots of tempting original trivets, coasters and tea cozies.

Need more culture? Head to the charming **Gibsons Public Art Gallery** (☎604-886-0531; www.gpag.ca; 431 Marine Dr; ◷11am-4pm Thu-Mon), which showcases the work of locals artists and changes its displays every month. Check the website

Victoria Inner Harbour

for show openings – always a good time to meet the arty locals.

 p297

The Drive » Continue along tree-lined Hwy 101; expect glimpses of sandy coves in the forests on your left. The highway leads through Sechelt (handy for supplies) then on to Earls Cove. Hop the BC Ferries service across Jervis Inlet to Saltery Bay. This achingly beautiful

DETOUR:
WILD PLAY ELEMENT PARKS

Start: ❺ **Chemainus (p293)**

Fancy zipping, swinging or jumping from a giant tree? It's an easy 21km (13-mile) Hwy 1 drive north from Chemainus to **Wild Play Element Parks** (📞250-716-7874; www.wildplay.com; 35 Nanaimo River Rd; adult/child CAN$35/20; ⏰10am-6pm mid-May–Sep, reduced hours off-season; 👪) for some woodland thrills involving canopy obstacle courses and a daredevil bungee-jump zone.

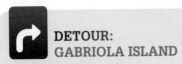

DETOUR:
GABRIOLA ISLAND

Start: ⑤ Chemainus (p293)

If you're tempted by those mysterious little islands peeking at you off the coast of Vancouver Island, take the 20-minute **BC Ferries** (☎250-386-3431; www.bcferries. com) service from Nanaimo's Inner Harbour to **Gabriola Island** (www.gabriolaisland. org). Home to dozens of artists plus a healthy smattering of old hippies, there's a tangible air of quietude to this rustic realm. Pack a picnic and spend the afternoon communing with the natural world in a setting rewardingly divorced from big-city life.

50-minute trip threads past islands and forested coastlines. From Saltery Bay, take Hwy 101 to Powell River.

⑦ Powell River

Powell River is one of the Sunshine Coast's most vibrant communities. It was founded in the early 1900s when three Minnesota businessmen dammed the river to create a massive hydroelectric power plant. Not long after, a pulp mill was built to take advantage of the surrounding forests and handy deepwater harbor, with the first sheets of paper trundling off its steamy production line in 1912. Within a few years, the mill had become the world's largest producer of newsprint, churning out 275 tons daily.

Today there's an active and artsy vibe to this waterfront town, including its historic **Townsite** (☎604-483-3901; www.powellrivertownsite. com; Dr Henderson's House, 6211 Walnut Ave; CAN$5) area, which is great for on-foot wandering. Many of Powell River's oldest streets are named after trees and some are still lined with the original mill workers' cottages that kick-started the settlement. The steam-plumed mill is still here, too – although it's shrinking every year and its former grounds are being transformed into parkland. Dip into this history at **Powell River Museum** (☎604-485-2327; www.powellrivermuseum.ca; 4798 Marine Ave; ⊙9am-4pm mid-Apr–Oct, 9am-4pm Mon-Fri Nov–mid-Apr), which covers the area's First Nations heritage and its tough pioneer days (check out the photos of early settlers).

If you spend the night in town, catch a film at the quaint **Patricia Theatre** (☎604-483-9345; www. patriciatheatre.com; 5848 Ash Ave), Canada's oldest continually operating cinema.

SUNSHINE COAST GALLERY CRAWL

Along Hwy 101, keep your eyes peeled for jaunty purple flags fluttering in the breeze. These indicate that an artist is at work on the adjoining property. If your eyesight isn't up to the task, pick up the handy *Sunshine Coast Purple Banner* flyer from area visitor centers and galleries to find out exactly where these artists are located. Some are open for drop-in visits while others prefer that you call ahead. The region is studded with arts and crafts creators, working with wood, glass, clay and just about everything else. For further information, check www.suncoastarts.com.

✖ ⊨ p297

Eating & Sleeping

Victoria ❶

✕ John's Place — Diner $$

(📞250-389-0711; www.johnsplace.ca; 723 Pandora Ave; mains CAN$9-17; ⌚7am-9pm Mon-Fri, 8am-4pm & 5-9pm Sat & Sun; 📶🖊; 🖥70) This friendly hangout is lined with quirky memorabilia, while its enormous menu is a cut above standard diner fare. They'll start you off with a basket of addictive housemade bread, but save room for pasta dishes, salads or a pancake or Tex-Mex brunch. A near-perfect breakfast spot.

🛏 Inn at Laurel Point — Hotel $$$

(📞250-386-8721; www.laurelpoint.com; 680 Montreal St; d from CAN$260; ✳@📶✖🐾; 🖥70) Tucked along the Inner Harbour a short stroll from the downtown action, this friendly, art-lined and comfortable hotel is all about the views across the waterfront. Spacious rooms come with private balconies. Owned by a local family, there's a resort-like level of calm relaxation.

Cowichan Bay ❸

✕ Hilary's Cheese — Deli $$

(📞250-748-5992; 1737 Cowichan Bay Rd; ⌚10am-5pm Sun-Tue, 10am-9pm Wed-Sat, reduced hours in winter) Now that cheesemaker Hilary has moved on, this inviting joint has become a purveyor of cheeses from around the world. And while the magic of having its own maker is missed, there's still good eats to be had here, including the cheese and charcuterie plate.

✕ True Grain Bread — Bakery $

(📞250-746-7664; www.truegrain.ca; 1725 Cowichan Bay Rd; ⌚8am-6pm, closed Mon Nov-Feb) Look for the old bicycle hanging over the entrance and follow your nose inside. From sourdough to raisin, the loaves are organic and milled on site (from BC-farmed grain). Be sure to pick up some sweet treats for the road, too.

✕ Masthead Restaurant — West Coast $$$

(📞250-748-3714; www.themastheadrestaurant. com; 1705 Cowichan Bay Rd; mains CAN$26-35; ⌚5-10pm) Push out the boat (not literally) on the patio deck of this charming, heritage building restaurant where the CAN$35 three-course BC-sourced tasting menu is surprisingly good value. Seasonal ingredients is the approach here, plus some good Cowichan Valley wines to try.

🛏 Dreamweaver — B&B $$

(📞250-748-7688; www.dreamweaverbedand breakfast.com; 1682 Botwood Lane; d from CAN$135; 📶) Perched on the edge of the village, just steps away from the restaurants and galleries, this Victorian-style home welcomes guests with three comfortable, rather floral rooms.

Gibsons ❻

✕ Molly's Reach — Breakfast, Burgers $

(📞604-886-9710; www.mollysreach.ca; 647 School Rd; mains CAN$8-16; ⌚9am-9pm) A popular local fixture, famous as a location for the legendary Canadian TV show *The Beachcombers*, this yellow-painted, pub-style diner is the perfect place to fill up on a heaping breakfast (crab cake eggs Benedict recommended) or a giant serving of fish 'n' chips. Aim for a seat on the patio to peruse the boats in the marina.

Powell River ❼

✕ Shinglemill Pub & Bistro — Pub Food $$

(📞604-483-3545; www.shinglemill.ca; 6233 Powell Pl; mains CAN$14-26) Built on piles over the lake at the edge of town, this historic pub knocks out hearty burgers, stir-fries and sandwiches. But the main reason to come here, especially in summer, is for a seat on the deck overlooking the glassy water.

🛏 Old Courthouse Inn — Hotel $

(📞604-483-4000; www.oldcourthouseinn. ca; 6243 Walnut St; d from CAN$129; 📶) Immaculately restored by new owners in recent years, this Tudoresque antique-lined hotel is a real charmer. Each room, individualized with its own knickknacks, feels like a cozy home-away-from-home decorated by a nostalgic aunt with artistic appreciation. Rates include cooked breakfast in the lovely Edie Rae's Diner.

Southern Vancouver Island Tour

28

Begin on the Gulf Islands among uncommon amounts of creativity and tranquility. Then cross through ancient, fern-lined forests to Vancouver Island's wild west coast.

TRIP HIGHLIGHTS

174 km

Botanical Beach
Explore vibrant tidal pools next to the crashing coastline

24 km

Red Tree Gallery
Be inspired by Pender Island's diverse artists in a quaint waterside gallery

● Sidney
START

6

 7

Jordan River

Victoria
FINISH

China Beach
Delve deep into the forest and emerge onto a huge sandy expanse

213 km

Salt Spring Island Cheese
Experience life on a forested gourmet cheese farm

61 km

4–5 DAYS
290KM/180 MILES

GREAT FOR...

BEST TIME TO GO
June to September for frequent ferries, warm weather and possible whale sightings.

ESSENTIAL PHOTO
Botanical Beach's crashing waves.

BEST FOR OUTDOORS
Salt Spring Island for cycling and hiking, and kayaking in sun-dappled lakes.

---

n De Fuca Provincial Park Beach camping

Southern Vancouver Island Tour

Whether you're standing on the deck of a Gulf Islands ferry or on the sandy expanse of China Beach, the untamed ocean is an essential part of life in this part of the world. It seems to foster pods of creativity – small islands where artisans practice crafts from pottery to cheese-making – and it salt-licks the dramatic coastline into shape, with sandy coves fringed by dense, wind-bent woodlands.

❶ Sidney

A short trip north of Victoria, the sunny seaside town of Sidney is ideal for wandering. Along the main street, an almost unseemly number of bookstores jostle for space with boutique shops and cafes. When you reach the water, you'll find the **Seaside Sculpture Walk** (www.sculpturewalk.ca) – showcasing a dozen or so locally created artworks – plus a picturesque pier with twinkling island vistas. Watch the sea for seals and herons or join a

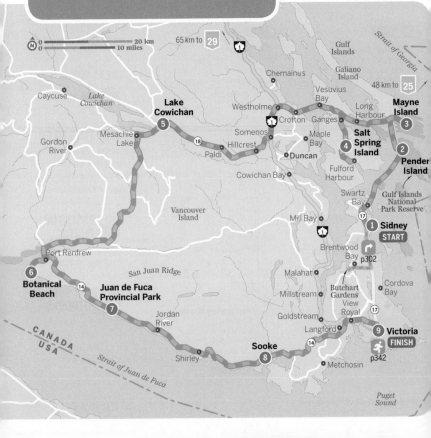

marine wildlife-spotting boat tour with **Sidney Whale Watching** (🕿250-656-7599; www.sidneywhale-watching.com; 2537 Beacon Ave; adult/child CAN$115/89; ☺Mar-Oct).

While you're at the waterfront, visit the compact but brilliant **Shaw Ocean Discovery Centre** (🕿250-665-7511; www.oce-andiscovery.ca; 9811 Seaport Pl; adult/child CAN$15/8; ☺10am-4:30pm). It opens your eyes to the color and diversity in the neighboring Salish Sea with aquariums, touch pools and plenty of hands-on exhibits. The staff are well versed and the gift shop is a treasure trove.

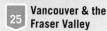 p305

LINK YOUR TRIP

25 Vancouver & the Fraser Valley

From the Gulf Islands, you can catch ferries to Tsawwassen on the mainland to connect with Hwy 1 into Vancouver or out toward Harrison Hot Springs.

29 Vancouver Island's Remote North

When you reach Hwy 1 after leaving Salt Spring Island, you can carry on north to pick up this even more off-the-beaten-track trip.

The Drive » Follow Hwy 17 (Patricia Bay Hwy) north to its end at the BC Ferries terminal. Board a boat for a beautiful crossing to Pender Island.

TRIP HIGHLIGHT

2 Pender Island

Disembarking the ferry onto this small island, you are quickly enveloped by a sense of tangible quietude. Narrow roads wind within deep forests where you'll see countless walking trails, quail crossings and confident deer.

Pender is actually two islands – North and South, joined by a small bridge. **Gowland** and **Tilly Point** on South Pender have beach access; head to Tilly Point for tidal pools and Mt Baker views. Sheltered, sandy **Medicine Beach** on the North Island has lots of clamber-worthy logs. While on the beaches, look out for bald eagles, seals and otters.

Pender is also home to many artists. Pick up a copy of the *Pender Island Artists Guide* on the ferry or on Pender for

a list of local galleries. A great place to start is the **Red Tree Gallery** (🕿250-629-6800; www.redtreegallery.ca; 4301 Bedwell Harbour Rd; ☺10am-4pm Tue-Sun Jun-Sep, 11am-4pm Wed-Sun Oct-Apr) in quaint Hope Bay. This arts cooperative displays the work of over 15 local artists, with everything from photography to glass art, jewelry, paintings and hand-spun wool.

For locally produced wine, head to delightful **Sea Star Vineyards** (🕿250-629-6960; www.sea starvineyards.ca; 6621 Harbour Hill Dr; ☺11am-5pm May-Sep). Using grapes from its own vine-striped hills, it produces tasty small-batch tipples plus a wide array of pickable fruit from kiwis to raspberries.

Also worth a look is **Pender Islands Museum** (www.penderislandmuseum.org; 2408 South Otter Bay Rd, North Pender; ☺10am-4pm Sat & Sun Jul & Aug, reduced hours off-season), housed in an original 1908 farmhouse. Explore the history of the island through its re-created rooms, vintage photos and evocative exhibits.

 p305

The Drive » Return to the ferry terminal on North Pender and board a ferry through the channel to Mayne Island.

❸ Mayne Island

As the boat pulls into Mayne Island, you're greeted with colorful wooden houses, quaint communities and lots of deer. Head to **Georgina Point Lighthouse** for ocean and mountain-filled views across Active Pass. The water literally bubbles here with the strength of the current. This is a popular spot for eagles to fish and you're also likely to see (and hear) sea lions resting on nearby rocks.

For a quiet retreat, visit the **Japanese Garden** (Dinner Bay Community Park, Dinner Point Rd), dedicated to the many Japanese families who settled on the island from 1900 onward. Once constituting a third of the population, they contributed more than half of the island's farming, milling and fish-preservation work. During WWII the government saw them as a national threat and forced their removal. The garden contains traditional Japanese elements within a forest, including shrines and a peace bell.

 p305

The Drive » Return to the ferry terminal and board a ferry to Long Harbour on Salt Spring Island.

TRIP HIGHLIGHT

❹ Salt Spring Island

When folks from Vancouver talk about quitting their jobs and making jam for a living, they're likely mulling a move to Salt Spring. Once a hippie haven and later a yuppie retreat, it's now home to anyone who craves a quieter life without sacrificing everyday conveniences. The main town of **Ganges** has it all, from grocery stores to galleries. If you're coming from Mayne, it'll feel full-on; it's a wonderful place to explore.

Salt Spring is also home to many an artisan, with everyone from bakers to carvers and winemakers. Stop in at **Waterfront Gallery** (☎250-537-4525; www.waterfrontgallery.ca; 107 Purvis Lane, Ganges; ⊗10am-5pm), which carries the work of many local artists with pottery, glassware, knitwear, candles and even birdhouses prominent. Also stop in at **Salt Spring Mercantile** (☎250-653-4321; www.saltspringmercantile.com; 2915 Fulford-Ganges Rd, Fulford; ⊗8:30am-6pm), which sells lots of local products, including Salish Sea Chocolates (try the cherry with hazelnut!), jars of fresh chutney and flower-petal-packed soaps.

If you're suddenly peckish, save time for **Salt Spring Island Cheese** (☎250-653-2300;

➤ DETOUR:
BUTCHART GARDENS

Start: ❶ Sidney (p300)

A 16km (10-mile) drive south of Sidney on Hwy 17, turning west on Keating Cross Rd, brings you to Benvenuto Ave and British Columbia's most famous botanical attraction. The century-old **Butchart Gardens** (☎250-652-5256; www.butchartgardens.com; 800 Benvenuto Ave; adult/teen/child CAN$32.10/16.05/3; ⊗9am-10pm, reduced hours off-season; 🅿75), which originated from an attempt to beautify an old cement factory site, has been cleverly planned to ensure there's always something in bloom, no matter what the season. In summer there are Saturday night fireworks displays and in winter the twinkling seasonal lights are magical. Whatever time of year you arrive, give yourself at least a couple of hours to enjoy the spectacle.

Salt Spring Island Cheese Tasting event

www.saltspringcheese.com; 285 Reynolds Rd; ⊙11am-5pm May-Sep, 11am-4pm Oct-Apr; 🚻) on Weston Creek Farm. Meet the goats and sheep that produce milk for the cheese, see it being made, and be awed by the beautiful finale – taste cheeses adorned with lemon slices, flowers and chilies.

Head to **Ruckle Park** for ragged shorelines, gnarly arbutus forests and sun-kissed farmlands. There are trails here for all skill levels, as well as great ocean views for a picnic. **Mt Maxwell** offers a steep but worthwhile hike and

Cushion Lake and **St Mary's Lake** are summertime swimming haunts. Fancy exploring sans car? Visit **Island Escapades** (📞250-537-2553; www.islandescapades.com; 163 Fulford-Ganges Rd; rentals/tours from CAN$40/65) in Ganges to rent kayaks and join excursions.

✗ 🛏 p305

The Drive » Explore the island's diverse landscape of rolling meadows and dense forest, heading north to Vesuvius Bay where you can board a ferry to Crofton on Vancouver Island. From the east coast, curve inland along Hwy 18 and the glassy-calm waters of Lake Cowichan.

5 **Lake Cowichan**

Hop out of the car at Lake Cowichan for some deep breaths at the ultra-clear, tree-fringed lakefront. This is a perfect spot for swimming or setting out for a hike along the lakeside trails. After the town of Lake Cowichan, it's another 64km stretch (without services) through the heart of the island. You'll encounter cathedral-calm old-growth woodland here where towering spruce and Douglas firs, many centuries old, dominate the landscape.

MARKET DAY

If you arrive on Salt Spring Island on a summer weekend, the best way to dive into the community is at the gigantic **Saturday Market** (www.saltspringmarket. com; Centennial Park, Ganges; ⊙9am-4pm Sat Apr-Oct) where you can tuck into luscious island-grown fruit and piquant cheeses while perusing locally produced arts and crafts.

The Drive » From Lake Cowichan, follow South Shore Rd and then Pacific Marine Rd to Port Renfrew and on to Botanical Beach, 66km (41 miles) from Lake Cowichan. Pacific Marine Rd is narrow and winding but takes you through breathtaking forest.

TRIP HIGHLIGHT

6 Botanical Beach

Feeling like the edge of the earth, it's worth the effort to get to Botanical Beach. Follow the winding road from Port Renfrew and then the sometimes steep pathway down to the beach. The tidal pools here are rich in colorful marine life, including chitons, anemones, gooseneck barnacles, sea palms and purple sea urchins. Surrounded by windblown coastline and crashing waves, this is also a favorite springtime haunt of orcas and gray whales, plus a feeding ground for harbor seals.

The rocks here can be slippery and the waves huge; take care and watch the tide.

✖ p305

The Drive » Head southeast on Hwy 14 to nearby Juan de Fuca Provincial Park.

TRIP HIGHLIGHT

7 Juan de Fuca Provincial Park

Welcome to the dramatic coastal wilderness of **Juan de Fuca Provincial Park** (✆250-474-1336; www.bcparks.ca; Hwy 14). There are good stop-off points along this rugged stretch, providing memorable views of the rocky, ocean-carved seafront where trees cling for dear life and whales slide past just off the coast. Our favorite is **China Beach**, reached along a fairly gentle, well-maintained trail through dense forest. The prize is a long stretch of wind-swept sand. **French Beach** is also popular with day-trippers and requires less of a leg-stretch.

The Drive » Continue southeast along Hwy 14, skirting the coastline to Sooke, 74km (46 miles) away.

8 Sooke

Once considered the middle of nowhere, seaside Sooke is gaining popularity and is a handy place to bunk down for the night. For an introduction to the area, stop at **Sooke Region Museum** (✆250-642-6351; www.sookeregion museum.com; 2070 Phillips Rd; ⊙9am-5pm mid-May–mid-Oct, closed Mondays mid-Oct–mid-May), which has intriguing exhibits on the district's pioneer past, including the tiny **Moss Cottage**, one of the island's oldest pioneer homes.

🛏 p305

The Drive » From Sooke, follow Hwy 14 (Sooke Rd) east, all the way to Hwy 1. Join the eastbound traffic, which will lead you on to nearby Victoria, 40km (25 miles) from Sooke.

9 Victoria

The provincial capital is vibrant, charming and highly walkable (p342). The picturesque Inner Harbour, magnetic boutique shopping and belly-thrilling cuisine make it understandably popular. Add an outgoing university crowd plus a strong arts community and you get an interesting, diverse population.

✖ 🛏 p297, p305

Eating & Sleeping

Sidney ❶

✖ Toast Cafe   Cafe $

(✆250-665-6234; 2400 Bevan Ave; mains CAN$6-12; ⏱6:30am-4pm Mon-Sat; 📶)
Serving the best coffee in Sidney, this corner joint also makes great breakfast wraps and thick-cut, superbly satisfying sandwiches.

🛏 Sidney Pier Hotel & Spa   Hotel $$

(✆250-655-9445; www.sidneypier.com; 9805 Seaport Pl; d from CAN$209; @📶🐾) This swish property fuses West Coast lounge cool with beach pastel colors. Many rooms have shoreline views, and each has local artworks on the walls.

Pender Island ❷

✖ Pender Island Bakery Cafe   Cafe $

(Driftwood Centre, 4605 Bedwell Harbour Rd, North Pender; mains CAN$6-20; ⏱7am-5pm; 📶) The coffee is organic, as are many of the bakery treats, including huge cinnamon buns.

🛏 Poet's Cove Resort & Spa   Hotel $$$

(✆250-629-2100; www.poetscove.com; Bedwell Harbour, 9801 Spalding Rd, South Pender; d from CAN$350; 📶🐾) This luxurious lodge has arts-and-crafts-accented rooms, most with great water views. It also has an activity center that books eco-tours and fishing excursions.

Mayne Island ❸

✖ Bennett Bay Bistro   Canadian $$

(✆250-539-3122; www.bennettbaybistro.com; 494 Arbutus Dr; mains CAN$12-22; ⏱11:30am-8:30pm) You don't have to be guest of the Mayne Island Resort to dine at its restaurant, which serves pubby classics. Go for the seafood, though; especially the velvet-soft seared sockeye salmon. Reservations recommended.

Salt Spring Island ❹

✖ House Piccolo   Canadian $$$

(✆250-537-1844; www.housepiccolo.com; 108 Hereford Ave, Ganges; mains CAN$27-34;

⏱5-10pm Wed-Sun) White tablecloth dining in a beautifully intimate setting, House Piccolo offers memorable dishes focused on local seasonal ingredients and the best drinks on the island.

🛏 Oceanside Cottages   Cottage $$

(✆250-653-0007; www.oceansidecottages.com; 521 Isabella Point Rd; d from CAN$135) These four unique cottages are nooks of bliss. Each is private and filled with eclectic artwork and creative flourishes.

Botanical Beach ❻

✖ Tomi's Home Cookin'   Cafe $

(✆250-412-6099; 7152 Parkinson Rd, Port Renfrew; mains CAN$6-10; ⏱7am-4pm Mon-Sat, 10am-4pm Sun) Simple, friendly and homey, this red-painted little landmark serves up delicious muffins, soups, wraps and burgers.

Sooke ❽

🛏 Sooke Harbour House   Hotel $$$

(✆250-642-3421; www.sookeharbourhouse.com; 1528 Whiffen Spit Rd; d from CAN$329; 📶🐾) Whether you opt for the Emily Carr or Blue Heron, each of the 28 guest rooms here has a tub or steam shower, while most also have wood-burning fireplaces, balconies and sea views. The hotel's Copper Room Bistro is also worth a stop.

Victoria ❾

✖ The Mint   Fusion $$

(✆250-386-6468; www.themintvictoria.com; 1414 Douglas St; mains CAN$9-23; ⏱11am-4pm Mon-Sat & 5pm-2am daily; 🚌70) Mint offers an eclectic, finger-licking menu of Nepalese, Tibetan and fusion delicacies that run from spicy lamb cooked with apricots to almond-and-cashew pesto fettuccine.

🛏 Abigail's Hotel   B&B $$$

(✆250-388-5363; www.abigailshotel.com; 906 McClure St; d from CAN$249; 🅿@📶; 🚌7) Behind its Tudoresque facade, accommodations range from flowery standard rooms to antique-lined suites with canopy beds. Adults only.

Vancouver Island's Remote North

Throw yourself head-first into Vancouver Island's natural side. Ancient forests, diving orca, wild sandy beaches, quaint villages and a peek into First Nations cultures make it a well-rounded trip.

TRIP HIGHLIGHTS

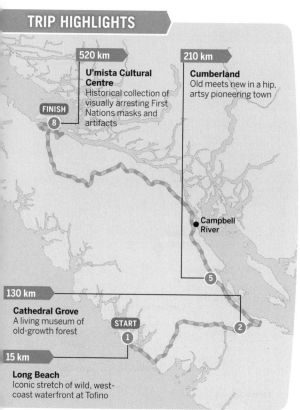

520 km

U'mista Cultural Centre
Historical collection of visually arresting First Nations masks and artifacts

FINISH
8

210 km

Cumberland
Old meets new in a hip, artsy pioneering town

Campbell River

5

130 km

Cathedral Grove
A living museum of old-growth forest

START
1

2

15 km

Long Beach
Iconic stretch of wild, west-coast waterfront at Tofino

2–3 DAYS
520KM/323 MILES

GREAT FOR...

BEST TIME TO GO
May to September for the most sunshine and the least chance of relentless rain.

ESSENTIAL PHOTO
The forest of totem poles watching over the sea at Alert Bay.

BEST FOR STORM WATCHERS
Watch massive, frothy waves crashing onto Long Beach, especially in winter.

MacMillan Provincial Park Cathedral Grove

29

Vancouver Island's Remote North

Following this trip is like following Alice down the rabbit hole — you'll feel you've entered an enchanted land that's beyond the reach of day-to-day life. Ancient, moss-covered trees will leave you feeling tiny, as bald eagles swoop above and around you like pigeons. You'll see bears munching dandelions and watching you inscrutably. And totem poles, standing like forests, will seem to whisper secrets of the past. Go on. Jump in.

TRIP HIGHLIGHT

❶ Tofino

Packed with activities and blessed with stunning beaches, former fishing town Tofino sits on Clayoquot (clay-kwot) Sound, where forests rise from roiling waves that batter the coastline. Visitors come to surf, whale-watch, kayak, hike and hug trees. For the scoop on what to do, hit the **visitor centre** (📱250-725-3414; www.tourismtofino.com; 1426 Pacific Rim Hwy; 🕘9am-8pm Jun-Aug, reduced hours off-season).

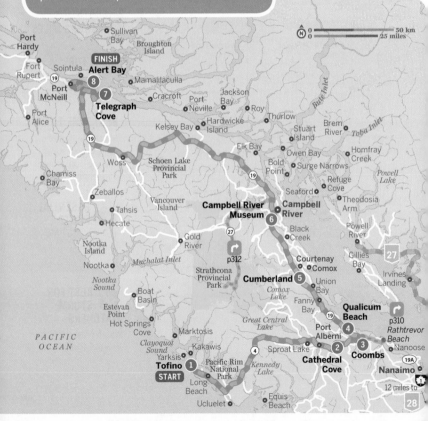

The area's biggest draw is **Long Beach**, part of Pacific Rim National Park. Accessible by car along the Pacific Rim Hwy, this wide sandy swath has untamed surf, beachcombing nooks and a living museum of old-growth trees. There are plenty of walking trails; look for swooping eagles and huge banana slugs. Tread carefully over slippery surfaces and never turn your back on the mischievous surf.

Kwisitis Visitor Centre (Wick Rd; ⊙10am-5pm Jun-Oct, 11am-3pm Fri-Sun Nov-May) houses exhibits on the region, including a First Nations canoe and a look at what's in the watery depths.

While you're in Tofino, don't miss Roy Henry Vickers' **Eagle Aerie Gallery** (📞250-725-3235; www.

LINK YOUR TRIP

27 A Strait Hop
From Qualicum Beach, travel south on Hwy 19 to Nanaimo, where you can hook up with this tour.

28 Southern Vancouver Island Tour
Drive east from Coombs on Hwy 4A and then south on Hwy 1. You can connect to this tour at Westholme.

TOP TIP:
PACIFIC RIM PARK PASS

First-timers should drop by the **Pacific Rim Visitors Centre** (📞250-726-4600; www.pacificrimvisitor.ca; 2791 Pacific Rim Hwy, Ucuelet; ⊙10am-4:30pm Tue-Sat) for maps and advice on exploring this spectacular region. If you're stopping in the park, you'll need to pay and display a pass, available here.

royhenryvickers.com; 350 Campbell St; ⊙10am-5pm), housed in an atmospheric traditional longhouse. Vickers is one of Canada's most successful and prolific Aboriginal artists.

Also visit **Tofino Botanical Gardens** (📞250-725-1220; www.tbgf.org; 1084 Pacific Rim Hwy; 3-day admission adult/child CAN$12/free; ⊙8am-dusk Jun-Aug, reduced hours off-season), 4.8 hectares of forest and coast complete with pocket gardens, art installations and a historic homestead.

A short trip from town is the **Maquinna Marine Provincial Park** (www.bcparks.ca), where 2km of boardwalks lead to natural hot springs. Transportation is readily available from Tofino. Also accessible from Tofino is mesmerizing **Meares Island**, home to the **Big Tree Trail**, a 400m boardwalk through old-growth forest that includes a stunning 1500-year-old red cedar.

✗ ⊨ p313

The Drive » Follow Pacific Rim Hwy 4 southeast, and then north as it turns into the Mackenzie Range. Mountains rise up on the right as you weave past the unfathomably deep Kennedy Lake (there are a number of vehicles resting unreachable at its bottom). The road carries on along the racing Kennedy River. Continue to the next stop, just past Port Alberni.

TRIP HIGHLIGHT

2 Cathedral Grove

To the east of Port Alberni, **Cathedral Grove** (www.bcparks.ca; MacMillan Provincial Park) is the spiritual home of tree huggers and the mystical highlight of MacMillan Provincial Park. Look up – way, waaaaay up – and the vertigo-inducing views of the swaying treetops will leave you swooning. Extremely popular in summer, its accessible **forest trails** wind through dense woodland, offering glimpses of some of British Columbia's oldest trees, including centuries-old Douglas firs more than 3m in diameter. Try hugging that.

DETOUR:
RATHTREVOR BEACH

Start: ❸ Coombs

It's only around 20 minutes from Coombs, but Rathtrevor Beach feels like it's a million miles away. Visit when the tide is out and you'll face a huge expanse of sand. Bring buckets, shovels and the kids, who'll spend hours digging, catching crabs and hunting for shells. The beach is in a provincial park just east of Parksville, and is backed by a forested picnic area. To get there from Coombs, drive east on Hwy 4A, connecting to Hwy 19 northwest and then turning off at Rathtrevor Rd.

KATE N / SHUTTERSTOCK ©

The Drive » Continue east on Hwy 4, past Cameron Lake, with swimming beaches and supposedly a resident monster. From Hwy 4, follow Hwy 4A for Coombs.

❸ Coombs

The mother of all pit stops, **Coombs Old Country Market** (📞250-248-6272; www.oldcountrymarket.com; 2326 Alberni Hwy; ⏰9am-7pm) attracts huge numbers of visitors almost year-round. You'll get inquisitive looks from a herd of goats that spends the summer season on the grassy roof, a tradition here for decades. Nip inside for giant ice-cream cones, heaping pizzas and all the deli makings of a great picnic, then spend an hour or two wandering around the attendant stores, which are filled with unique crafts, clothes and antiques.

The Drive » Continue east on Hwy 4A, crossing Hwy 19 to

Parksville on the coast. Turn left and follow the coastline west past pretty French Creek and on to Qualicum Beach.

❹ Qualicum Beach

A small community of classic seafront motels and a giant beachcomber-friendly bay, Qualicum Beach is a favorite family destination. This coastline is thick with shellfish; many of the scallops, oysters and mussels that restaurants serve up come from here. Wander the beach for shells, and look for sand dollars – they're readily found here.

🍴 🛏 p313

The Drive » While it's slower than Hwy 19, Hwy 19A is a scenic drive, following the coast north past the Fanny Bay Oyster Farm (stop in for a cookbook) and Denman Island (site of the famous chocolate factory). Just north of Union Bay, turn left to connect with Hwy 19. Turn right, continue north and take the exit for Cumberland.

TRIP HIGHLIGHT

❺ Cumberland

Founded as a coal-mining town in 1888, Cumberland was one of BC's original pioneer settlements, home to workers from Japan, China and the American South. While it's retained that small-town feel, with a main street that's still lined with turn-of-the-century wooden stores, it's also moved with the times. Instead of blacksmiths and dry-goods shops, you'll find cool boutiques, espresso bars

and even tattooists. Stop by **Dark Side Chocolates** (📞250-336-0126; www.darksidechocolates. com; 2722 Dunsmuir Ave; 🕙10am-4:30pm Tue-Sat) for truffles and bars, and be sure to visit the evocative and very impressive **Cumberland Museum** (📞250-336-2445; www. cumberlandmuseum.ca; 2680 Dunsmuir Ave; adult/child CAN$5/4; 🕙10am-5pm Jun-Aug, 10am-5pm Wed-Sun Sep-May). Explore more than 40 exhibits, including a replica coal mine and company store, brought to life by colorful stories

of Cumberland's early residents.

✖ p313

The Drive ≫ Carry on north on Hwy 19, with mountain and island views. Turn right onto Hamm Rd, heading east across farmland and passing a bison farm. Turn left onto Hwy 19A, which skirts Oyster Bay. The next stop is on your left, on the outskirts of Campbell River.

6 Campbell River Museum

Stretch your legs and your curiosity with a wander through the award-winning **Museum**

at Campbell River (📞250-287-3103; www.crmuseum. ca; 470 Island Hwy; adult/child CAN$8/5; 🕙10am-5pm mid-May–Sep, noon-5pm Tue-Sun Oct–mid-May). Hop behind the wheel of an early logging truck, explore a settler's cabin, see First Nations masks and watch footage of the removal of the legendary, ship-destroying Ripple Rock, which was blasted with the largest non-nuclear explosion in history.

The Drive ≫ From Campbell River, head northwest on Hwy 19. As you inch into Vancouver Island's north, follow the signs and an increasingly narrow road

DETOUR: STRATHCONA PROVINCIAL PARK

Start: ⑥ Campbell River Museum (p311)

BC's oldest protected area and also Vancouver Island's largest park, **Strathcona** (📞250-474-1336; www.bcparks.ca) is a 40km (25-mile) drive west on Hwy 28 from Campbell River. Centered on Mt Golden Hinde, the island's highest point (2200m), it's a pristine wilderness crisscrossed with trail systems that deliver you to waterfalls, alpine meadows, glacial lakes and looming crags.

On arrival at the main entrance, get your bearings at Strathcona Park Lodge & Outdoor Education Centre. It's a one-stop shop for park activities, including kayaking, guided treks and rock climbing for all ages.

for 16km to Telegraph Cove. En route, you'll pass Beaver Cove with its flotilla of logs waiting to be hauled away for milling. It's a beautiful drive, but isolated. Fuel up before you head out.

⑦ Telegraph Cove

Built on stilts over the water in 1912, Telegraph Cove was originally a station for the northern terminus of the island's telegraph. A salmon saltery and sawmill were later added. Extremely popular with summer day-trippers, the boardwalk and its many houses have been charmingly restored, with plaques illuminating their original residents. During the season, the waters off the cove are also home to orcas. See (and hear!) them

with **Stubbs Island Whale Watching** (📞250-928-3185; www.stubbs-island.com; adult/child CAN$99/84; ⏱May-Oct). You might also encounter minke and humpback whales as well as dolphins and porpoises.

✕ 🛏 p313

The Drive ≫ Return to Hwy 19 and carry on to Port McNeill, from where you can catch a BC Ferries vessel to Alert Bay on Cormorant Island.

TRIP HIGHLIGHT

⑧ Alert Bay

This welcoming village has an ancient and mythical appeal underpinned by its strong First Nations culture and community. In some respects, it feels like an open-air museum. On the

southern side is an old pioneer fishing settlement and the traditional **Namgis Burial Grounds**, where dozens of gracefully weathering totem poles stand like a forest of ageless art.

Next to the site of the now-demolished St Michael's Residential School is a much more enduring symbol of First Nations community. The must-see **U'mista Cultural Centre** (📞250-974-5403; www.umista.ca; 1 Front St; adult/child CAN$12/5; ⏱9am-5pm Jul & Aug, 9am-5pm Tue-Sat Sep-May) houses ceremonial masks and other potlatch items confiscated by the Canadian government in the 1920s and now repatriated from museums around the world.

Continue over the hill to the Big House, where **traditional dance performances** (⏱Thu-Sat Jul & Aug) are held for visitors. One of the world's tallest totem poles is also here. Alert Bay is home to many professional carvers and you'll see their work in galleries around the village.

Head to the **visitor center** (📞250-974-5024; www.alertbay.ca; 118 Fir St; ⏱9am-5pm Jul & Aug, 9am-5pm Mon-Fri Jun, Sep & Oct) for more information.

🛏 p313

Eating & Sleeping

Tofino ①

✗ Sobo   Canadian $$

(☑250-725-2341; www.sobo.ca; 311 Neill St; mains CAN$14-33; ⏱11:30am-9:30pm) The focus at Sobo – meaning Sophisticated Bohemian – is seasonal West Coast ingredients prepared with international influences. A brilliant place to dive into fresh-catch seafood, there's a hearty, well priced lunch menu if you need an early fill-up; try the chowder, fish tacos or gourmet pizzas.

⛱ Wickaninnish Inn   Hotel $$$

(☑250-725-3100; www.wickinn.com; Chesterman Beach; d from CAN$420; 🛜🍴) 'The Wick' is worth a stay any time of year. Embodying nature with recycled wood furnishings and natural stone tiles, the sumptuous guest rooms have push-button gas fireplaces, two-person hot tubs and floor-to-ceiling windows.

⛱ Ecolodge   Hostel $$

(☑250-725-1220; www.tbgf.org; 1084 Pacific Rim Hwy; r from CAN$159; @🛜) In the grounds of the botanical gardens, this quiet education center has a selection of rooms, a large kitchen and an on-site laundry. Popular with families and groups, there's a bunk room that's around CAN$40 each per night in summer for groups of four. Rates include garden entry.

Qualicum Beach ④

✗ Fish Tales Café   Seafood $$

(☑250-752-6053; www.fishtalescafe.com; 3336 Island Hwy W; mains CAN$12-25; ⏱11:30am-9pm Tue-Fri, 8am-9pm Sat & Sun) This Tudoresque landmark has the look of an old-school English tea shop, but it's been reeling in visitors with its perfect fish 'n' chips for years. If you arrive early enough, grab a table in the flower-studded, fairy-lit garden.

⛱ Free Spirit Spheres   Cabin $$

(☑250-757-9445; www.freespiritspheres.com; 420 Horne Lake Rd; cabins from CAN$175) These unique spherical tree houses enable guests

to cocoon themselves in the forest canopy. It's all about communing with nature. There's also a ground-level sauna, BBQ and hotel-quality showers. Book as far ahead as possible, especially in summer.

Cumberland ⑤

✗ The Wandering Moose   Cafe $

(☑250-400-1111; www.wanderingmoose.ca; 2739 Dunsmuir Ave; mains CAN$6-12; ⏱10am-4pm Thu-Sat & Mon-Tue, 9am-4pm Sun; 🛜) The stately exterior belies the interior of one of the town's coolest hangouts. Warm and inviting with a kid's corner and seating on the patio, it will satisfy coffee lovers with its locally roasted beans and refuel you with wraps, salads and gelati.

Telegraph Cove ⑦

✗ Seahorse Cafe   Cafe $

(☑250-527-1001; www.seahorsecafe.org; mains CAN$9; ⏱8:30am-7pm May-Sep) This popular little dockside cafe has plenty of outdoor picnic tables to relax at while you dig into barbecued Bavarian smokies, bison burgers, salmon burgers and home-cut fries. Breakfast brings pancakes, burritos and homemade granola.

⛱ Telegraph Cove Resorts   Resort $$

(☑250-928-3131; www.telegraphcoveresort. com; campsites/cabins from CAN$32/150) This well-established heritage resort provides accommodation in forested tent spaces as well as a string of rustic, highly popular cabins on stilts overlooking the marina. And what does rustic mean? No TVs or wi-fi.

Alert Bay ⑧

⛱ Alert Bay Cabins   Cabin $$

(☑604-974-5457; www.alertbaycabins.net; 390 Poplar Rd; d from CAN$135) A clutch of well-maintained cabins, each with kitchens or kitchenettes, this is a great retreat-like option if you want to get away from it. Call ahead and they'll even pick you up from the ferry.

Classic Trip

Okanagan Valley Wine Tour

30

Weave your way between golden hills and the shimmering Okanagan Lake. This route will leave you with a trunkful of first-class wine and, in the right season, juicy cherries and peaches.

TRIP HIGHLIGHTS

2 km

Mission Hill Family Estate
This wine finds its way into many a restaurant across BC; try it at its source

3 km

Old Vines
Dishing up all kinds of gourmet-prepared local produce on a vineyard terrace

● Kelowna

② ①
START

⑤

FINISH
⑦

Carmelis Goat Cheese Artisan
Whether in blue or gelato form, it's handmade and delicious

35 km

Summerhill Pyramid Winery
The pyramid experience is intriguing, as is the wine

27 km

2 DAYS
35KM/22 MILES

GREAT FOR...

BEST TIME TO GO
July and September bring hot sunny days that are perfect for a slow-paced meander.

 ESSENTIAL PHOTO
Snap the view from the terrace at Mission Hill Family Estate winery.

 BEST FOR FOODIES
Stop for fresh peaches, apricots, cherries, raspberries and watermelons in season.

Classic Trip

30 Okanagan Valley Wine Tour

Filling up on sun-ripened fruit at roadside stalls has long been a highlight of traveling through the Okanagan on a hot summer day. Since the 1980s the region has widened its embrace of the culinary world by striping its hillsides with grapes. Over 130 vineyards take advantage of the Okanagan's cool winters and long summers. Icewine, made from grapes frozen on the vine, is a unique take-home tipple. And when you're done soaking up the wine, you can soak up the scenery at the countless beaches along the way.

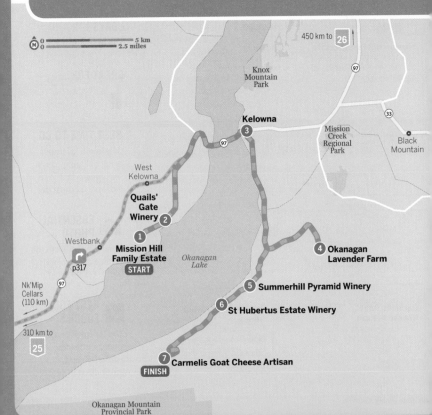

0 — 5 km
0 — 2.5 miles

450 km to 26

Knox Mountain Park

97

33

Kelowna 3

Mission Creek Regional Park

Black Mountain

West Kelowna

Quails' Gate Winery 2

Westbank
p317

1 Mission Hill Family Estate
START

Okanagan Lake

4 Okanagan Lavender Farm

Nk'Mip Cellars (110 km)

97

310 km to 25

5 Summerhill Pyramid Winery

6 St Hubertus Estate Winery

7 Carmelis Goat Cheese Artisan
FINISH

Okanagan Mountain Provincial Park

❶ Mission Hill Family Estate

Begin your leisurely taste-tripping trawl on the western shore of the 100km-long Okanagan Lake, the region's center-piece. Following Bouche-rie Rd north, between the lake and Hwy 97, will bring you to Westbank's award-winning **Mission Hill Family Estate** (☎250-768-7611; www.missionhillwin ery.com; 1730 Mission Hill Rd, West Kelowna; ⊙10am-6pm; P). The estate is a modernist reinterpreta-tion of mission buildings, reached through imposing gates. Several tours and tastings are available, in-cluding some that include lunch. Highlights include a film on the creation of

LINK YOUR TRIP

25 **Vancouver & the Fraser Valley**

Follow Hwy 3A and then Hwy 3 from the southern end of Okanagan Lake to Hope.

26 **Sea to Sky Highway**

Head northwest from the north of Okanagan Lake on Hwy 97 through Kamloops to Hwy 99, which leads southwest to Whistler via Lillooet.

DETOUR: NK'MIP CELLARS

Start: ❷ Quails' Gate

Add a day to your visit and sample one of the region's most distinctive wineries at **Nk'Mip Cellars** (☎250-495-2985; www.nkmipcellars.com; Rancer Creek Rd, Osoyoos), North America's only First Nations–owned and operated winery when it opened in 2003. Rather than being a novelty producer, it has since created some celebrated tipples from its pueblo-style, desert-fringed site in the town of Osoyoos.Sit on the view-filled patio and enjoy the inspired lunch menu with wine pairings. Or knock back some Pinot Blanc for a little courage before checking out the rattlesnake enclosure at the adjoining **Nk'Mip Desert Cultural Centre**. The winery is about 112km south of Westbank along Hwy 97.

---

wine in the region, a peek at an amazing Chagall tapestry, and a visit to the barrel cellars, where the only natural light comes from an oculus that sits above ground.

Outside is a terrace where you can sip wine, enjoy a meal and take in a great valley view, as well as a grassy amphitheater that hosts summer concerts (accompanied by wine, of course). You can also visit the shop for souvenir bottles. Try Oculus, the winery's premium and unique Bordeaux blend.

The Drive » Return to Boucherie Rd and continue north, following the coast.

---

❷ Quails' Gate Winery

Continuing north will bring you to **Quails' Gate**

Winery (☎250-769-2501; www.quailsgate.com; 3303 Boucherie Rd, West Kelowna; ⊙10am-8pm; P). Charm-ing stone and beam ar-chitecture reigns at this warm and welcoming spot. Tours run through-out spring and summer and begin in an on-site pioneer home built in 1873. Tastings are held throughout the day – the rhubarby Chenin Blanc and pleasantly peppery reserve Pinot Noir are recommended. The win-ery's **Old Vines** restau-rant is a foodie favorite, with a menu showcasing seasonal British Colum-bia ingredients and a commitment to sourcing sustainable seafood. Or you could just chill at vine-side picnic benches.

🍴 p323

The Drive » Cross the lake at the new William R Bennett Bridge and head for the 'east

MADDISON123 / SHUTTERSTOCK ©

coast' town of Kelowna, the Okanagan capital.

- - - - - - - - - - -

③ Kelowna

The wine industry has turned Kelowna into a bit of a boomtown. Property prices are surprisingly high for this part of the world, as is the growing skyline. A wander (especially along Ellis St) will unearth plenty of art galleries and lakeside parks, along with cafes and – delightfully – wine bars.

Continue your wine education at the **BC Wine Museum** (☎250-763-2417; www.kelownamuseums.ca; 1304 Ellis St; admission by donation; ⏰10am-5pm Mon-Sat, 11am-4pm Sun). Housed in the historic Laurel Packinghouse and newly expanded in 2016, the museum offers a look at celebrated bottles, labels and equipment, along with an overview of wine-making in the region.

With vineyards cozied up to Knox Mountain, **Sandhill Wines** (☎250-762-2999; www.sandhillwines.ca; 1125 Richter St; ⏰10am-6pm; [P]) – formerly known as Calona Vineyards – was the Okanagan's first winery, kicking off production in 1932. Its architecturally striking tasting room is an atmospheric spot to try the ever-popular, melon-note Pinot Blanc, along with the port-style dessert wine that makes an ideal cheese buddy. You'll find the winery north of Hwy 97.

✕ ⌂ p323

The Drive » Head south of Kelowna on Lakeshore Rd, keeping Okanagan Lake on your right. Take a left onto Dehart Rd and follow it to Bedford Rd. Turn right and then right again so that you're heading south on Takla Rd.

Okanagan Vineyards at sunset

④ Okanagan Lavender Farm

Visiting **Okanagan Lavender Farm** (☎250-764-7795; www.okanaganlavender.com; 4380 Takla Rd; tours CAN$5-15; ☺10am-6pm, tours 10:30am Jun-Aug; [P] [🚶]) is a heady experience. Rows and rows of over 60 types of lavender waft in the breeze against the backdrop of Okanagan Lake. Enjoy a guided or self-guided tour of the aromatic acreage and pop into the shop for everything from bath products to lavender lemonade. Your wine-soaked

LOCAL KNOWLEDGE: WHAT'S RIPE WHEN

Say that 10 times fast. It's even trickier when you've got a mouthful of plump raspberries. Farms sell their ripened fruit at stalls along the road, and fresh fruit and veggie markets are plentiful. Harvest times bring lower prices and top nosh. Here's what to watch for when:

Strawberries Mid-June to early July

Raspberries Early to mid-July

Cherries Mid-June to mid-August

Apricots Mid-July to mid-August

Peaches Mid-July to mid-September

Pears Mid-August to late September

Apples Early September to late October

Table grapes Early September to late October

Classic Trip

PENKA TODOROVA VITKOVA / SHUTTERSTOCK ©

WHY THIS IS A CLASSIC TRIP
RYAN VER BERKMOES, WRITER

You could spend days wandering the gorgeous Okanagan Valley and sampling products at its wineries. With over 140 to choose from, you're sure to find many that offer your perfect tipple. The lush green hillside vineyards are set against the cerulean waters of the lakes, making for visual delights as well. Many wineries have excellent restaurants, which combine farm-to-table goodness with fine wine and awesome views.

Top: Vineyard in Kelowna
Left: Red wine grapes
Right: Okanagan Lavender Farm

palate will be well and truly cleansed.

The Drive » Retrace your route back to Lakeshore Rd, heading south and then veering left onto Chute Lake Rd.

TRIP HIGHLIGHT

5 Summerhill Pyramid Winery

In the hills along the lake's eastern shore, you'll soon come to one of the Okanagan's most colorful wineries. **Summerhill Pyramid Winery** (☎250-764-8000; www.summerhill.bc.ca; 4870 Chute Lake Rd, Kelowna; ☼9am-6pm; ℗) combines a traditional tasting room with a huge pyramid where every Summerhill wine ages in barrels, owing to the belief that sacred geometry has a positive effect on liquids. The winery's **Sunset Bistro** is much loved and the Peace Chardonnay icewine is particularly delightful.

✕ p323

The Drive » Return to Lakeside Rd and continue south. The next stop is across from Cedar Creek Park.

6 St Hubertus Estate Winery

Further south, lakeside **St Hubertus Estate Winery** (☎250-764-7888; www.st-hubertus.bc.ca; 5225 Lakeshore Rd, near Kelowna; ☼10am-5:30pm May-Oct, noon-4pm Mon-Sat Nov-Apr)

BRITISH COLUMBIA **30** OKANAGAN VALLEY WINE TOUR

Classic Trip

✔ **TOP TIP:**
WINE FESTIVALS

The Okanagan stages four major multiday seasonal wine festivals (www.thewinefestivals.com) throughout the year. Time your visit right and dip into one of these:
Winter Festival Mid-January
Spring Wine Festival Early May
Summer Wine Festival August
Fall Wine Festival Early October

is another twist on the winery approach. Visiting is like being at a traditional northern European vineyard, complete with Bavarian architectural flourishes.

Despite its emphasis on Germanic wines, including Riesling, St Hubertus isn't conservative: try its floral, somewhat spicy Casselas and the rich Marechal Foch. While there are no formal tours, you can stroll around the vineyard or head to the complimentary tasting room to try four different wines. There's also a shop selling artisan foods and, of course, wine.

The Drive » Continue south on Lakeside and then take the left turning onto Rimrock Rd.

Follow it to a T-junction and take a right onto Timberline Rd.

- - - - - - - - - - - - - - -

TRIP HIGHLIGHT

❼ Carmelis Goat Cheese Artisan

End your tour by treating your driver to something they can sample at **Carmelis Goat Cheese Artisan** (☏250-764-9033; www.carmelisgoatcheese.com; 170 Timberline Rd; tours CAN$5; ⊗10am-6pm May-Sep, 11am-5pm Mar, Apr & Oct, closed Nov-Feb; **P** 🛦). Call ahead to book a tour of the dairy, milking station and cellar. Even without the tour, you can sample soft-ripened cheeses with names like Moonlight and Heavenly, or the hard-ripened Smoked Carmel or Goatgonzola. For those with a milder palate, there are super-soft unripened versions like feta and yogurt cheese. And then there's the goat's-milk gelato!

THE OGOPOGO

For centuries, traditional First Nations legends have told of a 15m-long sea serpent living in Okanagan Lake. Called the N'ha-a-itk, or Lake Demon, it was believed to live in a cave near Rattlesnake Island, just offshore from Peachland. People would only enter the waters around the island with an offering, as they believed the monster would otherwise raise a storm and claim lives.

Beginning in the mid-1800s, Europeans also began reporting sightings of a creature with a horse-shaped head and serpent-like body. Nicknamed Ogopogo, the serpent has been seen along the length of the 129km lake, but most commonly around Peachland. In 1926, 30 carloads of people all claimed to have seen the monster and film footage from 1968 has been analyzed, concluding that a solid, three-dimensional object was moving through the water.

Cryptozoologist Karl Shuker suggests that the Ogopogo may be a type of primitive whale like the basilosaurus. Keep your eyes peeled, but if you don't have any luck spotting it, you can visit a statue of the Ogopogo at Kelowna's City Park.

Eating & Sleeping

Quails' Gate Winery ❷

✕ Old Vines Restaurant   Bistro $$$

(☏250-769-4451; www.quailsgate.com; Quails' Gate Estate, 3303 Boucherie Rd, West Kelowna; mains CAN$20-35; ⏱11:30am-2pm, 5-9pm) Using only the freshest ingredients available, this terrace-style restaurant draws crowds. At brunch try Dungeness crab cakes with coconut, cilantro and pineapple, and daikon radish salad. Or dig into smoked quail or prawn risotto at lunch. Wash it all down with some of the region's top wine.

Kelowna ❸

✕ RauDZ Regional Table   Fusion $$

(☏250-868-8805; www.raudz.com; 1560 Water St; mains CAN$12-30; ⏱5-10pm) Noted chef Rod Butters has defined the farm-to-table movement with his casual bistro that's a temple to Okanagan produce and wine. The dining room is as airy and open as the kitchen. The seasonal menu takes global inspiration for its Mediterranean-infused dishes, good for sharing, and serves steaks and seafood. Suppliers include locally renowned Carmelis goat's cheese.

✕ Little Hobo   Cafe $

(☏778-478-0411; www.thelittlehobo.com; 438 Lawrence Ave; mains CAN$7-12; ⏱10am-2pm Mon-Fri) This unadorned sandwich shop is hugely popular and for good reason: the food is excellent. The custom sandwiches are good, but the daily specials really shine (meatloaf, pasta, pierogi etc) and the variety of soups is simply superb.

✕ Kelowna Farmers Market   Market $

(☏250-878-5029; cnr Springfield Rd & Dilworth Dr; ⏱8am-1pm Wed & Sat Apr-Oct) The farmers market has more than 150 vendors, including many with prepared foods. Local artisans also display their wares. It's off Hwy 97.

🛏 Hotel Eldorado   Hotel $$$

(☏250-763-7500; www.hoteleldoradokelowna.com; 500 Cook Rd; r CAN$180-400; Ⓟ❄☎️⚹) This historic lakeshore retreat, south of Pandosy Village, has 19 heritage rooms where you can bask in antique-filled luxury. A modern low-key wing has 30 more rooms and six opulent waterfront suites. It's classy, artful and funky all at once. Definitely the choice spot for a luxurious getaway.

🛏 Hotel Zed   Motel $$

(☏250-763-7771; www.hotelzed.com; 1627 Abbott St; r CAN$90-180; Ⓟ❄☎️⚹) An old Travelodge has been reborn as this funky throwback to a 1960s that never existed. The 52 rooms come in many shapes and sizes; all are in cheery colors. Extras such as free bike rentals, ping-pong, hot tub, comic books in the bathrooms and much more are way cool. It's perfectly located downtown and across from City Park.

Summerhill Pyramid Winery ❺

✕ Sunset Organic Bistro   Bistro $$

(☏250-764-8000; www.summerhill.bc.ca; 4870 Chute Lake Rd, Summerhill Pyramid Winery, Kelowna; mains CAN$15-30; ⏱11am-9pm) Acclaimed chef Alex Lavroff has created excellent locally sourced and organic menus for lunch and dinner. In between, there is an exquisite selection of small dishes, which go well with an afternoon of organic wine tasting.

Haida Gwaii Adventure

31

Far-flung and isolated, the lush Haida Gwaii ('Islands of Beauty') are steeped in superlatives – most stunning scenery, freshest seafood and most accessible First Nations culture.

TRIP HIGHLIGHTS

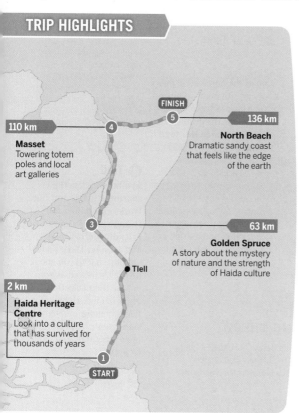

110 km
④

Masset
Towering totem poles and local art galleries

FINISH ⑤ **136 km**

North Beach
Dramatic sandy coast that feels like the edge of the earth

③ **63 km**

Golden Spruce
A story about the mystery of nature and the strength of Haida culture

● Tlell

2 km

Haida Heritage Centre
Look into a culture that has survived for thousands of years

① **START**

**2 DAYS
136KM/85 MILES**

GREAT FOR...

BEST TIME TO GO

July and August: the sun is more likely to shine and the wind is less vicious.

 ESSENTIAL PHOTO

Capture the islands' wilderness from Tow Hill's viewpoint.

 BEST FOR CULTURE

Gain insight into the resurgence of Haida culture at Haida Heritage Centre.

31 Haida Gwaii Adventure

You'll be welcomed to what feels like the edge of the earth. Once known as the Queen Charlotte Islands, this rugged northwestern archipelago maintains its independent spirit, evident in its quirky museums, rustic cafes, down-to-earth art and nature-loving locals. You'll feel closer to the natural world than ever before, and some of the Northern Hemisphere's most extraordinary cultural artifacts are found here.

TRIP HIGHLIGHT

① Skidegate

If you're not bringing your car, you can rent a car in advance of your **BC Ferries** (250-386-3431; www.bcferries.com) arrival in Skidegate on Graham Island (or air arrival in Sandspit). Spend some time perusing the clapboard houses or fueling up at the home-style pub or cafes in nearby Queen Charlotte. Save an hour or two for the unmissable: the **Haida Heritage Centre** (250-559-7885; www.haidaheritagecentre.com; Hwy 16; adult/child CAN$16/5; ⊙10am-6pm Mon-Wed, to 8pm Thu-Sun Jun-Aug, 10am-5pm Tue-Sat Sep-May), a striking crescent of totem-fronted cedar longhouses that's arguably British Columbia's best First Nations attraction. Check out ancient carvings and artifacts recalling 10,000 years of Haida history and look for the exquisite artworks of the legendary Bill Reid, such as huge canoes and totem poles.

Hitting Hwy 16, head north to explore the distinctive settlements that make latter-day Haida Gwaii tick. You'll wind along stretches of rustic waterfront and through shadowy woodland areas while a permanent detachment of beady-eyed eagles follows your progress.

The Drive » Follow Hwy 16 north along the shoreline. At around 19km (12 miles), watch for orange-and-white leading marks on the inland side of the highway, marking the end of the long bar that extends north all the way from Sandspit. At 35.4km (22 miles) you'll enter into the flat, arable land around Tlell River.

② Tlell

Just before Tlell, the charming Bottle and Jug Works exemplifies the region's pioneer spirit. Friendly potters John and Jennifer Davies will happily chat to you about life on the island as you peruse their selection of fat-bellied, Hobbit-friendly mugs and handsome rustic teapots. It's open irregular hours and by appointment from Monday to Saturday.

 p331

TOP TIP: GETTING THERE

From mainland Prince Rupert in northern BC, take the BC Ferries service to Skidegate on Graham Island. The crossing usually takes seven to eight hours.

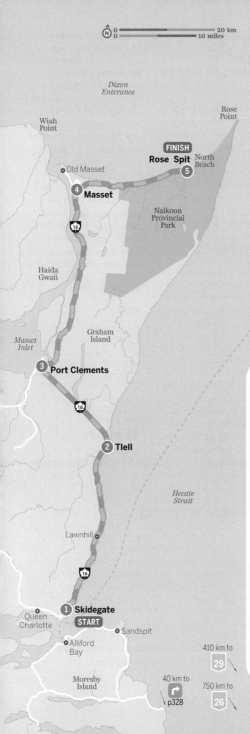

The Drive » Continue 21.7km (13.5 miles) northwest along Hwy 16. This incredibly straight route was a walking trail until 1920 when a road was built by placing wooden planks end to end along the ground. Watch for shrub-like Shore Pines along the now-paved route.

3 Port Clements

Just before you reach Port Clements, head down Cedar Ave to Bayview Ave and onto the logging road for 4.8km (3 miles). This brings you to a signposted, easy 3.2km (2-mile) trail through the forest leading to the banks of the Yakoun River and the site of the legendary **Golden Spruce** (p328).

LINK YOUR TRIP

26 Sea to Sky Highway

Head inland via Prince Rupert and hop on Hwy 16. Hang a right at Prince George and go 696km (432 miles) on BC-97 toward Squamish to pick up this trip.

29 Vancouver Island's Remote North

After a six-hour boat ride from Skidegate to Prince Rupert you travel along the inside passage on a 22-hour ferry to Port Hardy. From here drive 40km (25 miles) along Hwy 9 to Port McNeill to pick up this trip.

DETOUR:
GWAII HAANAS
NATIONAL PARK RESERVE

Start: ❶ Skidegate (p326)

Famed for its mystical élan, **Gwaii Haanas National Park Reserve** (www.parkscanada.ca/gwaiihaanas) covers much of Haida Gwaii's southern section, a rugged region only accessible by boat or floatplane. The reserve is the ancient site of Haida homes, burial caves and the derelict village of Ninstints with its seafront totem poles (now a Unesco World Heritage site). You should only consider an extended visit if you are well prepared. Facilities are sparse; other than three water hoses, composting toilets and maintained cultural sites, you're on your own.

It is essential to contact **Parks Canada** (📞250-559-8818, reservations 📞877-559-8818; www.parkscanada.ca/gwaiihaanas; Haida Heritage Centre at Kay Llnagaay, Skidegate; 🕑office 8:30am-noon & 1-4:30pm Mon-Fri) in advance, as access to the park is very limited and most visitors will need to work with officially sanctioned tour operators.

Tragically cut down in 1997 by a deranged environmentalist, the tree – a 150ft, 300-year-old genetic aberration with luminous yellow needles – was revered by local Haida as the transformed spirit of a little boy. The tree's death was traumatic for many island residents. You can see a seedling taken from a cutting from the felled tree in Millennium Park in Port Clements. For a gripping read, pick up *The Golden Spruce: A True Story of Myth, Madness and Greed* by John Vaillant (2006).

Head back to Hwy 16 to the village and nip into **Port Clements Museum** (📞250-557-4576; www.portclementsmuseum.ca; 45 Bayview Dr; adult/child CAN$3/free; 🕑10am-4pm Jun–mid-Sep, 2-4pm Sat & Sun mid-Sep–May), where you're welcomed by a forest of rusty logging machinery. Learn about early logging practices and check out toys and tools from pioneering days. You'll also encounter a stuffed albino raven, another genetic aberration that was also revered until it electrocuted itself on local power lines.

🛏 p331

The Drive » Head north along Hwy 16, which hugs Masset Inlet to the northern coast. Continue north to the settlements of Masset and Old Masset, 43.5km (27 miles) from Port Clements.

TRIP HIGHLIGHT

❹ Masset

Masset primarily occupies the rather stark,

THE STORY OF THE GOLDEN SPRUCE

Long ago a harsh blizzard buried a small village in snow. Supplies diminished and villagers died of cold and starvation. Eventually only a young boy and his grandfather remained and, with hopes of surviving, they dug themselves out and began trekking.

As they walked in search of a new village, the blizzard ended and spring arrived. The grandfather warned his grandson: 'Don't look back. If you do, you will go into the next world. A world where people can admire you, but will not be able to speak with you. You will be standing in this sacred place until the end of the world.'

Missing his home, the boy stole one last glance in the direction of the village they'd left behind. The boy was rooted to the forest floor. Seeing what had happened, the grandfather said, 'It is okay. Future generations will come and see you and remember your story.' The boy had become the Golden Spruce.

BRITISH COLUMBIA **31** HAIDA GWAII ADVENTURE

Gwaii Haanas National Park Reserve Sea lions

RETURN OF THE HAIDA

The Haida are one of Canada's First Nations peoples, and had lived here for thousands of years before Europeans turned up in the 18th century. Centered on the islands, these fearsome warriors had no immunity to such diseases as smallpox, measles and tuberculosis that were brought by the newcomers, and their population of tens of thousands was quickly decimated. By the early 20th century, their numbers had fallen to around 600.

Since the 1970s, the Haida population – and its cultural pride – has grown anew, and the Haida now make up about half of the 5000 residents on the islands. In 2009 the Government of British Columbia officially changed the name of the islands from the Queen Charlottes to Haida Gwaii ('Islands of the People') as part of the province's reconciliation process with the Haida.

Historically one of the most vibrant of First Nations cultures, the Haida have very strong narratives and oral history. Legends, beliefs, skills and more are passed down from one generation to the next and great importance is placed on the knowledge of past generations. Today the Haida seek to live in harmony with their environment. Traditional laws recognize the stunning nature of the islands and embrace both the past and look to the future.

To learn more about the Haida, visit www.haidanation.ca.

institutional buildings of a disused military base, while the adjoining **Old Masset** is a First Nations village where wood-fired homes are fronted by broad, brooding totem poles. There are several stores here where visitors can peruse and buy Haida carvings in argillite, a glasslike slate that is found only in this corner of the world.

Also in Masset is the **Dixon Entrance Maritime Museum** (☎250-626-6066; 2182 Collinson Ave; adult/child CAN$3/free; ◷1-6pm daily Jun-Aug, 2-4pm Sat & Sun Sep-May). Housed in what was once the local hospital, the museum features exhibits on the history of this seafaring community, with displays on shipbuilding, medical pioneers, military history,

and nearby clam and crab canneries. Local artists also exhibit their work.

✕ ⍩ p331

The Drive ≫ Head east off Hwy 16 along a well-marked logging road signposted for Naikoon Provincial Park. The next stop is 27.4km (17 miles) from Masset.

TRIP HIGHLIGHT

❺ Rose Spit

The region's wild northern tip is home to **Naikoon Provincial Park** (☎250-626-5115; www.bcparks.ca; off Hwy 16). This dense, treed park has more than 95km (60 miles) of white-sand beach and is the area's most popular destination for summertime nature fans.

Continue along the tree-lined dirt road until

you reach **Tow Hill**, a steep, dense and easily enjoyed short forest walk (1km/0.6 miles each way). Look out for trees where strips of bark have been carefully removed for Haida basket-making over the decades, then catch your breath at the summit while you gaze over the impenetrable coastal forest stretching into the mist.

Finally, head for the park's extreme coastal tip and **North Beach**. Leave the car here and tramp along the wave-smacked sandy expanse, where locals walk in the surf plucking Dungeness crabs for dinner. With the wind watering your eyes, you'll feel closer to nature than you've ever felt before.

✕ ⍩ p331

Eating & Sleeping

Tlell ❷

✘ Haida House   Seafood $$

(☏855-557-4600; www.haidahouse.com; 2087 Beitush Rd; mains CAN$20-30; ⊗5-7:30pm Tue-Sun mid-May–mid-Sep) This Haida-run restaurant has excellent, creative seafood and other dishes with island accents, such as Haida favorites with berries. Also rents plush rooms.

Port Clements ❸

▭ Golden Spruce Motel   Motel $

(☏250-557-4325; www.goldenspruce.ca; 2 Grouse S; r CAN$76-100; P 🛜) Urs, the owner of this simple yet comfortable motel, gives a warm welcome and has a good breakfast cafe. Some rooms have kitchenettes and there are fire pits outside for guest use. The motel has a car to rent.

Masset ❹

✘ Charters Restaurant   Seafood $$

(☏250-626-3377; 1650 Delkatla Rd; mains CAN$15-30; ⊗5-9pm Wed-Sun) The numbers are small: six tables, three mains. But the pleasure is great: simply delicious food, such as seafood fettuccine and fresh local halibut. The changing menu also features burgers, ribs, salads and more. The attention to detail is extraordinary: the greens used to ornament plates are grown under lights in the kitchen. Reserve ahead.

▭ Copper Beech House   B&B $$

(☏250-626-5441; www.copperbeechhouse.com; 1590 Delkatla Rd; r CAN$100-160; P 🛜) This legendary B&B in a rambling old house

on Masset Harbor is owned by poet Susan Musgrave. It has five unique rooms, and there's always something amazing cooking in the kitchen.

Rose Spit ❺

✘ Moon Over Naikoon   Bakery $

(☏250-626-5064; 16443 Tow Hill Rd, Masset; snacks from CAN$3; ⊗8am-5pm Jun-Aug) Embodying the spirit of its location, on a road to the end of everything, this tiny community center–cum-bakery is housed in an old school bus in a clearing about 6km from Masset. The baked goods and coffee are brilliant.

▭ All The Beach You Can Eat   Cabin $$

(☏250-626-9091; www.allthebeachyoucaneat.com; Km 15, Tow Hill Rd, North Shore; cabins CAN$100-190; P) On beautiful North Beach, five cabins are perched in the dunes, back from the wide swath of sand that runs for miles east and west. One, the lovely little Sweety Pie, has views that seem to reach to Japan. Similar to other properties with rental cabins out here, there is no electricity; cooking and lighting are fuelled by propane. It's off the grid and out of this world.

▭ Agate Beach
Campground   Campground $

(☏250-557-4390; www.env.gov.bc.ca/bcparks; Tow Hill Rd, Naikoon Provincial Park, North Shore; campsites CAN$18; P) This stunning, wind-whipped campground is right on the beach on the north shore. Frolic on the sand, hunt for its namesake rocks and see if you can snare some flotsam.

Circling the Rockies

32

Taking you through Kootenay, Banff and Yoho National Parks and dipping into Alberta, this trip shows off Mother Nature at her best: lofty snowy peaks, deep forests and natural hot springs.

TRIP HIGHLIGHTS

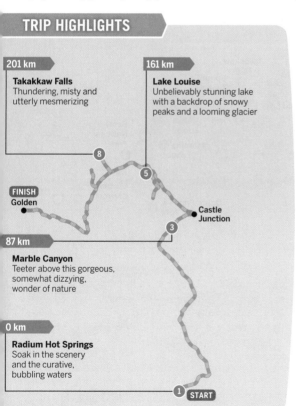

201 km

Takakkaw Falls
Thundering, misty and utterly mesmerizing

161 km

Lake Louise
Unbelievably stunning lake with a backdrop of snowy peaks and a looming glacier

FINISH
Golden

Castle Junction

87 km

Marble Canyon
Teeter above this gorgeous, somewhat dizzying, wonder of nature

0 km

Radium Hot Springs
Soak in the scenery and the curative, bubbling waters

START

3 DAYS
294KM/183 MILES

GREAT FOR...

BEST TIME TO GO

July and August when the snow has melted and all of the roads are open.

ESSENTIAL PHOTO

Mt Temple Viewpoint in Banff National Park for postcard-perfect mountain shots.

BEST FOR WILDLIFE

Watch for bears, elk, big horn sheep and plenty of moose.

32 Circling the Rockies

This route will give you a new perspective on nature. This is where mountains stretch up to the stars and where bears and moose own the woods (and sometimes the road). Waterfalls, canyons and gem-colored lakes lay deep in the forest, waiting to be discovered. It's impossible not to be awed, not to feel small, and not to wish you had longer to explore.

TRIP HIGHLIGHT

1 Radium Hot Springs

Set in a valley just inside the southern border of Kootenay National Park, the outdoor **Radium Hot Springs** (☎250-347-9485; www.pc.gc.ca/hotsprings; off Hwy 93; adult/child CAN$7/6; ⏰9am-11pm) has a hot pool simmering at 102°F (39°C) and a second pool to cool you off at 84°F (29°C). Originally sacred to First Nations peoples for the water's curative powers, these springs are

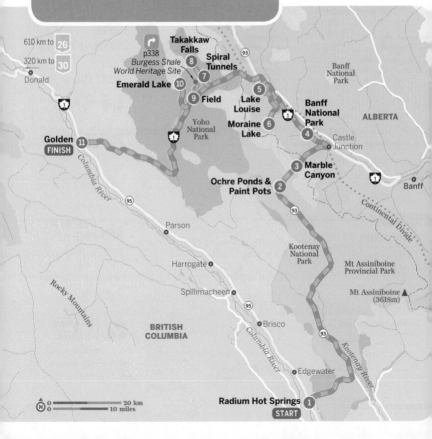

610 km to 26
320 km to 30

Donald

Takakkaw Falls

p338
Burgess Shale
World Heritage Site

8 Spiral Tunnels

7

Emerald Lake 10

9 Field

5 Lake Louise

6 Moraine Lake

Banff National Park

ALBERTA

Castle Junction

Banff

Golden 11
FINISH

Columbia River

Yoho National Park

3 Marble Canyon

Continental Divide

Ochre Ponds & 2
Paint Pots

Parson

Harrogate

Spillimacheen

Kootenay National Park

Mt Assiniboine Provincial Park

Mt Assiniboine ▲ (3618m)

BRITISH COLUMBIA

Brisco

Rocky Mountains

Columbia River

Kootenay River

Edgewater

N 0 ——— 20 km
0 ——— 10 miles

Radium Hot Springs 1
START

uniquely odorless and colorless. The large tiled pool can get crowded in summer. You can rent lockers, towels and even swimsuits.

The Drive ›› From Radium Hot Springs, it's a lovely 83km (52-mile) drive on Hwy 93 through the park to Ochre Ponds and Paint Pots.

TOP TIP: ROAD CONDITIONS

Weather is very changeable in the mountains. Be sure to carry chains outside of the summer months of June, July and August. Check http://drivebc.ca in BC for current road conditions; in Alberta check http://511.alberta.ca or dial [🎵] 511.

② Ochre Ponds & Paint Pots

As the road delves down into the woods along Hwy 93, a signpost leads to a short, flat interpretive trail. Follow this to the intriguing red-and-orange Ochre Ponds. Drawing Kootenay First Peoples for centuries – and later

European settlers – this iron-rich earth was collected, mixed with oil and made into paint. Further along the trail are three stunning crystal-blue springs that are known as the Paint Pots.

The Drive ›› Continue north along Hwy 93 for 3km (1.9 miles) to the next stop.

LINK YOUR TRIP

26 Sea to Sky Highway

Mountain-hop to the Coast Mountains by heading west from Golden on Hwy 1 and then taking Hwy 99 southwest to Whistler.

30 Okanagan Valley Wine Tour

From Golden, a lovely 214-mile (345km) drive along Hwys 1 and 97 will take you to Kelowna in the heart of the Okanagan Valley wine country.

TRIP HIGHLIGHT

③ Marble Canyon

This jaw-dropping stop is not for the faint-of-heart. An easy 15-minute trail zigzags over Tokumm Creek, giving phenomenal views deeper and deeper into Marble Canyon below. The limestone and dolomite walls have been carved away by the awesome power of the creek, resulting in plunging falls and bizarrely shaped cliff faces. The trail can be slippery. Take sturdy shoes and your camera.

🛏 p339

The Drive ›› Continue north along Hwy 93 and across the provincial border into Alberta to the junction with Hwy 1 (Castle Junction). Head west.

④ Banff National Park

More of a drive than a stop, the stretch of Hwy 1 running from Castle Junction to Lake Louise is one of the most scenic routes through Banff National Park. The highway runs through the Bow Valley, following the weaving Bow River and the route of the Pacific Railway. The craggy peaks of the giant Sawback and Massive mountain ranges sweep up on either side of the road. The resulting perspective is much wider than on smaller roads with big open vistas.

There are several viewpoint pull-offs where gob-smacked drivers can stop to absorb their surroundings. Watch for the unmissable **Castle Mountain** looming in its crimson glory to the northwest. The Panorama Ridge then rises in the south, after which the enormous **Mt Temple** comes into view, towering at 11,620ft. Stop at the **Mt Temple Viewpoint** for a good gander.

This stretch of the highway is only two lanes with no fencing to stop wandering animals from venturing into the road. Drive with caution.

The Drive ⟩⟩ The turnoff for Lake Louise Village is 24km (14.9 miles) from Castle Junction.

- - - - - - - - - - -

TRIP HIGHLIGHT

⑤ Lake Louise

With stunning emerald-green water and tall, snowy peaks that hoist hefty Victoria Glacier up for all to see, Lake Louise has captured the imaginations of mountaineers, artists and visitors for over a century. You – and the enormous numbers of other visitors – will notice the lake's color appears slightly different from each viewpoint.

Follow the **Lakeshore Trail**, a 2.4-mile (4km) round trip, or head up the gorgeous (though somewhat more difficult) route to **Lake Agnes** and its sun-dappled teahouse, perched 4.4 miles (7km) from Lake Louise's shore. For a more relaxed experience, rent a canoe from **Lake Louise Boathouse** (📞403-522-3511; canoe rental per 30min/1hr CAN$75/85; 🕐8am-8:30pm Jun-Sep, weather permitting) and paddle yourself through the icy waters.

The **Lake Louise Gondola** (📞403-522-3555; www.lakelouisegondola.com; off Hwy 1A; adult/child CAN$33/16; 🕐9am-4pm May-Jun & Sep-Oct, 8am-5:30pm Jul-Aug; 🚡) lands you at a lofty 6850ft for a view of the lake and the surrounding glaciers and peaks. En route you'll sail over wildflowers and possibly even a grizzly bear. At the top is the **Wildlife Interpretation Centre**, which hosts regular theater presentations and guided walks. Travel the 14-minute ascent in either an open ski lift or an enclosed gondola.

🍴 🛏 p339

The Drive ⟩⟩ From Lake Louise Dr, head south along Moraine Lake Rd for 14km (8.7 miles).

- - - - - - - - - - -

⑥ Moraine Lake

You'll be dazzled by the scenery before you even reach Moraine Lake, set in the Valley of the Ten Peaks. En route, the narrow, winding road gives off fabulous views of the imposing **Wenkchemna Peaks**. Look familiar? For years this scene was carried on the back of the Canadian $20 bill. In 1894, explorer Samuel Allen named the peaks with numbers from one to 10 in the Stoney Indian Language (*wenkchemna* means 'ten'); all but two of the mountains have since been renamed. You'll quickly notice the **Tower of Babel**, ascending solidly toward the heavens at the northeastern edge of the range.

HANS-PETER MERTEN / GETTY IMAGES ©

With little of Lake Louise's hustle or bustle and lots of beauty, many people prefer the more rugged and remote setting of Moraine Lake to Lake Louise. The turquoise waters are surprisingly clear for a glacial reservoir. Take a look at the surrounding mountains through telescopes secured to the southern shore (free!) or hire a boat and paddle to the middle for a 360-degree view. There are also some great **day hikes** from here, and, to rest your weary legs, a cafe, dining room and lodge. The road to Moraine Lake and its

Banff National Park Moraine Lake

facilities are open from June to early October.

The Drive » Return to Hwy 1 and continue west, across the provincial border and into Yoho National Park.

- - - - - - - - - - - -

7 Spiral Tunnels

Upon completion of the railway in 1885, trains struggled up the challenging **Kicking Horse Pass**, which you'll cross soon after the Alberta–British Columbia provincial border. This is the steepest railway pass in North America and wrecks and runaways were common. In 1909 the **Spiral Tunnels** were carved into Mt Cathedral and Mt Ogden and are still in use today. If you time it right, you can see a train exiting from the top of the tunnel while its final cars are still entering at the bottom. Watch from the main viewing area on the north side of the highway.

The Drive » Continue west on Hwy 1 and then turn north onto Yoho Valley Rd (open late June to October). This road climbs a number of tight switchbacks.

- - - - - - - - - - - -

TRIP HIGHLIGHT

8 Takakkaw Falls

Named 'magnificent' in Cree, **Takakkaw Falls** (Yoho National Park) is one of the highest waterfalls in Canada (804ft). An impressive torrent of water travels from the Daly Glacier, plunges over the edge of the rock face into a small pool and jets out into a tumbling cloud of mist.

En route to the falls you'll pass a second **Spiral Lookout** and the **Meeting of the Rivers**, where the clear Kicking Horse runs into the milky-colored Yoho.

The Drive » Return to Hwy 1 and continue west to Field.

DETOUR: BURGESS SHALE WORLD HERITAGE SITE

Start: ❾ Field

In 1909 Burgess Shale was unearthed on Mt Field. The fossil beds are home to perfectly preserved fossils of marine creatures, dated at over 500 million years old and recognized as some of the earliest forms of life. The area is now a World Heritage site and accessible only by guided hikes, led by naturalists from the **Yoho Shale Geoscience Foundation** (✆800-343-3006; www.burgess-shale. bc.ca; 200 Kicking Horse Ave, Field; tours adult/child from CAN$95/65; ◷mid-Jun–mid-Sep). Reservations are essential, as is stamina: it's a 12-mile (19.3km) round trip, ascending 2500ft.

❾ Field

In the midst of Yoho National Park, on the southern side of the Kicking Horse River, lies the quaint village of Field. This historic but unfussy railroad town has a dramatic overlook of the river. While Field may be short on sights, it's a beautiful place to wander around.

This is also the place to come if you want to organize an activity in the park – from dog-sledding in winter to canoeing and white-water rafting in summer.

✗ ⊨ p339

The Drive ❯❯ Continue west on Hwy 1 and take the first right. Continue north for 1okm (6.2 miles).

❿ Emerald Lake

Gorgeously green Emerald Lake gains its color from light reflecting off fine glacial rock particles that are deposited into the lake by grinding glaciers. It's a highlight of the park, so the lake attracts visitors year-round, either to simply admire its serenity or to fish, skate, hike or horseback ride. In summer, the water warms up just enough to have a very quick dip.

En route to the lake watch for the impressive **natural bridge** stretching across the Kicking Horse River.

⊨ p339

The Drive ❯❯ Return to Hwy 1 and continue to Golden, 54km (33.5 miles) from the turnoff.

⓫ Golden

With six national parks in its backyard, little Golden is a popular base. It's also the center for white-water rafting trips on the turbulent Kicking Horse River. Powerful grade III and IV rapids and breathtaking scenery along the sheer walls of Kicking Horse Valley make this rafting experience one of North America's best. Full-day trips on the river are about CAN$165; half-day trips CAN$65. Operators include **Alpine Rafting** (✆250-344-6778; www.alpine rafting.com; 101 Golden Donald Upper Rd; raft trips CAN$25-180; ◷Jun-Sep; 🚻).

Over 60% of the 120 ski runs at **Kicking Horse Mountain Resort** (✆403-254-7669, 866-754-5425; www. kickinghorseresort.com; Kicking Horse Trail; 1-day lift ticket adult/child winter CAN$90/36, summer CAN$41/21) are rated advanced or expert. It's 8.7 miles (14km) from Golden on Kicking Horse Trail.

The **Northern Lights Wolf Centre** (✆250-344-6798; www.northernlightswild life.com; 1745 Short Rd; adult/child CAN$12/6; ◷9am-7pm Jul & Aug, 10am-6pm May, Jun & Sep, noon-5pm Oct-Apr; 🅿) is a refuge for this misunderstood animal, which is being hunted to extinction. Meet a resident wolf or two and learn about their routines and survival.

Eating & Sleeping

Marble Canyon ③

🛏 Marble Canyon Campground
Campground $

(off Hwy 93, Kootenay National Park; campsites CAN$22; ⊙Jul-Sep) This high-country 61-pitch campground is situated near the Marble Canyon trail, and has flush toilets but no showers. Most sites have tree cover to shelter from the wind. The eastern side has the best views.

Lake Louise ⑤

✕ Lake Louise Station Restaurant
Canadian $$

(☎403-522-2600; www.lakelouisestation.com; 200 Sentinel Rd; mains CAN$20-45; ⊙11am-4pm & 5-9pm) Dine in the station's great hall or one of the dining cars, which are nothing short of elegant. Details like stacks of turn-of-the-century luggage and the stationmaster's desk take you back to 1910, when the station was first built. Dig into the first-class Rocky Mountain sausage plate, maple salmon or bison burger and soak up the almost palpable atmosphere. Reservations recommended.

🛏 Deer Lodge
Hotel $$$

(☎403-410-7417; www.crmr.com; 109 Lake Louise Dr; r from CAN$250; P🛜) Tucked demurely behind Chateau Lake Louise, historic Deer Lodge dates from the 1920s and has managed to keep its genuine alpine feel intact. The rustic exterior and maze of corridors can't have changed much since the days of bobbed hair and F Scott Fitzgerald. Lodge rooms are fairly tiny but quaint, while spacious Heritage rooms have smart, boutique-like furnishings.

The beautifully restored lounge and log-cabin sitting room, especially with its stone fireplace ablaze, make time travel feel like a real possibility. Tranquility here is ensured – you won't find a TV anywhere.

Field ⑨

✕ Truffle Pigs
Fusion $$$

(☎250-343-6303; www.trufflepigs.com; 100 Centre St; mains CAN$12-30; ⊙11am-3pm & 5-9pm Mon-Fri, 8am-3pm & 5-9pm Sat & Sun; 🛜) A legendary cafe serving inventive, high-concept bistro fare that's locally sourced and usually organic. The menu changes seasonally.

🛏 Kicking Horse Lodge
Hotel $$

(☎250-343-6303; www.trufflepigs.com; 100 Centre Street; r from CAN$120; ⊙Jun-Sep; P❄🛜) Field's only hotel is a timber building with heritage charm. The 14 rooms are fairly simply decked out, though. Some have small kitchens. The owners run the town's well-known restaurant, Truffle Pigs bistro.

Emerald Lake ⑩

🛏 Emerald Lake Lodge
Lodge $$$

(☎403-410-7417; www.crmr.com/emerald; Emerald Lake Rd, Yoho National Park; r CAN$250-450; P🛜) Commanding a picture-perfect five-hectare (13-acre) site accessed by a bridge and situated right beside the tranquil shores of Emerald Lake, this lodge couldn't have a better position. The interiors are disappointingly old-fashioned, however, so sit back on the porch and enjoy the lake view.

STRETCH YOUR LEGS
VANCOUVER

Start/Finish: Gastown

Distance: 10km (6.2 miles)

Duration: 3-4 hours

Wandering around Vancouver, with its visually arresting backdrop of sparkling sea and snow-dusted mountaintops, you discover there's more to this city than appearances. It's a kaleidoscope of distinctive neighborhoods, strongly artistic and just as bohemian as it is sophisticated.

Take this walk on Trips

Gastown

Crammed into a dozen cobblestoned blocks, trendy Gastown is where the city started. Century-old heritage buildings now house cool bars, hip boutiques and quirky galleries, with the landmark **steam clock** (cnr Water & Cambie Sts; S Waterfront) whistling to a camera-wielding coterie of onlookers every 15 minutes. Tucked along a handsome historic row nearby, **Salmagundi West** (☎604-681-4648; 321 W Cordova St; ⊙11am-6pm Mon-Sat, noon-5pm Sun; S Waterfront) features the most eclectic array of antiques and curios you will ever see. Steps away is **Brioche** (☎604-682-4037; www.brioche.ca; 401 W Cordova St; mains CAN$15-17; ⊙7am-9pm Mon-Fri, 8am-9pm Sat & Sun; S Waterfront), a colorful, comfy place to stop for coffee and drool-worthy baking.

The Walk ›› Follow Water St east, turning right on Carrall St and heading south for three blocks to Pender St and Chinatown.

Chinatown

North America's third-largest **Chinatown** (www.vancouver-chinatown.com) is an explosion of sights, sound and aromas. Check out the **Chinatown Millennium Gate** (cnr W Pender & Taylor Sts; S Stadium-Chinatown) and visit the **Dr Sun Yat-Sen Classical Chinese Garden** (☎604-662-3207; www.vancouverchinesegarden.com; 578 Carrall St; adult/child CAN$14/10; ⊙9:30am-7pm mid-Jun–Aug, 10am-6pm Sep & May–mid-Jun, 10am-4:30pm Oct-Apr; S Stadium-Chinatown). Save time for the **Chinese Tea Shop** (☎604-633-1322; www.thechineseteashop.com; 101 E Pender St; ⊙1-6pm Wed-Mon; ◻3), which has all the makings of a perfect cuppa, and slip into **Pak Chong** (☎604-633-2218; 506 Main St; ⊙9:30am-5pm; ◻3) for an eyeful of traditional Chinese medicine.

Have lunch at the deservedly popular, locally beloved New Town Bakery – and buy some pork buns to go.

The Walk ›› Follow Keefer St and Keefer Pl west, crossing the roundabout at the end and continuing to Beatty St. Turn left and walk three blocks to Robson St. Turn right, crossing Granville St, and continue along Robson St to Hornby St.

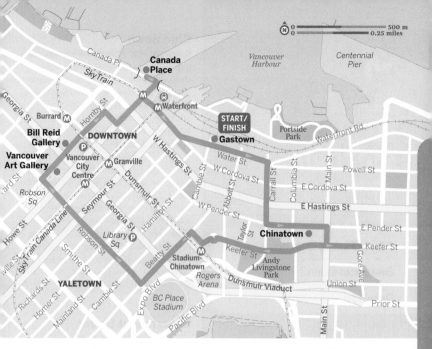

Vancouver Art Gallery

A former courthouse building, the grand home of the **Vancouver Art Gallery** (VAG; ☎604-662-4700; www.vanartgallery.bc.ca; 750 Hornby St; adult/child CAN$20/6; ⏰10am-5pm Wed-Mon, to 9pm Tue; 🚇5) showcases contemporary exhibitions, work by masters, and blockbuster international traveling shows. Check out **FUSE** (☎604-662-4700; www.vanartgallery.bc.ca/fuse; Vancouver Art Gallery; admission CAN$24; ⏰8pm-midnight; 🚇5), a regular late-night party event where you can hang out with the city's young art types over wine and live music.

The Walk » Exit the gallery on the Hornby St side and walk two blocks northeast along Hornby St.

Bill Reid Gallery

The **Bill Reid Gallery of Northwest Coast Art** (☎604-682-3455; www.billreidgallery.ca; 639 Hornby St; adult/child CAN$10/5; ⏰11am-5pm mid-May–Sep, 11am-5pm Wed-Sun Oct–mid-May; Ⓢ Burrard) showcases carvings, paintings and jewelry from Canada's most revered Haida artist as well as his fellow First Nations creators.

On the mezzanine level you'll view an 8.5m-long bronze of magical creatures.

The Walk » Continue up Hornby St to Pender St. Turn right and then left onto Howe St. Follow this towards the water.

Canada Place

Shaped like a series of sails jutting into the sky over the harbor, **Canada Place** (☎604-775-7063; www.canadaplace.ca; 999 Canada Place Way; Ⓟ; Ⓢ Waterfront) is a cruise-ship terminal, convention center and pier where you can stroll the waterfront and enjoy handsome views of the photogenic North Shore mountains. Save time to snap photos of the floatplanes landing and taking off alongside, framed by Stanley Park in the background. Next door, check out the grass-roofed convention-center expansion and the tripod-like **Olympic Cauldron**, a permanent reminder of the 2010 Winter Olympics.

The Walk » Backtrack up Howe St for one block and turn left onto W Cordova St. After three blocks, edge left onto Water St and back into Gastown.

STRETCH YOUR LEGS
VICTORIA

Start/Finish: Chinatown

Distance: 6km (3.7 miles)

Duration: 4-5 hours

It's not sugar coating – the seaside provincial capital really is as charming and beautiful as it first appears. Filled with funky boutiques, excellent museums, unique neighborhoods and a jewel of a park, Victoria makes for a blissful wander.

Take this walk on Trips

Chinatown

Settled in 1858, Chinatown stretches two packed blocks along Fisgard St. Grocery shops and inviting stores display exotic veggies, fans, fortune cookies and teapots. Pop into **Fantan Trading Ltd** (551 Fisgard St; ⏰10am-5:30pm Mon-Sat, 11:30am-5:30pm Sun) for a maze of made-in-China goods or **Fan Tan Home & Style** (www.fantanvictoria.com; 541 Fisgard St; ⏰10am-5:30pm Mon-Sat, noon-5pm Sun; 🚌70) for beautiful wooden and woven items. Dine at delightful **Venus Sophia** (☎250-590-3953; www.venussophia.com; 540 Fisgard St; mains CAN$10-19; ⏰10am-6pm Jul & Aug, 11am-6pm Wed-Sun Sep-Jun; 🍴; 🚌70), a tearoom with a vegetarian twist, then breathe in and slide along super-narrow **Fan Tan Alley**. It's home to many small boutiques and vintage shops.

The Walk » At Chinatown's gate, turn right onto Government St.

Government Street

With everything from designer shops to ice-cream parlors, Government St is a great stretch of pavement to pound. Visit **Silk Road** (www.silkroadtea.com; 1624 Government St; ⏰10am-6pm Mon-Sat, 11am-5pm Sun; 🚌70) for heavenly teas, and detour onto Johnson St for quirky independent stores. Hungry? Continue along Government, turn left onto Fort St and then around the corner onto Broad St for the phenomenal **Pagliacci's** (☎250-386-1662; www.pagliaccis.ca; 110 Broad St; mains CAN$12-25; ⏰11:30am-3pm & 5:30-10pm, to 11pm Fri & Sat; 🚌70), a pasta place locals try to keep secret.

The Walk » Continue eight blocks south on Government St.

The Inner Harbour

Watched over by the grand **Empress Hotel**, the handsome **Legislative Buildings** and the brilliant **Royal BC Museum** (p290), the Inner Harbour is Victoria's most photogenic location. Walk down along the waterfront promenade to check out the boats bobbling like candy-colored corks and enjoy a full roster of artisan market stalls and street performers.

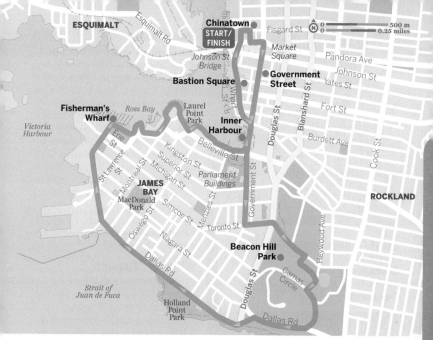

The Walk » Continue south on Government St to Toronto St. Turn left and follow this east for three blocks to Beacon Hill park.

Beacon Hill Park

An idyllic fusion of planted gardens and wild and woody sections, Beacon Hill Park is naturally popular. There's a playground, an excellent petting zoo and a heron-nesting zone worth cricking your neck to see. Head south and you'll find one of North America's tallest totem poles and eventually Dallas Rd, a breeze-licked oceanside walk where whale sightings aren't uncommon.

The Walk » Follow Dallas Rd to its end.

Fisherman's Wharf

At **Fisherman's Wharf**, fishing boats share dock space with a floating community of eclectic, colorful houseboats. Wander along the sun-dappled boardwalks and visit the galleries – then add a hunger-busting pit stop. Award-winning **Barb's** (☎250-384-6515; www.barbsfishandchips.com; 1 Dallas Rd; meals CAN$10-19; ◷11am-dusk mid-Mar–Oct; 🚌30) is hard to resist for fish 'n' chips, and kids' eyes will pop at the counter of **Jackson's Ice-Cream**.

The Walk » Follow the shoreline footpath east along the water from Fisherman's Wharf, all the way back to the Inner Harbour. Alternatively jump on one of the cute harbour ferries. From the Inner Harbour, follow Wharf St north.

Bastion Square

Historic Bastion Square hosts a popular seasonal artisan market along with cafes and buskers. This is also a great area to come for dinner. **Rebar** (☎250-361-9223; www.rebarmodernfood.com; 50 Bastion Sq; mains CAN$9-17; ◷11:30am-9pm Mon-Fri, 9:30am-9pm Sat & Sun; ✐; 🚌70) is a favorite among Victorians for good reason. Popular with vegetarians, it also serves up chicken and fish dishes to keep the carnivores happy. Love what you're eating? Be sure to pick up a cookbook on the way out.

The Walk » Carry on up Wharf St to Fisgard St to complete the loop.

STRETCH YOUR LEGS
WHISTLER

Start/Finish: Town Plaza

Distance: 2.7km (1.7 miles)

Duration: 3-4 hours

This super-scenic, gable-roofed village has some top cultural attractions plus enticing shops and restaurants where you can rub shoulders with ski bunnies and bike barons. Feeling energetic? The outdoor pursuits are virtually endless.

Take this walk on Trips

Town Plaza

There's something about the Whistler shopping scene that makes money run through your fingers like water. From boutique hat shops to Canadian brands like Roots and Lululemon, the options are an interesting (and often worthwhile) distraction here. You'll find plenty of the prerequisite sports-gear and souvenir stores, among less likely neighbors like cigar emporiums and fancy jewelry boutiques. Town Plaza is ringed with shops and is the best place to start browsing.

The Walk >> From Town Plaza, head west directly opposite the gazebo, between Deer Lodge and the Delta Whistler. Walk a block down Main St and swing a right to the museum.

Whistler Museum

The **Whistler Museum & Archives** (www. whistlermuseum.org; 4333 Main St; suggested donation CAN$5; ⏱11am-5pm, to 9pm Thu) features paraphernalia from the 2010 Winter Olympics, plus displays on geology, wildlife and village history. Look for exhibits on Myrtle Philip, one of the area's early pioneers. 'She battled bears, birthed babies and baked pies out on the trail.'

The Walk >> Return east up Main St towards the Village Stroll and carry on north to Olympic Plaza.

Olympic Plaza

Surrounded by cafes and home to a fantastic children's playground, Olympic Plaza is great for coffee and a bakery treat at **Purebread** (www.purebread.ca; 4338 Main St; baked goods CAN$3-6; ⏱8:30am-5:30pm). For something stronger, the Plaza's **Whistler Brewhouse** (www.mjg.ca/brewhouse; 4355 Blackcomb Way; ⏱11:30am-midnight Sun-Thu, 11:30am-1am Fri & Sat) offers smooth drinks such as Lifty Lager and 5 Rings IPA.

In summer, catch a performance at the plaza's outdoor theater. And save time for a selfie with the huge Olympic rings, a reminder of when the world came to party in the snow back in 2010.

The Walk >> Follow the footpath at the end of the Village Stroll – this leads to Lorimer Rd. Turn right

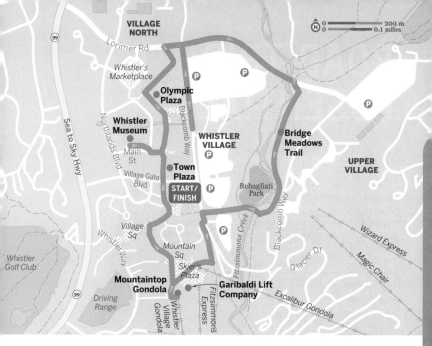

and follow it over the bridge, then turn right onto Blackcomb Way.

Bridge Meadows Trail

A few minutes' walk along Blackcomb Way brings you to the striking **Audain Art Museum** (p286) and its breathtaking BC and First Nations artworks. Afterwards, retrace your steps along Blackcomb and turn right onto Lorimer Rd for the nearby Squamish Lil'wat Cultural Centre (p283).

Next door, follow nature-hugging Bridge Meadows Trail south along Fitzsimmons Creek. Veer right at the covered wooden bridge and cross to Rebagliati Park, with its forest and waterside meadow views. Continue west through the woods to Blackcomb Way.

The Walk » Cross over Blackcomb Way and follow the footpath south until you reach a set of stairs. Turn right and descend back to the Village Stroll.

Mountaintop Gondola

Hop on the Whistler Village Gondola, sans skis. At the top, the **Peak 2 Peak Gondola** (📞604-967-8950; www.whistler blackcomb.com/discover/360-experience; 4545 Blackcomb Way; adult/teen/child CAN$57/50/29; 🕙10am-4:45pm) links Whistler with Blackcomb. This is the longest, highest unsupported lift span in the world – 3km (1.9 miles), at a height of 436m (1430ft). If you're feeling brave, wait for one of the two glass-bottomed gondolas.

The Walk » Return down to Whistler and the Village Stroll.

Beer at the GLC

If your knees are a little wobbly after all that gondola action, steady them with a beer overlooking the slopes at the **Garibaldi Lift Company** (GLC; 4165 Springs Lane, Whistler Village Gondola; 🕙11am-1am), the closest bar to the powder and a great place to hang out at the end of the day. The pub-grub menu includes hearty burgers, but if you're craving something fancier, swanky **Bar Oso** (www.baroso.ca; 4222 Village Square; small plates CAN$7-27; 🕙3pm-late) is a short walk away on Village Sq.

The Walk » Continue on the Village Stroll back to your starting point.

345

ROAD TRIP ESSENTIALS

The Pacific Northwest Driving Guide

Short on interstates, long on scenic byways, the Pacific Northwest yields some of the most beautiful drives on the continent.

DRIVER'S LICENSE & DOCUMENTS

If you're stopped by the police, you'll be expected to provide a valid driver's license and proof of insurance. Foreign visitors can legally drive a car in the USA for up to 12 months using their home driver's license. However, an International Driving Permit (IDP) will have more credibility with police, especially if your home license doesn't have a photo or isn't in English. Your national automobile association can provide one for a small fee, and they're usually valid for one year. Always carry your home license together with the IDP.

Driving rules in Canada are similar to the USA, although they vary slightly from province to province. Just like in the USA, you will need a driver's license and proof of insurance. A foreign license will suffice, though an IDP can save you headaches if your license is in a foreign language.

INSURANCE

Insurance is required by law. Without it, you risk financial ruin and legal consequences if there's an accident. Basic liability insurance covers damage you may cause to another vehicle. Rental companies are required by law to provide the minimum level set by each state, but it usually isn't enough in the event of a serious accident.

Many Americans already have enough insurance coverage under their personal car-insurance policies; check your own policy carefully. Foreign visitors should check their travel-insurance policies to see if they cover foreign rental cars. Rental companies charge about $15 per day for extra accident insurance.

Insurance against damage or loss to the car itself, called Collision Damage Waiver (CDW) or Loss Damage Waiver (LDW), can cost up to $25 per day (and may have a deductible). The CDW may be voided if you cause an accident while breaking the law. Again, check your own coverage to see if you have comprehensive and collision insurance.

Some credit cards cover CDW for rentals up to 15 days, provided you charge the entire cost of the rental to the card. Check with your credit-card company to determine the extent of coverage.

RENTING A CAR

Major international rental agencies have offices throughout the Pacific Northwest. To rent a car, you must have a valid driver's license, be at least 21 years of age and

---

Driving Fast Facts

→ **Right or left?** Drive on the right
→ **Legal driving age** 16
→ **Top speed limit** 75mph USA, 110km/h Canada
→ **Best bumper sticker** Sasquatch for President

Driving Problem-Buster

What should I do if my car breaks down? If it's a rental, call the service number of the rental company. If it's your own car, membership in an automobile association such as AAA will offer 24-hour roadside assistance.

What if I have an accident? If there are no serious injuries and your car is operational, move over to the side of the road. If there are serious injuries, call ☎911 for an ambulance. Exchange information with the other driver, including names, contact and insurance info, and license tag numbers. Then file an accident report with the police or Department of Motor Vehicles.

What should I do if I get stopped by the police? Stay in your car and keep your hands visible. They'll want to see your driver's license and proof of liability insurance. As long as you're not a serious threat, you probably won't end up in the pokey, although you'll probably get either a ticket or a warning if you've broken a road rule.

What if I don't have a room booked for the night? Not everyone reserves hotel rooms in advance. After all, spontaneity is a key ingredient of any road trip. Chain motels along the highway are a convenient solution if you're willing to go without up amenities. You can try to book a last-minute bargain on websites like www.priceline.com or www.hotwire.com.

present a major credit card or a large cash deposit. Drivers under 25 often pay a surcharge over the regular rental rate.

Agencies often have bargain rates for weekend or week-long rentals, especially outside the peak seasons or in conjunction with airline tickets. Prices vary greatly depending on the type or size of car, pick-up and drop-off locations, number of drivers etc. In general, expect to pay from $30 to $60 per day for a midsize car, more in peak seasons. Rates usually include unlimited mileage, but not taxes or insurance.

For rates and reservations, check the internet or call toll-free:

Alamo (☎800-222-9075; www.alamo.com)

Avis (☎800-633-3469; www.avis.com)

Budget (☎800-218-7992; www.budget.com)

Dollar (☎800-800-3665; www.dollar.com)

Enterprise (☎800-261-7331; www.enterprise.com)

Hertz (☎800-654-3131; www.hertz.com)

National (☎800-227-7368; www.nationalcar.com)

Rent-A-Wreck (☎877-877-0700; www.rentawreck.com)

Thrifty (☎800-847-4389; www.thrifty.com)

BORDER CROSSINGS

All crossings are open 24 hours except Lynden/Aldergrove, which is open 8am to midnight. During the week, expect to wait five to 20 minutes, an hour or more on weekends and during holidays. For up-to-date wait times, check www.cbsa-asfc.gc.ca/bwt-taf/menu-eng.html; it has links to other USA–Canada border crossings. Tips and directions can be found at www.vancouver.hm/border.html.

Many travelers also cross the border by ferry, principally on journeys from Anacortes to Sidney, BC (near Victoria), and from Port Angeles to Victoria.

Blaine/Douglas (aka Peace Arch) crossing The main overland point of entry from Washington to Vancouver, BC. It's at the northern end of I-5, which continues as Hwy 99 on the Canadian side. This crossing has the longest lines.

Pacific Hwy crossing Commercial trucks (and regular vehicles) use this crossing, 3 miles (5km) east of Blaine/Douglas; from I-5, take exit 275 (the one before Blaine). If you're entering Canada with duty-free goods, you'll need to cross here.

Lynden/Aldergrove crossing A good choice during busy times is this little-known crossing about 30 miles (50km) east of

Blaine/Douglas. Take exit 256 off I-5, just north of Bellingham, and follow Hwy 539.

Sumas/Huntingdon crossing Best for heading to BC's interior is this crossing 62 miles (100km) east of Blaine/Douglas. Take exit 255 off I-5, just north of Bellingham, and follow Hwy 542 and then Hwy 9.

- - - - - - - - - - - - - - - - -

FERRIES

Washington and British Columbia have two of the largest state-owned ferry systems in the world. Some boats are passenger-only, while others take vehicles and passengers. Summertime ferry routes can have long waits if you're in a car. Bring snacks, as ferry offerings are limited and expensive. You can almost always find a bathroom on board. For general information on the area's schedules and routes, check www.youra.com/ferry.

BC Ferries (☑888-223-3779; www.bcferries. com) Operates most of the ferries in BC. Primary links are between Tsawwassen (south of Vancouver) and Swartz Bay (on Vancouver Island), and to Nanaimo from Tsawwassen and Horseshoe Bay. BC Ferries services also link Gulf Islands to Tsawwassen.

Clipper Navigation (☑800-888-2535; www.clippervacations.com/clipper-ferry) The privately operated *Victoria Clipper*, a passenger ferry that connects Seattle with Victoria, BC, stops at the San Juan Islands in summer.

Washington State Ferries (WSF; ☑888-808-7977; www.wsdot.wa.gov/ferries) Operates most of the ferries that run in the Puget Sound area. Popular routes go to Bremerton, Bainbridge and Vashon Islands from Seattle. WSF also operates the ferry system through the San Juan Islands and on to Sidney (near Victoria, on Vancouver Island) from Anacortes.

- - - - - - - - - - - - - - - - -

MAPS

For a good road atlas or driving maps, try **Rand McNally** (www.randmcnally.com) and its Thomas Brothers city guides; both are stocked at many bookstores and some gas stations. If you are a member of an automobile association it will provide high-quality maps for free at regional offices.

Road Distances (miles)

	Seattle	Portland	Vancouver	Spokane	Eugene	Ashland	Seaside	Bend	ONP	Walla Walla	Whistler
Portland	172										
Vancouver	141	315									
Spokane	280	351	410								
Eugene	283	110	424	462							
Ashland	460	285	599	637	180						
Seaside	194	80	334	432	181	356					
Bend	330	159	470	396	120	186	247				
ONP	90	146	128	370	265	425	150	305			
Walla Walla	270	245	408	158	352	470	322	286	350		
Whistler	215	390	70	495	498	675	409	640	305	485	
Mt Rainer	85	136	179	212	204	325	279	195	175	173	300

Pacific Northwest Playlist

Kissing the Lipless The Shins

Roll on Columbia Woody Guthrie

You're No Rock 'N' Roll Fun
Sleater-Kinney

Float On Modest Mouse

Come as You Are Nirvana

Mass Romantic New
Pornographers

ROAD-TRIP WEBSITES

Road Conditions & Traffic

Oregon Trip Check www.tripcheck.com
**Washington State Department of
Transportation** www.wsdot.com/traffic
Drive British Columbia www.drivebc.ca

Driving Rules

Oregon Department of Transportation
www.odot.state.or.us/forms/dmv/37.pdf
**Washington State Department of
Transportation** www.wsdot.wa.gov/
LocalPrograms/Traffic/Laws
British Columbia Regulations www2.
gov.bc.ca/gov/content/transportation/
driving-and-cycling/road-safety-rules-and-
consequences

Automobile Associations

American Automobile Association
(AAA; ☎877-428-2277, emergency roadside
assistance 800-222-4357; www.aaa.com;
annual membership from $52) Get 24-hour
roadside assistance anywhere in the USA
plus free maps, trip planning and travel
discounts.

Better World Club (www.betterworld
club.com) Offers roadside assistance, plus
donates 1% of revenue to assist environmental
cleanup.

ROAD CONDITIONS

During winter months roads are sometimes closed to cars without chains or
4WD, so keep a set of chains in the trunk.
Make sure they fit your tires, and practice
putting them on *before* you're out in the
snow. Many car-rental companies prohibit
the use of chains on their vehicles.

Deer and other wildlife can be a hazard
on roads all around the region. Pay attention to the roadside, especially at night.

ROAD RULES

Cars drive on the right-hand side of the
road. The use of seat belts and child safety
seats is required. It's illegal to talk or text
on a mobile phone while driving, unless
you're on a hands-free device. The maximum legal blood-alcohol content for drivers is 0.08%; in Canada, it's 0.05%.

Speed limits vary depending on the
type of road: in the USA, it's generally
55mph –65mph on highways, up to 75mph
on the interstates, 25mph –35mph in cities
and towns, and as low as 15mph in school
zones. It's forbidden to pass a school bus
when its lights are flashing.

In Canada, speed limits are expressed
as kilometres per hour, so if you see a sign
that says 'Maximum 60', they don't mean
60mph. If you're watching your US odo-
meter, you shouldn't be traveling at more
than 37.28mph.

Speed limits are generally 70km/h –
90km/h on highways (or 43mph–56mph),
up to 110km/h (68mph) on expressways,
40km/h –50km/h (25mph–31mph) on
residential streets, and 30km/h –50km/h
(19mph–31mph) in school zones.

FUEL

Oregon law prohibits you from pumping
your own gasoline – all stations are full
service, so just sit back and enjoy it. Tips
are not expected.

Gas prices are fairly uniform, but tend to
get more expensive in remote rural areas
or near airports, where rental-car return-
ers don't mind paying extra. Within a given
area, prices might differ by about 10 cents
per gallon from one place to the next.

The Pacific Northwest Travel Guide

GETTING THERE & AWAY

AIR

Domestic airfares fluctuate significantly depending on the season, day of the week, length of stay and flexibility of the ticket for changes and refunds. Nothing determines fares more than demand, and when business is slow, airlines drop fares to fill seats. Airlines are competitive and any one of them could have the cheapest fare.

Most air travelers to the Pacific Northwest will arrive at one of the three main airports in the region:

Portland International Airport (PDX; ☏503-460-4234; www.flypdx.com; 7000 NE Airport Way; ☎)

Seattle-Tacoma International Airport (SEA; ☏206-787-5388; www.portseattle.org/Sea-Tac; 17801 International Blvd; ☎) Known locally as 'Sea-Tac'.

Vancouver International Airport (YVR; ☏604-207-7077; www.yvr.ca; ☎)

BUS

In car-oriented societies like the USA and Canada, bus travel takes second place. Service is infrequent or inconvenient, networks are sparse and fares can be relatively high. Air travel is often cheaper on long-distance routes, and it can even be cheaper to rent a car than take the bus, especially for shorter routes. However, very long-distance bus trips can be available at decent prices if you purchase or reserve tickets in advance.

The largest nationwide bus company in the USA and Canada, **Greyhound** (☏800-231-2222, international customer service 214-849-8100; www.greyhound.com) operates to major and minor cities throughout the Pacific Northwest; check its website for destinations and schedules. Tickets can be purchased by phone or online with a major credit card and mailed to you if purchased in advance, or picked up at the terminal with proper identification. Buying tickets in advance will save you money, as will traveling during weekdays and nonholiday times. Children, students, military personnel, veterans and seniors are eligible for discounts as well; check its website for details.

CAR & MOTORCYCLE

Although the quickest way to get to the Pacific Northwest is usually by plane, the best way to get around is by car. If you have time, it can be less expensive to drive to the Pacific Northwest than to fly and rent a car. And the region is blessed with many scenic highways that make driving long distances a feasible alternative.

Car Sharing

There are over two dozen car-sharing programs in the USA. These programs usually require a membership fee (one-time and/or annual), plus a per-hour car-rental charge. Two of the biggest are Zipcar and Car2go, but there are many that operate only within a city or a few cities. They can be an economical way to rent (or share) a car if you only need wheels for an hour or two at a time.

Note that driving regulations, such as speed limits and the permissibility of right turns on red lights or making U-turns, can vary somewhat from state to state.

TRAIN

The Pacific Northwest is well served by **Amtrak** (☎800-872-7245; www.amtrak.com) in the USA and **VIA Rail** (☎888-842-7245; www.viarail.ca) in Canada. Trains are comfortable, if slow, and equipped with dining and lounge cars on long-distance routes.

Amtrak's *Coast Starlight* links Los Angeles to Portland and Seattle via Oakland and other West Coast cities. The *Empire Builder* runs from Chicago to the Pacific Northwest via Minneapolis and Spokane, where it separates to reach Portland and Seattle. VIA Rail's *Canadian* runs between Vancouver and Toronto. Schedules can be very fluid: they become less reliable the further you are from the starting point.

Fares on Amtrak vary greatly, depending on the season and what promotions are going. You can beat the rather stiff full-price fares by purchasing in advance – the sooner you buy, the better the fare. Round trips are the best deal, but even these can be more expensive than airfares. Children, students, veterans, military personnel, seniors and even AAA members are eligible for discounts; check Amtrak's website for details, and for rail passes, which are a good option for longer travel periods.

DIRECTORY A–Z

ACCOMMODATIONS

Many lodgings have only nonsmoking rooms, but you can usually smoke outdoors. Air-conditioning is common at inland places but nearly nonexistent along the coast, which is much cooler. Many hotels take pets, but always ask beforehand (there's usually a fee). Wi-fi access is commonplace except in backcountry towns. Children (defined as anything from under six to under 18) can often stay free with their parents.

Except where noted, rates listed in this guide do not include lodging tax:

Washington Outside Seattle, lodging-tax rates vary by county but are generally around 12% for hotels of about 50 rooms or more. Smaller hotels or B&Bs usually include taxes in their daily rates and this is what we quote. Most Seattle hotel rooms are subject to a tax of 15.6%.

Oregon Outside Portland, lodging tax is 6% to 10.5%. In Portland it's 11.5% to 13.5%, depending on the size of the hotel.

British Columbia Lodgings in BC attract an 8% provincial sales tax (PST) plus a 5% goods and services tax (GST). Some BC regions levy an additional tax on overnight accommodations of up to 2%.

Sleeping Price Ranges

Room prices listed are high-season rates, excluding local taxes. Prices vary widely depending on the season, festivals and holidays, whether it's a weekend and sometimes even vacancy rates. Prices are generally highest in summer (or in winter at ski-resort towns), and some places have two- or three-night minimum stays. Always ask about discounts, packages and promotional rates, especially in low seasons. Some places give better rates if you book online.

It's always a good idea to see a room before paying for it. Rooms can vary widely within an establishment. Reserve ahead during festivals and holidays, or in summer (especially on the coast). If you plan on arriving late, let your hotel know or it might give away your room.

Accommodations fall into three categories (prices are for a double room per night):

budget	$	less than $100
midrange	$$	$100 to $200
top end	$$$	more than $200

ELECTRICITY

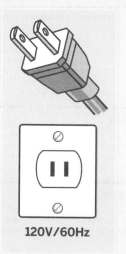

120V/60Hz

120V/60Hz

FOOD

Try to think of a food that isn't grown, raised or harvested in the Pacific Northwest, and you'll realize why in-the-know gourmands have been putting down roots in the region for decades. Outsiders, who have been slower to discover the abundance, now flock here for the food, seeking a taste of Northwest cuisine prepared by talented chefs who cook local, seasonal foods with an alluring simplicity.

The late James Beard (1903–85), an American chef, food writer and Oregon native, believed that preparing foods simply, without too many ingredients or complicated cooking techniques, allowed their natural flavors to shine. This philosophy has greatly influenced modern Northwest cuisine.

In some of Beard's writings, he describes his first tastes of wild mushrooms, herbs, truffles, berries and seafood, both in his hometown of Portland and on the coast at Gearhart, where he spent his childhood summers. Those tastes of foods at their seasonal prime shaped his reverence for quality ingredients.

In the spirit of James Beard, Pacific Northwesterners don't like to think of their food as trendy or fussy, but at the same time they love to be considered innovative, especially when it comes to 'green', hyperconscious eating. Don't be surprised if, when sharing a meal with locals, the conversation turns to how the food was prepared, grown, harvested, slaughtered or caught, which inevitably leads to conversations about the morals and ethics of its consumption. These are people who love to show off their homegrown vegetables, neighborhood-grown fruit, eggs gathered from backyard chickens and honey from nearby hives.

Farmed and Wild

The diverse geography and climate – a mild, damp coastal region with sunny summers and arid farmland in the east – foster all types of farm-grown produce. Farmers in these parts grow plenty of fruit, from melons, grapes, apples and pears to strawberries, cherries and blueberries. Veggies thrive here too: potatoes, lentils, corn, asparagus and Walla Walla sweet onions all feed local and overseas populations.

Other well-known farmed products include hazelnuts (also known as filberts; Oregon produces 99.9% of the hazelnuts grown in the USA) and herbs, especially lavender and spearmint. Hop farming is another regional specialty. The Northwest is the only region of the country with large-scale hop farms, which provide the sticky, fragrant cones that help add flavor, aroma

Eating Price Ranges

Restaurants are broken down into three price categories. These prices represent the average cost of a main course.

$ less than $10

$$ $10–20

$$$ over $20

---

and bitterness to many beers around the world.

Many wild foods thrive here as well, especially in the damper regions such as the Coast Range. Foragers there seek out the year-round wild mushrooms, as well as summertime huckleberries and blackberries.

LGBT TRAVELERS

The Pacific Northwest is generally a very gay-friendly place. As it is elsewhere, gay life is most tolerated in urban centers while attitudes tend to be less accepting in the hinterlands. In the major cities of Seattle, Vancouver and Portland, and even some smaller towns, such as Eugene and Victoria, travelers will find everything from gay religious congregations to gay hiking clubs, while in the rural areas they may want to keep their orientation to themselves.

The Capitol Hill neighborhood is the center of gay life in Seattle. In Vancouver, the West End is gay-centric, while Commercial Drive is more lesbian-oriented. Queer-integrated Portland has no specific gay neighborhood (Sam Adams, Portland's mayor from 2008 to 2012, was the first openly gay mayor of a large US city).

Seattle Gay News (www.sgn.org) A weekly newspaper focusing on gay issues.

Proud Queer (www.pqmonthly.com) Online news serving Portland's gay community.

Vancouver Pride Society (www.van couverpride.ca) Check out the events link.

Tourism Vancouver (www.tourism vancouver.com/vancouver/gay-friendly-vancouver) Resources for gay-friendly Vancouver.

MONEY

ATMs are widely available. Credit cards are accepted at most hotels, restaurants and shops.

OPENING HOURS

For sights, activities and information, we mostly list high-season hours. Mid- or low-season hours vary throughout the year.

Type of business	Standard opening hours
businesses	9am-5pm
post offices & banks	8am or 9am-5pm Mon-Fri, some 8am or 9am-2pm Sat
restaurants	7-11:30am breakfast, 11:30am-2:30pm lunch, 5-9pm dinner
shops	9am or 10am-5pm or 6pm (malls 9pm) Mon-Sat, noon-5pm Sun
supermarkets	8am-10pm, 24hr in large cities

PUBLIC HOLIDAYS

Holidays falling on a weekend are usually observed the following Monday.

New Year's Day January 1 (USA and Canada)

Martin Luther King Jr Day Third Monday in January (USA)

Family Day Second or third Monday in February (Canada)

Presidents' Day Third Monday in February (USA)

Good Friday Friday before Easter Sunday (Canada)

Easter Sunday in late March or early April (USA and Canada)

Easter Monday Monday after Easter (Canada)

Victoria Day Monday on or preceding May 24 (Canada)

Memorial Day Last Monday in May (USA)

Canada Day July 1, or July 2 if July 1 is Sunday (Canada)

Independence Day July 4 (USA)

Labor Day First Monday in September (USA and Canada)

Columbus Day Second Monday in October (USA)

Thanksgiving Day Second Monday in October (Canada); fourth Thursday in November (USA)

Veterans' Day November 11 (USA)

Remembrance Day November 11 (Canada)

Christmas Day December 25 (USA and Canada)

Boxing Day December 26 (Canada)

SAFE TRAVEL

The Pacific Northwest is generally a friendly and safe place to travel, though crime does exist – mostly in bigger cities. Take the usual precautions:

➡ Don't leave valuables visible in your vehicle, whether you're in a busy downtown street or at a remote hiking trailhead.

➡ Use ATMs in well-trafficked areas. In hotels, use safe-deposit boxes or place things in a locked bag.

➡ Ask around for neighborhoods to avoid. If you find yourself in a questionable place, act like you know where you're going, even if you don't.

➡ Pan-handlers are a problem in any city. Many suffer from psychiatric problems and drug abuse, but most are harmless. It's an individual judgment call whether to offer them anything – you might offer food if you have it. If you want

Local Leanings

Finding local products has become a popular pursuit for an increasingly food-aware, eco-minded population (most of whom believe that shipping food long distances wastes precious resources). The year-round availability of fresh produce has spurred a fanaticism for seasonal eating. Many of those food fanatics prefer organic, sustainably produced edibles, and conventional farmers and vintners are working to meet the demand by undergoing the two- to three-year organic-certification process.

Farmers markets have become the best examples of this new hyper-awareness of food sourcing, and a handful operate year-round. Some of the most popular markets go beyond offering produce, with everything from pastries, artisan cheeses, honey and jams to prepared foods like wood-fired pizzas, roasted peppers, and biscuits and gravy.

If you miss the markets, don't worry. Many grocery stores and specialty food markets prominently label local foods. Large-scale brands like Tillamook Cheese, which makes cheese, yogurt and ice cream in the coastal town of Tillamook, Oregon, have a devoted customer base that enjoys supporting local economies. So does the fast-food chain Burgerville, which buys ingredients for its menus from local sources – it offers Walla Walla onion rings, blackberry or hazelnut milk-shakes and Tillamook cheddar burgers.

Upscale restaurants also reflect the public's passion for local foods. Some menus name the farms and harvesters who supply specific ingredients. If you're curious, ask servers for details about a restaurant's sourcing practices – most likely they'll be used to such requests.

to contribute toward a long-term solution, consider donating to a reputable charity that cares for the homeless.

➡ If you're accosted by a mugger, always hand over the goods fast – nothing is worth getting attacked. Some people keep a 'false' stash of cash to placate a possible mugger.

Here are some tips on local livestock or wildlife:

➡ Drivers should watch out for loose cattle and horses in remote countryside areas.

➡ When camping in bear country, use bear containers/boxes or hang food correctly. While hiking in bear country, wear bear bells or talk loudly to avoid surprising them. Bears will generally avoid people when they can. Never feed bears or other wildlife!

➡ It's unlikely you'll even glimpse a mountain lion (also called a cougar or puma). Adult travelers aren't much at risk of an attack, but unattended children and pets can be. Loud noises and making yourself appear bigger (hold open your jacket) will usually scare them off.

➡ Rattlesnakes live in dry desert country and hikers can sometimes encounter them basking on trails. Give them a wide berth and they'll leave you alone. Wearing thick hiking boots offers some protection, as does staying out of thick underbrush.

TELEPHONE

The USA and Canada use GSM-850 and GSM-1900 bands. SIM cards are relatively easy to obtain in both countries.

TOURIST INFORMATION

Oregon, Washington and BC have state and provincial tourist bureaus that offer glossy guides, maps and plenty of other pertinent travel information. Individual cities, towns and regions also maintain visitor centers, which are often run by the local chamber of commerce.

Washington State Tourism (www.experiencewa.com)

Oregon Tourism Commission (www.traveloregon.com)

Destination British Columbia (www.hellobc.com)

TRAVELERS WITH DISABILITIES

If you have a physical disability, travel within the Pacific Northwest won't be too difficult. The Americans with Disabilities Act (ADA) requires all public buildings in the USA – including most hotels, restaurants, theaters and museums – to be wheelchair accessible. Most sidewalks in the Pacific Northwest are wide and smooth and many intersections have curb cuts and sometimes audible crossing signals.

Lift-equipped buses are the norm in Washington, Oregon and BC, and many taxi companies have wheelchair-accessible cabs. Some municipal bus networks provide door-to-door service for people with disabilities. Most car-rental franchises are able to provide hand-controlled models at no extra charge – but reserve well ahead. All major airlines, Greyhound buses and Amtrak trains allow service animals to accompany passengers (bring documentation for them). Airlines will also provide assistance for connecting, boarding and disembarking if requested with your reservation. Disabled travelers using Washington State Ferries should check www.wsdot.wa.gov/ferries/commuterupdates/ada for information on reduced fares and how to board.

Many state and national parks in the Northwest maintain a nature trail or two for use by travelers in wheelchairs. For a list of accessible trails in Washington state, see www.parks.wa.gov/adarec; for Oregon check www.traillink.com/stateactivity/or-wheelchair-accessible-trails.aspx. Meanwhile, BC has a good general website at www.hellobc.com/british-columbia/about-bc/accessibility.aspx.

The America the Beautiful Access Pass (previously known as the Golden Access Passport; these are still honored) is available free to blind or permanently disabled US travelers with documentation. It gives free lifetime access to US national parks and wildlife refuges and 50% off campground use. For more information see www.nps.gov/findapark/passes.htm.

Rolling Rains Report (www.rollingrains.com) An advocate for inclusive travel. Interesting blog.

Emerging Horizons (www.emerging horizons.com) An online magazine, with much information on accessible travel.

Whale-Watching

The Pacific Northwest is one of the world's premier spots for whale-watching. The shoreline is long, so if you want to see whales at their peak, pick a particular coastal spot, then find out when most whales will be passing through.

WASHINGTON

You can spot gray and humpback whales from Washington's coastline, especially from Long Beach (near the Oregon border), Westport and Ozette. The most famous kind of whale in this state, however, is the killer whale or orca.

About 90 resident orcas in several pods live year-round in the Puget Sound and San Juan Islands area, feeding on fish. The San Juan Islands in particular are the best place for spotting orcas, since they often swim close to shore. You can take boat tours from the islands or spot them from land – Lime Kiln Point State Park on San Juan Island is an especially good place. And while you're here, be sure to visit the **Whale Museum** (☑360-378-4710; www.whale-museum.org; 62 1st St, Friday Harbor; adult/child $6/3; ◷10am-5pm) in Friday Harbor.

The best time to spot orcas is from April to September; numerous charter companies run cruises from the San Juans, Puget Sound and Seattle. You might be able to spot orcas from a ferry too.

Out on the coast, any orcas you might see are part of transient pods that can roam from Alaska to California. These killer whales don't interact with resident pods, and their diet includes seals, sea lions and even small whales.

OREGON

Oregon's long coastline offers many opportunities for whale-watching (especially at promontories that jut out to sea), but Depoe Bay and Newport are especially dedicated to the activity. Here you'll find several tour-boat companies willing to take you out, but if you'd rather stay on land, that's fine too. An organization called **Whale Watching Spoken Here** rallies hundreds of trained volunteers to assist visitors in spotting whales at various sites all along the Oregon Coast. Check the website (www.whalespoken.org) for details.

And in Depoe Bay, be sure to check out the Whale Watching Center, which offers exhibits and sea views.

BRITISH COLUMBIA

Every March, Tofino and Ucluelet, the communities surrounding Pacific Rim National Park Reserve on Vancouver Island, put on the **Pacific Rim Whale Festival** (www.pacificrimwhalefestival.com), celebrating the northbound travels of the gray whale during its spring migration. With an estimated 20,000 whales passing through, you're likely to spot a few blowholes around here from March to May.

Another good place on land to try spotting whales is Telegraph Cove, where orcas can often be seen; visit the **Whale Interpretive Centre** (☑250-928-3129; www.killerwhalecentre.org; by donation adult/child $5/3; ◷9am-5pm mid-May–Oct) here. If you'd rather go for a super close-up, however, there are several boat-tour companies in Victoria.

Mobility International USA (www.miusa.org) Runs educational exchange programs in the USA and abroad.

Society for Accessible Travel & Hospitality (www.sath.org) Useful links and information specifically about travel.

VISAS

Requirements vary widely for entry to the USA and Canada. Check https://travel.state.gov/content/visas/en.html (USA) and www.cic.gc.ca/english/visit (Canada).

Practicalities

Radio NPR (www.npr.org) has a progressive yet impartial approach to news and talk radio.

Discount Cards If you plan on visiting many national or state parks or national forests, a recreation pass will save you money – check www.nps.gov/planyourvisit/passes.htm for details. For Washington, go to www.parks.wa.us/204/Passes-Permits; for Oregon, www.oregonstateparks.org/ckFiles/files/2012_pass_summary.pdf

Student Discounts If you're a student, bring along your student ID, which can get you discounts on transportation and admission to sights and attractions.

Hostels Many hostels in the Pacific Northwest are members of HI-USA (www.hiusa.org), which is affiliated with Hostelling International. You don't need a HI-USA card to stay at these hostels, but having one saves you a few bucks per night. You can buy one at the hostel when checking in.

Post The US Postal Service (www.usps.com) and Canada Post (www.canadapost.ca) provide dependable, timely service.

Senior Discounts People over the age of 65 (or sometimes younger) often qualify for the same discounts as students; any identification showing your date of birth should suffice. Folks who are 62 years or older and visiting national parks can get a Senior Pass (store.usgs.gov/pass/senior.html). For more information, contact the American Association of Retired Persons (www.aarp.org).

Smoking Banned in all indoor public spaces throughout the Pacific Northwest, including bars and restaurants.

Time Oregon (except most of Malheur County, near the Idaho border), Washington, and Vancouver, BC, are in the Pacific zone (GMT minus seven hours in summer, minus eight in winter).

Entering the USA

Getting into the United States can be complicated, depending on your country of origin, as the rules keep changing. For up-to-date information about visas and immigration, check the website of the **US Department of State** (www.travel.state.gov) and the travel section of **US Customs & Border Protection** (www.cbp.gov).

For the most part, all foreign visitors need a visa to enter the US. Exceptions include most citizens from Canada and Bermuda, certain North American Free Trade Agreement (NAFTA) professional workers and those entering under the Visa Waiver Program (WVP). Visitors should carry their passport (valid for at least six months) and expect to be photographed and have their index fingers scanned.

Entering Canada

Visitors to Canada from major western countries need no visa, but citizens of more than 150 nations do. Visa requirements change frequently, so check **Citizenship & Immigration Canada** (www.cic.gc.ca/english/visit/visas.asp) before you leave.

Officially, US citizens don't need a passport or visa to enter Canada by land; some proof of citizenship, such as a birth certificate along with state-issued photo identification, will ordinarily suffice. However, since the introduction of tighter border security, officials recommend that US citizens carry a passport to facilitate entry.

BEHIND THE SCENES

SEND US YOUR FEEDBACK

We love to hear from travelers – your comments help make our books better. We read every word, and we guarantee that your feedback goes straight to the authors. Visit **lonelyplanet. com/contact** to submit your updates and suggestions.

Note: We may edit, reproduce and incorporate your comments in Lonely Planet products such as guidebooks, websites and digital products, so let us know if you don't want your comments reproduced or your name acknowledged. For a copy of our privacy policy visit lonelyplanet.com/privacy.

WRITERS' THANKS

BECKY OHLSEN

Becky would like to thank Alex Howard, Celeste Brash, Mike Russell, Ryan at Beulahland, Patrick Goodall, Joel and Christina Ohlsen and everyone else she pestered with questions along the way.

CELESTE BRASH

Thanks to my husband Josh and kids Jasmine and Tevai, to the Irwins in Spokane, Jackie Caplan-Auerbach and family in Bellingham, the Joneses in Olympia, the Pilot/Forsters in Port Angeles, Iain on Orcas, park rangers, tourist info people, random people met along the ways and so many more!

JOHN LEE

Special thanks to Maggie for ensuring my sanity and delivering copious amounts of tea during the write-up for this project. Thanks also to our feline companion Max for grooming my beard on a regular basis. And cheers to my buddy Dominic for joining me on that elongated Vancouver Island road-trip. Sincere apologies to all my other Vancouver friends and family for being stuck to my keyboard for so long; I'm more than ready for a beer or two now.

BRENDAN SAINSBURY

Thanks to all the untold bus drivers, chefs, hotel receptionists, tour guides, and innocent bystanders who helped me during this research. Special thanks to my wife Liz and ten-year-old son Kieran for their company in on the road.

RYAN VER BERKMOES

The number of folks to thank outnumber Kermode bears but here's a few: Ben Greensfelder, my fearless co-pilot who kept the supply of good beer flowing. In Prince Rupert, I am beyond indebted to Bruce Wishart for literary food folks and fun. And words can't repay the car shuttle service. In Dawson, Tony and the gang almost made me forget my visit. Finally, to Alexis Ver Berkmoes, who I love even more than the giant beaver.

ACKNOWLEDGMENTS

Climate map data adapted from Peel MC, Finlayson BL & McMahon TA (2007) 'Updated World Map of the Köppen-Geiger Climate Classification', *Hydrology and Earth System Sciences*, 11, 163344.

Front cover photographs (clockwise from top): Moraine Lake, Richard Cavalleri/ Shutterstock©; Spoiled Dog Winery and vineyard, Whidbey Island, Danita Delimont Stock/AWL©; Classic Ford, Jacksonville, Oregon, Heeb Christian/Alamy©

Back cover photograph: Beach in Bandon, Oregon, Danita Delimont Stock/AWL©

THIS BOOK

This 3rd edition of Lonely Planet's *The Pacific Northwest's Best Trips* guidebook was curated by Becky Ohlsen, and researched and written by Becky Ohlsen, Celeste Brash, John Lee, Brendan Sainsbury and Ryan Ver Berkmoes. The previous edition was written by Mariella Krause, Celeste Brash, Korina Miller and Brendan Sainsbury. This guidebook was produced by the following:

Destination Editor Alexander Howard

Product Editors Vicky Smith, Ross Taylor

Senior Cartographer Alison Lyall

Assisting Cartographer David Kemp

Book Designer Katherine Marsh

Assisting Book Designers Gwen Cotter, Lauren Egan

Assisting Editors Sarah Bailey, Imogen Bannister, Michelle Bennett, Kate Chapman, Pete Cruttenden, Andrea Dobbin, Carly Hall, Victoria Harrison, Gabrielle Innes, Kellie Langdon, Ali Lemer, Kate Mathews, Kate Morgan, Lauren O'Connell, Kristin Odijk, Susan Paterson, Monique Perrin, Christopher Pitts, Saralinda Turner, Simon Williamson

Cover Researcher Naomi Parker

Thanks to Kirsten Rawlings, Luna Soo, Tony Wheeler, Dora Whitaker, Tracy Whitmey

INDEX

JOHN LEE

Born and raised in the historic UK city of St Albans, John grew up in the lengthy shadow of London, finding as many opportunities as possible to gorge on the capital's rich diet of museums and galleries. Slowly succumbing to the lure of overseas exotica, he arrived on Canada's West Coast in 1993 to begin an MA in Political Science at the University of Victoria. Regular trips home to Britain ensued, along with stints living in Tokyo and Montreal, before he returned to British Columbia to become a full-time freelance writer in 1999.

RYAN VER BERKMOES

Ryan Ver Berkmoes has written more than 110 guidebooks for Lonely Planet. He grew up in Santa Cruz, California, which he left at age 17 for college in the Midwest, where he first discovered snow. All joy of this novelty soon wore off. Since then he has been travelling the world, both for pleasure and for work – which are often indistinguishable. He has covered everything from wars to bars. He definitely prefers the latter. Ryan calls New York City home.

Read more at ryanverberkmoes.com and at @ryanvb.

Read more about Ryan at: lonelyplanet.com/ ryanverberkmoes

BRENDAN SAINSBURY

Originally from Hampshire (the 'old' one in England), Brendan has been covering Seattle and the Pacific Northwest for Lonely Planet for over a decade. He is currently based in White Rock, BC, 45 minutes south of Vancouver and just 2km from the US border. Researching for this book (his 45th for Lonely Planet) he enjoyed trying copious new beers, getting drunk on coffee and doughnuts, and taking his son (yet again!) to Seattle's legendary pinball museum.

Read more about Brendan at: lonelyplanet.com/ brendansainsbury

OUR WRITERS

OUR STORY

A beat-up old car, a few dollars in the pocket and a sense of adventure. In 1972 that's all Tony and Maureen Wheeler needed for the trip of a lifetime – across Europe and Asia overland to Australia. It took several months, and at the end – broke but inspired – they sat at their kitchen table writing and stapling together their first travel guide, *Across Asia on the Cheap*. Within a week they'd sold 1500 copies. Lonely Planet was born.

Today, Lonely Planet has offices in Franklin, London, Melbourne, Oakland, Dublin, Beijing, and Delhi, with more than 600 staff and writers. We share Tony's belief that 'a great guidebook should do three things: inform, educate and amuse'.

BECKY OHLSEN

Becky is a freelance writer, editor and critic based in Portland, Oregon. She writes guidebooks and travel stories about Scandinavia, Portland and elsewhere for Lonely Planet.

Read more about Becky at: www.lonelyplanet.com/beckyohlsen

CELESTE BRASH

The beauty of the Pacific Northwest coaxed Celeste back to the US after 15 years in Tahiti. For the last six years she's revelled in exploring her new back yard, its mountains, coasts, wineries and fantastic restaurants, while getting back in touch with her cowboy and Indian roots. Her award winning writing has appeared in publications from BBC Travel to Afar and Islands Magazine and she's contributed to nearly 60 Lonely Planet titles.

Read more about Celeste at: lonelyplanet.com/celestebrash

 MORE WRITERS

Published by Lonely Planet Global Limited
CRN 554153
3rd edition – Feb 2017
ISBN 978 1 78657 232 5
© Lonely Planet 2017
Photographs © as indicated 2017
10 9 8 7 6 5 4 3 2 1
Printed in China

MIX
Paper from responsible sources
FSC™ C021741

Paper in this book is certified against the Forest Stewardship Council™ standards. FSC™ promotes environmentally responsible, socially beneficial and economically viable management of the world's forests.